fP

ALSO BY ROBERT DRAPER

Hadrian's Walls
Rolling Stone Magazine: The Uncensored History

DEAD CERTAIN

———◆———

THE PRESIDENCY
OF GEORGE W. BUSH

ROBERT DRAPER

FREE PRESS

New York   London   Toronto   Sydney

FREE PRESS
A Division of Simon & Schuster, Inc.
1230 Avenue of the Americas
New York, NY 10020

First Free Press hardcover edition September 2007

FREE PRESS and colophon are trademarks of Simon & Schuster, Inc.

For information about special discounts for bulk purchases,
please contact Simon & Schuster Special Sales at 1-800-456-6798
or business@simonandschuster.com

Manufactured in the United States of America

1   3   5   7   9   10   8   6   4   2

Library of Congress Cataloging-in-Publication Data

Draper, Robert.
Dead certain : the presidency of George W. Bush / Robert Draper.—
1st Free Press hardcover ed.
p.   cm.
Includes bibliographical references.
1. Bush, George W. (George Walker), 1946–.   2. United States—Politics and
government—2001–.   3. United States—Foreign relations—2001–.
4. Pride and vanity—Political aspects—United States.   I. Title.
E902.D73   2007
973.931092—dc22   2007023471

ISBN-13: 978-0-7432-7728-0
ISBN-10:   0-7432-7728-7

Always there: my parents, Bob and Claire;
my brother, John.

CONTENTS

December 12, 2006

"You can't possibly figure out the history of the Bush presidency—until I'm dead."

George W. Bush slipped a piece of cheese into his mouth. "Let's order first." He took a quick glance at the day's menu prepared for him and his guest, saw nothing on it he cared for, and announced to the steward, "I'll have a hot dog. Low fat hot dog."

Then he slapped down the menu and asked, "What is the purpose of this book?"

He was edgy that day. Earlier that morning, Bush had decided that a major address slotted for next week was going to have to wait another month. The subject was Iraq, and he was, frankly, unsure of what to say on the subject. A bipartisan commission called the Iraq Study Group—cochaired by longtime Bush family consigliere James A. Baker III—had recently returned its report, which had labeled that country's condition "grave and deteriorating." Progress in that ongoing conflict had been inchwise even before sectarian violence began to develop its awful momentum in the spring of 2006 and threaten to tear the country apart. Bush had repeatedly said that the war was winnable. He had said that the American-led Coalition was, in fact, winning. No one, including Bush, was claiming imminent victory anymore.

So, what to say? Bush was a quarterback now playing defense. Five weeks before, the Democrats had seized back the House and the Senate in an election that even Bush had to concede was to some degree a referendum on the tragic misadventures in Iraq. The Democrats, with public backing, were clamoring for a change in course. So was the Iraq

Study Group. And so—with their tongues freshly loosened by the resignation of Defense Secretary Donald Rumsfeld—were the generals in whose trust Bush had placed the mission. Stung by this reality, Bush nonetheless was digging in his heels. The day after the midterms, he had announced his intention to replace Rumsfeld with Robert Gates. Beyond that, Bush would not veer in haste. He would take the holidays to think about it.

"If you're weak internally? This job will run you all over town," the president observed. He was sitting in the small conference room beside the Oval Office where his predecessor, Bill Clinton, infamously found leisure time with Monica Lewinsky. His back was to the White House lawn. He had flung himself into his chair like a dirty sweatshirt and continued to pop pieces of cheese into his mouth. Stress was hammered into his face. The subject was himself—how his leadership skills had evolved over time, and how he had dealt with disappointment and defeat, going back to his loss to Senator John McCain in the New Hampshire primary of 2000 and now, once again, in 2006.

Bush, as always, bridled at the request to navel-gaze. "You're the observer," he said as he worked the cheese in his mouth. "I'm not. I really do not feel comfortable in the role of analyzing myself. I'll *try*. But I don't spend a lot of time. I will tell you, the primaries strip you down to your bare essence, and you get to determine whether or not you're willing to fight through—to prevail. It's a real test of will, I agree to that. I think the whole process was responsible for testing my will. *No question* getting defeated was a powerful moment."

He added, "I've never run a race where I thought I wouldn't win. I thought we were gonna hold the House and the Senate in '06. I thought we'd lose nine or ten seats, and I thought we'd be one or two up in the Senate."

Bush had held that view, almost manic in its optimism, all the way up to election day, in defiance of all available polling data. At the very mention of such data, his face began to curdle. "I understand you can't let polls tell you what to think," he declared—one of his most frequently expressed sentiments, but now he went further: "And part of being a leader is: *people watch you*. I walk in that hall, I say to those commanders—well, guess what would happen if I walk in and say, 'Well, maybe it's not worth it.' When I'm out in the public"—and now he was fully animated, yanked out of his slouch and his eyes clenched like little blue fists—"I fully understand that the enemy watches me, the Iraqis are watching me, the troops watch me, and the people watch me.

"The other thing is that *you can't fake it*. You have to believe it. And I believe it. I believe we'll succeed."

In spite of his stated preference that he be viewed as a simple guy, Bush now and then would reveal subtle shadings or outright dualities in his character. Here he was, for example, saying that he would not be influenced by polls—and then, a sentence later, saying that the job *required* acute consciousness of public perceptions. His father was better known for discretion and attention to appearances, Bush acknowledged. "My dad was one time speaking to the Press Club," he reminisced. "And the last question is always kind of a funny question: 'Why are you wearing a blue tie?' And he kind of balked. I whispered, 'Tell him you spilled gravy on your red one.'

"Now I don't know how that happened. It popped in my head. I didn't train for the quip. By the way: He said it, and the place went wild. And then—typical George Bush—he said, 'Well, my son told me that!' He had to share the credit, instead of taking it and running with it!"

Interest in the relationship between the 41st and 43rd presidents was unquenchable, for reasons historical, political, and Oedipal. Despite their mutual love and their common experiences—which included such not-so-trifling matters as invading Iraq and appointing Dick Cheney to positions of high power—they were two profoundly different men. Above all, George W. had long emphasized, he was his own man. Seldom did he call on his father as a useful executive resource.

"Yeah, I asked him about it," he said when the subject turned to choosing Cheney as his vice president. "He said, 'You'll like working with him.' My relationship with my dad is, y'know—I don't call him and say, 'Give me your list of potential candidates, man!' Or, 'What are the five things *you* would do if you were me?' It's more, 'Y'know, I'm really thinking about Dick Cheney, Dad.' Or, 'I'm thinking about Bob Gates. You've worked with Bob Gates, what's he like?' He knows as an ex-president, he doesn't have *nearly* the amount of knowledge I've got on current things. I mean, I get briefed every day, twice a day sometimes. He knows that. And plus, once the president gets a strategy in mind—I mean, there's no need to *argue* about the Freedom Agenda! I'm sure he subscribes to a lot of it. Now, the rumors are that he and his people don't. But I don't necessarily think it's true. But, look, *you can't talk me out of thinking freedom's a good thing!*"

His hot dog arrived. Bush ate rapidly, with a sort of voracious disinterest. He was a man who required comfort and routine. Food, for him, was fuel and familiarity. It was not a thing to reflect on.

"The job of the president," he continued, through an ample wad of bread and sausage, "is to think strategically so that you can accomplish big objectives. As opposed to playing mini-ball. You can't play mini-ball with the influence we have and expect there to be peace. You've gotta think, think BIG. The Iranian issue," he said as bread crumbs tumbled out of his mouth and onto his chin, "is *the* strategic threat right now facing a generation of Americans, because Iran is promoting an extreme form of religion that is competing with *another* extreme form of religion. Iran's a destabilizing force. And instability in that part of the world has deeply adverse consequences, like energy falling in the hands of extremist people that would use it to blackmail the West. And to couple all of that with a nuclear"—as always, he pronounced it *nu-ku-ler*—"weapon, then you've got a dangerous situation. . . . That's what I mean by strategic thought. I don't know how you learn that. I don't think there's a moment where that happened to me. I really don't. I know you're searching for it. I know it's difficult. I do know—y'know, how do you decide, how do you learn to decide things? When you make up your mind, and you stick by it—I don't know that there's a moment, Robert. I really— You either know how to do it or you don't. I think part of this is it: I ran for reasons. Principled reasons. There were principles by which I will stand on. And when I leave this office I'll stand on them. And therefore you can't get driven by polls. Polls aren't driven by principles. They're driven by the moment. By the nanosecond."

A moment later, press secretary Tony Snow stepped into the doorway and immediately assumed a deferential tone. "When I go in front of the press," he said, referring to the daily briefing he was about to conduct, "can I just say, 'We will not be giving the speech until the New Year'? I mean—"

"The New Year," Bush cut in, "and the reason why is, the president still has other people to listen to, and there's a lot of work to be done on a very important task. And I think you oughta just say, 'He's gonna be very deliberate—and listen, he's not gonna be rushed.' "

"Yeah," said Snow.

"And if their argument is, 'Well, what happens if there's an attack in Baghdad?' You can say, 'He talked to his commanders today, and there's a *current* strategy in place.' "

"Right."

"Of dealing, protecting—whatever."

"Can we say you're moving in a direction and assigning tasks to people to try and work out—there are hard political issues—"

"Yeah." Bush's voice rose, as if facing the truculent press at that very moment: "I want to make sure before we put the policy in place that Gates—*I don't have a secretary of defense!*"

"Right, I'm working that out—"

" 'The president wants to make sure that all the key players on the national security team are well briefed, well versed, and ready to make a measured judgment,' " Bush finished.

"Good. Perfect. Sorry to interrupt," Snow said as he vacated the room.

"It's okay," remarked Bush. "This is worthless, anyway." Then, in a sudden bellow: "*I'd like an ice cream! Please!* You want some ice cream, Robert?"

Bush dived into his vanilla ice cream. "The presidency is—*you get tired*," he confessed. Then, leaning back from the bowl: "This is a *tiring* period we're in now. I've got Iraq on my mind. A *lot*. You know, every day I see the casualties, I get the reports—I am *immersed* in this war."

He was taking pains to sound factual instead of anything that could be construed as overwrought. "Look—it's war," he went on. "Listening to a lot of people right now. Plus the trips I've been on," referring to the late-November meetings in Eastern Europe and then Asia. "Plus the sixteen holiday events we're doing. Eight thousand, nine thousand hands I'll be shaking . . . I'm actually feeling pretty good," he insisted. "Exercise helps. And I think prayer helps. I really do."

Bush added, "I'm also sustained by the *discipline* of the faithful experience. I don't think I'd be sitting here if not for the discipline. I was undisciplined at times. Never over the edge, but undisciplined. I wouldn't be president if I kept drinking. You get sloppy, can't make decisions, it clouds your reason, absolutely."

Laughing, he said, "I remember eating chocolate in the evenings after I quit drinking, because my body was saying, 'Where's that sugar, man?' And so—I can still, interestingly enough, I still remember the feeling of a hangover, even though I haven't had a drink in twenty years."

Now that the speech had been postponed, the next days would be light for Bush before he spent Christmas at Camp David. One of the few events on his schedule was a trip to Walter Reed Medical Center to visit soldiers wounded in Iraq. Bush had met with more than a thousand such soldiers and grieving family members over the course of his presidency. It was one of those duties that the former Texas governor had not foreseen when he decided to run for office in 1999. The world was relatively peaceful back then. These days, Bush began each morning with a Presidential Daily Briefing. The first item was always Iraq, and the report listed the day's damage: this many killed and wounded, that many targets bombed. It had become Bush's habit to take out his pen and circle the number of casualties. Then to close his eyes for a moment. And then to turn the page.

He viewed it as the commander in chief's obligation to visit with those who had suffered loss as a result of his decisions. "Sometimes it's not pleasant, and I understand that," Bush said as he leaned back from his vanquished bowl of ice cream. "And they have every right to be unpleasant. Sometimes there are disagreements. . . . Yeah, it's hard. And to see the wounded, the head injuries. But that's part of the presidency, to immerse yourself in their emotions. Because they look at the president and they—most of them—say, 'My son or daughter did what they wanted to do.' The interesting thing is, the healer gets healed. I appreciate it."

The healer gets healed. Bush seldom if ever implied that he carried the burden of regret or self-doubt—that he required healing of any sort. Did the grieving sense that need in him? For, as he acknowledged, "I'm told by some politicians here that the people they meet with say, 'Get out now.' That just doesn't happen with me. A couple of wives I think in Fort Hood might've said, 'It's not worth it. Bring 'em home now.' Some say, 'Get 'em home as soon as you can—but my child volunteered, they're proud of what they're doing.' The interesting thing about this war is that our military understands better than most what's happening—and that we *are* making some progress there. No question, it's tough. But what *they* see is a different picture from what *America* sees. And *they are in the mission!*

"I tell people—I read an interesting book by [Richard] Carwardine—I'm on my eighty-seventh book this year." With rueful admiration, he added, "Rove's on, like, a hundred two. Anyway, this book [*Lincoln: A Life of Purpose and Power*] talks about the constituency that Lincoln had. And one was religious people who were going through this Second Awakening, that loved Lincoln's position that all men are created equal: there is a God, and all men are created equal by that

God, and so it's a moral position. And the military loved Lincoln to the point where," and Bush offered up a sly politician's grin, "Lincoln made sure that they were able to get to the polls in 1864.

"There's a parallel here. And that's that our military understands this. And a key constituency in the global war is for our military to be appreciated and respected, starting with the commander in chief. And they look at me—they want to *know* whether I've got the resolution necessary to see this through. And I do. I believe—I *know* we'll succeed. *And* I know it's *necessary* to succeed. And anyway. There wasn't a moment when I knew you were supposed to do that," he said, returning of his own volition to that irritating first question about the evolution of his leadership abilities. "I can't tell you the moment. I *can* tell you—that, uh . . . that, uh . . ."

For the first and only time in that seventy-minute monologue-dominated conversation, Bush fell silent for several seconds. "Yeah, well," he finally said. "When you're responsible for putting a kid in harm's way, you better understand that if that kid thinks you're making a decision based on polls—or something other than what you think is right, or wrong, based upon principles—then you're letting that kid down. *And* you're creating conditions for doubt. And you can't give a kid a gun and have him doubt whether or not the president thinks it's right, and have him doubt whether or not he's gonna be suppportive in all ways. And you can't learn that until you're the guy sitting behind the desk."

"There's no preparation for that," ventured the guest.

"There's none," said Bush.

He then pushed away from the table and abruptly strode back to the aforementioned desk in the Oval Office. His next visitor, Iraqi Vice President Tariq al-Hashemi, would not be terribly receptive to talk of "some progress" in that country. Hashemi's brother and sister had been assassinated in Baghdad earlier in 2006. A few weeks ago, another one of his brothers had been gunned down as well.

And Bush could not show doubt to this man, either. *I know we'll succeed*—he had to show that confidence, which would not be difficult, because he *did* know: America would succeed in Iraq because it *had* to succeed.

He would take the holidays to figure out how.

PART ONE

——◆——

BAPTISM

1

NEW HAMPSHIRE

The motorcade lurched to life just after seven on the morning of Monday, June 14, 1999. Like an ungainly serpent, it negotiated its bulk through the studied quaintness of Kennebunkport, Maine, clogging the narrow artery of Route 9. The inhabitants of Kennebunkport, where the Bush family have long kept their summer home, had grown more or less accustomed to such spectacles. For that matter, the sight of a caravan departing town for Interstate 95, southbound to New Hampshire, was unsurprising to those who followed presidential politics. George Herbert Walker Bush had literally been down this road before—once as a virtual unknown, then as a frontrunner, and a third time as a president seeking reelection.

But this was another era, another Bush. This was an altogether different beast.

Not counting state police escorts, the motorcade consisted of eight vehicles. Five of them—two vans and three buses—conveyed nearly two hundred reporters from around the world, supervised by an assortment of fresh-faced young Texans and veterans from the first Bush administration. Two other vans ferried an armada of political aides: gurus, money counters, truth spinners, image makers, stagecrafters, and a young man and young woman each assigned to the personal care of the candidate and his wife. The eighth vehicle—driven by a member of Texas's elite law-enforcement corps, the Rangers—contained four passengers: fifty-two-year-old Governor George W. Bush; his wife, Laura; Bush's cousin by marriage, Craig Stapleton of Greenwich,

Connecticut; and the governor's alter ego, muse, and message disciplinarian, Karen Hughes.

The oceanside town awaiting the motorcade, New Castle, normally
counted its populace as eight hundred. Fully two hours in advance of
the fleet's arrival, another six hundred New Hampshirites had begun
to congregate along the Commons—some holding miniature flags,
others carrying postcard invitations from the Bush campaign organization. A makeshift cityscape of camera crews and satellite dishes
lined the beach. The town's four cops were joined outside by five
ringers from the state police—the nine of them no doubt a fitting
squadron for a lilac-festival parade or a snowmobile pileup. Today,
they might as well have been scarecrows.

A heavy fog presided that morning. When the caravan at last
arrived on Wentworth Road, thirty minutes behind schedule, it did so
amid an uproar of disembodied hysteria. The sedan doors swung
open—a peeling back of the curtains as Act One of the 2000 primary
season began and its lead actor took the stage.

George W. Bush stepped out into the tidal wave of hands and
screams. For perhaps a second, it might have appeared that he didn't
warrant such a gathering. Though Bush cut a nimble figure in his fine
summer suit, he lacked the toothy ebullience of a Reagan or a
Kennedy, the eager charm of a Clinton. This candidate—and New
Hampshirites had met scores of candidates—seemed unexceptional in
dimension and bearing. Normal, really, in every way.

How to explain, then, the sonic force of his presence as he waded
among them? How his strong hand grabbed yours and pulled you into
his airspace so that the tanned and slightly bemused (*kinda weird,
isn't this?*) face was right in yours. Unaffected, big-brotherly, oddly
confidential as his keen blue eyes locked in on yours. *This* guy liked—
no, loved (but didn't quite crave) the crush of flesh. The New Hampshirites had seen them all. They'd seen another Bush, too. Decent
fellow. This one was different. A Bush, but not simply that. In New
Hampshire, like nowhere else in America, they got close, and they
could tell.

A few strides behind Bush, left in his wake, was his wife. Her eyes
betrayed a flicker of frailty as the crowd closed in on her. But then
Laura Bush composed herself. And she, like her husband, had something. Not rambunctious at all in the way of George W., but in her
oppositeness the two seemed of an intimate piece. "We're very excited
to be here"—over and over she said it, unable to find other words and

unwilling to fumble through them as her husband might. Still, you could see why he loved her, and why he depended on her, and why she would be, if not a force, then in her own way an asset.

The Bushes mounted a stage. Standing beside them, the preppy scion / Senator Judd Gregg bellowed, "So we are ready to ROLL!"— and then unscrolled a parchment, eight feet of it, lapping across the stage: some 250 names, effectively the New Hampshire political universe, all pledged to the cause of George W. Bush.

Under a white tent, the candidate took questions from the media. Someone asked about immigration. He answered in Spanish. Someone asked him about a litmus test for judicial appointees. There would be none, said the governor. Someone asked him about his famously ambiguous youthful indiscretions. Bush confidently demurred: "There is a game in Washington. It's called 'gotcha.' It's the game where they float a rumor and make the candidate prove a negative. And I'm not playing the game, Jack."

Later that morning, at the New Castle public library, Bush sat next to a little boy and asked him how he was doing. "Awesome," the boy replied.

"I'm awesome, too," said George W. Bush.

That week, a New Hampshire poll indicated that Bush's popularity surpassed that of all nine of his Republican opponents combined.

You could not be faulted for believing that this was, as the press often put it, a juggernaut—a bloodless, ever-calculating, unerring victory machine. By the end of the 1999–2000 election cycle, the Bush campaign would raise more money ($193 million) and spend more ($186 million) than any other in American history, by a long shot. Its elaborate campaign organization—a corporate/populist hybrid devised by Karl Rove and Ken Mehlman, replete with "metrics" and "viral marketing," a lexicon never before uttered in a presidential race—drove a stake into the flabby old model of hierarchies and smoke-filled rooms. And, as sheer merchandise, no political commodity could trump George W. Bush: son of a president, governor of a big state, ferociously disciplined yet engaging, a self-styled "different kind of Republican" but nonetheless with the full backing of his party, and with Rove and Karen Hughes—geniuses in their craft—to guide him at every turn.

You could track the juggernaut's progress from that first day in New Castle and find little during that summer of 1999 to challenge your belief in its invulnerability. The Bush monstrosity returned to New Hampshire a month later, on the Fourth of July. Other Republican presidential candidates attended the local parades. But among the aspirants, only George W. Bush walked astride a gauntlet of local heavyweights, all but carried on their shoulders.

And then in a third, almost mythical moment, on July 31, the Bush couple arrived by an antique wooden boat across the silky waters of Lake Winnipesaukee to the shores of Wolfeboro, passing under a bridge crammed with sign-waving fanatics. No fog besmirched the postcard this time. The advance men had slotted a half hour for mingling, but the candidate was feeling Wolfeboro's love—he was sweating and gabbing—and nobody wanted this to end. And so the entourage was late that afternoon arriving at a block party in the well-heeled town of Dover, where mounted police galloped forth to block off Quail Drive and the Bush Winnebago nearly mowed down a swarm of goggle-eyed children on bicycles. While the governor joshed and flipped burgers in a large backyard tent, two Texas Rangers wearing supersize belt buckles stood inside the house, transfixed by the spectacle of a stuffed and mounted indigenous moose's head . . . the absolute biggest goddamned thing they'd ever seen.

But as you took in the sight of these two tough legends gaping like choirboys at a dead animal on a wall, you realized what you were seeing—namely, that this Bush machine was not a machine at all. It was, at best, an army: prone to mortal wounds, fallible in judgment, flailing its way through an ungovernable war. And looking closer, beneath all that polished machinery, you could plainly see that this army's general, George W. Bush, sported no battle scars . . . and that for all his fine leadership portfolio, he did not really know what political combat was.

A competitor—he was that. He loved to smoke a jogging mate right before the finish line. He sulked after the Texas legislature denied him his property tax reform initiative. But Bush was neither by temperament nor by upbringing a warrior. Indeed, he disdained the bullying image of conservatism—"It's mean," was his view—and publicly sparred with the troglodytes in both the state and national Republican Party. By marketing himself as a Compassionate Conservative, George W. Bush was all but encouraging Americans to view him as a softie.

Oh, he promoted something called the Responsibility Era as his big idea: a tough-love tonic to the Boomers' Era of (as he never tired of saying on the stump) "If it feels good, do it, and if you've got a problem, blame somebody else." Every presidential aspirant, after George Herbert Walker Bush made the flip comment in 1992 about his lack of a "Vision Thing," needed one, and this was his. But Bush didn't communicate through ideas. (That was Rove's way.) He tended to act by impulse, without apology, calling himself a "doer," "decider," "provoker," "charger," and "not a very good psychoanalyst guy." Trusting one's gut was a good thing; gazing in the same anatomical area, at one's navel, struck him as an indulgence of the weak willed. And yet, in George W. Bush's masculine world, there was no shame in exhibiting sensitivity. He was, in addition to the above, a self-confessed "cryer." For all his gut checking, he spoke far more often of what was "in my heart."

Presence? Bush had it in abundance. At the same time, there was a thorough absence of grandiosity to the man—unless you counted his claim to be "a uniter, not a divider" . . . which, given his record of bipartisan accomplishment in Texas, not only had the force of truth behind it but bespoke an appealing modesty: *I'm here to bring us all together, not to hog the spotlight.* Whether or not he really was "a different kind of Republican," Bush was a different kind of *candidate*, one who had not coveted from birth the most powerful position in the known universe. Where one expected to find ego, one instead encountered a brotherly . . . was it sweetness? Whatever it was, to a nation fatigued by the bruising Clinton psychodramas, the affable compassion of George W. Bush was surely a welcome antidote.

This, at least, was the calculation of Karen, Rove, and Bush himself. Of course, they would play to win. But for all his competitive instincts, Bush harbored no lifelong yearning for this particular competition. And wasn't that—along with his terrierlike hair, his untutored posture, his goofy faces, and his daily disfiguring of the English language— proof that he was anything but a political animal? Wouldn't they see, and love, that he was *real*?

A compassionate general, evincing not so much as an ember of the warrior's fire in the belly—this was an advantage, wasn't it?

The bigness was the first problem.

After the triumphant swing through Wolfeboro and Dover that same July 31, the Bush caravan figured to round off the day with a visit to North Conway. This small town with a charming drugstore on Main Street was a veritable slice of Americana, eye candy for the evening news. The governor climbed out of the Winnebago and was immediately engulfed. Barricades, the media hordes, cops, and advance men hollering and shoving . . . Bush got as far as across the street from the pharmacy, couldn't penetrate any farther. He could only wave sheepishly at the drugstore employees, shake a few hundred outstretched hands, and then retreat to the Winnebago.

New Hampshire was about smallness. Being the last bastion of that quaint idyll, retail politics, New Hampshire cherished—*demanded*—being won over, as they loved to say, "one voter at a time." Elsewhere in America, the motorcade itself was the show, the roaring sirens and the gleaming limos and the chiseled broadcasters no less crucial to the experience than the candidate himself. New Hampshirites didn't give a damn about all that. They wanted face time. They wanted to be wooed.

Therein lay the tension. Because the Bush campaign wasn't about charming the folks of the Granite State, strictly speaking. It was about George W. Bush becoming president of the United States. And this meant several things.

It meant, for a fellow with only four years' worth of statewide governing experience, looking presidential—vaguely imperial, heavily endorsed, above the fray of the also-rans. And indeed, that was Rove's directive to advance chief Brian Montgomery when the latter was staging events: "Make it look presidential." Sweeping backdrops, all TV cameras poised to capture the candidate at iconic angles . . . and for God's sake, *tell the damn Ranger security force not to wear their goddamn cowboy hats!*

It meant playing things safe. *Like a hockey season*, wrote the campaign's pollster, Matthew Dowd, in an early 1999 memo, referring to these early primaries. *The regular season's sole practical function is to prepare the team for the playoffs—without sustaining injuries or exposing weaknesses.* So, no showing the whole playbook. No improvising. And no freaking out the voters with radical notions following the Clinton era of Peace & Prosperity. As Rove would proclaim with cherubic meta-irony, "We're the candidate of reasonable, cautious, prudent reform." (Or as Stuart Stevens, the bon vivant ad guy, would more smirkily put it: "Things have never been better. Vote for change.")

And it meant winning 270 electoral votes. "We're running a fifty-state campaign"—even Karen couldn't maintain the gusto every time she chanted Team Bush's mantra. But yes, a candidate with an obscene war chest could afford to spread the field and look down the road to

November 7, 2000. For the cash-poor opposition in the summer of 1999, America was a nation of five states: Iowa, New Hampshire, South Carolina, Michigan, and Arizona. And so they courted the early-primary voters with a hard-luck boy's fevered desperation . . . while the prince and presumptive nominee, anything but desperate, did not.

Of course, this strategy ran the risk of offending the flinty yet somewhat spoiled citizens of the First Primary State. But New Hampshire's fetish for giant killing was hardly a secret. Rove certainly knew it—and, courtesy of Bill Clinton and frontrunners past, knew this as well:

A giant could survive New Hampshire . . . provided (as in Clinton's case) the wounds were only of the flesh.

Sitting in the van, appraising his new state adviser, Tom Rath—who had come on board only after his first choice, Lamar Alexander, had given up the race—Bush chose his words carefully.

"I understand you know box scores better than anyone else around here," he said. "How many hits did Harold Baines get last night?"

"Two," said Rath.

"You stay right here with me, Rathbone."

He dispensed nicknames the way his attentive young bodyman, Logan Walters, whipped out the canister of hand spray after a round of gripping and grinning. "Hey, Barbarini!" to field director Barbara Russell. "Things okay, Robbyboy?" to state cochair Robb Thomson. Local admaker Pat Griffin was Griffey, U.S. Congressman Charlie Bass the Bassmaster. . . . In this way, the Texan closed the distance and his Granite State hired hands instantly became towel-snapping teammates.

To some, this might have seemed a hollow gesture, or even condescending. (Back at the Governor's Mansion in Austin, Bush had received the highly respected Ohio congressman and presidential hopeful John Kasich with a booming, "Johnnyboy!" Kasich wondered where the hell Bush got off reducing national figures to mascots.) Yet these politicos, hardly virgins—Reagan, Bush I, Dole, Alexander, and Gramm were among their past clients—felt a strange tingle in the presence of George W. They loved the guy. Loved the realness: pounding back the Cheetos, farting on the plane, gossiping about the sexual exploits of the traveling press. He was unfailingly kind to the B-teamers. Hated to keep anyone waiting—*always* on time. (Actually, almost always early. What was *that* about?) Stepping into his hotel room in the morning, they'd find him reading his Bible over breakfast. He revered his wife, was noticeably less jagged when Laura was traveling with him. And it was kind of sweet, his unabashed longing to be back home in Texas, and that feather pillow from the mansion he carried with him . . . a factoid that the press jumped on like starved hyenas.

New Hampshire, too, would love this guy. Of this the local deputies were convinced. But how to get him out there . . . how to let the people see George W. Bush the way they saw him . . . letting Bush be Bush—but at the same time, letting New Hampshire be New Hampshire . . .

His New Hampshire staff was having a hard time getting the Texans to understand the hokey imperatives of a campaign here. People *craved* yard signs, buttons, corny slogans, and garish T-shirts. Judd Gregg's pale-eyed chief of staff, Joel Maiola, loved churning this stuff out. Bush sheriff's badges, Bush baseball cards. Later in winter, T-shirts trumpeting the Reason for Freezin' campaign. And buttons sporting three big W's: WIN WITH W.

(The Texans vetoed that last one. Molly Ivins, the left's feline Will Rogers, had taken to calling Bush Dubya, an indelible slander. So no using the middle initial—EVER!)

The Texans, for their part, were having a hard time getting the local aides to understand: There was a strategy, and it would be followed. Period. *Must Stay on Message.* Overseeing this was the towering woman with the practical swimmer's hairdo, Karen Hughes. When Karen said of Message Discipline, "I don't know much, but this is one thing I think I'm good at," the governor's communications director was semi-nicely saying, *Fall in line, pal.*

Karen knew Message and she knew Bush. Of New Hampshire and national campaigns she was thoroughly ignorant. Someone—the local gurus blamed Karen; she blamed them—had failed to warn Bush about Boston News 7's Andy Hiller, a Harvard-bred trickster who finagled quality time with the candidate on November 1, 1999. Hiller began innocently enough, asking if the governor believed himself to be weak on foreign policy.

"No. I've got a clear vision of where I want to lead America," came the reply—forceful but general, a sign that his answers to the next questions would be disastrous.

"Can you name the president of Chechnya?"

"No. Can you?"

"Can you name the president of Taiwan?"

"Yeah. Lee. Wait a minute—is this Fifty Questions?"

"No. It's four questions of four leaders of four hot spots."

The leader of Pakistan? "The new Pakistani general. Just been elected—he's not been elected," Bush corrected himself. "The guy took over office. . . . It appears he's going to bring stability to the country, and I think that's good news for the subcontinent."

Hiller interrupted the filibuster: "And you can name him?"

"General—I can name the general . . ."

"And it's . . ."

"General," Bush concluded miserably.

Finally: How about the prime minister of India?

"Uh . . . no."

His competitive juices seething, Bush countered with a question he no doubt wished Hiller had asked: "Can *you* name the foreign minister of Mexico?"

With an undertaker's half-smile, Hiller replied, "No, sir, but I would say to that, *I'm* not running for president."

As soon as Hiller was done, Karen accosted him. He needed, it was his *duty* as a supposedly *objective journalist*, to administer the very same quiz to all the other candidates.

Hiller was unsympathetic. Breathlessly, Karen phoned Josh Bolten back at 301 Congress in Austin. "Do you know the answers to any of those?" she demanded.

"Well, Musharraf," replied Bolten. (He'd lived with a Pakistani guy once.)

Karen hung up, started fielding the press calls. "Even our policy director didn't know the answers!" she began.

("Great, Karen," muttered Bolten when this spin job got back to him. "Now we *all* look like idiots.")

Once composed, Karen summoned the Message: Her boss was "seeking to be the leader of the free world, not a *Jeopardy!* contestant."

Too little too late. And so tonight it might be a good idea to give the governor some time alone.

The great thing about him? Tomorrow, he would let it go. Which was not the same thing as forgetting. For weeks thereafter, they'd hear it from Bush, at the beginning of this or that briefing:

"Okay, you guys are supposed to be so smart. Who's the president of Trinidad?"

*　　*　　*

Karen wasn't like other communications directors. She wasn't like Gore's Chris Lehane, only too happy to dish with the press over cocktails. Not that she wasn't fond of a nice chardonnay, and of . . . well, some of the reporters. (She'd been one herself, after all.) But Karen was, to use her word, an "advocate." The press didn't seem to get this. The cause she advocated was not that of warm and fuzzy media relations. It was that of George W. Bush: her friend, whose moods and preferences she could anticipate with Doppler accuracy. Though she was blessed with a gratifying life of family and faith back home in Austin, there was in fact no other cause for Karen. She would not be re-upping with some other campaign should the governor somehow lose. Though she had done time in the early 1990s flacking for the Texas Republican Party, Karen wasn't Rove—she wasn't a political animal. In this way, she was very real . . . just as in her thorough understanding of the needs of a man not her husband, she was rather unreal.

The governor needed downtime. He needed naps and he needed to jog. The governor needed loyalty more than expertise. Karen, Rove, Logan Walters; Israel "Izzy" Hernandez, the first Walters, now a valued utility player who knew no politics other than Bushworld; Mark "M-Cat" McKinnon, a lifelong Democrat admaker who'd sworn off politics until a dinner with the governor in 1997 left him hopelessly smitten; Dan Bartlett, whose entire adult life had been spent in the service of Rove and Bush; the young press aides, smooth Gordon Johndroe and Mindy "Xena Warrior Princess" Tucker (so nicknamed for the way the Amazonian redhead personally blockaded gubernatorial opponent Garry Mauro when he tried to crash a Bush press conference) . . . All Texans, all talented—but it was their belief in him, their omnipresence in his corner, and their desire never to let him down that the governor most needed.

The governor needed to know the point of things. Not the details. Just: *What is the particular purpose in this fourth stop on our schedule today, who's thought this through, what is the strategy behind going into another one of these diners, and if there isn't one why the HELL are we doing it— KARL!*

Bush's local ambassador, Senator Judd Gregg, understood this about him. *We're going to Merrill Lynch and Fidelity,* Gregg would patiently explain, *because business offices are fast becoming the town halls of the twenty-first century.* Which struck the Texans as a load of horseshit—the governor standing in an insurance company cafeteria in front of a thousand people in suits, all the pageantry of an Amish funeral . . . but Gregg had a point, if not much of one.

(Actually, Gregg's unspoken point was this: *If you showed up in New Hampshire more often, we wouldn't have to jam a thousand voters into every event. If you were willing to let him get up close and personal with the voters, you'd have more pageantry than you knew what to do with. If you were actually running to win the New Hampshire primary, rather than running not to lose the election . . .*)

The governor needed not to be made a fool of. He could laugh at himself, but only if the joke was of his instigation. One evening in Bedford, Bush mingled with well-heeled contributers at the $3.1 million home of Dean Kamen, the dark-eyed eccentric whose inventions included the Segway. Kamen had been a generous supporter, and, being a politician, it was the governor's tendency to indulge such benefactors. The schedule had been murder, however. Last night he'd been in Iowa. Tomorrow there would be a debate. The inventor seemed unaware of this. He seemed intent on touring Bush through every corner of his fifteen-thousand-square-foot abode. Checking out his swimming pool . . . his softball field . . . his closet . . . his helicopter hangar . . .

It was getting close to nine-thirty, past the candidate's bedtime, when Kamen said, "I want you to sit in this wheelchair."

The contraption was another of Kamen's inventions. It could literally climb stairs. Ingenious, but, well heck, look at the time . . . Against his better judgment, Bush sat. Kamen moved the control switch. The wheelchair bucked, its two front wheels in midair. Bush's eyes went wide with panic. Then the chair, with the governor in it, clunked its way up Kamen's staircase.

When Bush got out of the chair, he fixed the night's handler, Tom Rath, with a look that could have curdled plutonium. But just in case Rathbone hadn't gotten the message, the governor delivered it aloud, as soon as they had thanked their host and returned to the car:

"Don't ever do that to me again."

The ride back to the hotel was very quiet.

The governor needed there to be no surprises. This was, of course, a tricky matter for Karen and the others to arrange in a fifty-state campaign. And besides, New Hampshirites *longed* for the unscripted encounter. They would stand before Bush while he unspooled all the cornpone canned jokes that went over so well in Iowa. . . . Scowls. So he'd start riffing on Social Security . . . and the people in the audience *took notes!* And then he'd catch himself, go back to the script. . . . More scowls.

The local staff said he needed to do radio shows, so Bush did radio shows. During one call-in program on a Keene station, a fellow grilled Bush on abortion. The governor recited his pro-life stance. The next caller grilled him further. "I've said all I'm going to say on that," Bush pushed back, "my position's clear. I'd like to talk about education, some of the other things we've done in Texas. . . ."

But because the press had been all over Bush about abortion and whether he would apply a *Roe v. Wade* litmus test to judicial nominees, the radio grilling continued, and Bush was unable to get back on message. In frustration, the governor flung the phone at a local aide. "You got any more bright ideas, smart guy?" he snapped.

For the most part, however—and this was what made the whole business of avoiding surprises particularly dicey—Bush often *excelled* when he was flying blind. Sure, there would be errors, some more gruesome than others. ("Rarely is the question asked: Is our children learning?") And the press would titter, while ordinary folks would nod and say, *Ol' George, he's one of us.* The local gurus marveled at Bush's "eternal handshake," but it wasn't a question of stamina or stunts—it was just a natural skill: Up close, the man could flat win you over.

But the governor didn't want that. He wanted predictability. Surprises put him on edge. And so it fell to the advance men, after handing out flyers and knocking on doors and calling businesses on behalf of the soon-to-be-coming-to-your-town frontrunner George W. Bush, to answer the inevitable query: "Is he going to stand there and take our questions?"

And the reply was: "No, he's not going to."

When the Londonderry Chamber of Commerce expressed its indignation, which the local aides duly reported to Austin—*This is insane, he's in New Hampshire, for Christ's sake*—deputy campaign manager Maria Cino relented, but only barely. If the governor got tripped up, she warned darkly, there would be hell to pay. Meekly, the aides got back to the folks in Londonderry and asked, *Uh, could you submit your questions in advance?*

Later, the Texans gave slightly more ground. The governor would take questions. . . . *Except, here are what the questions will be.* On orders, the New Hampshire staff began to plant questioners in the audience.

The deck stacking unsettled even some of the Texans who so believed in their boss. Why was it necessary, they wondered quietly among themselves, to embed loudly cheering Texans at every event? Couldn't their guy inspire the crowd on his own? If a twice-elected governor couldn't handle a few impromptu questions, the odd heckler . . . should he really be running for president? Was this any way to audition for leader of the free world?

But in point of fact, there was one other thing the governor needed. He needed to win. Bush did not like to lose. Couldn't stand even thinking about it, or hearing his aides ratchet down the expectations. Which is why, while slouching in a chair and examining a speech draft, he would growl, "What's this '*if* I'm elected'?"

Herein lay the most bedeviling conundrum, however:

Though the victory strategy was to play it safe, George W. Bush could not win by playing it safe. It was basic to the man: He needed the adrenaline rush of competition. Without the whiff of defeat in his nostrils, he tended to lose focus, seeming to forget what distinguished him from all the other fortunate sons.

And Bush didn't detect that alarming whiff in New Hampshire. Quite the opposite, really. By August 1999, according to a *Wall Street Journal* poll, 59 percent of the respondents preferred the governor as the Republican nominee for the presidency.

Somewhere far down the list was a senator from Arizona by the name of John McCain, with 3 percentage points.

"Boys," said the senator, "remember the words of Chairman Mao: It's always darkest before it's totally black."

Husky cascades of laughter—the jaunty melody of a candidate with absolutely nothing to lose. That was the soundtrack to John McCain's Straight Talk Express.

It was what he'd promised aides like Mike Dennehy and Roy Fletcher—really, the only thing he had promised: "We might not win, but we're going to have a hell of a lot of fun." A novel pledge, if ultimately naïve. Broke, sleep deprived, ignored by the press, and in the end snubbed by the voting public . . . underdog campaigns were typically about as fun as smallpox. And yet here they were, trundling across the Granite State like Ken Kesey's busload of giggly acid testers—at that point in time, the happiest campers in American politics.

At the back of the bus, the candidate sat in a maroon swivel chair. A burly sixty-three-year-old fellow with thinning silver hair and ruddy cheeks who could make even a good suit look ill tailored, his appearance did nothing to warrant attention until you noticed how natural he was basking in it. Usually at his side hunched an unkempt figure straight out of a Grateful Dead jam session, strategist Mike Murphy . . . though at other times the second chair would be occupied by one of McCain's other archbishops, like the dour John "Sunny" Weaver or Mark Salter, the senator's quiet but intense wordsmith. The other half-dozen or so seats at the back of the bus would be filled by reporters. For eight, ten, fourteen hours, they fired questions at the candidate. And the candidate would answer—on the record, off the cuff, all day long, until finally the reporters had to excuse themselves so that they could go file their stories.

Back in 1997, when the seeds for his candidacy were first planted, the concept was to present McCain as the Honest John antidote to Slick Willie Clinton. And throughout the campaign, the senator's most consistent applause line was, "My friends, I'm going to beat Al Gore like a drum." Still, reporters who'd been fed a spartan diet of Message Discipline could not help but regard this banquet of verbiage as clear and welcome evidence of the Anti-Bush.

"McCain's base"—that's what the press became for the senator. Where Bush seemed most comfortable bantering with reporters about sports or the perils of child rearing, McCain welcomed multi-hour exchanges on tax cuts, campaign finance reform, Social Security, and the like. Not all the senator's positions were deeply felt. Though staunchly anti-abortion, he seemed uncomfortable when asked what he would do if his daughter were pregnant. His health care reforms were so poorly thought through that his press aides kept stammering out freshly modified numbers to exasperated reporters. And, on occasion, word would filter up to the front of the bus: *He's, uh, putting his foot in his mouth.* At which point Weaver would stalk down the aisle. "Senator? Hate to interrupt. Cindy's on the phone for you."

The press loved this Straight Talk shtick and did nothing to jeopardize it. Aboard the bus, Weaver and Salter openly discussed ad scripts, almost defiant in their confidence that the press would keep mum. But was this gentleman's agreement necessarily a bad thing? Warhorses like Curtis Wilkie from the *Boston Globe* enthused that this was what it used to be like, back when movies cost a dollar and candidates didn't have handlers. . . . *The Boys on the Bus* revisited! Yet it felt postmodern rather than retro, this high-wire insurgency . . . which was why the dispatches from the Straight Talk Express began to take on a life of their own, throughout New Hampshire and beyond.

The first of John McCain's 114 town hall meetings convened in April 1999 at an American Legion hall in Manchester, before a crowd of thirteen. They were veterans—the only natural McCain constituency that the Bush Machine hadn't tapped into—and they had been lured by flyers promising free ice cream. For the next two months, McCain's ice cream socials drew anywhere from fifteen to twenty-five brothers-in-arms. Somewhat to their surprise, the attendees found a candidate who wasn't terribly interested in speechifying. The senator would clear his throat for a couple of minutes, then ask the small audiences to say what was on their minds.

The main question at that point was: Who the hell is John McCain, and what if anything does he stand for? Beyond Arizona and the Beltway, two things were known of him: He'd been a prisoner of war in Hanoi, and he'd been implicated in a savings-and-loan scandal a decade or so ago. Nothing about that heavy-cheeked face and reedy tenor hinted of the rousing drama the three-term senator would bring to an otherwise paint-by-numbers campaign season.

McCain's maverick raison d'être was to cleanse the befouled campaign process, bringing the PACs and lobbyists to heel with serious reform so that well-intentioned public servants could concentrate on the nation's business rather than that of their sponsors. As a charter member of the Keating Five (the five senators compromised to varying degrees by savings-and-loan operator Charles Keating), McCain knew whereof he spoke. The repenting-sinner aspect was an especially deft touch, imbuing the senator with added authority while indemnifying him against charges of sanctimony.

He chose not to overplay the war hero persona. At the 1992 Republican National Convention in Houston, the senator was just about to take the stage to give his speech supporting the reelection of President George H. W. Bush when a youthful-looking fellow grabbed him by the arm. *You've gotta hammer Clinton on the draft dodging*, the man said.

Sorry, McCain replied to George W. Bush. *That's not my thing.*

In early June 1999, a McCain event at the Derry VFW hall drew fifty-five locals, not all of them veterans. Some of the questions were nutty, and McCain's pugnaciousness was on free display. Later that month, a hundred elected representatives showed up to a free face-feed across from the statehouse. A buzz had commenced, and it grew exponentially in August, with the release of McCain's memoir, *Faith of My Fathers*. When Random House held McCain to the contractually stipulated three weeks of book promoting, the candidate's lieutenants feared that this would pose a fatal disruption in an already precarious campaign.

They thought different after seeing two thousand book buyers standing in line at a Barnes & Noble in Atlanta.

Still, the McCain insurgency was a pauper's operation.

While the frontrunner amassed and lavished fortunes throughout America, McCain's moneyman, Rick Davis, deposited a hard-earned $3 million in the bank, the interest from which was intended to be their budget for New Hampshire. The Bush campaign employed two full-time opposition researchers. McCain relied on AskJeeves.com. Bush had the Texas Rangers for security. McCain's detail consisted of a large fellow named Bob who ordinarily worked at a dry cleaner's and who carried with him a gym bag that may or may not have contained a firearm.

Comparisons to the frontrunner's apparatus were irresistible. McCain did nothing to discourage them. By all rights, the Texan should have been the outsider, the eighteen-year veteran of Capitol Hill the emblem of the status quo. But Bush had all the money, all the endorsements, and none of the outsider's romanticism. Not that McCain himself didn't try to woo the kingmakers. Not that his gurus, when calling think tanks like the Heritage Foundation to request policy expertise, were altogether thrilled to hear the reply, "Sorry. We're committed to Bush."

Goliath's role having already been taken, McCain deftly resorted to the slingshot. As Weaver would tell his subordinates, "We've got two things going for us: a better candidate, and a faster operation." By seven each morning, deputy press secretary Todd Harris would be disseminating talking points to morning radio shows, well before the local Bush offices were even lit up. Running rings around the frontrunner became the favorite event in Team McCain's decathlon. *Bush is doing two events today? Hell, let's do ten!* A more obliging foil could scarcely be imagined. Bush's equivalent to the Straight Talk Express was his press plane, emblazoned AIR ACCESS but dubbed by its sullen inhabitants "No Access." McCain's boys simply referred to it as the Stalag—a continuing play on the metaphor peddled by Murphy: "We're the French Resistance. They're the German army."

Even the senator, while professing a thorough distaste for negative campaigning, delighted in coy observations such as "Some would tell you" or "Others in this campaign"—and no one took these to be putdowns of Orrin Hatch. Officially, of course, he and his subordinates insisted that they had no beef of any kind with the governor. Respected the man, respected the operation, fully intended to obey Reagan's Eleventh Commandment about not speaking ill of a fellow Republican, etc. It was far from that simple. McCain's ranks included various individuals who had, at least implicitly, been snubbed by the Bush Machine. Particularly bad blood ran between Rove and his fellow Texan John Weaver, owing to some ancient Hatfield-McCoy dispute going back to when the two were among the few Republican consultants in a vast state that nonetheless seemed not big enough for them both.

But above all, if this was to be a crusade, a certain moral superiority had to be mustered. And so McCain's boys took few pains to conceal their disdain—to "scratch the man who would be king, see if he bleeds to death," as Murphy so delicately put it. The day that the *New York Times'* Frank Bruni reported on Bush's feather pillow—"Don't you all bring your own pillows?" the governor was quoted as asking the press—was a day that found Weaver howling with laughter on the Straight Talk Express. And the day that Rick Berke, also of the *Times*, obliged Todd Harris's suggestion that the reporter look into a possible rift between Bush's New Hampshire operation and its Austin office, resulting in a page-one Sunday story . . . well, the boys on the bus said what they always said when outrageous good fortune plopped into their maverick laps:

"What a fucking *caper!*"

Bush's New Hampshire staff could feel the ship listing as the weather turned cold. With it came a creeping seasickness familiar to those deckhands who'd sunk with the elder Bush in 1980 and with Bob Dole in 1996. They could see it in the numbers, hear it on the evening news: New Hampshire was in full swoon, and not for George W. Bush.

The temptation was to blame it all on Joe Allbaugh—Pinky, as Bush called him, though the campaign manager preferred to be known as The Enforcer, since it fit his gym coach's scowl and drill sergeant's flattop. (Before this image makeover, the Oklahoman had sported a ponytail.) Allbaugh showed a predilection for tough love. Though

tasked chiefly with keeping Rove on a short leash, The Enforcer was
never too busy to humble the lowly—as when he presided over a
seminar for unpaid interns and held up a business card with his burly
digits, growling, "Everything I have to say to you can fit on this. Every
one of you is replaceable—doesn't matter who you are, I've got a hundred résumés sitting on my desk." With particular relish, it seemed to
the local aides, Allbaugh said no to the uppity first-primary minions.
No to a request for one more day for Bush in New Hampshire. No
to a request for yard signs. No to a request for name badges. No to a
request for soap and toilet paper for the Concord office.

They wanted to blame Allbaugh, or mother-knows-best Karen,
or the ad guys like McKinnon whose wizardry was nowhere in evidence in the blasé spots that showed Bush and Laura sitting on a
couch in Crawford. And while certainly no one *wanted* to blame
Laura, it peeved them when she wowed the Concord Rotary Club on
October 12 with her pastoral charms—and then, in the manner of her
husband, departed the event without taking a single question.

Alas, there was little doubt as to where the fault truly lay by late
September, when George W. Bush informed his staff that he had no
interest in attending the first presidential primary debate in New
Hampshire on October 28.

*Big mistake—they'll take it as a slight, they're gonna call us arro-
gant. . . .* Bush didn't care. He hated debates. He hated them for the
same reasons that he hated press conferences and voter Q&A's. They
were all about preening, a transparent exercise in *gotcha*, a chance for
some bit player to seize the stage and disrupt the governor's Message.

And anyway, these Republican primary debates weren't even
debates. How could they be? At one time, Bush had ten rivals scrap-
ping for the daily sound bite. By October 1999, five contenders of low
to middling promise—Lamar Alexander, Dan Quayle, Elizabeth Dole,
Bob Smith, and Pat Buchanan—had given up the ghost. But that
still left McCain, Steve Forbes, Alan Keyes, Gary Bauer, and Senator
Orrin Hatch vying for the role of not-Bush. Why spend an hour
onstage brawling for the microphone with mud wrestlers like Bauer
and Keyes?

*Because that's part of it—showing them you're not afraid, that you don't
need a script. It's just, you can't not show up. . . .*

The governor's aides pushed back: *It's too soon, there's no upside, he
needs to stay above the fray, fifty-state campaign. . . .* Privately thinking: *He
could lose the debate.*

After days of internal bickering, the Bush camp issued its regrets: Alas, the governor would be in Dallas that evening, watching his wife, Laura, receive an award at her alma mater, Southern Methodist University. "I'm sorry I'm not there," Bush said on TV that day, not terribly convincingly.

In the days that followed, he would be sorrier.

By early November, John McCain had vaulted ahead of Bush, 37–35, in the *Time*/CNN poll. Karen announced that despite the campaign's earlier refusal to participate in any debates before January, the governor would in fact show up at the next such event, on December 2 in Manchester. His performance that night was not what it needed to be. Virtually every one of Bush's answers included a reminder that he was "the governor of the second biggest state" and "the twelfth biggest economy in the world." More than once, he ran out of things to talk about and so concluded his answers early—a sensible, even admirable gesture, had George W. Bush not already been under suspicion of having little to say for himself.

Winter brought unaccustomed misery. On the icy roads, the Texas Rangers wrecked three cars. The right-wing Manchester *Union-Leader*, never adoring of Bushes, spat out particular venom in its endorsement of Steve Forbes: "Bush is a nice guy but an empty suit with no philosophical underpinning." A half-dozen prominent supporters proudly announced their defection to the McCain camp, while several others quietly followed suit. The Judd Gregg eight-foot Roll Call of Endorsees, unraveled by Gregg only five months ago in New Castle, was now a fast-shriveling parchment. And even as Liddy Dole dropped out of the race and threw her support behind Bush—"a proven leader with optimism and faith," she drawled with, it seemed, distinctly vice-presidential vigor—the evidence was clear that *her* supporters were heading in the opposite direction, toward the senator from Arizona.

Nothing worked, except to opposite effect. On January 24, Bush took the Iowa caucus. But what he termed a "record-shattering victory" was only a 41–30 triumph over the dreary Forbes—with McCain, who had eschewed Iowa altogether, getting five points anyway.

On the Friday before primary day, the former New Hampshire governor and Bush 41 chief of staff John Sununu at last lumbered out of his indecision and declared himself a supporter of the Texas governor. As to the lateness of the endorsement, there were two theories: Either Sununu was hoping to be cast as the gallant difference-maker, or he was exacting a pound of flesh for having been fired as the elder Bush's chief nine years earlier. (Sununu's former deputy, Andy Card, had done the actual firing, but George W. had long bragged that he himself had dropped the hammer on his dad's behalf.) The reason, whichever it might be, was all about John Sununu, and the event—staged, for reasons only Judd Gregg could explain, at the offices of an insurance company—fell flat.

Desperate for a momentum swing, and after much internal hand-wringing, the gurus did what they'd sworn not to do: They brought in Bush's father.

"How's he doing?" George Herbert Walker Bush asked Tom Rath as they stared out into the impressive crowd assembled at the Milford Athletic Club on Saturday, January 29.

"Well, he's pretty sick," said Rathbone. Which was true—the governor was fighting off the flu—but was not really what the ex-president meant.

The father then turned to Pat Griffin. "Can we pull this off?" he asked.

"I think it can still happen," replied Griffey. But he could see worry in the old man's face. After all: If things really were fine, then what the hell was Dad doing here?

The governor was summoned to the microphone. A thousand rapt attendees, waiting all day to hear the candidate speak. But Bush felt like crap, had nothing in the tank. Three minutes of *We're gonna win on Tuesday*, and he gave things over to George Herbert Walker Bush.

Who spoke from the heart, his eyes tearing with pride, a quavering defiance in his voice: "This boy—this son of ours—is not going to let you down. . . ."

And if you stood amid the audience, your heart melted with theirs. But if you sat in the rafters with the media—heard the chortles, saw the cell phones flip open—you knew that Daddy's boy was screwed.

Monday, the day before the primary, the fateful Final Push, began in Manchester at a pancake flip-off. A competition, Bush's thing.

"Watch this," the governor called out, and, flipping a pancake well above his head, he affected a centerfielder's nonchalance as he caught it with his spatula.

"I'm gonna do it again," he declared to no one in particular. A flick of the wrist, the edible disk soaring . . . then neatly thudding onto Bush's spatula.

Gary Bauer attempted the feat, and promptly fell off the riser.

Bush won the flip-off hands down.

Then the frontrunner's motorcade headed for the town of Exeter, where the candidate and his wife would mingle with the natives at a diner called the Loaf & Ladle, and afterward spend an hour walking door to door, the cameras capturing the Texas governor in full command of retail politics as he and his charming wife implored the good people of Exeter to join the Bushes in ushering in an era of Compassionate Conservatism and Personal Responsibility. That was the plan. That is what was on the schedule. But along the way, Bush's director of travel logistics, Brad Blakeman, got word from his boys on the ground that a gaggle of union protesters bused in from Massachusetts were standing in front of the Loaf & Ladle, holding up signs.

Blakeman, Judd Gregg, and Joe Allbaugh huddled for about a millisecond. They knew well that nothing so rankled George W. Bush as being heckled. "We're turning around," Blakeman muttered into the radio.

But to where? The campaign now had two hours to kill. Joel Maiola made a call, then informed the other staffers: Madden's Family Restaurant in Derry would be happy to receive the governor.

Which turned out to be the case—except that the proprietor had neglected to inform Maiola that the diner was virtually empty. For fully an hour the candidate and his entourage sat stewing in the booths, listening to the clock tick.

Pat Griffin came up with the bright idea: "Why don't we go sledding at Ragdon Farm?"

Advance reported back: The popular Amherst slope was packed with kids and their parents making merry in the snow. *A New Hampshire moment, take off the coat and tie, put on the windbreaker—yeah!* The locals had been pining for just such a photo op.

The Texans thought this had to be a joke. *You're saying the governor should spend his final campaign day . . . SLEDDING?*

"Sure, let's do it," Bush grinned.

Upward of a thousand people were crawling across the slope that crisp afternoon when the caravan settled in along the highway. State troopers converged, their bellows parried by the irresistible force of Texas Rangers plowing a swath for the governor, his wife, his parents, and his daughters. At the top of the hill, a couple of kids were led to the candidate. Bush introduced himself, shook their hands. Then he challenged them to a race.

Mounting his sled, the governor took off downhill. The snow had hardened into a carpet of ice. Bush zoomed ahead of his two fellow sledders, losing as well his daughters and the advance team, jubilant even as he grimaced against the cold. Reporters in pursuit fell on their asses. The Rangers, positioned near the bottom of the slope, watched Bush fly past them and then stumbled after their boss in their cowboy boots.

Bush rose from his sled. Sure enough, he had been the first one down.

"Let's go again!" he exulted . . . then was reminded, in the gentlest possible words, that in sixteen hours, people would be standing in line to vote on whether George W. Bush—fine downhill sledder and pancake flipper though he may be—had what it took to be president of the United States of America.

The Bush campaign wrapped up the day's activity at a candlepin bowling alley in Nashua. That evening, Americans in the Granite State and beyond took in the televised spectacle of the two leading Republican presidential contenders. There was John McCain, the master of the town hall, being mobbed in Peterborough, delirious followers hanging from the balcony like schoolboys; McCain the war hero at a rally in Portsmouth, serenaded by the horn of a mighty naval vessel.

And there was George W. Bush, the president's son, sledding and bowling.

"You ready to win tonight?" the governor called out early the next morning, February 1, 2000, to one of his advance guys, who thought, *Not a freaking chance.*

Bush wanted to believe it. Rove tried to believe it. The New Hampshire lieutenants like Maiola could not, even in their wildest delusions, believe it, figuring nonetheless that the margin of defeat would be 4, perhaps 5. . . .

The first exit polls came in around noon.

Studying them, McCain's strategist John Weaver murmured, "They can't be true."

Hearing them from Rove over Chinese food, Mark McKinnon replied, "Oh, shit."

Receiving them by phone, Joel Maiola turned to Pat Griffin and informed him, "We're getting killed."

Wolfeboro, six months ago the site of the Bush couple's Tolkien-like arrival by boat at a shoreline swelling with worshippers . . . had swung to McCain by a margin of 21.

Both sides figured the numbers had to be off. Which they were.

The next wave of numbers came in: McCain by 19.

"Are you *sure?*"

That was Bush, sitting in his suite at the Merrimack Residence Inn, the expression on his face matching his words. Karl Rove had been the deliverer, a task no sane man would have relished.

Rove indicated that yes, he was sure.

Bush was at a loss for words. His ordinary reflex action, lashing out at his two favorite targets, Rove (because he usually had it coming) and his bodyman Logan Walters (who never did, but who just always happened to be handy)—*What the hell do you mean, why wasn't this done, give me a goddamn straight answer*—did not fit the present circumstances. No. A complete and total humiliation . . . he couldn't point fingers. He couldn't hide, any more than he could quit.

He sat there in the suite for a while with his wife—watching, sort of, the Weather Channel. It was Laura who first spoke up. And when she did, people tended to listen, since the former librarian largely kept to her parallel universe. Never scheduling herself into policy meetings, always deferring—or simply shutting it all out, as when five staffers and the Bushes crammed into a tiny plane for an event in Albuquerque, and in the middle of a gin rummy game heavy on profane trash-talking, there sat the First Lady of Texas with her face in a book.

"You got defined," she now told her husband. Her tone wasn't sympathetic. "And you need to make up your mind whether or not you're going to go down there and tell people who *you* are. Instead of letting people define you."

Bush didn't argue with her.

He preferred the Merrimack hotel for its environs, which were better suited for jogging than the downtown alternatives. Today, however, it was freezing, and in any event the governor needed to sweat somewhere out of public view. The Rangers drove him to a strip-mall gym. Huffing on a treadmill in his sweats, the plainclothes emblem of middle-age stress—Bush gave himself that hour to pity and punish and reconstruct himself. Then he showered and instructed his Rangers to take him back to the hotel.

There he marshaled his Texans—Rove, Karen Hughes with her

teenage son, Robert, McKinnon, Blakeman, a few others—and explained to them what all of this meant. "We're going to lose today," Bush told them. "Look, if anybody wants to blame someone, blame me. I don't want anybody blaming anyone in New Hampshire. These people did a good job for us. We're gonna need them in the general."

He said to Karen, "Draft a statement. I want it to be a *celebratory* statement."

Surveying the pallor of their expressions, Bush was more emphatic: "This thing ain't over. We're gonna fight, okay? Don't let 'em smell defeat when you walk out there. People are gonna read your body language."

The governor was still working on his.

In his suite at the Nashua Crowne Plaza, John McCain stood beside a window, rehearsing the victory speech Mark Salter had written for him. Weaver and Salter entered the room, handed him the 5:00 P.M. exit polls.

McCain had left that final rally in Peterborough last night confident that he would win. Five points, eight points. But *these* crazy numbers . . . Studying them, the senator said quietly, "This has . . . implications."

"Uh . . . like you might be president?" ventured Salter.

McCain smiled. He turned his gaze toward the window for a moment. Then he looked back down at his speech.

Later, McCain's press secretary Todd Harris received a call from a friendly reporter in the Bush camp. The Bush people, she told Harris, were asking around for a line to McCain. He passed on the number of the senator's pollster, Bill McInturff, whose phone then rang.

"Rove's on the phone," McInturff announced.

"Tell him consultants don't concede," scoffed Weaver.

A second call came through. It was the governor. Cindy McCain was crying as her husband took the phone. Sharing this historic moment with Cindy and McCain's inner circle were, fittingly, a handful of thoroughly embedded reporters like Jake Tapper and Tucker Carlson, along with a clutch of liquored-up veterans.

In times of crushing malaise or irrational exuberance, McCain and his fellow POWs fell back on an old sailor's admonition: *Steady strain, boys. Steady strain.* Accordingly, the rope line of his emotions stayed just slightly taut as he listened to the governor—his expression less that of a victor than of a man on the phone with his insurance agent.

"Okay, George. Okay. See you in South Carolina. Thank you, George. Okay. Goodbye, George."

Doing what she did best, Karen spent the afternoon spinning a rhetorical web of gold in her draft of the concession speech: *The road to the Republican nomination is a long road. Mine will go through all fifty states, and I intend it to end at 1600 Pennsylvania Avenue. . . .*

Doing what he did best, Rove placed a conference call to the South Carolina offices before the news had hit the wires: "The governor's taken responsibility for it. We made some mistakes, but we're gonna regroup. And you're gonna help us do it."

Doing what he did best that night at Saint Anselm College's not-Victory Party, Joe Allbaugh took note of the spread of food that no one had mustered the appetite to devour and thereupon chewed out a young staffer for her profligate spending.

And doing what had been bred in his bones, George W. Bush, having been dealt a 50–32 drubbing, wound down that miserable evening in a state of Bushian graciousness as he spoke to the local faithful one by one:

"You're a good man."

"You guys worked your asses off. We're gonna pull this together."

"I'm gonna learn, I'm gonna get better."

"You go out and buy yourself a red dress and come to Washington, because we're gonna win."

What a guy—he knew just the right things to say. It meant so much to them.

But did it mean anything else?

2

TEXAS

He was not, by any meaningful measure—and certainly not by presidential calculus—a tested man.

The travails of George Walker Bush fell somewhat short of mythic. He was the eldest son of an accomplished, arguably great man—a man who loved his son, wishing for his son a good life while subliminally suggesting greatness as a standard; a man who was often gone, reappearing now and then in newsprint; a man whose few imperfections were magnified by his fame, in turn setting for his son a kind of double standard, of how to be and how not to be, when even the imperfect standard was greater than could be expected of most offspring. All of which, for the son, had to be hard. Had to feel like struggle. But not a severe test—not really.

From one womb he entered the extended Bush womb—sprawling, loving, enriching in every meaningful way. In the summer of 1948 at the age of two, his parents spirited him away from Greenwich, Connecticut, leaving him without memories or Yankee affect, but with his birthplace's Rolodex already there for the asking. Between Midland's flat earth and its vast sky, young George sprouted semiupright, a perfectly normal lad in this strange utopia known as the Texas oil patch. If he was too young to be scarred by the death of his kid sister Robin from leukemia, he saw how his mother grieved—and so he responded just as two other future performers, comedians Jim Carrey and Stephen Colbert, would while watching their mothers suffer: He played the goofball, yearning to coax out a laugh from Bar. And in return, he would say, "I learned from my mother how to put people at ease. She was the greatest person about walking into a room full of intense people and enabling them to relax, so that you could communicate with them."

It was never a boy's idea to be yanked away from a safe haven such as Midland to an unfamiliar colossus like Houston . . . or, two years later, in 1961, to be shipped off to the Phillips Academy in Andover, Massachusetts. But all Bush princes went to Andover, and George W.'s affability—a somewhat crude hybrid of Poppy's tutored patter and Bar's stiletto tongue—transferred well there. With average grades he got into Yale, and later into Harvard Business School. His skills were not, nor ever would be, of the academic sort. Even trying his best in his schoolwork—and he really did try—something short-circuited in the boy's agile but unsophisticated motherboard: He mangled his words, got impatient, smoke all but streamed out of his ears. Dipping Copenhagen in the classroom was George W.'s way of serving notice that he did not, truthfully, need to take shit from the ivory tower. Like he needed A's!

No, young Bush's particular genius—the facility for wiping out in milliseconds the distance separating himself from total strangers— would more than compensate. What drew the other boys to him was that instant familiarity: remembering their names (or, if one's surname twisted the tongue, assigning a nickname), flinging arms around shoulders, acute eye contact, a gruff yet seductive whisper. . . . Formality never suited him—he wasn't *really* a prince, just a senator's grand-kid—so George W. swept it aside. As a freshman, he befriended seniors. In the clique-obsessed world of adolescence, he kept largely to his jock tribe but never bullied those left out of the game. At Andover, he formed a stickball league, thereby rewriting all the rules in his favor: Now the school's most popular pastime would *mock* the other sports at which George W. was only mediocre . . . oh, and guess who would serve as the league's "high commissioner"? During one game, the brilliant but athletically challenged Alan Wofsey flukishly made a circus catch in left field—prompting High Commissioner Bush to stop the game and award Wofsey a moment of solemn congratulations. It was a gesture reminiscent of the other George . . . except, of course, that Poppy would've never made such a show of it.

The first George Bush to attend Phillips Academy (class of '42) had been universally regarded as brilliant, athletic, and gorgeous. George the Second, less so. Everything about him suggested asymmetry.

Exhibit A was the off-center grin that was intended to reflect bashfulness or bemusement or his taste for the absurd, but that instead came off as an arrogant sneer. His posture was awful; blazers hung from his frame like ancient undergarments. Even with no reason to hurry, George W. bustled, somewhat crab-armed, and when he tried to saunter he looked like a boy pretending to be . . . well, his father. He edged into people's airspace. He interrupted. His hands latched on to cheeks, biceps, necks . . . grabby bastard! And some would infer from his wretched manner of dress that this was Bush's version of prep school rebellion—but no, the evidence in his dorm room told the real story: He was a complete and total slob.

But he didn't give a damn. Young Bush—DKE pledge, Skull and Bones legacy, baseball team benchwarmer—was committed to, if nothing else, having an excellent time. The Yale alma mater's lyrics extolled "the shortest, gladdest years of life." Mission accomplished for George W., despite the fact that his short/glad years coincided with the cultural tumult of the sixties. Introduced as a freshman in 1964 to the campus chaplain, antiwar activist William Sloane Coffin Jr., the chatty young fellow his Andover chums dubbed "the Lip" was rendered speechless when Coffin said, "I know your father, and your father lost to a better man." (The elder Bush had just been defeated in his first U.S. Senate race by incumbent Ralph Yarborough, a darling of the libs whom Bush had attacked for supporting the Civil Rights Act.) But for that storied encounter, George W. might have passed his college years largely unacquainted with that decade's controversies.

The Yale he experienced more closely resembled the Yale of Poppy's day than Berkeley with its gun-toting Black Panthers and its ranting Mario Savio. He didn't much know what to make of Vietnam. The posturings of history professor Staughton Lynd—who'd gone to Hanoi with a band of fellow antiwar activists to negotiate a separate peace—riled Bush's conservative impulses. After Lynd returned to campus in 1966, George W. went to hear him speak, figuring that Lynd's words would piss him off, and he wasn't disappointed. Around that same time, George W. sat on the Green, unpersuaded by the liberal jabber of Vice President Hubert Humphrey. Still, he didn't join the Young Republicans, didn't pass out leaflets. Didn't succumb to "any kind of heaviness of the moment." Occasionally he would wonder what it must be like to be one of those fretful types who worried about nuclear war and such. Long after his graduation in 1968, he would reflect on the other events of that year: "Race riots, assassinations, the Vietnam War, the Chicago convention—it was pretty rough." But not for him.

Like many of his generation,, George W. found casual virtue in the era: you could spend less money at the barbershop, you could dress like a vagrant and the ethos of the times meant that your chances of sexual gratification were greatly improved. At parties where one walked through curtains of marijuana smoke—and where one's refusal to partake implied that one was a narc—he blended easily as always, despite invariably having the shortest haircut in the house. (And despite preferring to hear country singer George Jones over whatever psychedelic gibberish the host had spinning on the turntable.) Even with diploma in hand, George W. Bush was far, far from adulthood. He still played touch football on a Houston neighbor's lawn with his younger brothers. He still hopped from one local girl to the next. (His engagement to a Rice student died of inertia.)

And, famously, he enlisted in the National Guard, a preferred combat-avoiding gambit in the days well before Iraq. Leapfrogging ahead of five hundred applicants wait-listed for the remaining four slots, 2nd Lt. George Walker Bush joined the 147th Fighter Group in September 1968 with the aim of flying planes as his war-hero father had. By November 1970, his commander, Lt. Col. Jerry Killian, couldn't believe what a catch he'd landed: "Lt. Bush is a dynamic outstanding young officer. . . . He is a natural leader . . . should be promoted well ahead of his contemporaries."

But George W. wasn't up for leading just yet. Sure, he'd written the Guard a letter of intent, stating, "I have applied for pilot training with the goal of making flying a lifetime pursuit." What else was he going to say? And anyway, politics now held his attention. Between basic and pilot training in 1968, a friend had hooked him up with Congressman Ed Gurney of Florida, who was running for the U.S. Senate. Bush became Gurney's personal aide; among his duties was to carry the candidate's pillow. Gurney walloped his opponent for speaking ill of segregation. Two years later, George W.'s dad again ran for the U.S. Senate, losing when Democrat Lloyd Bentsen ran to Poppy's right. Looked pretty simple, really. George W. himself had considered running for the Texas State Senate in '71. Instead, he signed on as political director for Red Blount's 1972 Senate race in Alabama, masterminding Blount's way to a 62–33 thumping in the general election.

Meanwhile, Lt. Bush's commanding officers were wondering why their ace flyboy had skipped his May physical. The pilot-errant called five days after the deadline and said, according to his commander's memo, "he wants to transfer to Alabama to any unit he can get in to. Says that he is working on another campaign for his dad . . . I advised him of our investment in him and his commitment . . . I told him I had to have written acceptance before he would be transferred, but think he's also talking to someone upstairs." The once "dynamic out-standing young officer" had officially become a pain in the ass. He was suspended from flying duty in September 1972. A year later, George W. requested an early discharge from the Guard. No one stood in his way.

He could avoid any number of things, but not the recognition that he was falling well short of his father's trajectory. That Dad never pushed him, never verbalized his disappointment—well, that only made it worse, in a way. Like success had never been expected of him to begin with. (Jebby, yes. But Georgie, the family chucklehead?) Sure, he had it lucky, having it all laid out for him: Andover, Yale, piloting.

Was that lucky?

And if it wasn't—if this wasn't what George W. wanted . . . well, what, then?

His dad was running the RNC during the Watergate doldrums of 1973 when George W. drove up to their home in Georgetown one night, amid a clattering of garbage cans. He'd taken his fifteen-year-old brother, Marvin, out drinking, as Poppy could plainly see when the noise brought him outside. The father's expression of displeasure was too much for the eldest son to bear. And thus, the immortal words: "You wanna go *mano a mano* right here?"

Reminded of this anecdote by a friend a quarter century later, Barbara Bush would lower her spectacles and with trademark brutality observe, "Georgie would've never won that fight."

Which the son knew, of course. And so he never threw a punch that night.

Instead, he let the old man hook him up with a volunteer gig at a nonprofit of which Poppy was honorary chairman. Driving up in his white Skylark to the office of Project PULL on McGowan Street, in the bowels of Houston's inner-city Third Ward—not so far away at all from his pals' homes in lush River Oaks—George W. must have fig-ured that Dad was really sticking him with the tough love this time. But it turned out to be a pretty sweet gig, playing big brother to ghetto kids: a little table tennis, some hoops, hanging out with a few Houston Oilers also volunteering their time, didn't have to wear socks with his shoes. . . .

It could've been that, and only that. And, because it was baseball season, his bosses were frankly worried that George W.'s fondness for Nickle Beer Night at the Astrodome would get the better of his work ethic. But the thing was . . . the kids *loved* him. Loved his banter, his spirit—nothing like the other white men in their lives, i.e., cops—but especially loved his love. The way he showed up every day, threw his arms around them, didn't talk down . . . Not one of them knew, or could have known, that their George, with his ratty T-shirts and his Skylark full of smelly clothes and gum wrappers, was a guy who had it made.

And he, in turn, loved being looked up to. On top of which, he had never been around a bunch of black kids, much less impoverished black kids. Not quite the Andover experience, horsing around with a twelve-year-old whose waistband suddenly reveals a revolver. Not quite the Dekes, these toughs he'd see when he toured his boys through a juvenile jail. There was a cute little kid named Jimmy Dean who stood on the curb waiting for George W.'s arrival every morning. Little Jimmy lived in a pesthole with a zoned-out mama. George W. saw it once when he dropped the kid off: all that smoke, all those loser males. . . . Bush always considered himself an optimist. Still: Jimmy Dean making it out of this tar pit? Now *that* would be a test.

(Alas, Jimmy failed. Jimmy got shot to death as a teenager. George W. learned about this in 1988, the year he spent helping his father get elected president of the United States.)

To be one's own man is every man's test, and for some time it was all the test George W. Bush could handle. His parents paid his way to the Harvard School of Business, which got him out of the Guard early and enabled him, for the first time ever, to tread soil that did not already bear the deep footprints of George Herbert Walker Bush. And insofar as he could ever flourish in an academic setting, he did so. He hit the books with surprising relish. A self-styled Ivy League Bubba with his cheekful of Copenhagen, George W. made himself memorable in the classroom, once bringing in a friend who'd gone to work in his father's mill in the middle of a strike to talk about what it was like to be a scab.

Yet, no sooner had he staked out his own path than he scampered back to Poppy's, tossing his worldly goods into the back of his Cutlass following graduation in 1975 and driving solo westward to the Texas oil patch. The men who took him in—providing him with an office, a desk, an accountant, an apartment, and the basics of the oil business— had all been paid calls by one Bush or another. Not that this guaranteed prosperity by any means. The Ivy League–trained businessman would be cutting his teeth as one of 150 or so landmen fanning out across the Permian Basin: cold-calling ranchers, barging in on coffeehouse conversations, foraging through courthouse records in search of a score ranging from mineral rights or a land swap to the almighty gusher.

Though he barely knew a derrick from a dipstick, George W. was made for this job. It was all about the things he did best: remembering people's names, getting to the heart of the matter, and covering the terrain like a demon. "George was at our house," a rancher told one of Bush's mentors. "He's the nicest fella! I wonder if he'd like to meet our daughter?"

He looked like a genius, arriving when he did—$3 a barrel to $11 to $30 in the span of three years, with all the major oil companies playing at Midland's table and all the local bank execs dispensing loans like kindly grandfathers. "I've been talking to Dad—I wish he'd get politics out of his head, we could make a *lot* of money!" George W. enthused to a friend. And indeed, having arrived in Midland with a net worth of about $50,000, he would depart it eleven years later with about $2 million in assets.

But if his success was ensured, it didn't feel that way at the time. When a visiting friend asked him that first year, "Do you make any money?" George W. shrugged. "I had a pretty good week last week," he said. "Made a hundred bucks in a poker game." The big score would elude him throughout his time in the oil patch. Yet it felt ever within reach in this Texas boomtown. Fancy houses shot up, along with a Rolls-Royce dealership. Fellow scrappers were now buying racehorses and jetting off to Vegas. You could not help but feel optimistic, ripe for reinvention in this blank slate of a city. Nature threw up no barriers, no looming reminders of one's mortal puniness. Any and all distinction and beauty in Midland were manmade . . . while that big sky was heaven, and it was the ceiling.

Most important, he was returning to his people. The mannered playing field of the Ivy League had not favored his visceral style of play, and (very much unlike him) he never quite got over it—ridiculing, even as president, the very institutions whose elite network had provided him with an unsurpassable education (despite his less-than-deserving academic qualifications), underwritten his businesses, and donated heavily to his campaigns. Bush would chide his aides for their Harvard affiliations. Epic wooing on the part of Yale's president was required to lure him back to his alma mater in 2001 to give a commencement speech, in which he grudgingly declared, "That's how I've come to feel about the Yale experience—grateful."

The Midlanders-versus-Ivy-Leaguers paradigm would become a lasting binary contrast of virtue in Bushworld. "You guys from Midland never bother him," White House chief of staff Andy Card would appreciatively tell one of them—adding, "Those jerks from Yale and Harvard call him all the time!" The town had no pretense, which was perfect for a very young twenty-nine-year-old man who was known to wear the same pair of socks three days in a row and to accept hand-me-downs from friends and relatives without the remotest shame. He cut a fine if slovenly figure in Midland. And beyond: George W. was more than happy to be fixed up with dates in Dallas, Houston, Austin, and wherever else his friends' weddings were held. He was just as content going to Mardi Gras with his pals as camping out in Big Bend National Park. As a counterweight to his partying, he'd taken up jogging and ran at a blazing clip through the streets of Midland during the lunch hour. The balance was not always perfectly struck, as when he threw up after being overserved at the country club one evening. Still, no one in Midland viewed George W. Bush as a screw-up, any more than they envisioned him as president.

He had, in fact, screwed up badly once, though not in the oil patch. Two months after his thirtieth birthday, in 1976, George W. got caught in a speed trap while driving from a bar in Kennebunkport back to the family compound on Walker's Point. With him in the car were tennis star John Newcombe—not a good idea, trying to match an Australian beer for beer—along with his sixteen-year-old sister, Dorothy, and his dad's longtime press assistant Pete Roussel, who hopped out of the car and told the cop, "Do you know who you just arrested? That's George Bush." Undeterred, the policeman subjected George W. to a field sobriety test, which he failed, and then placed him in his squad car.

The next day, Bush called one of his oil partners, who reported to another colleague, "Well, they got George last night on a DUI." That day the son also faced his father, who stoically observed that George W. would have to take his lumps. That meant a $150 fine and a license suspension in Maine. Years later, the elder Bush would run into the arresting officer and tell him that the DUI was the "best thing that could have happened" to young George. In truth, it was a non-happening, a nontest, and certainly a nonissue two years after the DUI, when George W. Bush ran for the open seat of the 19th U.S. Congressional District.

Allies far and wide lined up to dissuade him from running. "You can't win against Kent Hance," warned former governor Allan Shivers, referring to the West Texas lifer and conservative Democrat who would face no serious oppostion in his primary.

"Well, I think I can," replied George W.

"The district's not right," Shivers tried to explain.

"Well, I appreciate it," said Bush. As he would later reflect: "You can't learn lessons by reading. Or at least I couldn't. I learned by doing. I knew it was an uphill struggle. But see, I've never had a fear of losing. I didn't *like* to lose. But having parents who give you unconditional love, I think it means I had the peace of mind to know that even with failure, there was love. So I never feared failure."

His unmade bed of a life was starting to achieve coherence, thanks to a brunette librarian with catlike eyes named Laura Welch. Among the few things she and Bush had in common were that she was thirty-one, a Midlander (they'd attended junior high together), she had never married, and she was easily underestimated. Though outwardly a goody-goody, Laura was wry and curious and had effortlessly taken to Austin's bohemian sensibility. Her boyfriend was a restaurateur, and her friends, being Austinites, were music fans and stoners. (A tell-all book would launch the dubious claim that she had been a "go-to girl for dime bags" of pot while at SMU. Still, Laura's protestation to a staffer—"What's a dime bag?"—was a case of innocence feigned.) Only after her boyfriend dropped her in the summer of 1977 did Laura finally relent to the oft-made suggestion of her friends, Joe and Jan O'Neill, that they set her up with their pal George. On that first date—burgers in the O'Neills' backyard—George W. Bush did something they'd never quite seen before. He stayed up past midnight. The next day, Bush proposed that the four of them go paint the town red with a round of miniature golf.

For the next few weekends in August, Bush descended on Austin, ratcheting up his charm offensive. When the family's summer vacation in Kennebunkport intruded, Bush phoned Laura incessantly from Walker's Point—and, as Bar would remember, "A man would answer, or Laura would say, 'George, I can't talk right now.' So he left here after three days—then came back here in September with this darling girl! . . . He lived in what looked like a slum. Terrible! Such a sloppy fellow! And now he's Mister Clean. I tell you, we owe so much to Laura!"

They married on November 5, 1977, less than three months after their first date. Newly stabilized, Bush had even less reason to "fear failure." Still, failure in his next venture was likely. His political base was Midland, where friends in the oil biz were more than happy to volunteer their time and open their wallets. But the 19th District also encompassed vast rural swaths peopled by haters of Yankees and oil-men, of which Bush was both. George W. the genial landman might have won them over. And he certainly tried, tirelessly canvassing the region with his shy new bride in tow—so juiced by all that meeting and greeting that he barely seemed to notice the many doors slammed in his face, or that folks weren't following his dark rantings about President Carter's tilting toward European-style socialism with the Fuel Use Act of 1978 . . . because, well, this fella on the doorstep was wearing a tie, and who ever wore a tie in Muleshoe, Texas?

He prevailed in the primary against Jim Reese, the seasoned Odessa mayor, whose backers included Ronald Reagan and Gerald Ford, and who had excoriated Bush's father for his membership in the Tri-lateral Commission, with its ominous notions of a one-world govern-ment. Basking in victory, George W. gloated that he "wasn't given a Chinaman's chance of winning this thing." But, as Shivers and others had tried to tell Bush, beating Reese was the easy part. His Democra-tic opponent in the general election, the wily Hance, knew how to out-country the oilman. Bush tended to talk fast, and his pitch rose with the velocity. When stumped by a question, his face would turn, as one friend would put it, "red as a coffee can." His TV ads showed him jogging, presumably meant to convey vigor . . . or was he running *from* something? The drawling Hance gleefully painted Bush as Daddy's boy, *not from around heah*, and ran so far to the Republican's right that by the end of it all, George W. looked like Eugene McCarthy.

The showing—47–53—was respectable for a novice candidate, particularly in a part of America unaccustomed to voting Republican. But George W. took the defeat hard. Two years later, Bush called to console a friend who had just been beaten in a congressional race of his own. "Aw, I'll get over it," the friend muttered.

"You don't ever get over losing," George W. Bush replied.

Nonetheless, when Bush in 1979 opened his own oil practice, Arbusto Inc., following his defeat, he assured his bookkeeper that he wouldn't be closing shop to run again anytime soon. He was now married. Two years later, he would be both a father and the son of the vice president of the United States. (Parenthood did not come swiftly, Laura would say: "We wanted kids and in fact started going to the Gladney [Center for Adoption in Fort Worth] because we had trouble getting pregnant.") Time to be a responsible provider. And this he achieved, though more through the providence of his connections than through business acumen. Years later, Governor George W. Bush would confide to a writer that his firm had been "floundering." Karen Hughes pulled the writer aside for a rephrasing: "We consider it a *successful business.*" What was successful about it was that Bush got out, and got out ahead—selling to Harken Oil & Gas even as Arbusto verged on insolvency—just as the bust was collapsing most of Midland. Though the town had been good to him, George W. had nowhere left to go in Midland, as either an entrepreneur or an ambitious Republican.

Once again, Dad provided him with an easy out. As expected, Reagan's vice president had presidential designs of his own. The elder Bush had fabulous fund-raising and strategic support. What he lacked in Washington was a loyalist. He needed family watching his back. Brother Jeb—regarded both in the family and in the party as the Bush ascendant—had just been appointed Florida's secretary of commerce. George W., of course, was encumbered with twin five-year-old daughters and a wife with deep Midland roots. Yet here was an opportunity to which, for a variety of reasons, he could not say no.

The offer to move to Washington had actually been presented by the father's chief strategist, the thirty-four-year-old guitar-picking Strom Thurmond acolyte Lee Atwater. George W. had openly challenged Atwater: "How do we know we can trust you?" *So come hang out at the Washington office,* was the reply—a gesture of appeasement, but also classic Atwater, who knew from past campaigns how valuable a family pipeline could be.

Months before situating himself at the desk beside Atwater's, George W. quit alcohol. The occasion had been the morning after his fortieth birthday—July 6, 1986—at the Broadmoor Hotel in Colorado, where, with his close Midland pals Joe O'Neill and Don Evans and their spouses, "we just stayed up all night and drank," he would later say. Hangovers such as this one were competing with his energy, he told friends. Laura—herself a study in moderation, be it wine or cigarettes—had "been telling him for a few years that I thought it was necessary" to quit, she would recall. "George is pretty impulsive and does pretty much everything to excess. Drinking is not one of the good things to do to excess. And we had little girls, and in fact that's what I remember most, having these two little babies, and drinking really didn't fit. . . . Another factor was that we were going to move to Washington. He knew he couldn't move there and work on his dad's presidential campaign and keep drinking like that. You just can't take that kind of risk."

Bush could not bear the thought of again embarrassing his dad, as he had that night in Kennebunkport. Even before his birthday at the Broadmoor, he'd spent months in a very un-Bushian state of introspection—aware, he would later say, that "obviously I was searching for something in my life." The Reverend Billy Graham took a stroll with him one afternoon at Walker's Point. Their dialogue was memorable not for what was actually said—and in fact George W. was never able to recall Graham's words that day—but for the minister's calming presence, his assurance that Bush would not be confronting his struggles alone.

And so Graham's eighteen months as family confidant to the eventual forty-first president of the United States saw George W. Bush harnessing his energies to sober and purposeful if free-ranging effect. When Atwater fired his field director, Mary Matalin, Bush urged that she be given a second chance in a race in Michigan, saying, "Let her gut it out." When some brainiac at a preconvention rally replaced one of the VP's grandsons as introducers ("Ladies and gentlemen, the next president of the United States of America, my granddad!") with the droning South Carolina Governor Carroll Campbell, an apoplectic George W. tried in vain to reverse the decision. And when, as his mother would recall, "people had to move on, he moved them on. They would've gone eventually, and George gave 'em the help." He served as his father's gatekeeper, speechmaking surrogate, liaison to Atwater, and (when the press disparaged Dad) avenging angel. Laura would later tell a Texas reporter that it was during this campaign that father and firstborn son at long last filed down the barbed edges of their relationship. For once, the old man *needed* Georgie. And for once, George W. could be counted on.

But with this surge of responsibility came a determination to be, once and for all, his own man. This became evident to those who received handwritten notes from George W. scrawled on his per-

sonal campaign stationery. The letterhead read, GEORGE BUSH, JR.—
or at least it had before the son drew firm pen strokes through those
last two letters.

"George, you've got no base here. All you've got is a famous name."

This time, George W. listened when Texas political operatives like
his longtime friend Jim Francis warned him about running for office.
It was early 1989, and ever since the previous Thanksgiving the president-elect's son had been discussing with friends the 1990 gubernatorial race. He'd now distinguished himself on a national stage. Lee
Atwater had made some calls to Texas kingmakers on George W.'s
behalf. Among those who believed the son could prevail in a contested
Republican primary and then slay the dreaded Ann Richards was
another Atwater protégé, Austin direct-mail specialist Karl Rove.

But if Rove was wrong . . . George W. would be twice defeated,
probably broke, publicly ridiculed as a man whose only achievement
was to be born a Bush. . . .

Instead, he moved to Dallas and bought a baseball club.

As stairways to a governorship go, George W.'s was as original if
not quite as cinematic as that of Teddy Roosevelt abandoning a life of
letters and bureaucratic appointments to lead the Rough Riders up
San Juan Hill. Seeing the Bush name as instant credibility, baseball
commissioner Peter Ueberroth gave the imperial wink to the group
George W. began assembling to buy the Texas Rangers in April 1989.
Of the $89 million asking price, Bush himself could pony up only
$500,000—the subject of much smirking in some circles—but the
Rangers' group was hardly hurting for money. What it needed was a
managing general partner who could generate some local excitement
about this sad-sack American League franchise. It needed a fellow like
the Andover cheerleader, the Midland landman who could walk into
a stranger's living room, kick off his shoes, and cajole his way into a
free lunch and a mineral-rights lease. It needed a First Fan.

Beginning with that first season in 1989, George W. planted himself
in Arlington Stadium—not up in the air-conditioned VIP suite where
Laura and the twins occasionally sat, but right behind the home-team
dugout adjacent to first base. He made it a point to sit through all nine
innings, no matter the score, no matter how brutal the summer heat.
He sat there sweating right through the shortsleeved dress shirts that
Laura had helpfully bought him, scarfing down peanuts and hot dogs,
autographing literally thousands of his own personalized baseball card

for fans who lined up hoping for a moment with Pudge Rodriguez or Pete Incaviglia, but settling for the signature of a president's son. He'd call out to the batboy, "Hey, Bat, you got some bubble gum?" and distribute the fistful to those nearby. Just as the umps could expect a daily ribbing from George, so could the home team's many Hispanic players—Pudge and Jose Hernandez and Ruben Sierra and Juan Gonzales and a half-dozen others—rest assured that their appearance in the on-deck circle would be hailed with an "*Oye, amigo, como estás?*" And though the seats surrounding him were typically filled with Secret Service detail and the odd celebrity guest, Bush was never averse to inviting some random fan—*Hey, George! When're ya gonna get a half-decent lefthander?*—to join him down in front, where together they would bask in the luster of the national pastime.

The way George W. saw it, this wasn't small ball. He was, he would later maintain, *changing the culture* of baseball in the Dallas/Fort Worth Metroplex. A new stadium was in the works. Community outreach in the manner of all Bushes. And speeches—he'd darken every Rotary Club's door in the region, always talking about the *family experience* and *building traditions*, and it didn't seem to matter how larded with hokum it was, ticket sales always shot up after the managing general partner ran the circuit. What other baseball owner did that sort of thing?

To other tasks as baseball exec, George W. was less suited. He could barely sit still during the lengthy stadium-construction meetings, and he left the tough personnel decisions to others. (This included the infamous Sammy Sosa trade to Chicago—though at the time neither Bush nor anyone else in the Rangers organization thought that manager Bobby Valentine was dealing away a home-run king.) His preferential treatment of the great Nolan Ryan—excusing the forty-two-year-old pitcher from certain road trips, letting Nolan's boys romp around in the clubhouse—rankled a few teammates. Now and again he made untoward comments to the press, such as when he predicted that the Rangers would win the pennant in 1992, or when he expressed an interest in Boston Red Sox pitcher Roger Clemens, leading Boston's front office to accuse Bush of tampering.

Still, it was a straight-up relationship that George W. enjoyed with the local sportswriters. He dressed as they did—horrendously—and he didn't pretend that his fancy title connoted a mastery of the game. (On the contrary, Bush enjoyed reminiscing about his days as a Yale benchwarmer. "I was a relief pitcher for the freshmen," he'd say.

"Williams is ahead 12–1, it's my big chance, I'm all loose. Coach points in my direction. And as I start walking in, I realize he's pointing to the second baseman, who's never pitched before. That's when I knew I wasn't destined to be a big league ballplayer.") If a column in the morning paper riled him, he would retaliate with a snippy wake-up call but revert to his backslapping mode that afternoon at the stadium. And he could get as well as he gave. When the owners convened a press conference after announcing that the newly erected ballpark in Arlington would be called . . . wait for it . . . the Ballpark In Arlington, Bush could see that the local press didn't share his appreciation of simplicity.

"Well, I guess you don't like it," he observed. "What about you, Galloway?"

Said columnist Randy Galloway, "I hate it."

"Well, what would you have named it?"

"Ann Richards Field."

That he took the job seriously, that he went the extra mile, that he made a difference—that he was *consequential* . . . all true. Still: Could it really be called a test, this sweet gig as the Metroplex's Jocksniffer in Chief? "I'll never forget," he would say of opening night of his first season as owner, "being in the center of the mound, when Eddie Chiles, me, Rusty Rose, and Tom Landry were all introduced. I turned to my partner Rusty Rose—and I was *used* to crowds; you know, I'd campaigned for my dad—I turned to him and said, 'How cool is this?' I was living a dream."

If anything, his job description was an invitation to regress. He could hang out in the cafeteria jawing with the veteran scouts about the lineup of the 1962 Pittsburgh Pirates. He could stride into the announcer's booth and have a snicker with Bob Uecker or Phil Rizzuto. He could fill shelf after shelf in his office with baseballs autographed by the game's legends. He could sit for nine innings with Muhammad Ali or Ben Crenshaw. (Or, well, Senator Phil Gramm.) He could play cards with the manager. He could work out in the players' training room. He could attend owners' meetings with George Steinbrenner. He could spend weeks touring the nation's great ballparks for "research." He could let Jenna and Barbara play whatever music they wanted over the stadium loudspeakers. He could wear cowboy boots garishly bearing the Rangers logo and not be viewed as pathetic.

He could do all this *and* get filthy rich, his $606,302 total investment ballooning into a sellout check for $14.9 million less than a decade later.

But there was more.

Now George W. Bush had an identity, name recognition in his own right. This did not escape the attention of his Dallas adviser Jim Francis, who ordered Bush's assistant Shari Waldie to begin marking the Ranger exec's speaking appearances on a map, after which Francis would visit Bush's office weekly and help him select future talks according to locale, much as one would do when diagramming a campaign . . . which, of course, this came to be, and on the Rangers' dime.

Nicely done, this transition from private to public life, from somebody's son to man in full. More than merely a feat of uncommon dexterity, it counted as a defining moment, insofar as Bush had begun, at long last, to define himself.

But apart from what he knew he *could do*, did he really know what he was *made of*, deep down?

Not yet.

Was it possible to beat Ann Richards, fulfill every campaign promise, become the darling of the Republican Party, and win reelection for governor of America's second-largest state with 68 percent of the popular vote . . . and still, somehow, not demonstrate his fitness for the crucible of a presidential campaign?

The humiliation of his father's defeat to Bill Clinton in 1992 had only begun to subside when George W. told Rove, "The great irony is, Dad's defeat makes it possible for me to consider running."

He needed a reason, of course. It wasn't enough simply to take down the helmet-haired dragon lady who had suckerpunched his father—really, the whole Bush family—with her acid quip at the 1988 Democratic National Convention: "Poor George. He can't help it. He was born with a silver foot in his mouth." His dad had overcome Queen Ann's jab with a vicious counterpunch of his own, in the form of a general election mudfest that left poor hapless Michael Dukakis looking like a man whose chief contribution as Massachusetts governor was to teem its streets with recently furloughed rapist-murderers. But four years later, the old man's lack of what he offhandedly termed the Vision Thing sealed his fate. George W. absorbed the lesson.

And he noted as well how Governor Richards's vision had stalled. Even Ann's admirers could plainly see how little interest she had in governing—how she preferred the role of Mother of Texas as the state's weathered yet progressive public face, all too happy to escort visiting Hollywood royalty around her New Texas but reluctant to soil her hands with the muck of policymaking. She was what the cantankerous lieutenant governor, Bob Bullock—himself a Democrat—considered, perhaps uncharitably, "a show horse, not a work horse."

George W. was driving around Dallas one day, listening to the radio, when he heard Richards say that she had frankly no idea of how to solve the mess that the Texas school financing system had become. "I can't *believe* a governor would say, 'I don't know what to do!'" was his sputtering refrain thereafter. At the same time, it occurred to Bush—and to Rove—that he had better figure out what to tell Texas voters about *his* Vision Thing.

He summoned to his office a Democrat and Dallas school board trustee named Sandy Kress. When Kress told him that he wouldn't endorse a Republican, Bush replied, "I didn't ask you here to back me. I want to know these things." And George W. read from a notepad containing his scribbled lines of inquiry: *How do we hold schools accountable? What difference does money make? Who are the best experts?*

He summoned as well a Tarrant County judge named Hal Gaither. "Teach me about juvenile law," Bush said. "I'll make the time." When asked by the judge why a baseball-team owner would care to know about determinate sentencing and recidivism rates, George W. replied evenly, "Because I'm going to be the next governor of Texas."

And he showed up at Karl Rove's shabby Austin office to meet with Marvin Olasky, the author of *The Tragedy of American Compassion*, which in two years Newt Gingrich would hail as the single best case made for welfare reform . . . but which Rove, being Rove, had already digested. George W. pelted Olasky with questions—but not the usual how-do-we-cut-the-welfare-rolls dreariness: He'd been thinking all this through, way outside the box, dispensing with small ball. "How can we reform welfare to *help* people?"

Availing himself of their expertise became part of his early campaign regimen. And to the three issues involving reform of education, juvenile justice, and welfare, Rove suggested a fourth—tort reform—and arranged for him to hear a few lawsuit horror stories from Texans for Public Justice. With Vision Thing amassed, and after having met with the various other Republican aspirants to inform them politely that they didn't stand a warbler's chance against him, George W. Bush kicked off his candidacy in the summer of 1993. Already, the challenger was a mere eight points behind the incumbent.

Publicly, he assured the doubters—including his mother—that he had every expectation of winning. Here, though, were his instructions to his campaign manager, Jim Francis: "Don't let this campaign end up in the red. I don't want to lose this election and end up owing money."

For years thereafter, Bush's stunning 53–46 victory over the mighty Richards would be seen partly as a referendum on Clinton, part of the Newt Gingrich tidal wave that washed away scores of Democrats great and small. Mainly, though, it would be hailed as a triumph of ferocious discipline—the challenger inseparable from those four issues, his roman-candle temper never once igniting as he waded obliviously through the rivers of kerosene Governor Richards poured with her incessant references to "Shrub" and other Molly Ivins inspirations. It would be remembered for Rove's crafty incursion into the yellow-dog Democrat territory of East Texas, where allegiances to Hollywood Ann were wobbly, what with her alleged posse of lesbians and her rumored druggie past.

Unremembered would be the Bush campaign's missteps—so many of them early on that Francis and Rove sacked nearly the entire staff in the spring of 1994, bringing in the burly Joe Allbaugh from Oklahoma and a former TV reporter and state Republican Party director named Karen Hughes to right the foundering vessel. Forgotten as well the klunky early speeches Rove wrote for George W., and the latter's tendency to bark out alarming declarations on the stump like *"I am a capitalist!"* before the Message Dominatrix curbed his tongue. For all the Rove/Hughes/Allbaugh Iron Triangle's shrewdness, the Bush campaign was far from seasoned. Its policy director, Vance McMahan, had not worked a day in politics or government. Karen herself had no experience in any campaign, Allbaugh none in Texas. And the man on whom George W. would most frequently rely for clarifying issue sticking points—and for delving into Bush's past so as to anticipate questions about his bachelor days and his service in the National Guard—would be a twenty-three-year-old UT graduate named Dan Bartlett, who happened to be the only one in the office when the candidate would call at seven in the morning, asking, "It says general crime's gone up in Brazos County by 36 percent, but how do we know that?"

This first Bush Machine was more akin to a children's crusade, and Richards had ample opportunity to squash it. But the governor preferred her exquisite putdowns to an engaged campaign. For months she paid her opponent no heed while he laid out the four defining issues. (But only those four. George W. had no life experience in matters such as health care, and it did not occur to the Richards camp to expose his ignorance early on.) For the same period, she spent little from her huge Hollywood-endowed war chest when she could have forced the Bush camp to drain its lesser coffers. And Richards assumed that areas of Texas in which Republicans from time immemorial had been gaily tarred and feathered did not require her attention. She had forgotten one of her favorite aphorisms, that 80 percent of life is just showing up. That formula seldom holds true in politics, but it did in Texas in 1994: George W. showed up, Ann did not, and that made 80 percent of the difference.

From that moment on, he was a star. And he seemed properly fit for stardom the very next day after his election, when he stood in the Austin Hyatt and faced the national media with aplomb and grace. Before being sworn in, he responded to California's enactment of Proposition 187—denying benefits such as public schooling to illegal aliens—with the stirring promise, "In Texas, *we're* gonna educate the children."

But there was a bit of swagger to that declaration as well, a hint that George W. Bush had arrived somewhat unready for the realities facing a state's chief executive. And indeed, at an event for Republican governors in Williamsburg, Virginia, shortly after his election, he came off to some as a good-time Charlie rather than a man of gubernatorial stature. The leadership in the state capital picked up on the cocksure mien as well. And a Texas reporter was startled to hear the newly elected governor tell him, "Blacks didn't come out for me like the Hispanics did. So they're not gonna see much help from me."

But among George W.'s lifelong attributes were his awareness of his own limits and the willingness to surround himself with able (though loyal!) experts. The very first of these, after winning the election, was his tailor.

He knew that he was an awful dresser—had to know, the many times it was pointed out to him: first in Midland, where a golf tournament offered a George W. Bush Award presented to the worst-dressed participant; and later in Dallas, where his co-owner Rusty Rose would mercilessly observe, *Gee, didn't you wear that shirt yesterday, George?* It never really bothered him much. Comfort was all-important . . . whereas fashion, pretty much by definition, was the province of those who felt insufficiently comfortable with themselves. Of course, Laura was comfortable and at the same time immaculately turned out. Bless her heart, she had given up the fight on George W.'s wardrobe long ago.

Now, however, he was on a stage where such things mattered. "It's part of the *discipline*," Jim Francis would say. And so one day Francis called tailor Barry Smith, who arrived at George W. Bush's Dallas home on Northwood just after the 1994 election.

Knowing that it was time for a proper schooling, George W. listened. "I know you don't like clothes—I can tell that," began Smith. The governor-elect did not take umbrage, so he continued: "But we need to figure out what's going to work well for you, because you're entering a public profile. So, three things we need to think about. One, what is what you're wearing going to look like on camera? Two, what are your best colors? And three, what do *you* like?"

"Well, obviously, I need dark suits," George W. said. "I don't do a lot of patterns."

"Then let's stick to basic blues and grays, get you inaugurated, and we'll go from there."

They stood in his walk-in closet and appraised his current wardrobe. It was a horror show. The tailor fingered the polyester Haggar Sansabelt slacks (the Haggar family were friends of his) and said, "I don't think these portray the right kind of image you're looking for."

"I like them. I don't much care for belts."

"But they don't take you to the next level. I'm not saying you have to throw them away. Wear them around the house if you want."

Drawing the line, the governor-elect said, "I don't like cuffs. They always get caught on something." Smith assured him that he could do cuffless trousers.

Footwear: boots. A couple of pairs of loafers (which once had tassels, but he had cut them off), several pairs of running shoes . . . but otherwise, boots. He would be wearing them with his suits. Case closed.

They moved on to his dress shirts, all of which were white—or had been at one time. "These have seen better days," George W. chuckled as he noted the yellow rings under the arms.

They looked at his suits. A couple of them, purchased at a Dallas haberdashery, were quite nice. But George W. didn't like them. "These jackets, they're grabbing me," he said. "So I'm just not gonna wear 'em."

Smith suggested that they take all his suits out of the closet. In one pile they would place the suits to be retained. The other pile would be donated to his church. In the end, the church made out like a bandit. Two suits were culled from the junk—and they were the uncomfortable ones, but they cost so damned much that it seemed a pity to just toss them out.

They found Laura in her pool-house office. Displaying some fabric samples for suits—dark navy herringbone for the Inaugural, postman-blue and skipper-blue suits for the days to follow—the tailor said to her, "These are what we think makes sense for now."

Implacable as always, Laura replied, "Great. I like all those things."

It was done. Having already achieved success, George W. Bush would now begin dressing for it. And fevered from the breakthrough, George W. went a little crazy that afternoon, also ordering from Barry Smith several pairs of socks, belts, ties, shirts, sportcoats, and even a couple of basic lace-up cap-toe shoes.

But he kept some of the polyester Sansabelts. So *comfortable*!

He would succeed as governor because he wanted to get big things done and refused to allow the legislative process to water down his big things into little things. He would succeed because he would capitalize on Ann Richards's alienation of her own tribe and befriend several Democratic legislators, inviting them to cookouts at the Governor's Mansion and UT basketball games. He would succeed because he thought to bring in conservative Big-Thinkers like James Q. Wilson and David Horowitz to push him and his staff with heady queries: *What changes behavior? What is the government's role in bringing hope to its citizens? How do we break the cycle of despair?*

He would also succeed because Bob Bullock would not let him fail.

The famously difficult, onetime ragingly alcoholic lieutenant governor loved Texas and hated incompetence in equally high measure. Bullock demonstrated both in one of his many epic firings, bellowing to one ex–chief of staff, "You're not even from Texas, *are you?* I can tell the blood of William Barret Travis is not in your body! If you'd been at the Alamo, you would've gone over the back wall!"

Bullock and House Speaker Pete Laney busted down the forty-eight-year-old governor's insouciance and were happy to find a receptive pupil. His was the constitutionally weak office; they controlled the committee assignments and had the votes. When the legislature was in session, the trio breakfasted together every Wednesday. Whatever was discussed did not leak out. Bullock appreciated that Bush wasn't full of himself. And if he viewed Ann Richards as the preening younger sister who couldn't be counted on to do house chores, he saw in George W. Bush a son with whom he could start fresh, with no past to regret, availing only fatherly virtues.

And so in that historic first legislative session of 1995, Bush and Bullock and Laney succeeded in passing the whole agenda: tougher juvenile-justice laws, greater accountability in education, tighter restrictions on welfare, and civil-suit reform. It was true that the first three initiatives had been moving through the legislative pipeline prior to Bush's arrival. The fact still remained that George W. Bush campaigned to accomplish four things, and he had made good on his promise. Karl Rove divined in this a strong whiff of national electability. And on George W.'s fiftieth birthday, in 1996, Bob Bullock gave full voice to it, telling a large audience at the mansion, *I've served with four governors. And* this *one here has the stuff to be president of the United States!*

Bush imposed on the governor's office a style of management that was not quite strict and not quite casual. By 7:45 A.M. he was in his office, signing letters, working his way down the call list. His subordinates knew to be in earlier (and never to be late), but also knew that the governor's door was open—they didn't have to grovel for face time via chief of staff Allbaugh. They knew as well that the governor preferred his meetings short. "Give them an hour, they'll take an hour," he would say. "Give 'em ten minutes, they'll focus better." They knew that it was better not to bring him the heavier policy stuff right after lunchtime, when he would have just returned from a jog under the broiling sun. They knew that he could be quite impatient and peevish but that unpleasantness did not fester in him. "Well, don't you think you ought to know that sort of thing from now on?" he would say to the blunderer in question. And after eliciting the correct reply, the governor would move on.

What perhaps George W. Bush had himself not known was that he could love this job. Though he lived in a public building that gave tours, and a naked person would occasionally streak across his lawn, he could also sit on the second-floor balcony facing the Capitol at night, smoke a stogie, and listen to the Rangers' game on the radio. Mansion dinners offered the opportunity to host foreign dignitaries, admiring fellow governors, and his dad (whom, with other guests present, he referred to as "Mr. President" throughout the meal). Though he was now quite the public figure, it was hardly a confining thing. He could shop for his own running shoes, run his six miles on the hike-and-bike trail, and let someone else do the driving. (Though he would not make it pleasant on his Ranger detail if they got stuck in traffic.) As with everywhere else he went, George W. transformed the governor's office into his own personal frat house, bestowing nicknames like Prophet (Karen) and Pinky (Allbaugh) and Turdblossom (Rove) and Hawk (legislative director Albert Hawkins).

But it was his energy rather than his banter that most transformed an office that had customarily been regarded as ceremonial. When someone made the mistake of observing that George W. Bush was custodian of a weak office, his tart reply would be, "Only for a weak person."

Still: Was the job big enough?

Could he be of greater consequence?

Early on the afternoon of February 18, 1998, Bush and Karen Hughes arrived at a juvenile prison in Marlin, Texas. Because the governor was running that year for reelection—and after that, who could say?—Karen had arranged for the local and national presses to attend. This was an extraordinary situation, since the identities of criminal youths were protected by state laws. But the photo op of Governor Bush dispensing tough (but Compassionate!) love to his young wards was irresistible, and Karen wanted it out there in the public domain. So the youth-prison officials painstakingly obtained signed waivers from the parents of twenty-two juveniles, half of whom now sat in their orange jumpsuits beside Karen's boss. While the TV cameras rolled, one boy after the next recited his litany of criminality—*I'm Jimmy, I'm from Mineral Springs, at the age of thirteen I did steal the next door neighbor's car and I did run over my grandma with it, which did cripple her permanently*—followed by his acknowledgment that he, rather than society, was to blame and his pledge to do better.

This was the Responsibility Era personified, as Bush well knew. It was also exploitative, and he knew that as well. This prefab moment was about winning votes by broadcasting images of a human transaction that had never been. And so it was with an odd mixture of relish and embarrassment and finally impatience that he sat there, fidgeting a bit as the dreary litanies proceeded. At 1:15 he had to be out of there. Other photo ops and glad-handings awaited in Terrell, Kaufman, Greenville, Richardson, and Garland, before the governor's private plane at last angled back south to Austin at 8:50 that evening.

Still, when the last preselected urchin had concluded his recitation, Bush and everyone else sat there for an uncomfortable moment as if at the end of a bad blind date, searching for something nice to say about a thoroughly meaningless encounter.

A scrawny fifteen-year-old black kid raised his hand.

"Can I ask the governor a question?" said the boy, a petty thief from Tyler named Johnny Demon Baulkmon.

The juvenile-prison officials blanched. Johnny had crossed a forbidden line, for which he could be punished later. But nothing could be done about it now.

That familiar, jagged half-smile appeared on the governor's face. "Sure you can," he said.

"What do you think about us now?"

Only the popping of camera flashbulbs disturbed the dead silence. The question—so economically phrased, in so small a package, as to pierce him like an arrowhead—registered so personally that Bush (and Karen) thought the question had been: *What do you think of ME now?*

Bush fumbled with his fingers. He had no speech at the ready. No bubble to protect him. The cameras brought there to facilitate the photo op now bore down on George W. Bush, the most powerful man in Texas, at strange parity with a juvenile delinquent. And yet . . . that was a gift, wasn't it? A rare invitation to be himself? Or no, a demand: *Make a connection. A statement.*

Only fifteen days earlier, he had passed on the chance to grant a stay of execution to internationally renowned ax murderer and born-again Christian Karla Faye Tucker. "I have concluded judgments about the heart and soul of an individual on death row are best left to a higher authority," the governor had said in the prepared statement that sealed her fate. Nothing in it reflected the anguish that had compelled him to clear his entire calendar on the date of Tucker's execution. That was the way it was. A leader had to be impersonal at times. He had to keep it in. Had to be . . . a policy.

But right now, staring at Johnny Baulkmon, Bush felt that he was about to cry.

His words, when he at last found them, sounded almost confessional: "You look like kids I see every day. And I'm impressed by the way you're handling yourselves here. I think you can succeed. The state of Texas still loves you all. We haven't given up on you. But we love you enough to punish you when you break the law."

That was the answer to the question.

A strange euphoria overtook Bush and the other adults in the dormitory. Something had just taken place here that did not ordinarily occur, either in youth prisons or on the campaign trail. A sense of institutions humanized, of possibility. The Texas Youth Commission officials hugged and high-fived one another when the governor departed. But it was George W. Bush who could not get over the encounter. For weeks thereafter, he recounted it to aides and friends the way other men might rhapsodize about a fishing tale or a chance barstool flirtation with Sharon Stone.

Except that it was not myth. It was not braggadocio. It was anything but trivial. No: it was Big Picture collapsed into a singular, frail human moment. It was the Responsibility Era, Compassionate Conservatism—*it was why he was in this*. And when Bush was this seized by inspiration, the ever-attuned Karen knew what to do next. There had been a similar moment four years ago, when her boss was first running for governor—a welfare mom he'd met in Dallas, or something like that, she couldn't remember—and Karen had made it a point to put skeptical reporters in a car with George W. so that they wouldn't have to take it from Bush's paid flack that the guy was *absolutely passionate about this stuff!*

So she proceeded to work the Marlin tableau into his speeches, in language that one seldom heard from the lips of any politician, much less a conservative: "Each of us holds a piece of the promise of America. That young man at the jail in Marlin wasn't sure. He wasn't sure the promise was meant for him. He didn't know whether he still had a shot. Yet some spark was alive. He was willing to risk asking the governor, What do you think of me? He meant, Is there hope for me? Do I have potential? Can I make it? Do I own a piece of the promise of America? In the mightiest and wealthiest and free-est nation in the world, he still wasn't sure. And that's a tragedy."

(Johnny Baulkmon "still wasn't sure" for a reason, as it turned out. Some time after his chance encounter with George W. Bush, the boy was raped by another juvenile offender. Though the meeting in Marlin would become a centerpiece of Bush's nomination-acceptance speech in 2000, Baulkmon did not learn of his fleeting fame until years later. Apparently unconvinced by "the promise of America," he would become an adult petty criminal. In 2006, from a Beaumont prison visitation room Johnny Baulkmon would appraise Bush thus: "He doesn't care about anything but himself. He's complete trash, a horrible evil person.")

*   *   *

People were talking about him, and that was fine. But as heady as it all was, Bush had just gotten comfortable in Austin and was not of a mind to make any sudden moves. When his dad's old campaign manager, Bob Teeter, came to town in 1997 and visited with Rove, Karen, Don Evans, and others about the possibility—just the possibility—of the governor running for president, and what the sequence of preliminary steps should be, Karen shut down the whole thing. "This is *way* out in front of where I think the governor is," she said. And Rove faced some pushback from the boss when he suggested that they do a little reelection fund-raising out of state, since *that* money could be transferred to, well, a federal contest. Of course, George W. could clearly see what long-nurtured yearnings danced in Rove's eyes. Not Bush's problem.

Still, he let Rove talk him into a road trip.

The swing through California began innocently enough with a couple of fund-raisers in Los Angeles on April 22, 1998. The next morning, Bush—accompanied by Laura, Rove, Logan Walters, Don Evans, and his wealthy L.A. bachelor pal Brad Freeman—flew to San Francisco, where they met up with the twins and Bush's cousin Craig Stapleton. A luncheon, a couple of receptions, one dinner with all two hundred of the Bay Area's Republicans, a second dinner with the family. . . . Hectic and gratifying on a number of fronts, but none of this was why he was really there.

On Friday, April 24, at two in the afternoon, the governor arrived at the Palo Alto residence of former Secretary of State George P. Shultz. Inside were the Big-Thinkers of Stanford University's ghetto for conservatives, the Hoover Institution: former Reagan economic advisers Martin and Annelise Anderson, economist John Cogan, the college's impressive young provost and Sovietologist Condoleezza Rice, and the man who had organized the meeting, former Council of Economic Advisers director under the Bush administration Michael Boskin. In an earlier phone conversation, Boskin had suggested an agenda focusing on budget policy, taxes, the economic outlook, entitlements, Social Security, and international affairs. Bush came prepared, but he was relaxed as he made the introductions. Noticing that Shultz had a Hispanic housekeeper, the governor spoke to her in her native tongue, to her tittering delight.

They sat in Shultz's living room, where coffee and cookies were laid out on a table. The host began by saying, "Some of you may remember another meeting we had here with a sitting governor." That governor had been Ronald Reagan, back in 1979, when many of these same Big-Thinkers were sniffing Reagan out to discern whether he was really the dunce everyone said he was. They came away thinking entirely the opposite, and thus did the conservative intelligentsia throw its gray matter behind Reagan's 1980 campaign.

And now here was George W. Bush, about to provide a powerful dose of déjà vu. After listening to the others give their presentations—and, being professors, they all went overtime—Bush spoke his piece. "I've spent a lot of time thinking about these things—some of them back when I was working on my dad's campaign," he said. "I'm thinking about running, but I'm not here to make any announcement. I'll be making up my mind over the next few months."

He talked about Social Security: "I'm going to spend the political capital necessary to fix it." He agreed with Cogan's comment that budget surpluses usually ended up getting spent by Congress: "Yeah, that's a problem with all legislative bodies, isn't it?" He expressed great interest in India, which none of them had expected of a Texas governor. For several minutes he listened intently as Shultz, Boskin, and Rice debated whether the International Monetary Fund should be reformed or abolished altogether. (The next morning, at a gathering in Pebble Beach, someone would ask Bush about the IMF. "Well, there are two schools of thought," he replied, then proceeded to regurgitate the meat of the reform-versus-abolish debate before concluding with his own viewpoint.) And though he asked numerous questions, the Hooverites noticed that he did not frame them as what-should-I-do, but rather: "Here's what I'd do. What do you think?"

When it was over, Shultz rather giddily took George W. Bush aside. He told Bush that back in 1979, after Reagan's talk had concluded, Shultz had brought him to the very spot where they now stood, and said, *Run. We will support you.* And now, Shultz said, he wished to say the same thing to Bush.

"The thing is," said Bush, "I have to be sure that my family's comfortable with it. Also, I want to make sure there are significant things that I want to accomplish as president."

Which only made Shultz giddier: *My God, just like Reagan. An Agenda president.*

He was on the bubble now, keeping everyone guessing. "I'm doing everything in my power to convince him to run," Allbaugh assured one inquirer.

"He's definitely gonna run," said Brad Freeman to another.

"I don't know," Jeb Bush confessed during a round of golf with Dan Quayle, whose presidential hopes rested largely on George W. staying out of the race so that the Bush Rolodex would fall his way. "He sort of says he's not. But he's not doing anything to discourage the talks, either."

"I'm just not gonna do this," said Bush himself one summer afternoon to Karen Hughes as the two of them drove to an interview in Dallas. "I want my girls to have a normal life."

He was genuinely torn: flattered by all the beseeching Republicans showing up at his doorstep, indulging the national press with his clarion calls for the Responsibility Era . . . but remembering well how 1992's daily muggings in the press left the entire Bush family reeling. Why put everyone through it again? *He didn't need this.*

And yet there was an oddness to his fevered campaigning for reelection in 1998—a million points ahead of Garry Mauro and still sweating completely through his clothes at a diner in Beaumont. As if imbued with particular restlessness. Or seeking the unabashed, seemingly unanimous love of his fellow Texans one last time. Or maybe, just maybe, running up the score so as to qualify for the Big Tournament.

The 1998 campaign seemed at once a silly formality and overwrought with portent. National reporters tailed him everywhere. The DNC was giving Mauro all the support necessary to at least knock Bush down a notch. Meanwhile, and very quietly, a Dallas attorney named Harriet Miers was overseeing an extensive in-house opposition research effort, gathering all the goods against her friend George W. Bush so as to be ready for the onslaught.

This, of course, included the DUI incident in 1976. "What do you think we should do about this?" Karen asked Bartlett and Mindy Tucker one day.

The two agreed: *Get it out there. If that's the worst there is, we can deal with it.*

But Bush had already made his decision. While submitting to jury duty, the governor was approached by a reporter who asked, "Were you ever arrested for drunken driving?"

"I did a lot of stupid things when I was young," Bush replied.

He left it at that. Bush's daughters were just beginning to drive at the time. "I'd made a conscious decision not to spend time talking to them about stupid things I'd done," he would say. "And so I made the decision there on the spot—this is without any consultation, not sitting around with the Bartletts or the Hugheses of the world on how to handle it."

Rove would regard his failure to change Bush's mind on the subject as his biggest mistake of the presidential campaign.

The gears began to whirl after November 3, 1998. Mike Boskin from Stanford began to prepare briefing books on every national issue. Straining at the leash of strategic ambiguity, Rove's mind thrashed as he contemplated *the primaries before the primaries: the primary of money, the primary of ideas—in an era of Peace & Prosperity, gotta show that we're both innovative and for God's sakes prudent. . . . He's only dealt with state economic issues, his foreign policy's limited to Mexico, his four big issues we've gotta blow out to national scale. . . . We need a policy shop, building on what we did with Judge Gaither and Sandy Kress and Marvin Olasky. . . . Bring 'em in, let 'em teach but let 'em also be impressed like the Hooverites, they'll be part of our cheerleading squad. . . .*

Bush's language had changed, leaning more toward yes—"I'm thinking very seriously about it"; "Keep your powder dry"—but even with decision-making time absolutely upon him, the man who seven years later would refer to himself as The Decider was anything but. And though Laura had come on board—in many ways showing less reluctance than she'd displayed before the gubernatorial campaign—the girls remained in revolt. "You're ruining our lives!" Jenna said through angry sobs. She and Barbara had seen how the press lampooned Chelsea Clinton. How could a father put a daughter through such humiliation? And so it was not an easy time at the old hacienda.

"My attitude was, 'Someday you'll understand why,' " Bush would recall of these impasses. "Laura did a lot of that, too." The twins did not go quietly. Shortly after the election, an adviser visiting the Governor's Mansion could not help overhearing Bush upstairs having a yelling match with Jenna. The issue was whether or not his daughter could spend Thanksgiving with friends in Mexico. The father was trying to explain that, considering what was at stake here, gallivanting off to Mexico might not be a very good idea.

Jenna responded with her own unbiased prognostication: *"IT'S NOT LIKE YOU'RE GONNA WIN!"*

In truth, victory seemed almost certain. Seemed, compared to the average campaign marathon, an effortless stroll. A poll released a week before Bush's reelection in 1998 showed him 22 points ahead of his nearest Republican rival, Elizabeth Dole, and 18 points ahead of Al Gore.

The morning of Governor Bush's second inaugural ceremony, he sat with his family in an Austin church for what he had assumed would be an obligatory prayer service. But pastor Mark Craig had something else in mind. *People are starved for leadership*, Craig declared. *Starved for leaders who have ethical and moral courage . . . And it's not always easy or convenient for leaders to step forward. Even Moses had doubts. . . .*

"He was talking to you!" Bar stage-whispered into her eldest son's ear at the conclusion of the service. And though ever-modest Laura countered with, "He was talking about *all of us*," Bush was in the full throes of epiphany. Like that, the pastor's words became the godly hands that pushed him clean off the prepresidential bubble.

Bush declared his exploratory committee open for business in March 1999, at which point the very shadow of his candidacy began to suck the life out of campaigns already in progress. Quayle, the elder Bush's former vice president, began to get the message after multiple versions of, "Sorry, Dan, I gotta stick with the family." Quayle, Lamar Alexander, John Kasich, and Bob Smith would barely make it to the summer before turning off the respirators.

In the first 120 days of the campaign, Bush's finance chieftains Don Evans and Jack Oliver trotted out George W. Bush before the moneyed faithful, who would later be dubbed Pioneers, hoping in that span of time to raise perhaps $20 million. Before long, FedEx boxes full of checks began to accumulate in the office of Oliver's assistant, Kate Walters. On the first of July, at a campaign stop in San Jose, Bush announced the tally, to astonished gasps: $35 million.

("That's three times the amount my dad raised," he later pointed out to a family friend.)

Back in Austin, the governor presided over one last legislative session, adding another $1 billion tax cut to his portfolio. He showed up late to the August Iowa straw poll and rolled over the opposition anyway, ten points ahead of Forbes. Then he returned home, and to lengthy "policy time" meetings at the mansion with the nation's most prominent conservative economists, domestic policy innovators, and foreign affairs sages. He was getting schooled, but so were they. The governor was not the passive recipient—his "useful impatience" (as one participant would put it) ever on display, rather delighting in his ability to outwit the brainiacs, drilling down to profound simplicity with questions like, "What do we have an army for, anyway?" and never letting these Big-Thinkers forget who was in charge. (During one dinner meeting at the mansion to discuss economic policy, Bush led off by saying, "If the American people wanted an economist for president, you guys would be running and not me. But they don't.")

Fortified with Big Thoughts, and deployed with exquisite choreography by Rove, Bush would materialize in Los Angeles or Indianapolis or Charleston or some other carefully chosen venue and, amid a riot of TV cameras, roll out some new proclamation of Bush policy. The speeches, penned by newly hired scribe Mike Gerson, were freighted with detail and lofty allusions, and in some other context would have seemed pompous. But *this* was a campaign already starched up as a presidency—so inevitable, so forceful and precise as to appear almost preexisting . . . as if George W. Bush, the governor of the nation's second-largest state, had practically been running the nation for some time already. As if this man who would presume to improve upon an era of Peace & Prosperity had already passed all the requisite tests.

Which, you could say, he had.

For he had started at the bottom of the oil business and wound up a millionaire. (A test of his entrepreneurship . . . or of his extraordinary connections.)

He had distinguished himself as a dynamic co-owner of a baseball team. (A test of his executive shrewdness . . . or of his cheerleading skills.)

He had waged a successful underdog campaign against a popular governor. (A test he inarguably passed . . . and which Ann Richards and the Democratic Party indisputably failed.)

And he had become a bold and popular governor. (Whose agenda depended on the efforts of the far more powerful Democratic leadership.)

These were the tests George W. Bush had passed with flying colors. He'd made it all look easy. None of it was easy.

None of it was enough.

3

SOUTH CAROLINA

There was no snow on the ground in Greenville, South Carolina. That was the first bit of good news to greet the vanquished Bush camp when the plane landed on the morning of February 2, 2000.

"Logan?" said Warren Tompkins, the Bush team's chief local strategist, as he threw a meaty arm around the candidate's personal aide. "We gonna win this down heah. We gonna win this thing *huge!*"

The temperature was below freezing but did not feel that way. It felt like home. And it felt that way for a reason. Barbara Bush had attended boarding school at Ashley Hall. Poppy had spent many of his early Christmases on a plantation in Barnwell. Campaigning both for themselves and on behalf of others, the Bushes had logged untold hours in the Palmetto State. The governor had even said it to the TV cameras on his way out of New Hampshire: "South Carolina is Bush country." They were family here, and in desperate need of the family treatment.

Don Evans had joined the team in Greenville. The campaign's finance chairman knew nothing about national campaigns. But he was Bush's best friend, dependably cool-headed. He was also a certifiable adult. The soon-to-be-legendary divide between Karen and Rove would require his supervision. Sidling up to Tompkins, Evans asked quietly, "How bad's it gonna get?"

Tompkins knew he was referring to the local fallout from the drubbing in New Hampshire. "I'm not sure," he said. "We may lose ten to twelve points."

Each one cast an anxious glance at the candidate, searching for signs of panic or anger or self-pity or resignation. They had not seen Bush this way before. Like a pitcher who had given up a grand slam in the first inning, he appeared neither unaffected nor unhinged, instead maintaining an expression of determined casualness while gears whirled and clicked somewhere beneath. On the flight over to Greenville, the candidate had mingled freely with reporters—cracking a few jokes, offering no excuses. "Mindy," he'd said to his young press aide en route, "we got our asses kicked." But to Mindy Tucker and everyone else's relief, Bush left no sacrificial guru on the Manchester tarmac.

Instead, Dan Quayle arrived to stop the bleeding.

To bring in the former vice president—he of the deer-in-the-headlights moment during the 1988 debate when Lloyd Bentsen charged, "You're no Jack Kennedy"; he of the "potatoe"-spelling gaffe during a visit at an elementary school; he of the feckless, golf-obsessive empty-suitedness that constituted the caricature; but most of all, he of Daddy Bush's administration—was not a decision reached lightly. But the campaign needed an immediate boost, and Quayle was the campaign's only face card in its hand.

Bush had visited Quayle in Phoenix to receive his endorsement a few weeks prior, on a beautiful January day back when everyone but the local gurus thought New Hampshire was in the bag. While Rove fidgeted nearby (they had other appointments in Phoenix that day), the ex-VP and his former boss's son talked politics in the fantasy-baseball manner common to Beltway geeks. "You're gonna win this thing," Quayle assured Bush. "Gore's weak." He promised his endorsement—which both men figured could be announced some-time later, perhaps just before Super Tuesday in early March—and the two then went on to discuss who would be suitable cabinet members in a Bush administration.

That leisurely backyard chat, redolent of infinite possibility, was now inoperative. Rove called the veep on Tuesday, February 1, as the grim tallies mounted in New Hampshire. The next morning, there Dan Quayle sat in a sedan with Bush, driving to the Hyatt in down-town Greenville, where Quayle would deliver his endorsement. The governor seemed no less upbeat than he'd been in Phoenix. Now, however, Bush was focused. No more talk about cabinet positions. Much of what Quayle had to say on the way to the hotel and then in a holding room before their press conference—*No need to panic, keep your loyal Texans*—Bush had already figured out on his own.

But among the redundancies was one worth reiterating, and Karen was there to take notes as Quayle uttered it: "Look, *you're* the reformer. You've done it in Texas. So start talking about it."

Still, Dan Quayle knew he hadn't been brought into this southern state to talk about Bush's reformist credentials. Instead, the man who had droned on throughout the 1988 campaign about "midwestern values," and later excoriated the single-mom TV show *Murphy Brown* for its values deficit, now stood before the cameras and declared, "We know that we have prosperity today. But let us be very clear that prosperity without values is no prosperity at all. Governor Bush has the values to be president of the United States."

When it came Bush's turn, the governor repeatedly used a phrase that no one could recall him using during his tenure of reaching across the aisle and appealing to all segments of society. He did not speak of "armies of compassion." He did not speak of being "a uniter, not a divider." He did not speak of how the mission of America was to "change one heart, one soul, one conscience at a time."

Instead, George W. Bush spoke of *the base*.

Then he left the one-on-one interviews to Quayle and climbed back into the sedan, bound for Bob Jones University.

Why was it a big deal? Rove argued that it shouldn't be. Reagan had gone there. Poppy Bush had gone there. And one of the opposition's South Carolina advisers, Congressman Lindsey Graham, had been conferring with university officials for weeks, so that John McCain could go there as well.

It should not have been a big deal, except that Bob Jones had decreed that Catholics were diabolical and that interracial dating be banned from campus. The latter didn't sit well with Bartlett, Mindy Tucker, and other young Bush aides. Their colleagues included an interracial couple, Mark Lampkin and Emily Kurtz. Rove, Tompkins, and the other middle-aged white dudes didn't get it, they thought. They'd been drawn to the governor's humane core. To them, Bush was why it was okay to be a young conservative. He was a man of faith but not of sanctimony. He was a regular guy but not a redneck. There were gays on his staff—and there was an interracial couple, *and, Karl, how do you think they're gonna feel—wouldn't you be offended. . . .*

The debate, which spanned three weeks and took place largely in cyberspace, was one the younger staffers stood no chance of winning. The socially conservative youth vote of which Bob Jones was patron saint—Bush had to have that bloc. *And* they had to have an upbeat, telegenic moment following the misery in New Hampshire. That was all Karen Hughes had cared about. She envisioned an outdoor rally, lots of happy families, signs everywhere, her boss shaking hands, oozing compassion, instead of standing behind a podium where, frankly, he did not ooze. . . . Rove punctured the balloon: *There'll be five thousand Republican students packed in a convention hall for their convocation. They're there! Tell me how we're gonna get that many people to leave work and school on a Wednesday afternoon!*

As was often the case, Rove and Karen were both right. Bush gave his speech, a thoroughly unremarkable rehash of pledges to "restore honor and dignity to the White House, so help me God!" The audience roared, Rove checked a box, and, at the time, the media found little to say about the incident, one way or the other.

After leaving campus, Bush went for a run. Meanwhile, a conference took place in one of the Hyatt suites. All the heavies were present. Rove. Karen. Media guys McKinnon, Stuart Stevens, and Russ Schriefer. Bush's new press secretary from Liddy Dole's camp, Ari Fleischer. Plus local chiefs Tompkins, Heath Thompson, Neal Rhodes, Tucker Eskew, Attorney General Charlie Conin, Lieutenant Governor Bob Peeler, House Speaker David Wilkins, and former Governor David Beasley. All in all, some of the finest Republican minds in a sickly huddle, like a supper club just now dawning to the awareness of the sour meat in their mouths.

Rove started with a schedule update. The governor had to campaign for the upcoming Michigan primary the day after tomorrow. Then in Texas for the weekend, followed by a half-day's worth of campaigning in Delaware for that state's primary. *Otherwise, he's yours for the next sixteen days.* The fifty-state campaign, Rove knew, had come down to South Carolina.

Tompkins had tasked Thompson and Rhodes with an ad hoc strategy. "Throw in the kitchen sink, whatever you want, just put it all on paper," he'd told them. The South Carolina boys had known what they were up against for months now. Bush could say that their state was Bush country. It also hosted four hundred thousand veterans. They'd focus-grouped McCain's bio and ads last fall; the numbers were off the charts. Let McCain be McCain, and it could be New Hampshire all over again.

But they wouldn't let that happen. Heath Thompson read from the list:

They needed to stymie the momentum of McCain's campaign. Make this about values, not popularity.

They needed to identify and emphasize issues where Bush was strong and McCain was weak.

They needed to attack McCain's supposed strengths, if only to throw him off stride.

They needed a microtargeted message campaign. Not just the uniter-not-a-divider pap. Go after the social conservatives and the veterans right out of the box, using tactical telephone and radio strikes.

They needed to break out those groups into lists that an aggressive get-out-the-vote drive could exploit.

They needed well-respected in-state messengers like Attorney General Conin seated here—who, just last night, as the New Hampshire returns came in, went on the air assailing John McCain's conservative credentials. Let Conin, former Governor Carroll Campbell, and others put the wood to McCain, so that Bush could claim the high road.

They needed Bush to claim, but not maintain, the high road. He needed to get out there, contrast himself to his opponent whenever possible, not wait for McCain to throw the first punch.

They needed to extend the psychological warfare into procedural matters such as the February 15 debate in Columbia. Contest the lighting, the candidate positioning, the order of questions. Give no ground.

Eskew, Rhodes, and Tompkins added a few other points. All of them fell under the same admonition: *No more finesse. This is a brawl.*

Nothing got rejected.

Karen and Fleischer passed notes back and forth but said nothing. They were way out of their depth here, pacifists dumped into a war zone—like McKinnon, the Democrat who was fond of bohemian hats and alternative rock bands and iconic TV ads of Bush hooking a bass, and who now gaped, thinking, *Jesus. They're letting the dogs off the chain.*

Even South Carolina politicians like Beasley and Wilkins had never been present for such a pugnacious call to arms. They excused themselves early, muttering something about getting some ice cream.

Later, the door swung open. It was the governor, soggy and fragrant from his jog. Grinning, he said, "Well, boys, it looks like we've got some work to do."

There was laughter, and the very sound of it dissolved the tension in the room.

"But I feel like I'm with the right guys in the right place," Bush continued. "Y'all have been down this road before. You just load me up and tell me where to go. I'm ready to win."

The candidate left the room without asking what his advisers had agreed upon. He didn't need to. All he needed to know was what he told some of them that evening:

"If we don't win this, it's over."

The Zogby poll numbers came in the next day, just after Bush's speech in Fort Sumter. No one had envisioned a scenario this night-marish. The governor had been ahead of McCain by 19 points a week ago, before the New Hampshire primary. Now he was down by 5. Bush had fallen through the floorboards.

It fell to Karen to deliver the news to the candidate in the holding room. He gave the numbers a glance—then, "Aaaahhh," waved them off.

Karen stammered, "I just wanted to make you aware—"

"Whatever. But we're not gonna lose here. I can tell."

Bush was feeling his oats, fresh from a moment the full significance of which had not yet registered with him. He'd given a rousing speech on the Sumter County Courthouse steps, surrounded by several hundred residents and a host of retired generals and Medal of Honor recipients—morphing, essentially, into John McCain: "We're going into political battle. . . . It is inexcusable to have the men and women who wear our uniforms on food stamps. . . ."

But the moment in fact belonged to a man Bush had never met before. His name was J. Thomas Burch Jr., and between him and John McCain the blood was very bad. Burch was a lawyer (his partner at the time was former *Good Morning Vietnam* disc jockey Adrian Cronauer) and headed an outfit called the National Vietnam & Gulf War Veterans Coalition. Among other things, the coalition solicited money from the loved ones of missing-in-action soldiers who Burch insisted were still imprisoned in 'Nam, and who could be retrieved, if only politicians like John McCain hadn't given up the fight to do so. The coalition therefore considered McCain to be a traitor. McCain considered them to be Rambo wannabes and con artists. His chief of staff, Mark Salter, had gotten into a fistfight with one of them, Ted Sampley, in the hallway of the Senate Russell Office Building. Sampley used to show up at Senate committee meetings relating to POWs and shoot McCain the finger. McCain's back would stiffen, and his fellow senator and Vietnam vet, John Kerry, would put a hand on McCain's knee to steady him.

Burch himself had never agitated before on behalf of George W. Bush—and after the 2000 primary, never would again. The Bush campaign was fine with this. Burch simply called Warren Tompkins's office, asked if he and a few veterans could show up at an event and say a few words, and was told to be the campaign's guest.

Tom Burch was in fact permitted to give some introductory remarks as Bush stood nearby. Burch had little memorable to say about his chosen candidate. Instead, he railed at McCain, declaring, "We admire his war service. But he has never, ever sponsored or cosponsored a piece of veteran's legislation that means anything to Vietnam or Gulf War veterans. . . . [H]e goes over to President Clinton and stands with him and gives him political cover [by favoring the lifting of the trade embargo with Vietnam]. . . . He had the power to help the veterans. But he came home, forgot us."

Then Burch and Bush shook hands.

Somewhere, the late Lee Atwater was grinning like a jackass eating bees. Tompkins, like Rove and George W. Bush himself, had apprenticed under the Dixie "art of war" strategist. Atwater had always made it his business to get under the opponent's skin—make them scratch away at themselves, spill their own blood. He and Tompkins used to send out two or three outrageous brochures to friends of the opponent's campaign manager, or place a creepy call to his neighbor . . . and it worked every time: The other guy's guru would be in orbit, off message, playing defense.

McCain's temper was not exactly classified information. Seemingly every other page in *Faith of Our Fathers* alluded to his hotheadedness. So, in the Bush camp's let-it-all-hang-out South Carolina strategy, it became axiomatic that if McCain started burning, the governor wasn't going to hose him down.

Thus, when other veterans demanded that Bush condemn Tom Burch's remarks, Bush coolly averred, "He's entitled to his own opinion."

The next day, Friday, the Bush campaign released its first pushback TV ad. The subject was tax cuts. But the subtext was the war hero's veracity:

"John McCain's ad about Governor Bush's tax plan isn't true, and McCain knows it. . . . McCain's plan? A tax cut smaller than Clinton's—and not a penny in tax cuts for thirty million Americans.

On taxes, McCain echoes Washington Democrats, when we need a conservative leader to challenge them."

McKinnon, Russ Schriefer, and Stuart Stevens knew exactly what they were doing using McCain's name and Bill Clinton's in the same sentence. They tossed the match and then headed back to Austin for the weekend.

Karen was on her way to the hairdresser, thinking, *Reformer. Reformer.*

Quayle had made the point, and Bush had immediately incorporated it into his remarks to the press, saying, "I'm the person who's been the reformer. It's hard to be the reformer if you've spent your entire career in Washington, D.C., which he has done."

She phoned 301 Congress, where Rove had convened a weekend staff meeting. "George W. Bush is the real reformer in this race," she said in the conference call. "The difference is, he's a reformer with results."

Reformer With Results . . . Rove looked around the room with an expression that said, *Not bad.* McKinnon didn't think it passed the smell test. Stevens thought it was worse than dubious: "It's fighting on McCain's turf, so he automatically wins," he said. Bartlett and Tucker liked the slogan. It was a new narrative, a shiny object for the press to ogle. Rove decided to go with it.

Ari Fleischer offered up a contribution that had come from Republican lobbyist and Bush consultant Ed Gillespie. How best to tag McCain as a Washington insider who, for all his posturings as a maverick, chaired the Senate Commerce Committee? Call him "The Chairman," Gillespie recommended to Fleischer.

Mike Gerson and fellow speechwriter Matthew Scully would have a field day with that.

But the main strategic shift discussed at that meeting was physical, not rhetorical. Rove, along with finance directors Jack Oliver and Don Evans, was obsessed with Bush's magnetic performance in the Iowa caucus and why that had not spilled over into New Hampshire. They were tempted to blame it all on Judd Gregg's top-down campaign structure—as opposed to the grassroots organization, replete with team leaders and viral marketing strategies, that Ken Mehlman had executed to perfection in Iowa. But here was where the Texans knew they had blown it: They had protected their candidate from the hyperinquisitive New Englanders. In Texas, things had been so cozy and bipartisan that Bush's message had scarcely been challenged. And he felt so instantly comfortable with the Iowans that he mingled with them for hours on end. Not so the frigid New Hampshirites. So they had kept him in the bubble, on message, at his peril. That would have to change. Bush would have to try his hand at Straight Talk.

And so they called in head of advance Brian Montgomery, who sketched out a semicircular stage that would accompany the candidate and lend a suggestion of intimacy, more or less like a boxing ring. And they told Ari Fleischer to signal these changes to the press, with the promise of greater access and a new story to tell, which was: George W. Bush, once a supine frontrunner, was now on the offense and taking to the air.

Before the meeting broke up, McKinnon mentioned to Rove a TV ad that a special-interest group had sent over to Warren Tompkins's office for approval. It was an attack ad suggesting that John McCain had not supported legislation that would have saved the lives of thousands of women with breast cancer. McKinnon thought the ad was way out of line.

Karl Rove smiled. "Let's let the locals do it their way," he said.

"That's not right," said John McCain, shaking his head in disgust. "That's not honorable."

His aides had informed him of Bush's breezy remark about Tom Burch's diatribe. In McCain's view, the Bush camp had to know who Burch was. They had to know that something low and evil was bound to tumble out of his mouth. And Bush stood there, right next to the bastard . . . heard him say that John McCain "forgot" his Vietnam brothers . . . and all Bush had to say about that blasphemy was, *He's entitled to his own opinion?*

And then saying John McCain *echoes Washington Democrats?* Comparing him to *Bill Clinton?*

The sinews of temperament that were snapping in the McCain camp were not just those of the candidate. Salter, Weaver, Murphy, Harris, Davis, Fletcher—all of them were outraged, even more so than Senator "Steady Strain." Drunk on the heady elixir of a political crusade, the McCain campaign had every reason to exult rather than fulminate. The polls that two months ago showed him down by as much as 45 now had him dead even or ahead of Bush. Campaign money was gushing in from the Internet. Crowds every bit as vast and giddy as that last Granite State rally in Peterborough now swooned over the senator in Charleston and Myrtle Beach. In response to the

Bush campaign's whistling-in-the-dark characterization of New Hampshire as "a bump in the road," McCain trotted out this new applause line: "They call it a bump in the road. My friends, it was a land mine."

McCain had predicted that things would get "a bit nasty" in South Carolina. He was not going to become the oblivious, unarmed front-runner that Bush had been in New Hampshire. And so the McCain camp's first South Carolina ad was a counterpunch to McKinnon, Schriefer, and Stevens's opening salvo:

"This is George Bush's ad promising America he'd run a positive campaign. This is George Bush shaking hands with John McCain, promising not to run a negative campaign. This is George Bush's new negative ad attacking John McCain and distorting his position. Do we really want another politician in the White House America can't trust?"

Even before the ad ran on Monday, February 7, McCain's media consultant Greg Stevens had cooked up another, spicier ad. Its title was "Desperate." Mike Murphy had toned down the script, but only somewhat. Together they previewed the clip to McCain aides in the Columbia office of local McCain strategist Richard Quinn. In the ad, the senator wore an expression of statesmanlike chagrin:

"I guess it was bound to happen. Governor Bush's campaign is getting desperate, with a negative ad about me. . . . His ad twists the truth like Clinton. We're all pretty tired of that."

The roomful of strategists whooped and clapped when the spot concluded. Among them, only Lindsey Graham protested. "For the very reason y'all are sitting cheering it, that's the reason we shouldn't do it," the congressman cautioned.

No one listened to Graham. Airtime was bought for Tuesday, February 8.

"We've gotten to him!" yelped Tompkins when he saw the "Desperate" ad.

Bush had an altogether different response: He was pissed off.

It was one thing to question a man's stances on the issues of the day. And the odd personal swipe was to be expected in a contested race—he knew that, courtesy of Ann Richards. Bush had spent more time than any national candidate since Dan Quayle in 1988 defending his own intelligence. And character—well, yes, a presidential contender was expected to defend that as well. The McCain camp had excelled at implied contrasts: *Their* man wasn't beholden to special interests, *their* man had proudly served, etc. Bush had an answer for this after New Hampshire. He'd taken to saying that McCain, the reformer with no reforms under his belt, "says one thing and does another." It was a dig, just like the comparison to Clinton on tax cuts was a dig.

But to invoke the infernal C-word *in the context* of character— "twists the truth like Clinton"—was beyond the pale. McCain might just as well have called Bush a sexual predator. And to say it in South Carolina, of all places . . .

Of course, Tom Burch had come all the way down from Virginia to deliver his low blow to McCain in South Carolina as well. Letting that happen without a word of rebuke, Bush knew he had lost the high ground. Now John McCain had forfeited it as well. By resorting to name-calling, he'd become just another politician. Bush knew an opportunity when he saw one.

It was good to be pissed off.

The morning after the "Desperate" spot aired, Rove met with McKinnon, Stevens, Schriefer, and pollster Matthew Dowd down the block from headquarters, at a popular Mexican joint called Las Manitas. Rove didn't mince words: *The governor wants to do a response ad right away. As in, shoot it tomorrow.*

The admen really could not afford the luxury of panic. A script was dashed out by Stevens and McKinnon while Schriefer flew to South Carolina to scout a location for the forty-five-minute window Bush would have to shoot the ad between stops in Rock Hill, Fort Lawn, and Columbia. On Thursday, the day of the shoot, McKinnon flew to Charlotte, where he hooked up with a Mississippi cinematographer named Jim Dollarhide. The two drove to meet Bush, Schriefer, and Karen at a state park just outside of Fort Lawn. Bush had just finished bantering and shaking hands with seven hundred South Carolinians at a fish fry. He was feeling the rush from it—and this was not a good thing. He needed to be angry. Karen and Schriefer were tense. The whole thing was looking ad hoc to a major fault—their guy standing in the woods wearing a blue suit, trying to summon anger that wasn't there at the moment. . . . They and McKinnon huddled with the governor at the video-assist monitor to discuss wording and emphasis.

The moment the film rolled, Bush's placid mood disappeared. His voice became high and agitated and strained all at once. After two takes, Dollarhide approached the candidate. Straightening the governor's tie: *Sir, in my humble opinion . . . maybe a little less angry, this once?*

Bush nodded. The third take worked, and after that Bush decided to go for a jog. He was feeling juiced, so much so that Karen called Heath Thompson and told him to drum up a rally in an hour somewhere nearby, which after a frenzy of phone calls brought the candidate to a food court in a Lexington County mall. . . . And seeing the candidate standing on top of a picnic table, his face aglow as upward of five hundred locals went ga-ga as if gathered into the halo of Jesus Christ Superstar himself, you would never have guessed that this man was the same fellow who only a couple of hours ago had stood in front of a camera, snake-eyed and hammer-jawed, his voice betraying both hurt and reason but most of all indignation, as South Carolinians would hear for themselves the following day:

"Politics is tough. But when John McCain compared me to Bill Clinton and said I was untrustworthy, that's over the line. Disagree with me, fine. But do not challenge my integrity."

They would hear it again and again. And so would folks in Michigan and California—places where they'd never seen the ad that had triggered such self-righteousness to begin with, for John McCain had long since taken it down . . . though well after the damage had been done.

The night Bush's "Integrity" ad aired, Karen Hughes sat in a hotel bar in Columbia with Tucker Eskew, nursing a glass of white wine. Downcast, she sighed, "It might just be that we're not supposed to win."

Her boss had been campaigning all day, Ladson to Kiawah Island to Charleston to Columbia, road-testing the campaign's new format, "One on One with Governor Bush." The governor was now out there, fully exposed on Brian Montgomery's semicircular stage: no notes, taking questions, dispensing with the safety net. And doing great—though it was brutal for Bush's Message Disciplinarian to watch her friend, so driven by the need for comfort, get waylaid by harsh questions about his soft stance on illegal aliens and McCain's valor.

Most of all, the new format meant constant media access. And today, the governor was getting hammered on push polls. At one of his town hall meetings in Spartanburg the preceding afternoon, McCain listened to a distraught supporter describe a telephone call at home that her fourteen-year old Boy Scout of a son had recently received. "He was so upset when he came upstairs and he said, 'Mom, someone told me that Senator McCain is a cheat and a liar and a fraud,' " the woman tearfully recounted.

"What you just told me has had a very profound effect on me," a grim-faced McCain said after she was finished. Then he said, "I am calling on my good friend George Bush to stop this now. Stop this now. He comes from a better family. He knows better than this. He should stop it."

And so the media went chasing after the governor for an explanation, throwing him off message, which pained Karen to see. ("If anybody in my campaign has done that, they're going to be fired," Bush had said, while copping to the fact that his campaign had made "advocacy" phone calls.) But she wasn't seeing the larger picture, which was: They'd gotten to McCain. For at the conclusion of the Spartanburg town hall meeting, the voluble senator refused to chat with the press, saying only, "I'm a little rattled, frankly, by what happened to that young boy."

And once he'd climbed aboard the Straight Talk Express, McCain had a terse message for his aides: "I want the negative stuff off. Take them down."

McCain's ashen-faced aides tried to explain that this was tantamount to unilateral disarmament. He didn't care. He said to them, with his thirty-three-year-old daughter, Sidney, present, that he wanted to run a campaign that she would be proud of. It was bad enough that he'd already given a mealymouthed answer on whether the Confederate flag should be flown on state property. Fine for Bush to duck the moral question and say, "As an American, I trust the decision to the people of South Carolina." A McCain didn't duck. And a McCain didn't hit below the belt. He would take down his ads now and challenge George W. Bush to follow suit.

Bush got word of McCain's challenge after a rally at the College of Charleston. Scoffing, he said, "That's an old Washington trick. It's a bait-and-switch trick. He runs ads for eighteen days defining me for something I'm not, then all of a sudden says, 'Okay, let's all quit.' I'm going to make sure people understand exactly what I believe, exactly where I stand."

But even with that comment, Bush was slyly reminding South Carolinians that where *he* stood was no longer the focus. No, it was "the Chairman," the purveyor of "old Washington" sleaze, who would stay under the magnifying glass until February 19. Just after the "Integrity" ad had hit the airwaves on Friday the 11th, Tucker Eskew had seen McKinnon exiting Bush's hotel room and cornered him, saying, "We gotta keep the ads coming."

"He agrees," McKinnon had assured Eskew. A new spot was on its way, casting the champion of campaign finance reform as a grateful recipient of lobbying funds, one who "will say one thing and then do another."

No, Bush would not disarm. Quite the contrary: The aerial bombardment would now reach Dresden-like intensity.

South Carolina had earned its reputation as a firewall that immolated underdogs. It had taken down John Connolly in 1980, dispensed with Pat Robertson in 1988, and buried Pat Buchanan in 1992 and 1996. But just as Karl Rove had discounted the perils of New Hampshire, so too did he discount the need for a firewall in the Palmetto State. The heralded machine of former Governor Carroll Campbell had its grassroots army in place but no one from Bushworld to steer them, nor any funds to galvanize their energy. The Texans hadn't figured it necessary. By their calculations, the momentum from a victory in Iowa would sweep Bush through New Hampshire . . . and after that, South Carolina would be a gimme.

"We have a huge, huge problem," said Sara Taylor to Ken Mehlman by phone when she arrived in Greenville just after Bush's loss in New Hampshire. The Bush campaign's Greenville office was manned by a single apologetic-looking kid with a single rotary phone. Taylor, who had codirected the Iowa campaign, was appalled. Where were the precinct chairmen? Where were the grassroots models, the metrics, the tracking systems, the . . . *Where the hell was everyone?*

Within seventy-two hours, everything changed. Austin began dropping bodies into South Carolina like rations into a famine-stricken country. Events that previously had taken an act of Congress for funding approval from Joe Allbaugh now got ratified in an instant— "Just do it and send us the bill," came the word. Jack Oliver and Don Evans's Pioneers were prepared to dig deeper for the candidacy in distress. Supremely confident that it would never want for money no matter how dire the situation, the Bush campaign had passed on federal campaign funds and therefore did not have to suffer a cap on its spending in South Carolina as McCain did. So, millions upon millions poured in unabated. Within days, Sara Taylor had her Iowa model in place: team leaders, battle-tested pols as county managers, armies of door-knockers, phone banks. . . . The once-barren Greenville office was now a tangle of phone lines and dozens of volunteers working around the clock, with round-faced ladies parading through after sunset, bearing trays and singing out, "Here's a ha-am!"

McCain's hard-earned $3.4 million might as well have been Confederate money here. Bush had bought up all the TV time. *The Chairman . . . Says one thing and does another . . . Do not challenge my integrity!* You could not turn a radio dial without hearing an ad—or, more likely, a caller wondering aloud whether McCain really *had* taken down his negative ads, whether he really *was* a conservative . . . seeing as how they'd heard he was for abortion, and he'd fathered a colored child out of wedlock, and his wife, Cindy, was a druggie, and all that. . . .

Who could say for certain where all the dirt had come from? Some were proud to leave their tracks uncovered. In *World Magazine*, the publication edited by Bush's Compassionate Conservatism adviser Marvin Olasky, Bob Jones himself had penned an article titled "Explaining McCain." In it, Jones described the senator as "a calculating and conniving politician" with a "Clintonesque philosophy" who used "liberal-even-Marxist terminology," who dumped his loyal wife for a "rich, attractive and well-connected . . . twenty-five-year-old former cheerleader" who later became "addicted to barbiturates."

One of Jones's professors went both underground and over the top, disseminating an anonymous four-page e-mail that encouraged readers to "feel free to copy and/or send it to others." Among his accusations was that McCain "chose to sire children without marriage." When CNN's Jonathan Karl accosted him and suggested that McCain had no illegitimate children, the professor protested, "Oh, wait a minute. That's a universal negative. That's a universal negative. Can you prove that there aren't any?"

Make the bastards deny it. LBJ's old gambit was of timeless value. McCain's foes—the National Right to Life Committee, the Christian Coalition, the National Smokers Alliance, a ragtag Confederate flag advocacy group called Keep It Flying, and Tom Burch's gaggle of veterans, among others—had for the most part announced themselves. Connecting them to the dirty work being done on Bush's behalf was less straightforward. Flyers materialized on car windshields at McCain events, featuring, without commentary, a photograph of the senator holding the presumed black love child. (It was his and Cindy's adopted Bangladeshi daughter, Bridget.) Radio talk-show hosts were hit with waves of calls that had obviously been choreographed. Seldom was the subject George W. Bush's attributes. Instead, the callers laid into McCain for his pro-abortion leanings (when in fact the senator's stance was precisely that of Bush) or savaged the pill-popping Cindy (who had confessed her former addiction years before).

The thousands of push-poll calls sweeping the state had to be orchestrated by the Bush camp, McCain's staffers figured. After all, it was Bush's patron Carroll Campbell who first won his congressional seat in 1978 by besting the well-liked Jewish mayor of Greenville, Max Heller, in part due to a push-polling drive that asked callers, "Would you vote for someone who did not accept Jesus Christ as his Lord and Savior?"

Warren Tompkins listened to the sputterings of Weaver, Murphy, and the other McCainites and had himself a good guffaw. Of course the Bush camp was "testing messages" by phone. Spending tons on it! But Tompkins had nothing to do with the stuff on Cindy and the black kid, and he was glad not to know who the responsible party was . . . though he certainly had ideas. Working for Poppy Bush in 1988, he'd seen how Pat Robertson's crusaders spread their message from one church to the next, until ministers all across South Carolina were sermonizing as one, a single-throated Hallelujah for His Patness. Now Robertson's Christian Coalition had proxies in all forty-six counties—absolutely bent, like so many others encamped there in South Carolina, on destroying John McCain.

And it was all working, that unending avalanche of Bush money coupled with the insidious pursuits of the anti-McCain denizens. McCain was sliding in the polls. His aides quietly discussed busting the Federal Election Commision spending cap, though of course the consequences—*Campaign Finance Reform Champion Flouts Campaign Finance Laws*—would be ghastly. It seemed that all they could do was flail, ranting to the press about Rove and Tompkins, neither of whom was on the ballot. At one event, chief of staff Mark Salter had chased a man distributing leaflets full of scurrilous talk about Cindy's family. Salter caught up to him and raised his fist, with NBC's Linda Douglass and a cameraman poised to feed the action to a nationwide audience, when Lindsey Graham caught up and pulled Salter away.

The steady strain was gone. On February 15, Bush unfurled his own campaign finance reform package—scripted, unlike all the other weighty policy roll-outs, entirely by Karl Rove. Bush's mischievious Boy Genius "didn't just steal a page out of our campaign finance reform playbook—he stole the whole library," a McCain aide would later grumble. Though a fairly thoughtful fusion of the McCain-Feingold bill and Texas's own campaign finance law, the only real purpose in introducing it was to further agitate John McCain on this, the pivotal day of his debate with Bush in Columbia.

News of Bush's proposal caught the senator off guard. "He's come a long way," he observed edgily to reporters. "The next thing you know, he's going to be moving to Arizona."

Later in the day, the senator hardened his response, calling the Bush plan "a joke." McCain was already cranky from exhaustion and the attacks on his wife, Cindy. Just before the debate, CBS's Dan Rather had gone on the air with a report that the senator had flown gratis thirty-five times on private jets from thirteen different companies. (Bush was a more frequent flier—seventy-nine trips courtesy of thirty-five companies—but no one seemed to be holding him to the maverick's same pious standard.) Arriving at the Seawell Banquet Center in Columbia that evening, McCain was greeted by five hundred sign-waving Bush supporters—the kind of morale-sapping stunt McCain's New Hampshire staffers had employed before every debate there. The senator propped up a thin smile as he waded through his detractors and into the debate arena.

Alan Keyes had been allowed to participate, much to McCain's chagrin: Keyes was a windy know-nothing with a tendency to interrupt and get way out there on the subject of abortion. All of which he did that Tuesday evening, a Chihuahua swiveling between the two big dogs—yapping with such persistence about homosexuals shaming the military and how he would insist that his daughter have a rapist's baby that the moderator, Larry King, at one point admonished him, "Don't dominate, Alan."

But McCain's problem wasn't Keyes. It was Bush, who himself appeared punchy and ill humored from the accelerated pace of the primary. "Let me finish," the governor snapped repeatedly throughout the ninety-minute contest when the moderator or the other two contestants stepped on his monologue. Still, Bush had a surprise for McCain that evening.

McCain walked right into it after Bush was asked by King whether the campaign had turned dirty. "Well, it's kind of politics," the governor said in a genial but disappointed voice. "And John and I shook hands and we said we weren't going to run ads and I kind of smiled my way through the early primaries and got defined. I'm not going to let that happen again. And we shook hands and unfortunately he ran an ad that equated me to Bill Clinton. He questioned my trustworthiness."

When it came McCain's turn, the senator uncorked his musty displeasure. "Well, let me tell you what happened," he said, the blood rising through his jowls as he proceeded from this ad in New Hampshire to that name-calling surrogate in South Carolina, at which point he alighted on the wound that festered most: "But let me tell you what really went over the line. Governor Bush had an event, and he paid for it, and standing—and stood next to a spokesman for a fringe veterans' group. That fringe veteran said that John McCain had abandoned the veterans. Now, I don't know if you can understand this, George, but that really hurts. That really hurts. And so five United States senators, Vietnam veterans, heroes, some of them really incredible heroes, wrote George a letter and said, 'Apologize. You should be ashamed. . . .' "

"Let me speak to that," Bush said calmly.

"You should be ashamed," McCain repeated, and said the phrase twice more as Bush tried to reply, before Larry King insisted that the governor be given a chance to respond.

"The man was not speaking for me," Bush said evenly. "If you want to know my opinion about you, John, you served our country admirably and strongly, and I'm proud of your record, just like you are. . . . But let me say something. If you're going to be—hold me responsible for what people who work for me say, I'm going to do the same for you. And let me give you one example. [Former senator] Warren Rudman, the man who you had as your campaign man in New Hampshire, said about the Christian Coalition that they're bigots. He talked about the Christian Coalition in a way that was incredibly strong. I know you don't believe that, do you?"

"George, he's entitled to his opinion on that issue," McCain said.

"Well, so is this man," said Bush of Tom Burch.

"You *paid* for an event—"

"So is this man," Bush said triumphantly, and for the first time that evening, the audience applauded for a candidate.

McCain persisted—"You *paid* for an event"—until Alan Keyes interjected solemnly, "Larry, I'm sorry. I really am sitting here wondering, because I said we were going out to two hundred and two countries, and is this kind of pointless squabbling really what we want them to see? We're talking about electing the president of the United States!"

And again the audience applauded—first for Bush, now for Keyes, who then proceeded to tick off the *real* issues of concern: "killing babies in the womb every day"; "an income tax system that enslaves its people"; "a school system that needs to be put back into the hands of parents. . . ."

"Let's discuss the issues," agreed Bush. "Let's discuss the issues."

But McCain's train of thought had a raging locomotion all its own. "Let me finish up, okay?" he asked, though not really asking.

There was laughter from the audience, but John McCain did not join in. "So here's what happened," he said, and proceeded to describe the town hall meeting in Spartanburg five days earlier—the anguished mother of the fourteen-year-old Boy Scout who had told his mom that John McCain was his hero until that night the telephone rang and a caller told the boy that, as the senator now put it, "John McCain is a liar, a thief, and a cheat. . . ."

The Bush people had never bought this story. They were certain that the mother had been planted by McCain's flunkies. But they had said nothing, holding back for a moment such as this, when McCain concluded the tawdry tale by saying with saintly solemnity, "Well, that night I called my people together. I said, 'Take down our response ad. We're running nothing but a positive campaign from now on.' I commited to that. I promise that. . . . But I know the attacks go on."

Bush lunged.

"You didn't pull this ad," he said, holding aloft a piece of paper.

"Yes, I did," said McCain, looking somewhat bewildered.

"This had ended up in a man's windshield yesterday—"

"Yes, I—"

"That questions my—this is an attack piece!"

A part-time auto mechanic living downstate had discovered the flyer on his windshield. On the day of the debate, the mechanic showed the flyer to a Bush field rep, who faxed it to Heath Thompson in Columbia, who walked it over to Bush's hotel. Rove's eyes lit up as he read it. "We've got to get the original," he said. Thompson dispatched an aide to fetch it up. The original document made it into Bush's hands about an hour before the debate.

Now an oppressive silence prevailed as McCain afforded himself a quick glance at the flyer. In fact, it was not an "attack piece" at all. Rather, the paper compared the two candidates' positions on Social Security.

But McCain instead said, "That is not by my campaign."

"Well," said Bush, the document now back in his hands, "it *says*, 'Paid for by John McCain.' "

All but drowned out by cascades of laughter, McCain blustered, "It is not by my campaign."

A few minutes later, Larry King called for a commercial break. During it, Bush reached over to McCain, beginning a kind of apology: "Buddy . . ."

McCain pulled away, angrily informing the governor that they were not buddies.

(Whether he added a profanity, as would later be rumored, was a matter to which McCain would coyly demur. "I'm not exactly sure I said that," he would say, "but I didn't accept his sort of little outreach there.")

When the debate was over, the senator was ferried to a residence in Columbia for a "victory party." The press had been alerted by Tompkins's people and met McCain on the curb, wanting to know about his association with the party's host, a man who had made a fortune peddling video lotteries throughout South Carolina.

Meanwhile, Bush's people had located a gathering of three hundred high-school football coaches in a restaurant near the University of South Carolina. The governor passed the evening gleefully swapping jock tales, running out the clock.

It was all over, and yet it was not, and yet it was.

Four days after the Larry King debate, George W. Bush crushed John McCain in the South Carolina primary, 53–42. No one from the losing side could fault the voters for apathy. Over six hundred thousand had voted in the Republican primary, more than double the turnout in 1996. The McCain campaign had felt certain that such responsiveness could only benefit them. They were certain that Democrats and independents would cross over in record numbers. Instead, a dormant Republican base had been jolted to life and flocked to the polls, intent on defeating the man who had been said to favor abortion, to have fathered an illegitimate black child, and to have excoriated the gun and tobacco lobbies while gladly pocketing money from a host of other special interests.

The governor's victory speech that night offered a more lofty interpretation. "It is the victory of a message that is compassionate and conservative," he proclaimed to a cheering crowd in Columbia. "And it is the victory of a messenger who is a reformer with results."

"I congratulate Governor Bush on his victory here and wish him a happy celebration and a good night's rest," McCain retaliated at a rally in North Charleston. "He's going to need it, my friends, for we have just begun to fight and I cannot wait for the next round. . . . I will not take the low road to the highest office in the land. I want to win in the best way, not the worst way."

The biting concession speech was penned by Salter and aimed squarely at Michigan voters, where the next primary would be held a mere seventy-two hours later. That state's Republican governor, John Engler, was a Bush man. He had long ago declared that Michigan would be the Bush campaign's ultimate firewall. He had pledged to Karl Rove that the Engler machine would deliver the goods—that every key precinct was locked up, that the get-out-the-vote operation would be a wonder to behold.

Instead, McCain succeeded in turning Michigan into a referendum on the South Carolina mud wrestle, causing Democrats to cross over in droves. The senator won, 51–43, on February 22. That night was Karen Hughes's worst of the campaign. Rove was pale and devastated. When he and Mark McKinnon stepped out to meet Engler for a postmortem with the media, they found that the governor of Michigan had disappeared.

(Months later, after also failing to deliver his state in the general election, Engler reappeared in the White House, waiting in vain for an audience with Bush chief of staff Andy Card. "He'd promised the moon and delivered nothing," a White House official would recall. "And now he had his bags packed—he wanted to be a cabinet secretary. It became almost a comedy. Here's this guy with the balls to show up and think you're going to be welcomed with open arms after your poor performance. It's the Bush radar thing. If you bullshit this guy, you're dead.")

But McCain had won with Democrats and independents, which was no way to become the Republican candidate for president. After Michigan, he had run out of open primaries. In a desperate attempt to energize moderates, the senator lit into the religious right in a speech at Virginia Beach, calling out Pat Robertson and Jerry Falwell as "agents of intolerance." The crowd went crazy, just as thousands had stood in the rain outside the military base in Bremerton, Washington, five days earlier to hail the war hero as he drifted by on a naval cruiser with the granddaughter of his idol, Teddy Roosevelt, by his side.

Bush beat McCain in Washington, 58–38. He beat him in Virginia, 53–44. And a week later, on March 7, 2000, Bush carried New York, California, Ohio, Georgia, Missouri, and Maine—all across the nation, affirming the fifty-state campaign Bush had vowed to run all along. Broke, disorganized, and despondent, McCain had blown his

only chance in South Carolina . . . though later, when the state's former Republican chairman Henry McMaster confided to McCain that
the effort to defeat him in South Carolina had cost about $35 million,
which was more than ten times the amount McCain had spent
there . . . well, the senator could tell himself: *I guess I never had a
chance there, either. Never had a chance at all.*

But now did the victor have a chance?

The loopy narrative arc of the 2000 primaries would prefigure the
remainder of George W. Bush's political life. In New Hampshire, he
had lost his edge and his base, and thereby nearly lost the presidency.
In South Carolina, he had regained both his focus and his core support, but at the expense of what had made him a uniquely appealing
elected official to begin with. After that Machiavellian triumph on
February 19, the "different kind of Republican," the "uniter," the
"Compassionate Conservative," found himself with a lot of explaining
to do. He began on February 26, with a letter of apology to New
York's Cardinal John O'Connor for having attended Bob Jones University fully twenty-four days earlier without critcizing the school's
anti-Catholicism. Bush wrote, "On reflection, I should have been
more clear in disassociating myself from anti-Catholic statements
and racial prejudice. It was a missed opportunity causing needless
offense, which I deeply regret."

The Bush campaign told Pat Robertson to quit making nasty phone
calls about McCain's associates. The governor himself appeared on
The Late Show with David Letterman and awarded the host a
"Dweebs for Bush" T-shirt. He visited the Simon Wiesenthal Center
in Los Angeles, donned a skull cap, and pledged to fight "all forms of
religious bigotry." On March 24, Bush showed up at Central High
School in Little Rock, where federal troops had been stationed in
1957 to enforce desegregation, and acknowledged the "tremendous
gap of achievement between rich and poor, white and minority." He
pledged not to close down the Department of Education, and to
devote $2.9 billion to improve teacher training.

Bush's policy staff, headed by Josh Bolten, feverishly endeavored to
churn out new initiatives to bring the governor back toward the center. In Milwaukee, he delivered his first address on education in more
than four months. Then came a "new prosperity initiative" relating to
health care insurance for low-income workers. Then an Earth Day
statement committing Bush to "improving the quality of our environ-

ment." In April he at last agreed to meet with members of the gay Log Cabin Republicans. Bush was now where he needed to be—different, uniting, compassionate, all over again.

But he still needed to convince John McCain of that.

McCain's gurus, figuring he could use some distance from the Bush pageantry, had sent the defeated senator away to Tahiti to lick his wounds. But McCain was going nuts there, phoning his staff at all hours. After five wasted days he returned to Washington and stalked off to the Senate floor to talk about Kosovo. A couple of weeks later, McCain returned to South Carolina, because his wishy-washy stance on the Confederate flag issue had been torturing him all this time and he wanted to apologize to the state's citizens for his cowardice. Then McCain went off to Vietnam. He was, of course, aware that the Bush campaign was desirous of his endorsement. He was also aware that Bush had told the *New York Times* that McCain "didn't change my views." McCain figured that Bush could stand to twist in the wind for a while longer.

After days of negotiations between Rove and one of McCain's surrogates, Nebraska Senator Chuck Hagel, the two candidates met at last in a hotel in Pittsburgh on May 9, 2000. That Bush's imminent nomination would receive the senator's blessings was preordained, and so the governor did not feel the need to lather his opponent with flattery. ("What's he gonna say—'I think you're a great American'?" McCain would later laugh.) Instead, for forty-five minutes Bush discussed his campaign strategy and where he believed the senator could help him. He also acknowledged, three months after the fact, that he had regretted not denouncing Tom Burch for his disparagement of McCain.

"Thank you," said McCain.

And after that bloodless encounter, the two men faced the press outside. After McCain's opening statement of support, a reporter noted that the senator had failed to use the word *endorse* in his remarks.

John McCain set his jaw, stared glassily ahead, and said through his teeth, "I endorse Governor Bush. I endorse Governor Bush. I endorse Governor Bush. I endorse Governor Bush. I endorse Governor Bush. I endorse Governor Bush."

Love was in the air.

And it carried Bush through August, and swept into the convention hall in Philadelphia, where the Compassionate Conservative recited, above a rapt stillness, the words he had heard from that boy in the Marlin, Texas, juvenile facility: *What do you think about me?*

"A small voice," said the newly nominated Republican presidential candidate. "But it speaks for so many. . . . We are their country, too. And each of us must share in its promise, or that promise is diminished for all. If that boy in Marlin believes he is trapped and worthless and hopeless, if he believes his life has no value, then other lives have no value to him. And we are all diminished.

"When these problems aren't confronted, it builds a wall within our nation. On one side are wealth, technology, education, and ambition. On the other side of that wall are poverty and prison, addiction and despair. And, my fellow Americans, we must tear down that wall."

Said George W. Bush, "This is what I mean by 'Compassionate Conservatism.' And on this ground, we will lead our nation."

There he stood, resolutely defined, seemingly insurmountable . . . until two weeks later, when the Democratic candidate, Al Gore, prefaced *his* acceptance speech by planting a lingering kiss on the lips of his wife, Tipper—stunning proof of Gore's humanness, vaporizing Bush's postconvention bounce. Then a strange and sickly tailspin in September, righted in October by Bush holding his own in three debates against his pedantic, sighing opponent . . . only to be upset by the mother of all October surprises: the 1976 Kennebunkport DUI, leaked by a Democratic lawyer—prompting a confessional by Bush, and with it, a silent groan from perhaps millions of social conservatives who now saw a shade of Clintonian recklessness in their candidate and resolved to stay home on November 7, Election Day . . .

. . . Which, of course, turned out not to be Election Day at all, but rather the first of a thirty-seven-day wrangle for the highest office in the land, a contest of lawyering and partisan gutfighting staged in the ballot-contested state of Florida, from which George W. Bush largely removed himself—hibernating at his ranch in Crawford, away from the cameras, jogging and cutting brush and performing a few gubernatorial tasks while discussing presidential appointments with Rove and his running mate, Dick Cheney, and of course taking daily calls from his chief Florida strategist, Dad's old warrior, James A. Baker III. . . . Now he took comfort in his refuge, his family, his faith. For he had done all he could. He had bounced back from defeat, united his party, taken on the Clinton era of Peace & Prosperity, and received Al Gore's concession, only to have it retracted on that most exasperating of nights—a night when Rove's boast of 320 electoral votes proved wildly optimistic; a night when they snatched West Virginia and Tennessee right out from under Gore's nose but had New Mexico stolen away from them (so Rove believed) by voter irregularities; and of course, the night when Florida went the other way and then his way and then dangled like a question mark for over a month . . .

. . . From which he emerged on December 13 the winner, a single electoral vote ahead of the 270 required for election—prevailing by a margin of one in the U.S. Supreme Court and by a margin of 537 in the contested state of Florida, while losing the national popular vote by 543,895.

This was the state of the country that George W. Bush had pledged to unite.

Had he been tested for this?

Could anyone be?

PART TWO

——◆——

"THROUGH OUR TEARS"

4

The Building
of Bushworld

The White House could be a creepy place.

Even for a man whose family had enjoyed a dozen years of access to 1600 Pennsylvania Avenue, the 132-room behemoth was many things other than home: workplace, public property, major tourist attraction, symbol of might and hubris, museum, mausoleum of administrations past. Bush had gained an appreciation of the latter quality in the spring of 1992, when he was spending his days in Washington applying Band-Aids to his father's hemorrhaging reelection campaign.

On this particular evening, Poppy and Bar were away for the evening. For the first time ever in his life, Bush had the run of the White House. The Secret Service detail gave the president's son a few pointers on their way out the door. *There's some security downstairs. And the steward's on call.* Otherwise, he was on his own.

Bush had the steward bring him an early dinner. He intended to catch a baseball game on the tube. But the emptiness of the third floor only jostled his preternatural restlessness, so he changed into his grubby attire and headed to the small exercise room in the southeast wing. Bush turned on the TV, mounted the stationary cycle, and proceeded to burn through the fidgets. Eventually he got tired of that as well. Sweating, he stepped out into the hallway in his T-shirt and gym shorts with a towel around his neck.

The usher had turned out most of the lights. Bush took a few strides down the hallway and found his steps slowing. At the entryway

to the Lincoln bedroom, he froze. What had he just seen? Something.
No. Nothing. No!

Ghosts. He saw ghosts—*coming out of the walls!*
Or were they portraits?
Or ghosts coming out of the portraits?
Rubber-legged, he retreated to his bedroom and shut the door.

When he told that story to an acquaintance later in 1992, George W.
Bush had neither the ambition nor the wherewithal to be the future
inhabitant of the White House. For the most part, he possessed a normal man's sensibilities and a normal man's résumé. The ghosts in
the Lincoln bedroom Bush took as further proof of Washington's
inhospitality to normal life. "Kind of weird," would be his takeaway
of a Beltway event. Not that he, as a green-card resident of the sixties,
didn't appreciate weirdness. He had a six-toed cat named Ernie (so
named for Ernest Hemingway's famous spawn of similarly
appendaged pets). He loved to quote the preposterous detective/sex
symbol from the *Austin Powers* movies, and to mimic Powers' nemesis, Dr. Evil. And as governor he befriended a ponytailed El Paso biker
named Lico Subia—"You don't show two faces," Bush told him
admiringly—and later as president he appointed Lico to sit on the
board of the Legal Services Commission, customarily reserved for
well-toned attorneys and party hacks.

But Bush was not one to test the boundaries of his own life. He
knew who he was. He jogged daily and danced never. He professed no
curiosity about the loud music his daughters played. Though he was
not above asking a decidedly straight male staffer whom he was sleeping with, he very much did not wish to know about the private lives of
his gay staffers. At the Governor's Mansion, he demanded a fruit
salad every day, along with what the chef would describe as "uncomplicated, simple . . . American food." At his fishing lodge in East
Texas (where he spent weekends before purchasing his Crawford
property in 1999), Bush would gravitate to the same fishing holes,
where he would inevitably catch and release the same bass, over and
over, to the point where he had actually named the fish who were his
constant prey: "Let's see what ol' Henry's up to."

This was the normal life with which George W. Bush would part
company. Now he would be living among ghosts, in a town toxic with
ill will. It was Bush's determination to change the climate of Washington—he had pledged to do so, over and over.

Never, though, had he pledged to adapt to the climate. It was not his way.

Nor was it Dick Cheney's way.

It was early 2000 and Bush was still battling John McCain in the primaries when Joe Allbaugh flew to Dallas, and Cheney received him at his Halliburton executive's office. Bush's campaign manager inquired as to whether Poppy Bush's former secretary of defense would be interested in becoming the son's VP candidate. Cheney told Allbaugh that he wasn't the right guy for the job: He was happy in private life, he had suffered heart attacks in the past. . . . And then there were two thorny political realities. First, two oilmen as running mates did not a balanced ticket make. And second, the Twelfth Amendment to the U.S. Constitution forbade having two residents of the same state on the presidential ticket. Cheney didn't leave room for further discussion, and Allbaugh thanked him and returned to Austin.

Later that spring, Bush called Cheney. Would he be willing to help select Bush's VP? Cheney said that he would, and thereupon began to gather information on various governors and senators, which the Halliburton exec would then review with the help of a tax lawyer and a doctor provided by the campaign. Not everyone whom Cheney contacted wished to be considered. Florida Senator Connie Mack warned him, *If you put me on the list, I'll never speak to you again.*

Those who did make the cut and met with the governor nonetheless failed to satisfy Bush's two principal needs. First, as Bush would recall telling Cheney, "I don't know what's going to come on my desk, but I'm going to need somebody who's seen things before, who can give me advice to make good decisions." Second, he wanted a nominee whose own political ambitions would not supercede his loyalty to Bush. He could not help but notice how, in policy meetings with the other Vulcans, Cheney "didn't say a lot, but when he spoke, people listened. He's a thoughtful guy, he has the respect of the people around the table, and what he said made sense. And plus, *he didn't want it.*"

Bush knew that the former SecDef, Wyoming congressman, and chief of staff to President Ford had flirted with the top job shortly after Poppy's defeat. Cheney had set up a political action committee and did some 160 campaign events during the Republican-friendly election cycle of 1994. He'd concluded that the marathon was not for him. Cheney was done with politics. And Bush loved that about Dick Cheney.

"You know, you're the solution to my problem," Bush told Cheney the weekend before the Fourth of July as they sat on the back porch of the Crawford ranch. He had told Cheney this before, and Cheney had pretended not to hear. But now they had been through the entire list of candidates together, and it was clear that Bush didn't wish to choose any of them. Cheney agreed to jump through the requisite hoops: get a fresh medical checkup, look at the Twelfth Amendment, figure out how to divest from Halliburton. . . . And, of course, he would talk to his wife, Lynne, though Bush had nothing to worry about there: She had been disappointed that Dick withdrew in '94.

Rove thought it was a bad idea to pick Cheney and told Bush so. Selecting Daddy's top foreign-policy guy ran counter to message. It was worse than a *safe* pick—it was *needy*. As for sizzle: Cheney was old and bald and Beltway and ideologically retro, a political Jurassic Park. On top of which, Wyoming's three electoral votes weren't in danger of falling into Democratic hands.

Bush didn't care. He was comfortable with Cheney. He would be comfortable with his VP running the transition, vetting key personnel, sitting in on every Oval Office meeting, building his own national security apparatus and integrating his senior staff with that of Bush— sharing speechwriters, mouthpieces, and legislative aides—so that no bright line fell between Number One and Number Two as it had between Reagan and Poppy. . . . Secure in the knowledge that Cheney would be Bush's man and not his own, the president saw no harm in giving his VP unprecedented run of the place.

Dick Cheney's first run was to Capitol Hill, immediately after *Bush v. Gore* fell the way of the Texans. Pennsylvania's Senator Arlen Specter had invited the newly anointed VP to lunch with him and other moderate Republicans from the Northeast: Jim Jeffords from Vermont, Olympia Snowe and Susan Collins from Maine, and Lincoln Chafee from Rhode Island. Throughout the lunch, the senators brought up the matter of the contentious Florida recount. It was clear to Cheney that they had bought in to the conventional wisdom prevailing around town—namely, that the Bush/Cheney conservative agenda would have to trim its sails.

Cheney disabused them of this notion straightaway. He was polite but blunt: *We got elected, and we're not going to moderate our positions. Full speed ahead.*

Lincoln Chafee was astonished. It didn't sound to him like the new men in town were bent on uniting.

*   *   *

Bush had seen enough of Washington to know that it wasn't his kind of place. Three days before his inauguration, the president-elect flew on a government plane from outside his Crawford ranch to Midland—the town where he became a businessman, first ran for office, met his wife, raised children, found God, and in every other meaningful way formed his identity. It was a chilly day in the oil patch, and as ten thousand West Texans turned out to cheer on their native son with the fervor of a Friday night football crowd, the object of their applause was noticeably sentimental, even wistful. "In a way, Laura and I will never quite settle in Washington," Bush said. His voice became thick, and he paused.

Then he continued, "I'm leaving Texas, but not forever. . . . There is only one reason on earth that would cause me to leave, and that is the great privilege given me by the people of our country, to serve as your president."

Bush had not yet arrived in Washington and was already hinting at his eagerness to leave it.

He had dropped into town less than a week after *Bush v. Gore*'s resolution. Al Gore received him at the VP's residence adjacent to the Naval Observatory, but they found that they had little to say to each other, and fifteen minutes later Bush departed. By contrast, Clinton was only too happy to receive the president-elect at the White House. The former had plenty of reason to view the latter with hostility. Since 1997—when, at the dedication of his father's presidential library at Texas A&M, then-Governor Bush said of 41 in 42's presence that he had "entered the political arena and left it with his integrity intact"— Bush had made a living contrasting Clintonian crassness with the Bushian "honor and dignity" that would soon be restored to the White House. (". . . So help me God!")

But no one could kill with kindness quite like Bill Clinton. He greeted the Bushes in the diplomatic reception room—grinning, with a sidelong "Nice tie" to Logan Walters the bodyman, and then leading the entourage past the nurse's station and down the garden-room hallway, joking about the press huddled in the Rose Garden to their left, and then into the Oval Office through the side door, by which time George W. Bush was already in Clinton's sway. The two men dined upstairs for ninety minutes. They talked about the transition, about the economy (which Clinton maintained was strong; Bush had received briefings to the contrary but held his tongue), and about

North Korea, where Clinton was considering a visit to negotiate an end to that country's missile program.

Bush had something else on his mind. "With all due respect," he said, "you used not to be so great a speaker." The president-elect offered, as Exhibit A, then-Governor Clinton's Bataan death march of a nominating speech at the 1988 Democratic National Convention, in which thunderous applause had greeted the phrase *In closing. . . .* But, Bush noted, "You're good now." He was asking Clinton for pointers.

Clinton happily obliged him. Pacing was the key, he said, and Bush listened with gratitude as the outgoing president walked him through elocution techniques.

Bush's turn to show off his oratorical skills came on Saturday, January 20, 2001. The inaugural address penned by Mike Gerson was self-consciously marbled with homages—"And an angel still rides in the whirlwind and directs this storm"—and did not sound like anything that Midland's Own would ever utter. It rained throughout that day, and Bush hadn't even noticed, as befitted a man elected a scant thirty-seven days earlier. A few hours after his speech, his mother-in-law, Jenna Welch, sat in her daughter's new bedroom in the White House, watching with a certain perplexity as government contractors hauled out the mattress on which the Clintons had slept. They then replaced it with a virgin mattress—which Bush slept on that night, after a few reluctant turns on the dance floor.

Further eradication of the Clinton legacy began the next day. At 10:30 on the morning of Sunday, January 21, 2001, the West Wing remained a jumble of carpet rolls, stacked desks, and paint cans. But the walls were already covered with framed photographs of the preceding day's inaugural festivities. Not a single image of the Clinton presidency remained. When Bush walked in to work on Monday at dawn, he would know whose White House this was.

He left the carpeting choices to Laura—as long as the color scheme reflected optimism. Bush paid far more attention to retrofitting the White House gym on the third floor of the residence, down the hall from the dreaded Lincoln Bedroom. Conferring with head usher Gary Walters, Bush went through catalogs and ordered a raft of new weights and treadmills.

Bush had assigned the grind of White House staffing to his old Andover and Yale chum Clay Johnson, who, since the spring of 1999, had quietly been interviewing George Shultz, James A. Baker III, and other sages about how to avoid the bunglings of Clinton's transition team. Johnson and a half-dozen other campaign aides had flown from Austin to Washington on the evening of December 3, 2000—fully ten days before Gore's second and final concession—to begin the process for a presidency that might never eventuate. Jack Oliver raised the money from obliging Pioneers to pay for the McLean, Virginia, office, Liz Cheney rounded up furniture and staffed the building with volunteers, and her dad moved in to the second floor to oversee the operation. This rather audacious ramp-up proved wise, since the thirty-six-day Florida recount meant that Bush's cabinet and senior staff posts, not to mention some five hundred other positions culled from eighty thousand applicants, would have to be filled in half the ordinary time.

Though both Bush and Johnson wanted the transition process to be unmarred by the intrusions of self-important Republicans, Rove as always was looking ahead: *If you shut out the usual suspects, they'll write and say bad things about us.* Thereupon Johnson created "advisory agencies" in which the entitled could dispense all the advice their lungs could expel, secure in their delusion that attention would be paid.

Clay Johnson was among the disciplehood of Texans with which George W. Bush could not part as he began his Washington adventure. Rove, of course, did not need to be asked. Nor Karen—though she was less suited than Rove to a city teeming with power seekers. Bush's bodyman Logan Walters, who had once been an intern in the governor's office and still looked the part, would remain Bush's personal assistant. Walters's predecessor, Izzy Hernandez, was practically family—he'd lived with the Bushes in Dallas after someone broke into his garage apartment—so Rove claimed him as his assistant. Another former intern, Ashley Estes, became Bush's personal secretary. And loyal Dan Bartlett—no one, not even Laura, knew as much about Bush's past—became the White House communications director at the green age of twenty-nine.

Mindy Tucker, Scott McClellan, Gordon Johndroe, Jill Foley, Andi Ball, Jenna's old boyfriend Blake Gottesman . . . young workhorses, their filial allegiance unassailable. Somewhat higher up the totem pole, Bush sought a trusted cabinet intermediary, so he installed as its secretary his former legislative director, Albert "Hawk" Hawkins. He wanted a familiar face during overseas travel, so he recruited childhood buddy Donald "Enzo" Ensenat to be his chief of protocol. Though a reliable dispenser of antilawyer wisecracks, Bush, like everyone else, found his own attorneys indispensable. Alberto Gonzales became in Washington what he had been in Austin—Bush's general counsel—while the voraciously bureaucratic Harriet Miers, upon receiving her appointment as White House staff secretary, immediately set to work investigating the antics of Clinton's departing staffers. (A few *W*s removed from keypads, phone lines redirected, a few obscenities inscribed into desk drawers—though in hers, Ashley Estes found a charming good-luck note from Clinton's former personal assistant, Betty Curry.)

That left two other valued Texas friends Bush had to have on board. The first was his best friend, Don Evans. Don had helped manage every one of Bush's political campaigns, going back to 1978. He was rich and handsome and quietly astute, ambitious in only the most casual sense—a quintessential peer, born three weeks after Bush, a Midland oil field *arriviste* two years before the latter, a fellow Methodist, married to Laura's former roommate. The question was never *if* Evans would serve in a Bush cabinet, but in what capacity. A week after *Bush v. Gore*, the suspense ended: Don Evans would be his secretary of commerce.

Less visible than Evans during the 2000 campaign was Margaret LaMontagne. She dwelled in the bowels of the Austin-based policy shop with the propeller-heads who cranked out position papers on education, on which she had been the governor's leading adviser. But LaMontagne was not of the nerds, seeming instead to be Bush's fraternal twin: cheerfully profane, belligerently Texan (though, like Bush, not born there), suspicious of Beltway "expertise," more passionate about results-based education reform than ideological purity, and proud to have a life of family rather than a life of aspiration. LaMontagne's sole field of expertise was education—and the political jigsaw dictated that this cabinet post would go to Rod Paige, an African American and native of segregated Mississippi with a much better story to sell than that of a forty-three-year-old divorced white mother of two. But Bush wanted her in Washington badly enough that Clay Johnson informed her shortly before the election, "I think they want you to be the domestic policy adviser."

"You've got to be shitting me," said LaMontagne. But Johnson was not. Later, Andy Card made the formal job offer—warning, in Card's sweet, solicitous way, "You'll never see your children."

"Don't run off the mothers!" Bush later hollered at Card.

That Andy Card had been awarded the coveted post of White House chief of staff was an unexpected departure from Bush's Texcentric inclinations. Not that Bush had been an unyielding stickler for Lone Star credentials. Two of the campaign's most integral advisers had been foreign policy guru Condoleezza Rice from the West Coast and policy director Josh Bolten from the East Coast. They now occupied two of the most powerful offices in the West Wing: Rice as national security adviser, Bolten as deputy chief of staff for policy. A third outlier, New Jersey–bred Mike Gerson, was brought in as Bush's chief speechwriter—though this title was misleading: Bush liked to make policy in his addresses, so Gerson's job ultimately entailed providing an intellectual and moral framework for Bush's presidency. The final non-Texan to join the inner circle was Joe Hagin from Cincinnati, who became Bolten's counterpart, deputy chief in charge of operations. Probably the single most versatile White House staffer, Hagin was also, even by Bushian standards, mythically loyal: presidential candidate George H. W. Bush's bodyman in 1980, a member of his advance team in '88, then President 41's appointments secretary, and later coaxed out of the private sector by Poppy in 2000 to help mastermind his son's campaign schedule that year.

Andy Card's abiding loyalty also trumped geography. Like Hagin, the Maine native had been in 41's orbit since the latter's failed presidential campaign. He'd met George W. back in 1979, carrying with him forever the image of the slovenly Midlander wearing torn jeans and a flannel shirt, spitting tobacco juice into a Styrofoam cup while mother Bar yelled at him from the porch at Kennebunkport. Some twenty years later, Card penned Bush a fan note: *I hope you'll run for president. If you don't want me involved, that's okay. But I'm still going to suppport you.* Contacted later by Rove, Evans, and others, Card's refrain was, "I'll do anything I can to help."

He helped first by managing the 2000 Republican National Convention in Philadelphia. On the night of his nomination, Bush insisted that Andy Card walk with him into the convention center. Whereupon the nominee said, "I want you to keep your dance card clear."

When the campaign asked Card to assist in presidential-debate negotiations, he did so—a decision that did not delight his wife, since staying with the Bush campaign meant severing relations with his current employer, General Motors, and thereby losing his pension and stock options. Though deeply devoted to his wife, Kathy, a Methodist minister, his ceaseless rhapsodies about the candidate caused her to erupt one morning with, "Are you married to George W. Bush, or are you married to me?"

It was a fair question, especially considering that the phone rang a minute later, and after hearing the first syllables, Kathy said, "Yes, Governor," and with a smirk handed the receiver to Andy—who told Bush that of course, certainly he would fly to Austin to see Clay Johnson right away . . . a meeting that ultimately led to Bush offering Andy Card what the former termed "the big one."

Yet there was already a man seemingly in line for "the big one"—his chief of staff in the governor's office and manager of the presidential campaign, Joe Allbaugh, the third side of the Texas Iron Triangle. By ordinary measure, Allbaugh was a Bush devotee. But by the prevailing standard, he fell well short of Karen Hughes, who never left the candidate's sight, and who home-schooled her son Robert on the campaign plane rather than choose between loyalties. And though Rove's ambitions seemed at times ungovernable, when Bush told him to sell off Rove + Associates in Austin so as to dedicate himself exclusively to the cause of George W. Bush, Rove did not hesitate.

Allbaugh's wife, Diane, did not make the same sacrifice with her lobbying business. It was hardly a scandalous thing in Washington that a high government official might be related to someone whose job it was to seek largesse from the government. Senate minority leader Tom Daschle's wife, Linda, was a lobbyist. So were Andy Card's brother and sister-in-law. But Card's fealty could not be questioned. Fairly or not, to the Bush team Allbaugh gave off the reek of an opportunist. For that matter, he had no experience in Washington—unlike Card, who had served as deputy secretary of transportation under Reagan and as deputy chief under 41.

In short, Allbaugh had topped out. Bush exiled his former chief far from the West Wing, to the top post of the Federal Emergency Management Agency, where it was figured that Allbaugh could do little harm. Proof that he was not Andy "I'll do anything I can to help" Card came in March 2003, when FEMA merged with the newly formed Department of Homeland Security. Suddenly aware that he would no longer have direct access to the president, Joe Allbaugh immediately announced his resignation.

Bush never had a lengthy conversation with him again after that.

Rove was, of course, as they say in Texas, like a pig in manure.

At a 2001 conference hosted by the American Enterprise Institute, moderator Norm Ornstein asked Karl Rove when George W. Bush had begun actively to consider running for president. Rove gave a meandering reply. It was sometime after the governor's 1995 legislative session, he said, but it was hard to pinpoint, because Governor Bush really was quite content with his present job—didn't yearn for the high calling, didn't want to put his family through the ordeal. . . .

"And when did *you* begin to think seriously about it?" Ornstein pressed.

Rove didn't hesitate. "December 25, 1950," he said, reciting his date of birth.

How long, really, had he dreamed of such a moment? In 1960, nine-year-old Karl Christian Rove informed the little girl living across the street in Arvada, Colorado, that he was a Nixon man. The little girl's family was Catholic and loved Jack Kennedy. She knocked him to the sidewalk and smashed his nose. At that moment, politics-as-blood-sport ceased to be an abstraction for young Karl.

He first laid eyes on George W. Bush in 1973. The son was a work only barely in progress: unmarried, no career, no pronounced ambitions of any kind. And yet the younger Bush already had everything Karl Rove did not: a stable nuclear family (Rove's biological dad he had yet to meet; his adoptive father had only recently walked out on his mother, who later committed suicide), a college education, a pedigree, and a swagger the source of which the twenty-three-year-old Rove did not think to deconstruct. At the time, Rove was working for the elder Bush. The latter was toiling as the head of the Republican National Committee during the Watergate era, while the former had it worse: "Imagine being the *college* chairman during that time," he would say. " 'C'mon, guys! We're gonna change the world! Nixon's the One! Sock it to me!' "

Still, the charisma he observed four years later in George W. Bush did not strike Rove as the foreshadowing of political distinction. He was a little surprised when Bush announced his congressional candidacy in 1977, a little unsurprised when Bush lost a year later. By this time, Rove was tooling around in a single-engine plane with Bush's dad, who was exploring a presidential bid. Rove had married a Bush intern who nonetheless was not amused by her husband's incessant travel to Iowa and New Hampshire. "Your great reward is I'll win and you'll be in the West Wing of the White House," Poppy Bush had consoled Rove. But Reagan stomped Bush in the 1980 primaries, and Rove's first marriage ended that same year.

He relocated to Austin and founded a direct mail consulting shop, Rove + Associates. His fourth-floor office in the Vaughan Building was a snake pit of tangled orange extension cords feeding out from an armada of printers. Rove's national clients included Utah Senator Orrin Hatch and Pennsylvania Senator John Heinz. But he made his indelible mark in Texas, giving that state's conservative leanings a decisive push into Republican territory. Rove did his best work with photogenic ciphers who knew not to stray from the simple presentation he'd developed for them. Along the way, rumors persisted of nefarious tactics . . . but this was Texas, where Democrats from "Landslide Lyndon" Johnson to consultant George "Dr. Dirt" Shipley were long accustomed to building majorities by any means necessary. Karl Rove just happened to be the first Republican strategist with an equal talent for the hard low blow.

"What do you think?" George W. Bush had asked Rove in 1989, after Bush the Elder had been sworn in as president and the son began to contemplate the soon-to-be-open governor's seat. Rove responded that he thought Bush could prevail in a contested primary and wallop Ann Richards in the general. It turned out to be only a tease for Rove: Bush opted out of that election cycle and stuck to baseball. But, after Clinton dethroned Poppy in 1992, Rove began to make calls.

In later years, Rove liked to remind people that he'd gotten there well before Karen and Allbaugh—that there'd been no Iron Triangle in the beginning, only he and George W. . . . and though Rove never failed to rhapsodize over Bush's written answer to Rove's why-do-you-want-to-run question—"I wished to God I'd saved it, because it would be an incredible treasure"—he also could not resist adding that to Bush's three-pronged Vision Thing (reform of welfare, education, and juvenile justice), he, Karl Rove, had supplied a fourth: lawsuit reform.

Barely nine months into George W. Bush's career as an elected official, Rove began to summon presidential visions for the man. Despite all his early scheming, the 2000 campaign would be riddled with conspicuous misjudgments on Rove's part. The vaunted "fifty-state campaign" cost Bush New Hampshire and seemed idiotic even to some of his trusted colleagues—a wasteful flaunting of Rove's network of cronies from the College Republican days. Millions of dollars would be squandered in California, where Bush stood no chance. Meanwhile, in the deeply contested state of Florida, Rove overrode Governor Jebby, who had been pushing for big attention-getting rallies. Rove insisted on smaller, message-controlled events. Better to play it safe. After all, Rove had begun to boast, Bush was on track to garner 320 electoral votes, the state of Florida's among them.

The DUI October surprise undid Rove's prediction. On the other hand, it was Rove who squelched the panic when the news broke—striding through Austin headquarters, hollering with mock hysteria, "FREE FALL! FREE FALL!" At such times, the campaign's young lieutenants took their cues from Rove, since he'd hired many of them. One such acolyte was Coddy Johnson, a twenty-two-year-old Yalie bound for Oxford when Rove instructed him, "Get your ass down here. This will change your life. Twenty-five years from now, you'll look back, and this will be the thing that set you on your course."

Johnson ascended to the position of campaign political director for the region that included West Virginia, where registered Democrats outnumbered Republicans two to one. *If you spend more than thirty seconds of your time thinking about West Virginia, you'll be fired,* Rove essentially told him. But the kid thought that socially conservative and pro-coal messages would play well there. In the spring of 2000, he put together a long, statistics-driven argument for pouring resources into a state that had gone Republican only twice in the past seventy-five years.

OK, wrote Rove at the top of Coddy Johnson's memo. In came the resources. The Gore campaign seemed not to appreciate what was happening before their eyes. When they quietly shut down their Ohio operation in early October, Rove shut down Bush's as well—and threw *those* dollars into West Virginia, too. The number of volunteer offices in the state went from 2 to 28. Cheney was brought in on October 10 to pledge to the steel workers that Bush the free trader would impose tariffs. That was the coup de grâce, and none of it would have happened had Karl Rove not urged a fresh-faced lad to forget about Oxford and think big.

On December 13, 2000, *Bush v. Gore* made the electoral tally official: 271–266. West Virginia's five electoral votes—and Rove's *OK* that swung them Bush's way—made all the difference.

Rove's title—senior adviser to the president—was itself a triumph of the opaque. No one was more senior; no one advised so expansively. Yet that role encompassed scarcely a fraction of his domain. There was a reason why the administration's Web page "Ask the White House" offered up interviews with virtually every senior staffer except Rove. In "Ask the White House," citizen-questioners tended to ask the interviewee what he or she did. In the case of Karl Rove, that was a question best left unanswered.

Rove oversaw the Office of Political Affairs and its director, Ken Mehlman. Mehlman ordered goodbye to the days of the OPA doling out White House tours and trinkets to campaign donors. Mehlman devoted his time to selecting and promoting Republican candidates in battleground states. In those states, the OPA reached out to pivotal constituencies. How could it help the steelworkers in Ohio? How could it assist water flow to farmers in Missouri? Mehlman and Rove weren't asking out of charity. Their objective was singular: grow Bush's power by widening the Republican majority.

Rove oversaw the Office of Public Liaison. The "regular Americans" who sat onstage with Bush to discuss the desirability of his tax cuts, and the experts or celebrities or special-interest champions who would be awarded a visit to the Oval Office, were selected and screened by the OPL. But Rove didn't want his public liaison director, Lezlee Westine, to be simply "an in-box." The four hundred events that the OPL staged annually couldn't just be one long receiving line or a disjointed string of photo ops. That was the way Bush's dad had run the OPL. Rove pounded it into Westine: *We are doing big things. Build coalitions. Push the president's agenda.*

Rove oversaw the Office of Intergovernmental Affairs. That department had been its own satellite, but Rove simply took it over. Whenever a mayor or a governor reached out to the White House, or vice versa, Rove made it his business to supervise the give and take.

Rove oversaw the Office of Strategic Initiatives—which only made sense, considering that he invented it. Rove envisioned an in-house think tank for the White House. He believed that presidencies tended to forget the reason for their existence. They tended instead to get lost in their own quotidian mire. It occurred to Rove that there ought to be a nexus for long-range planning—and it occurred to him as well that he ought to be in charge of it.

Every other week or so, his OSI deputy, Barry Jackson, prepared an agenda and accompanying PowerPoint presentation of two or three looming issues. Rove would then convene an evening "Strategery" meeting—purposefully away from the West Wing's self-absorption— and instead in the OEOB's one secure office, room 208. Attending would be the president's seventeen assistants—among them Rove, Karen, Card, Rice, Nick Calio, Bolten, Larry Lindsey, and Cheney's chief of staff Scooter Libby. Discussion would focus not on the day's crisis—that was for the morning senior-staff meetings—but instead on the bigger picture. How would they manage the imminent economic downturn? How could the president's schedule be modified to suit the agenda while minimizing his discomfort? How would they use the polling data gathered by Barry Jackson to shape the strategy? (Despite Bush's incessant pledge that he would never "govern by polls," his administration did precisely that—though the president had the benefit of plausible deniability, since he was never briefed on what took place at Strategy meetings.)

All seventeen assistants had a say. But the agenda was designed, and thus largely controlled, by Karl Rove.

These were the offices Rove oversaw. The other White House offices he simply . . . hovered over, descending swiftly and none too subtly whenever something offended his calculations. The Presidential Personnel Office, responsible for doling out more than four thousand White House jobs, knew Rove well. So did the Office of Legislative Affairs. And the Office of Faith-Based and Community Initiatives. And the Office of Scheduling. (As the architect of Bush's First 180 Days—the first week on education, the second week on faith-based initiatives, then the economy, then national security—Karl Rove *was* the scheduler.) And Karen and Bartlett's Office of Communications. And the Domestic Policy Council. And . . . what else was there?

Cheney's office. Rove didn't push it.

"The danger for me," he volunteered to a reporter in 1999, "is to operate in a way that doesn't irritate my colleagues." Alas, there was little avoiding it.

Rove did not readily project his insecurity. He pretended to be indifferent to, or even delighted by, his daily accrual of enemies. "Fabulous!" he would boom in that hay-fever baritone, and hail acquaintances with "Dude!" or, less frequently, "Dudeness!" Reporters took his quiver full of playful insults and torrent of scolding e-mails at face value. At work, Rove cut an approachable, egalitarian figure—one who kept insane hours and responded to co-workers' beseeching e-mails in the blink of an eye. He was anything but a Beltway social climber, preferring the occasional hunting trip, or time at home with his wife, Darby, and son Andrew, to a night watching others get plastered. (Rove's last drinking binge had been on the infield of the Kentucky Derby, fully eleven years before Bush gave up the sauce.)

But the self-made, stiff-upper-lip product of a broken home and the palpably self-conscious power grabber were two sides of the same coin. And here in the West Wing, in the office once occupied by Hillary Clinton, at the absolute zenith of a political operative's powers, Karl Rove's constant proximity to the president of the United States served only to aggravate his insecurity. It would be said publicly that he and Bush were "like brothers"—that implicit in their banter was a remarkable closeness. And this was so. But to the extent that a sibling kinship existed, the hierarchy was plain: the president was the big brother, Rove the kid brother, and lest the latter forget—as he almost seemed to, from time to time—the former would apply the towel-snapping reminder.

"Karl!"

It was a meeting of economic advisers at the Governor's Mansion in 1999. Rove was going on and on about something, a moment of self-enthrallment, and Bush was not amused.

"Karl," said the governor. "Hang up my jacket."

The others looked around. Was this a joke? If it was, the man telling it was not laughing. Nor was Rove.

Amid the sickly silence, Rove walked over, picked up Bush's jacket, and hung it on a coat rack.

No one took the battering from Bush that Rove did. (And, in turn, no staff in the West Wing weathered the abuse that Rove's staff suffered.) Their affection and ease around each other was undeniable. So, however, was the insecurity each fostered in the other. Rather than fraternal, the bond suggested more a precarious symbiosis, like that of the handsome college quarterback and the campus geek who penned the former's term papers. Each's presence served to remind the other of who he was not and never would be.

"I'm glad to have you, but I don't *need* you," Bush was fond of telling staffers—not unkindly, but simply by way of reminding them that there was only one chief executive elected by the people, and beneath him, all others were dispensable. No one could remember Bush ever saying such a thing to Karl Rove. Instead, the two often engaged in an odd public burlesque. They would josh in front of others about Rove's imminent firing—how Karl's ass was on the line here, and if this vote didn't pan out or that public appearance turned out to be a dud, *well* . . . the kind of joke only an invulnerable employee could play along with.

Karen and Condi Rice—their devotion was reflexive and abiding. They were family. Rove was not family. He was staff. And to discern this, one needed only to observe Laura's wary regard for the senior adviser, whom she called Pigpen—a nickname bestowed fondly, she would insist, except that the first lady was a sensitive soul unaccustomed to doing anything that might be construed as mean, and whose edge revealed itself only when her husband or daughters required her protection.

"Let's ask Bush's Brain what *he* thinks about it," she was heard to say—the moniker coming from a takedown book about Rove, though the subtext was the notion that Rove did Bushie's thinking for him . . . which Laura (a) found to be galling and (b) suspected Rove of perpetuating. She knew of Pigpen's subterranean connivances; they were not Laura's cup of tea. One of her good friends was Nelda Laney, whose husband, Texas House Speaker Pete Laney, had been Governor Bush's second most important political ally after Bob Bullock. In 2004, Laney would be stripped of his speakership in a power play that the Laneys believed Rove had helped orchestrate. Commiserating with Nelda, Laura would later express her own distaste for Pigpen Rove. There was more hate than love in her love/hate regard for Bush's top adviser. Still, it wasn't Laura's style to channel Nancy Reagan, who demanded that her husband's chief of staff Don Regan be sacked.

Nor was Laura naïve. Her husband had pledged to "restore honor and integrity to the White House." Karl Rove had not taken the same pledge. And as Laura was fond of saying, "Everything happens for a reason."

Bush didn't share Rove's obsession with presidential history, but he had studied the last two Republican administrations at close proximity. He remembered well how his father's aides were so shut out by chief of staff John Sununu that they took to begging Vice President Quayle to bring up this or that urgent morsel during Quayle's weekly luncheons with 41. He remembered Don Regan's megalomania, Dick Darman's sense of superiority, Jim Baker's gift for self-promotion. These were men with agendas of their own. There would be none of that in this Bush administration.

In Austin, Bush had purposefully restrained Joe Allbaugh from behaving like a gatekeeper. He didn't desire one at the White House, either. At his insistence, a memo was generated listing those who had "walk-in access" to the Oval Office. Not including family members, over a dozen staffers were on the list, significantly more than those who had walk-in access during his father's administration. On the other hand, Bush disdained the chaos of the Clinton administration, where seemingly anyone could stroll into the Oval, wearing any manner of dress. Clinton's three deputy chiefs of staff readily acknowledged to the Bush transition team that there was little distinction between each's duties. In the Clinton White House, correspondences were answered within three months. Bush would not abide such lapses in discipline. He mandated coats and ties in the Oval, clearly drawn lines of authority among the staff, and all letters responded to within forty-eight hours.

For all the Clinton-Gore whiz-kid, father-of-the-Internet pretensions, the Bush administration's technology was stranded in the eighties, replete with IBM 386 woolly mammoths that practically required kick-starting. But obsolete computers were the least of it. During Bush's third week in office, a uniformed division officer stepped into Joe Hagin's West Wing office. "Mr. Hagin," he said, "you'd better come out in the hall."

"Why's that, Ed?"

"Well, there are people on the South Lawn shooting at us."

In fact, it developed that there was a single shooter—a deranged accountant from Indiana who had scaled the fence and fired a few rounds in the general direction of the residence before being kneecapped by a Secret Service marksman. Still, it occurred to Hagin not long after the incident: *Why are we relying on some Paul Revere galloping from room to room? Shouldn't the White House have an evacuation-alarm system?*

The following month, Bush was traveling to Camp David by car and decided to exercise the presidential prerogative of making a phone call. The sedan was equipped with two receivers. Bush grabbed the first one. Nothing. He was handed a second phone. Also a mechanical failure. Finally, an agent offered the president his cell phone. There was no signal. Bush couldn't believe it. All the way up to Camp David and all the way back, the leader of the free world was incapable of reaching an outside party.

"You've got to fix this," he ordered Hagin upon returning. And the deputy chief proceeded to do so—though at no small cost, and with results that were not in place until well after the month of September 2001.

Bush's subordinates applied their own zealous touches to his imperatives. His scheduler, Brad Blakeman, tasked a brainiac intern with developing a software system that vetted those who wished to host the president at some event. Had this steel executive committed OSHA violations, or said something racially insensitive, or consorted with Democrats? The Maestro system would spit out the answer—rejecting 99 percent of the would-be hosts, who would then be farmed out to a reliable Bush surrogate.

Harriet Miers, the staff secretary, understood her boss's penchant for exactitude and enforced it with relish. "You know the president believes that everything is important," she tsk-tsked others when the documents that crossed her desk for Bush's perusal were judged too wordy or equivocating or in some other way less than flawless. While other senior staffers judged speeches for content or rhetorical effectiveness, Miers would fire back distinctly protective comments: Would the president feel comfortable going out on such a limb? Had he ever said anything quite like this before?

Ken Mehlman, the Rove protégé who had himself mentored the administration's sharpest young talents during the 2000 campaign, was the obvious choice as White House political director. Mehlman understood George W. Bush's elemental compulsion: He needed to accomplish big things. Mehlman lent an assist by abolishing the traditional patronage system of appointments. It wasn't enough for White House job seekers to be Republicans, or even friends of Bushes—they had to agree with George W. Bush's ideology. More important, Mehlman reversed the Clinton administration's triangulating tendency to run away from its own party. To advance the Bush agenda, Republicans had to stay in power. And so by February 2001, Mehlman was already scouring the country for candidate recruits by which the GOP could expand its frail majority in the 2002 midterm elections.

All such activity took place in an atmosphere that was decidedly corporate if quietly slavish. This was not the Clinton White House of brat-geniuses, nor was it the Bush 41 White House of upper-management tyranny, nor the Reagan White House of merciless factions. Seminars and power jousting were indulgences of an undisciplined staff, or of incorrigible egos. If the administration of George W. Bush did not quite call to mind Kennedy's Best/Brightest valedictorians, at least it resembled a National Honor Society of highly competent overachievers who played by the boss's rules and dedicated themselves to his cause.

The Bush way meant routine. He would arrive in the Oval each morning by seven and spend the first thirty minutes of his day calling world leaders. By seven thirty, while Andy Card was conducting the daily senior staff meeting in the Roosevelt Room, the president would be receiving his intelligence briefing. From that point until lunch, staffers would file in for fifteen- or twenty-minute visitations. The afternoons would be devoted largely to policy time, supervised by Miers, and administrative time, in which he and Hagin would confer on various White House projects. Bush would knock off for the day no later than six thirty, dine in the residence at seven, and be in bed by nine. And though the time at which he chose to exercise would depend on the day's events, understood and inviolable was this: The president would exercise for one to two hours, six days a week, and was not to be disturbed.

Punctuality was ordained. Visitors to the Oval could expect to find Logan Walters standing in the anteroom, staring furiously at the second hand on his watch . . . and then at the preordained moment, swinging open the door to a waiting executive whose patience it was not wise to test. The president hated long meetings, long presentations, long anything. (Except runs or bike rides.) Smarter staffers knew to rehearse their pitches several times the night before. Even so, the First Interrupter would inevitably seize upon something they had not considered. "You don't know, do you?" he would challenge them. And it was never wise to fake it. At least, they could console themselves, they had displayed their befuddlement in a timely manner.

The president often described this fidelity to schedule as a courtesy bestowed on others. "Whether it's John McCain or an average citizen, they shouldn't be kept waiting," he would say. When candidate Bush first received Secret Service protection and arrived for a campaign event in Florida, it dismayed him to see the miles of blocked-off streets, just as he hated to hear old ladies at the rope line greet him with, *I waited five hours in the sun just to get a chance to shake your hand!* Was any of this really necessary? he would ask his staff.

Then again, no one really minded waiting for a president. (Or for his proxies: West Wing guests certainly became accustomed to waiting in the lobby for chronically overbooked senior staffers like Card, Rove, Bolten, and Hagin.) And in any event, it was not exactly a courtesy to begin and end a presidential meeting or event *early*. Bush moved through his schedule with type A vengeance. He was restless and he hungered to compete. For a man thought to be leisurely, he seemed forever to be racing the clock. He did not eat a meal so much as disappear it. Eighteen holes of golf—why not make it a contest of speed as well as skill? George W. Bush always did. It seemed a point of pride to him that he could arrive at a finish line—any finish line—faster than the next guy. And if there was no other guy, only him . . . well, get it over with regardless.

On the morning of January 31, 2001, Bush received a bipartisan gathering of senators in the Cabinet Room. Three minutes before it was to start, Bush arrived. Seeing members milling around in the hallway, he said, "What's wrong? Let's go."

One of the senators explained that not everyone had arrived.

"Well, why aren't they?" the president demanded.

"I'm not sure, sir. Maybe traffic's bad." Or maybe—though no one said it aloud—they had become accustomed to Clinton keeping them waiting for a half hour or more.

Bush said, "Let's start. Next time they'll know not to be late."

Not long after that, Bush strode like clockwork into the Roosevelt Room to conduct a meeting with his newly confirmed cabinet. He noticed that one chair—that belonging to Secretary of State Colin Powell—was empty.

"Lock the door," he instructed.

A few minutes later, the sound of a hand testing the doorknob could plainly be heard. The Cabinet Room erupted with laughter. Bush gave the signal, and the lock was turned for the secretary of state. Amid the levity, the president had made his point—although there were really two points, the second one being: Colin Powell, whose popularity had far exceeded George W. Bush's, whom the incoming president needed far more than the other way around . . . was nonetheless not the big dog any longer. A contest of sorts had just taken place. And Bush had won.

The presidency required many things of George W. Bush. Then again, what, really, was required? State dinners? He couldn't stand them. They were for drinkers and night owls and socialites and bloviators. Bush held a grand total of one state dinner in 2001, and precisely that number the following year. For that matter, foreign hosts would receive polite but firm word from the White House: *Sorry, monsieur, but the president will not be attending the nine-thirty dinner. He's got to start the day early.* (Lo and behold, the host country would blink. Dinner would be changed to eight.)

Press conferences? For whose benefit were they, in the end? Or, as Bush said to an aide, "Why should I put on makeup just so David Gregory [of NBC] can show the American people how smart he is?" (He took acrid delight in watching the TV correspondents spray their hair and apply their powder as if prepping for the prom.) It didn't matter that Bush could be quite deft in fielding questions.

(And also quite flat-footed—though usually when pitched a softball question, such as whether Bush had said or done anything he later regretted.) What mattered was that it was a waste of the president's time. That, and an opportunity for him to lose control of his message. And so Bush determined to stage press conferences only on those rare occasions when he deemed them useful in promoting his agenda.

As Andy Card smoothly put it, "The press doesn't represent the American public any more than other people do."

Of course, such obstinacy would scarcely endear the Bush White House to the Fourth Estate. The president's calculation was that the press's affections could never be counted on anyway. He had seen how *Newsweek*'s Margaret Warner, long a family favorite, had stuck the knife in with a 1987 piece on Poppy titled "Fighting the Wimp Factor." (Warner had offered her tearful excuses. But Bush happily accepted the executioner's role: "Sorry, Margaret, you're cut out.") For that matter, *New York Times* columnist Maureen Dowd had been chummy with his parents but unsparing to him. Though he could discern individuals within the institution of the Grey Lady—Bush was fond of the *Times*' Frank Bruni, dubbing him "Panchito," while famously referring to Bruni's colleague Adam Clymer as a "major league asshole"—he saw little percentage after the campaign in granting that bastion of eastern liberalism any interviews. And so he did not.

Would that rile the *Times*' editorial board? Bush didn't lose sleep over it. As he told a friendly journalist, "I don't spend a lot of time seeking out shallow opinions."

During one Oval Office meeting early in his presidency, a few staffers discussed the potential political fallout from the Card Memo, in which the chief of staff had placed a thirty-day review period on Clinton's many eleventh-hour regulations, which included a ban on wilderness road construction and new controls on air-conditioning efficiency. Though widely viewed throughout the White House as deliberate provocations, Bush insisted that they review each order on its merits. Some he was inclined to support, such as former EPA administrator Carol Browner's December, 6, 2000, decision to dredge the PCB-befouled Hudson River. But the rule banning wilderness road construction and the edict raising the energy efficiency of residential air conditioners and heat pumps Bush would not sign on to.

"We're going to get clobbered in the editorials," someone sighed.

"Don't read the editorials," Bush snapped. "They're never going to like what we do. Just try to figure out what the right answer is."

5

DOING A
FEW THINGS RIGHT

Despite all evidence by those who knew and worked for him that this would be an administration driven by a single willful chief executive, conventional wisdom persisted that George W. Bush would be a puppet—of Rove, of Cheney, of his father. Or that, given his reed-thin margin of victory, his would be a weakened presidency . . . or that it *should* be.

Bush endeavored to dispel these notions with a vengeance.

"I know there's a lot of talk out there about who's in charge around here. There's not going to be any *question* about who's in charge. Decisions are going to come to my desk, and I'm going to be the one making them."

This was George W. Bush in the inner office of Senate minority leader Tom Daschle, one week before the inauguration. Daschle had been prepped for the heralded Bush charm offensive. The incoming president was "really not a bad guy—he's someone we can work with," Daschle had been told by no less an authority than Ben Barnes, the Texas Democrat power broker who claimed to have assisted George W.'s ascent on the National Guard waiting list. And indeed, the president-elect had passed through Daschle's reception room that January day shaking hands with every minion, and then had joshed about the fine portraits on the walls—"a lot of good Democrats keeping you company, I see." And he'd begun his sit-down with the minority leader by reminiscing about his relationship with Texas

Lieutenant Governor Bob Bullock, recently deceased—how close the two had been, and how Bush would like such a relationship with Tom Daschle as well.

Then, as Daschle would remember it—though Bush would later doubt having used such harsh verbiage: *I hope you'll never lie to me.*

Daschle didn't know what to say. Of course, the third-term senator from South Dakota had not achieved his stature without some measure of caginess. But: *lie?*

Daschle later walked into his chief of staff's office. When asked how it went, he managed, "It was weird."

Republican House majority leader Dick Armey, a fellow Texan, also found the new president to be surprisingly indisposed to conciliation. The two had met to discuss Bush's tax cut initiative. Armey, who fancied himself a supply-side purist, told Bush that he appreciated that the proposed bill had worked as a Roveian campaign instrument—*but now that we're all elected, could we sit down and write a serious tax bill, or at least a MORE serious one, without all this pandering to the working mother of two or whatever?*

"No, Dick," Bush said firmly. "I'm going to run on the campaign talk."

Even before his election, the governor had approached Armey, who had openly feuded with Bush the Elder over the latter's capitulation to a tax hike. "You know, Dick," George W. had told him then, "I'm more like Ronald Reagan than my dad. The difference is, my dad was raised in the East, and I was raised in Texas."

Bush truly seemed to believe this distinction. But it was also true that the allusion to his dependence on Poppy rankled him. Even as 41 often visited 43 during his first few weeks in the Oval Office, a Republican elected official was shocked to hear Bush openly ridicule "my dad's Vision Thing."

He was a president's son with no federal governing experience and no popular mandate whatsoever . . . and he was not sharing the presidency with anybody.

Still, Bush believed in the virtues of unity, and in his own abilities as shaman to the partisan divide. On the day that the Supreme Court validated his presidency, Bush gave his victory speech while standing beside Democratic House Speaker Pete Laney in the chamber of the Texas House of Representatives—"because it has been a home to bipartisan cooperation. . . . The spirit of cooperation I have seen in this hall is what is needed in Washington, D.C. It is the challenge of our moment. . . . I am optimistic that we can change the tone in Washington, D.C."

On January 22, 2001, Bush's first day in office, six wise men from the Democratic Party—former DNC chair Robert Strauss, former Carter press secretary Jody Powell, former Senators Paul Simon and John Glenn, former Vice President Walter Mondale's chief of staff Richard Moe, and former Congressman Bill Gray III—were ushered into the Cabinet Room. (On time—a pleasant surprise to Simon, who had been accustomed to being kept waiting by Clinton.) Most of them were veterans of the Hill, where Bush aspired to influence people if not win friends. "In my administration, I hope to create bipartisanship," he told them in his introductory remarks. "In Texas I was able to do that. I recognize there'll be times when we have partisan battles. But what I'd like is to ask your opinion on those issues where we might be able to find common ground."

The others ticked off a few suggestions, such as the desirability of reaching out to African Americans who felt disenfranchised by the Florida recount debacle, and lessening the bureaucratic hassle of entering government service. Several of them brought up education, which of course was music to the new president's ears. Turning to Bill Gray—the only African American among the participants—Bush pledged to increase aid to historically black colleges. Karl Rove lunged forward and thrust some figures in front of the former congressman's face.

"What do you think of these increases?" said Rove.

Twenty percent. Impressed, Gray said, "That's the right direction."

But, Gray, Glenn, and Simon all warned Bush, civility was no longer a hallmark of their cherished institution. Members bashed colleagues, both in the media and on the floor. "Restoring honor and decency to the White House" was one thing. "Changing the tone in Washington" was another.

"It's not going to be as easy to do as you think," one of them observed darkly. "This is not Austin."

After the photographers had memorialized the moment and the wise men had been led out, press secretary Ari Fleischer confidently told the media of the gathering, "Get used to it."

Then he added a telling non sequitur: "He's going to continue to identify those Democrats who are most willing to work with him." That, of course, was not quite the same thing as changing the tone in Washington.

Nine days later, Bush invited the Congressional Black Caucus into the Cabinet Room. The president, who had received 9 percent of the African American vote, knew what he was getting into. Andy Card had already been up on the Hill to meet the Caucus. They had kept him waiting for half an hour, and shortly after letting him in, several Caucus members had stormed out in protest. Wisely, Bush phoned a Texas member, Congresswoman Eddie Bernice Johnson of Dallas, to get advance word of what he might be asked about.

Johnson assured him that he would hear an earful about the recount, and about his nominee for attorney general, John Ashcroft, an evangelical conservative whose sympathies to civil rights issues were considered highly suspect. At the end of the listen, Johnson brought up Africa.

"Africa?" Bush asked, somewhat startled.

"Yes," said the congresswoman. "We call that our motherland."

"Well, okay."

A number of the more partisan Caucus members like Maxine Waters refused to attend the January 31 meeting. But those who did found Bush personable and attentive. (Vice President Cheney, on the other hand, sat mute throughout the event.) Charlie Rangel talked about trade issues. Johnson pressed Bush to fund her election-reform legislation. The Ashcroft nomination indeed came up. The president reminded them that his nominee had been elected to the House, the Senate, and the governorship; clearly the good people of Missouri had judged him to be fair-minded. When several members registered concern about the reauthorization of the Voting Rights Act, Bush confessed, "I've got to see what that's all about. I'm not up on that."

Just as the meeting was about to break up, Bush protested: "Wait. We're not leaving yet. You said you wanted to talk about Africa. Colin and Condi got me up on it, so we're gonna talk about it."

Bush assured the Congressional Black Caucus that his administration would be very engaged on Africa. The members found his words convincing.

He also said, "This will be the beginning of hopefully a lot of meetings. I hope you come back, and I'll certainly be inviting."

The next visit of the Congressional Black Caucus to the White House would be more than three years later, on February 25, 2004.

Strictly speaking, the president had kept his word: Eddie Bernice Johnson would be invited back to the White House, and so would

Charlie Rangel—each of them willing to play ball on a White House issue of the moment. This was the shaded version of bipartisanship to which Ari Fleischer had alluded. George W. Bush had an agenda to advance, and any Democrat willing to sign on with that agenda would be proffered as a partner in tone-changing.

If this wasn't the opposition party's idea of "uniting," it wasn't what Bush had in mind, either. Three men in a room putting their differences aside for the sake of the people—he'd seen it happen, he'd lived it, and, well . . . now he knew that when Card referred to the ten football fields' worth of distance separating the White House from the Capitol, his chief wasn't just being literal. Bush's aides briefed him on Daschle—how he was shifty but also prone to caving under pressure, and in any event unable to control key members of his caucus. Tom Daschle was no Bob Bullock. Was House minority leader Dick Gephardt akin to Pete Laney? Frankly, Bush didn't need to find out. The brawny Republican House leadership would deliver majorities on demand.

Was this approach to governance unseemly, given the circumstances of Bush's ascension? No one on his team thought so. Clinton never got a majority of the popular vote and still was sworn in twice. And as for the threadbare hold on the Capitol—six seats up in the House, dead even in the Senate—the Republicans had known far worse: Bush's dad had faced a seventeen-seat deficit in the Senate and a House minority by fifty-eight.

Anyway, the gridlocked circumstances worked to Bush's favor. With every senator's vote crucial, the president could wheel and deal. He could peel a few choice Democrats away from the corpus. Exert his Midland landman's charm. Make them feel special. And get his legislation.

First on the agenda was education. This was no coincidence. It was a feel-good, different-kind-of-a-Republican issue and one that fully engaged the president. More than that, really: Bush was an unremitting nerd on the subject. Though he privately disdained Al Gore— "That guy's the exact opposite of me," he observed after reading Nicholas Lemann's *New Yorker* profile of Clinton's VP—Bush could sound every bit as in-the-weeds as the fellow Poppy Bush termed Ozone Man on the topic of education reform. The "oligopolistic" state educational systems, the need to avoid "prescriptive documents" from government while at the same time mandating "disaggregation of data," the glorious possibility of "voice-interactive virtual reality stations using the same technologies that hook kids on games to teach reading, where the program will constantly adjust to the child"—words and concepts that might ordinarily paralyze his tongue or jangle his patience emanated freely, even stream-of-consciously, from George W. Bush. During foreign-policy meetings, he often deferred to Cheney. But the tables turned when his pet subject was raised: It was Cheney who sat quietly while Bush became the star pupil, the know-it-all.

He *did* know it all. While sitting in on the Josh Bolten–led "policy time" meetings on education, Bush and Margaret LaMontagne would exchange exasperated glances as they listened to Diane Ravitch and Chester Finn and the other so-called experts: *Uh, excuse us, but here in Texas, we've already DONE reform.* Bush's father had once halfheartedly offered himself up as "the Education President." But George W. Bush had spent the last seven years taking on the unaccountable teachers' unions, excoriating "social promotion" (the practice of passing a clearly failing child on to the next grade level), insisting that schools "disaggregate" (reveal how ethnic and low-income groups were performing), and challenging schools to perform acceptably or risk being closed down. The failure was nationwide, evidence of a systemic malaise. Mike Gerson had a name for it—a bit of a mouthful, not to mention visually elusive, but Bush seized upon it, repeating it time and again: *the soft bigotry of low expectations.*

And if they weren't ready to hear it—if members of his own party were squeamish about an aggressive federal role in public schools . . . well, could they really expect no less from him? As he said, "I *am* an activist. And I don't understand—people saying they're against government: Then why are you *going in?*"

A month before he took over the White House, Bush invited federal legislators to the Governor's Mansion in Austin to explain why *he* was going in. Rove had put together the list of attendees. He believed that his boss had to gain traction with an early legislative success. And with sly pleasure Rove sat and watched as Bush performed his passionate riff—at one point swiveling in the direction of Democratic Congressman George Miller (soon to be dubbed Big George, or Jorge Grande) and saying, "I know how you've been calling for disaggregation of the data and I know how important that is. . . ." Miller looked stunned: *Had a Republican just said DISAGGREGATE?*

The Republicans at the mansion held back their protests. One of them, Senate Education Committee second-ranking Republican Judd Gregg, had little time for education reform unless vouchers lurked at the heart of it. Another, likely House Education and the Workforce chairman John Boehner, had lobbied to eliminate the Department of Education. They'd rejected much of what they were now hearing just last year, when the reformer's name was Clinton.

But Bush was their pal. Gregg, of course, went way back with the Bushes. The New Hampshire senator had spent the preceding fall playing the role of Al Gore in Bush's practice debates—mimicking his pedantic prissiness with such excruciating fidelity that Karen Hughes would interrupt him, wailing, "Stop doing that! Please stop!" And Boehner used to play poker with Bush when the latter traveled to Washington for National Governors Association events. He had lent an entire squadron of Ohio zealots to the Florida recount effort. Boehner and Gregg were heavily invested in Clinton's replacement— and knowing how badly their friend needed a fast start out of the gate, neither man doubted that they would ultimately have their say in the bill's outcome.

No, this meeting was more about seducing the Democrats. And it seemed to have worked. But Rove had miscalculated. He'd invited primarily the so-called New Democrats—Evan Bayh, Zell Miller, Jeff Bingaman, Tim Roemer—none of whom had anywhere near the influence of the man who later contacted George Miller, saying he'd like to be dealt into this game: Ted Kennedy.

On January 23, 2001, Bush's second full day on the job, he welcomed his first four congressional visitors to the White House: Boehner, Gregg, Senate Education Committee chairman Jim Jeffords, and Kennedy, the committee's ranking Democrat. There was no question as to whom Bush was performing for that morning. Before replaying his soft-bigotry shtick, he led Kennedy over to his Oval Office desk.

"Your brother used this desk," the president told the senator—who might have been less moved had Bush also mentioned that the desk had been built in 1880 and used by twenty-one of the last twenty-four chief executives. Or perhaps not: Bush seemed genial but also sincere to the Massachusetts Democrat, who had spent the last few years on a failed mission to pass a meaningful education bill.

"I want to help you do this," he assured Bush.

At the conclusion of their meeting, Bush sidled up to Kennedy. And in the manner of another Texas president with whom Kennedy was well familiar, Lyndon Johnson, Bush got into his airspace: *Look, we're gonna have our differences on choice and other things. But the reporters are out there waiting, and I want to ask you a favor. I'll pledge to you that we'll work together. And when they start asking you questions outside, I'd like you to emphasize that, rather than our differences. Because we're gonna resolve our differences.*

"I'll do that," said Kennedy. And a few minutes later the senator waded through the scrum of reporters, with CBS's John Roberts hollering in his face about vouchers . . . and Kennedy did not go there, of which Bush took due notice.

He had only just begun to plaster on the charm. Two days later at an elementary school on the minority-dominated northeast side of the District, Kennedy and Big George Miller gazed agog as the president sat on the edge of a table, his legs dangling as he and the school principal bantered like think-tank geeks about accountability and results interpreting. . . . Kennedy left the building saying, "I don't think we need any more hearings. We can work together on this."

Yet Bush kept laying it on. He invited the Kennedy family—not only Ted, his wife, Vicki, and his son Patrick, but also the senator's Portuguese water dog, Splash—to the White House for an advance viewing of *Thirteen Days*, about John Kennedy's handling of the Cuban missile crisis. A few months later, Bush signed on to renaming the Department of Justice building after Kennedy's other famous brother, Robert F. Kennedy. The veteran senator knew he was being worked, of course. He knew all about the Bush–Bullock alliance. He knew as well that Daschle was being left out of the picture, while in the meantime Bush's legislative team was working back channels with New Democrats like Joe Lieberman and Bayh, in case Kennedy pulled out altogether.

But Ted Kennedy was the least of Bush's worries. Conservatives like Pete Hoekstra and George Voinovich saw the No Child Left Behind package as an insult to their ideological purity. So did House majority leader Armey, who was appalled that Bush was willing to sacrifice vouchers, the one dignity-preserving facet of federal education reform. And, as expected, the teachers' unions yapped while civil rights groups declared their general wariness of a Republican-sponsored initiative aimed primarily at low-income schools.

Amid the crossfire, it was easy for Bush to overlook the welling discontent of Jim Jeffords. The Vermont senator had receded in significance as Kennedy's influence grew. It was axiomatic that Democratic congressional staffs were superior to their Republican counterparts when it came to social issues. In the case of education, the difference between Ted Kennedy's learned and aggressive lieutenants and Jeffords's staffers—one of whom memorably lectured a White House aide, "You know, these big bills just take a lot of time"—was almost embarrassing. Besides, Jeffords had a singular dog in this hunt—special education—and when he demanded a whopping $200 billion commitment to this matter, the White House reacted as if the Education Committee chairman was in need of some special education himself.

Jeffords didn't think he was being unreasonable at all. After all, even as George W. Bush was appeasing the center-left with No Child Left Behind, he was heaving a considerable bone to the right in the form of a $1.6 trillion tax cut proposal. Like other moderates, Jeffords found the cut alarmingly high. And if the rich deserved such a giveaway, he figured, didn't disabled kids as well? Though Jeffords had been a fair-weather friend at best—he refused to be the Vermont chair of Bush's 2000 primary campaign, then pushed aside chairman Jim Douglas during the convention—he felt slighted when the administration neglected to invite him to the White House ceremony honoring a Vermont educator as Teacher of the Year. Bush aides insisted that no insult was intended. Senators were never invited to such functions. (Though both Georgia senators were present at the Rose Garden in 2003 for a Georgia teacher's reception of the award, and the same for a Rhode Island recipient the following year.) Jeffords was not mollified. He confided to a colleague, "This is not the George Bush I thought I knew. This guy is a right-winger from Texas!"

That colleague, Nebraska Senator Chuck Hagel, paid a call to Andy Card in early May. "Andy," he said, "you've got a problem here. I suggest you have the president call Jeffords down to the Oval Office. Have him say, 'You and I both care about education, you're chair of the committee, I'll work with you'—and then give him something to make it work, and I think he'll be okay if you do that. Just give him some respect. Make this a partnership."

Replied Bush's chief of staff, "He doesn't deserve that."

Three weeks later, Jim Jeffords bolted from the Republican Party. Suddenly, the Democrats controlled the Senate—the committee chairmanships, the legislative calendar, influence over judicial nominees . . . and Tom Daschle, George W. Bush's not-Bullock, was now majority leader.

Karen Hughes anxiously phoned Republican leaders on the Hill, begging them not to point fingers at the White House. It was a little late for that. Bush, Rove, Card, and Director of Legislative Affairs Nick Calio knew they had badly underestimated Jeffords. Throughout the end of May, a sense of shock gripped the West Wing. How this would all play out was difficult to assess. Jeffords's defection was a blessing for the No Child Left Behind lieutenants, who far preferred working with Kennedy's people anyway. Tax cuts—Jeffords wasn't going to make a difference there, either. In fact, Bush's tax relief package, rather than education, would turn out to be his first big victory.

Here the numbers clearly favored Bush. No Republican was going to vote against tax cuts—not even the northeast's Mod Squad of Lincoln Chafee, Susan Collins, and Olympia Snowe, despite Snowe's agitating for child tax credits and triggers and other centrist baubles. Bush simply had to peel away a few Democrats. Over dinners at the White House, he cajoled Louisiana's John Breaux, who had already been flattered with an offer back in December to be Bush's secretary of energy. Bush deputized Andy Card to work Breaux (as well as Card's fellow Maine native, Olympia Snowe), and day after day he did so. At one point, the two men sat in the green room of CBS's *Face the Nation*, sketching out compromises on a napkin.

Above all, Bush took advantage of an offer made to him at the inaugural by Montana Senator Max Baucus, the ranking Democrat on the Finance Committee. "I want to be helpful—I want to be a different kind of Democratic leader," Baucus had said that day after introducing himself to the new Republican leader.

"Sure, Maxie," Bush had replied. He knew that Daschle and Baucus loathed each other. (The latter had been the only western Democrat to cast his ballot not for the former but instead for Chris Dodd as Senate minority leader in 1994.) He also knew that Baucus was up for reelection next year in conservative Montana. The four-term Democrat had to come up with some candy for the voters. Even before Bush took office, Baucus and the Finance Committee chair, Chuck Grassley, had been scheming in weekly meetings to get a tax bill passed. Now Bush deputized Grassley: *Take care of Maxie*.

And Maxie—who, thanks to the Jeffords defection, replaced Grassley in May as chairman—responded by taking care of Bush. "I'm representing the '02 Democrats," he defiantly informed Daschle, and proceeded to solicit the appetites of vulnerable midterm incumbents Jean Carnahan from Missouri, Max Cleland from Georgia, Mary Landrieu from Louisiana, and Tim Johnson from Daschle's state of

South Dakota. Then Baucus handed the laundry list of their pet items to Grassley, who handed it to Calio, who walked it over to the Oval Office.

Calio had worked for Bush's dad—who, having served in Congress himself and having developed the pragmatic sensibility that comes with being a member of the minority party, reflexively nurtured friendships with those on the Hill. This Bush, Calio learned early on, was satisfied with the friends he already had. "I'm the president, they're the Congress," he told Calio. "We can be friendly, but they don't have to be my friends."

The first Bush had famously caved on a Democratic tax hike. This Bush had declared in New Hampshire, "This is not only, 'No new taxes' "—the pledge his dad had reneged on—"but 'tax cuts, so help me God!' " He was not about to crawfish.

That said, the rationale for a major tax cut had strayed from Bush's campaign stump speech. Throughout 1999 and 2000, Bush's message was unwavering: The projected $4.6 trillion surplus through 2010 was "the people's money," and it ought to be given back to them. He said it when John McCain was scolding Bush's plan for not saving "one new penny for Social Security or the debt." And he said it when Al Gore continually asserted that Bush was foisting a "risky tax scheme" on the American public. ("Risky tax scheme! Risky tax scheme!" Bush would say with mock panic in his eyes every time he ran into his young economic aide Marc Summerlin—whom eventually Bush would nickname Risky.)

But even throughout the campaign season, the economic outlook was darkening, and the prospect of a new president returning sackloads of cash to the people began to lessen. Bush's chief economic adviser, Larry Lindsey, had been warning the governor of this scenario since 1997. When Lindsey brought up the matter of the high-tech bubble, Bush's eyes lit up. "I know about bubbles," he said, and proceeded to recall aloud Midland after the oil bust—friends losing jobs, neighbors having their mortgages foreclosed.

"There's a good chance it'll burst while you're president," Lindsey predicted. To which Bush with exasperation replied, "If you're right, then why do I want to *be* president?"

But that unhappy scenario was not occurring throughout 2000. "How's that bubble doing, Lindsey?" Bush would snicker. "Gonna burst any day now?"

Unfortunately, yes. By the resolution of *Bush v. Gore* in December, it was clear that George W. Bush would be presiding over an injured economy. Now, Bush argued, tax cuts weren't a virtue but a necessity. The very same plan that he had promulgated during the campaign as a good-faith return of "the people's money" Bush now recast as "an integral part of economy recovery."

Calio had cautioned the new president early on not to get too hung up on the magic number of $1.6 trillion for a tax cut. "You can offer that," he advised, "but if you insist on it, you'll end up not getting everything else you need in the package."

George W. Bush leaned across the table that separated them. "We're going to say $1.6 trillion," he replied. "And we're going to keep saying $1.6 trillion. And we're not going to back off. And we're not going to talk about compromising. And we're going to piss some people off. And eventually we may have to back off of the $1.6 trillion. But the longer we say it, the less we'll end up having to back off."

Beneath the intransigent rhetoric, Bush was backing off of all sorts of things. The House Republicans were not pleased. They wanted the White House to hold firm on lowering the top tax rate from 39.6 percent to 33 percent. They pushed for deeper cuts and fewer low-income giveaways. Bush didn't care. He simply rolled DeLay, Armey, and House Ways and Means Committee chairman Bill Thomas. The mods and the '02 Democrats got some if not all of what they wanted. And in the end, Bush backed down from the $1.6 trillion, settling for $1.35 trillion—which passed the Senate 58–33, accruing fully a dozen Democratic votes.

George W. Bush put his signature to his administration's first major piece of legislation, and the first major tax cut since the Reagan administration, on the morning of June 7, 2001. At the signing ceremony in the East Room, Democrats as well as Republicans grinned for the cameras. One of them was Maxie Baucus, and he had particular reason to smile: Administration aides had turned the other way while Baucus's people smuggled in a video camera, a practice absolutely forbidden in the White House. The ensuing footage—Baucus standing beside Bush, hailing the passage of tax cut legislation—went on the air in Montana that same month. And just like that, at least one '02 Democrat had nothing to worry about.

(Not that this stopped the White House from sending Cheney into Montana in 2002 to campaign for Republican senatorial candidate Mike Taylor, which infuriated Baucus. "Max," Andy Card assured him by phone, "it's just politics. You're gonna win.")

*　　*　　*

By early summer 2001, Karen was losing the message war.

Her boss was no longer a constitutionally weak governor or a one-man campaign act. "Government should do a few things and do them right"—it was pretty to think so, and a fine stump slogan . . . but now both George W. Bush and his counselor knew different: The president was the executive of a bureaucratic colossus and unwitting author of a thousand policy narratives, not to mention the leader of the Republican Party. It was one thing for Karen to control the White House's daily message. But how was she expected to harness, say, Tom DeLay, if she couldn't bring Message Discipline to one of Bush's own cabinet secretaries?

While in Trieste, Italy, for a G-8 summit in March, Environmental Protection Agency administrator Christie Todd Whitman—the former governor of New Jersey and a moderate counterweight to Secretary of the Interior Gale Norton—had proudly announced to her European counterparts that the Bush administration was prepared to designate CO_2 as a pollutant. In so doing, power plants that emitted carbon dioxide would be subject to EPA regulation. Whitman had not intended to make administration policy. The policy had already been made, on the campaign trail, described in a rollout speech Bush had delivered in Michigan. Josh Bolten, chief of the propeller-heads, had signed off on the speech and had included the mandatory cap on CO_2 emissions in the Transition 2001 policy notebook.

The problem was that Bolten had erred. The intended designation for CO_2 was "emission," not "pollutant." Whitman didn't know this. She knew only that Europe was seething over the United States' refusal to ratify the Kyoto Protocol. Bush wasn't alone in his objection to the protocol aimed at reducing greenhouse gas emissions: The Senate had rejected the treaty by a vote of 95–0 four years prior. All the same, hostility awaited Whitman at the G-8 meeting, so she delighted in the discovery of this little policy gem in her Transition 2001 notebook. She took it and ran with it to Trieste.

Driving to the White House one morning, National Economic Council adviser Larry Lindsey answered his cell phone and was stunned to hear an aide say, "Larry, did you hear? We're about to declare CO_2 a pollutant."

Scoffed Lindsey, "I'm exhaling CO_2 right now!"

Lindsey wasn't the only red-faced attendee at that morning's senior staff meeting—which, as a fanny-pat to the non–West Wingers, was being held at a conference room in the adjacent Old Executive Office Building for a change. Rove and Cheney had been getting an earful from the utility companies. Andy knew how his former co-workers at General Motors would react. Office of Management and Budget director Mitch Daniels agreed with Lindsey that designating CO_2 as a pollutant was not exactly what the sputtering economy needed.

Karen was apoplectic. The policy nerds weren't getting it. She argued a metadefense of the absent Whitman: *They're hammering us on the environment! Saying we're walking away from the Kyoto treaty and don't care about global warming . . . saying we're poisoning our children by lowering standards for arsenic in drinking water. . . . We can't let them DO THIS!*

The policy nerds had difficulty responding to Karen when she got this way. The issues were largely lost on her. And it was a disarming combination, that womanly sentiment barreling out like a boot-camp ultimatum: *The president is a COMPASSIONATE LEADER! HE CARES ABOUT CHILDREN AND THE ENVIRONMENT!*

Later, they took the matter into the Oval Office. Bolten came clean. "Calling CO_2 a pollutant in the campaign document was my mistake," he said.

Cheney, usually silent at domestic-policy meetings, forcefully argued that a cap on CO_2 emissions was bad energy policy and would only worsen the rolling blackouts occurring in California. Whitman wasn't there to make her case. Nor was Secretary of State Colin Powell.

"If it's a mistake, it's a mistake," said Bush. A few days later, on March 16, he reversed policy.

In an April strategy meeting, Karen told other senior staffers that the White House's perceived indifference to the environment was "killing us." She demanded some show—any show—of Green Bush. So the president was hustled out into the Rose Garden that month to announce his support for the Stockholm treaty negotiated by Clinton, which restricted the use of persistent organic pollutants. Later in April, Bush turned a perfunctory appearance at an Environmental Youth Awards reception into an opportunity to insist that "my administration has a commitment to clean air and clean water and good soils." Taking the presidential bubble into the wilderness, Karen led Bush to events at Sequoia National Park, the Everglades, and a state park in Birmingham. Bush joked that his counselor had become his "lima green bean." She was, in any event, a bean with significant influence. When the administration announced its support for a nuclear waste site at Nevada's Yucca Mountain, Karen insisted on some green shading. The EPA responded by adding a groundwater-protection standard for the area that would last ten thousand years—a panacea that drew smirks from the policy nerds inside the White House, and that went largely unappreciated outside it as well.

Bush's approval ratings began to sink. Karen could find little traction. It was bad enough that her "different kind of Republican" boss was being skewered as an appeaser of the right wing. (She could expect no less when Bush, on his first day as president, reinstated a Reagan-era clampdown on federal funding for international family-planning services that offered abortion counseling. It *did* surprise her that Bush's choice for attorney general, John Ashcroft, had been depicted by *Newsweek* as a holy warrior. Ashcroft had been a popular governor in Missouri. Couldn't they give the guy the benefit of the doubt?) And she had correctly predicted a public relations fallout when, over her protests, Cheney insisted on not releasing the names of those who would testify before his energy commission.

To question Bush's presidency was one thing. Much worse was that they questioned whether it was *his* presidency. Throughout the late spring and early summer of 2001, alternative theories abounded as to who provided the kinetic force to the administration's policies. It was Dick Cheney's White House. Or Karl Rove's. Or the Religious Right's. Or perhaps Poppy Bush's.

Anyone inside could see it: George W. Bush was singularly in charge. But outside, they weren't buying it.

And so Karen decided to draw back the curtain and invite America to view the silent movie of Bush deliberating on the subject of federal funding for stem cell research.

Well before the message crisis, stem cells had quietly been on the White House agenda. In March, Bolten tasked Office of Management and Budget counsel Jay Lefkowitz with studying the scientific and ethical implications of using discarded embryos for research. By late spring, Bush was calling him on his cell—"Lefky, where are you?"—for impromptu discussions. He asked Lefkowitz what other countries were doing with stem cell research. He told him to research how the different religious traditions treated the issue. The president was fascinated by the ethical dilemmas posed by stem cell research. If an embryo was going to be discarded anyway, how could it *not* be morally advantageous to use its stem lines to save a living human? On the other hand, could this rationale be used to justify, say, harvesting a death row inmate's organs just before the lethal needle went in? At one point, Lefkowitz brought a copy of Aldous Huxley's 1932 classic, *Brave New World*, into the Oval Office, and read aloud to his bemused boss the author's conjurings of human "hatcheries" nurtured in test tubes. That world had arrived.

"We're tinkering here with the boundaries of life," Bush murmured to Lefkowitz. "We're on this precipice. One step, and we fall into the abyss."

Beneath the intellectual exercise lay political dilemmas as well. Republican patriarch emeritus Ronald Reagan suffered from Alzheimer's disease, and his wife, Nancy, passionately asserted that a cure for the affliction might come from stem cell research. Pro-lifers were just as vigorous in their opposition to any research that involved tampering with a human embryo. Though Bush was firmly on record as an opponent of abortion, it had never been his pet issue. Both his mother and his wife were pro-choice. As governor, he gave strong indications to moderate aides that he would never be a right-to-life firebrand. But that was before the New Hampshire primary, where Bush learned the costs of straying from the Republican base.

"We've done a lot of polling on this issue," a member of the National Right to Life Foundation had said to the president, and held out the numbers. Bush literally swatted them out of his face. "We're not talking about public opinion," he snapped. "I'm trying to figure out what the right thing to do is." But since no easy answer was forthcoming, he proceeded to take a poll of his own.

He asked Andy Card. He asked Colin Powell. He asked speechwriter Mike Gerson. He asked Bolten. He asked Laura. He read a letter penned by Nancy Reagan and hand delivered by Andy. He sat in a limo and heard out South Carolina's ninety-eight-year-old senator, Strom Thurmond. He asked the White House doctors. He asked the deans at Notre Dame and Yale when he went to both campuses to deliver commencement addresses. During a briefing on the economy, he asked Larry Lindsey. On the way back from a political event in Virginia, he asked two members of his advance staff.

The more he asked, the less consensus he found. Gerson had been urging Bush to see his presidency as one that advocated a "culture of life," and the notion of harvesting human embryos seemed anathema to this. Then again, social conservatives like Senator Orrin Hatch strenuously defended the morality of stem cell research. The drumbeats began on both sides of the debate by early summer. It was at this point that Karen took over.

She instructed Lefkowitz to schedule Oval Office meetings with experts. Karen wanted Bush to be seen as properly deliberative, as opposed to hand-wringing. For once, Bush himself cared very much about appearances as well. He was struggling with an issue, and he believed people should know that he was struggling—that he wasn't a pawn or a dunce, that this was a decision not reached lightly.

"I must confess I am wrestling with a difficult decision," Bush said on July 9 to bioethicists Leon Kass and Daniel Callahan in the Oval Office. Both men were deeply opposed to funding for new stem-cell colonies, and Kass led Bush through a Socratic dialogue. Did Bush believe that a human embryo had life potential? Did that then entitle the embryo to some greater respect than an inanimate object? Could good therefore be promoted when it came at the expense of a human embryo?

Kass and Callahan didn't issue an explicit recommendation. They didn't need to. Bush left that meeting ready to embrace a middle ground. For some time now, Health and Human Services Secretary Tommy Thompson had advised confining federal funding to existing stem-cell lines. Kass had told him that five such lines existed, and that they would suffice for research purposes. Bush had Lefkowitz call the National Institutes of Health. They informed him that there were in fact thirty existing lines. Bush believed he had his answer.

On August 2, he met with one more bioethicist, Dr. LeRoy Walters of Georgetown University. Rove, Lefkowitz, and Card also sat in. Walters was an advocate for using new as well as preexisting stem-cell lines, but he wasn't going to push it. His fear was that Bush would ban *all* stem cell research.

"I think it's really important that the president be a moral educator on issues like this," Bush said.

"I agree," said Walters. "And actually, *Time* and *Newsweek* have both run cover stories on stem cells, and I think they've done quite a good job of presenting science to the public."

"I haven't read either of those articles," Bush said dismissively.

One of Bush's men volunteered that members of the NIH had been in the Oval Office earlier that day. The scientists had announced an encouraging discovery: There were in fact upward of sixty existing stem-cell lines. Walters was stunned. He knew that such a high number could not possibly be accurate. (Later he spoke with the NIH officials who had visited Bush and was told by them that such a number hadn't been mentioned—that after their meeting, it had apparently been supplied to the White House by the NIH's director. The NIH's website would later report the number of existing lines as twenty-two.)

The middle-of-the-road approach was likely to displease both sides, as Bush saw when he met with Karen, Card, Bolten, Rove, the newly remarried Margaret LaMontagne Spellings, and others. Amid the arguing, Card—whose father had died of Parkinson's disease and whose mother was a casualty of Alzheimer's—interrupted: "Mr. President, if that's where you are, it's okay."

Karen informed Gerson that she would write the speech. It was the only speech she would ever write for the president from start to finish. Bush ran through it a few times while vacationing in Crawford. On the morning of August 9, the White House contacted the major networks and requested time for Bush to address the nation. He went jogging with Lefkowitz on the ranch that morning and still was thinking through how his decision would play out. Rove placed a few calls a half hour before the address to let leaders on the Hill know what Bush would say.

His speech that evening was a mere eleven minutes long, dense with scientific expostulation and delivered clumsily, as if for the first time, with an unusually tentative conclusion: "I have made this decision with great care, and I pray it is the right one."

As Karen Hughes would later tell the media, "Several people told him, 'This may be the most important decision of your presidency.' "

Which said a lot about the state of the nation in August 2001.

6

THEN . . .

Education reform, tax cuts, stem cell funding. Commissions to reform energy policy and Social Security. A sweeping plan to promote federal funding for religious social services. A prescription-drug-care proposal to cover all senior citizens on Medicare. You could not say that his was a timid agenda. Yet something was missing. The pre–South Carolina primary George W. Bush was missing. How was he a "different kind of Republican"? Yes, he believed strongly that a federal government had a role in educating children. And that was not a small thing. But it was only one thing—and, as it would develop, an underfunded thing at that. How else was he "different"? His White House was more efficient, more stubborn, and more secretive than the previous two Republican administrations. Was *that* what voters had signed on for?

He seemed strangely accidental, undersized, disinterested. You saw a flash of the man's passion that day at Merritt Elementary School. You saw the discipline he imposed on his staff. You saw his political dexterity in simultaneously pursuing a tax cut policy coveted by Republicans and the No Child Left Behind education package desired by the opposition party. You saw his plainspoken decency when he stood before a group of African American law enforcement officials and said of racial profiling, "It's wrong in America, and we've got to get rid of it." And you saw him bear up graciously when he marked his one hundredth day with a luncheon for all 534 congressmen, which almost every Democrat boycotted.

What you no longer saw was the *purpose*.

"It's like the pig and the chicken with someone making ham and eggs," Governor George W. Bush had told a reporter in the summer of 1998 as the two of them sat in his office and discussed the risks and rewards of a presidential run. "The pig takes off, and the chicken says, 'What's the matter?' He says, 'For you, it's a contribution. For me, it's one hell of a commitment.' It's actually—this cultural issue, to me, is a reason. It's a reason. You've gotta have a reason. A mission. You've gotta have a reason to be out there. And you've gotta paint a picture."

Three years later, the picture lacked coherency. "A Compassionate Conservative" promulgating "the Responsibility Era"—what had happened to this man? Where was his Vision Thing?

Only one aspect of the Vision resonated sharply throughout his first eight months in office. During the second presidential debate with Al Gore, on October 11, 2000, George W. Bush promised a less interventionist foreign policy than that of the Clinton-Gore administration—one, in keeping with his Responsibility Era, that would encourage self-reliance while curbing its own meddlesome Great Power impulses. "I am worried," Bush said then, "about overcommitting our military around the world. I want to be judicious in its use. . . . I think what we need to do is convince people who live in the lands they live in to build the nations. Maybe I'm missing something here. I mean, we're going to have kind of a nation-building corps from America? Absolutely not. Our military is meant to fight and win war; that's what it's meant to do. And when it gets overextended, morale drops. . . . I'm going to be judicious as to how I use the military. It needs to be in our vital interest, the mission needs to be clear, and the exit strategy obvious."

But Bush wasn't finished. When the topic turned to reform of the International Monetary Fund, candidate Gore went on a Wilsonian roll, saying to moderator Jim Lehrer, "I just think, Jim, that this is an absolutely unique period in world history. The world's coming together, as I said. They're looking to us. And we have a fundamental choice to make: Are we going to step up to the plate as a nation the way we did after World War II, the way that generation of heroes said, 'Okay, the United States is going to be the leader.' And the world benefited tremendously from the courage that they showed in those postwar years."

"Let me comment on that," Bush said, and then countered with his own, far less grandiose proposition: "Yeah, I'm not so sure the role of the United States is to go around the world and say, 'This is the way it's gotta be.' We can help. And maybe it's just our difference in government—the way we view government. I mean, I want to empower people. I don't—you know, I want to help people help themselves, not have government tell people what to do. I just don't think it's the role of the United States to walk into a country, say, 'We do it this way; so should you.' "

The governor cited the example of Russia in the age of Putin. "The only people who are going to reform Russia are Russians," he said. "They're going to have to make the decision themselves. . . . We can work with them on security matters, for example, but it's their call to make, because I'm not exactly sure where the vice president's coming from, but I think one way for us to end up being viewed as the ugly American is for us to go around the world saying, 'We do it this way. So should you.'

"Now, we trust freedom. We know freedom is a powerful, powerful—a powerful force much bigger than the United States of America, as we saw in—recently in the Balkans. But maybe I misunderstand where you're coming from, Mr. Vice President, but I think the United States must be humble and must be proud and confident of our values, but humble in how we treat nations that are figuring out how to chart their own course."

It was an honest, plainly yet resolutely stated vision of a noninterventionist America. And on this promise, the president had made good in his first months in office.

His first foreign visit was in February, to Mexico, the kind of trip he might have taken as governor of Texas. One difference was that on the day of his visit with President Vicente Fox in San Cristóbal, American fighter planes bombed targets in Iraq in retaliation for violating the no-fly zone. But Ari Fleischer emphasized that this was "a routine enforcement," and the message remained one of restraint.

Bush's next foreign trip, on April 21, was across the northern border, to Quebec, for the Summit of the Americas. As he had in San Cristóbal, Bush showed off his Spanish and talked about free trade.

Earlier that month, a U.S. Navy EP-3 Aries spy plane surveilling international airspace over the South China Sea collided with a Chinese fighter aircraft and crash-landed on Hainan Island. A quiet frenzy ensued as Andy and Powell tried in vain to reach Chinese officials—any Chinese official—by phone to determine the safety of the plane's twenty-four passengers. Bush made a statement demanding their safe return. The Chinese in turn demanded an apology for the collision. It was an opportunity for bellicosity. Bush passed on it, and instead instructed his ambassador to China, Joseph Prueher, to say in a letter to the Chinese foreign minister that the United States was "very sorry." Ten days after the incident, China released the crew, and Bush emphasized that the two countries had "common interests"— and that he would "approach our differences in a spirit of respect."

Watching the rescued Navy pilots on the morning talk shows, Karen and Bartlett could barely contain their exhilaration: *Hey, when we run for reelection, we can say we passed the foreign-policy test!*

On those occasions when Bush's foreign policy did not emphasize humility, the subtext was never aggression—or at least not intentionally. While on Charlie Gibson's *Good Morning America*, the president made the careless remark that if China ever attacked Taiwan, America would respond with "whatever it took to help Taiwan"—a jolting departure from the United States' long-standing one-China policy. Just after the gaffe, Colin Powell phoned Senator Joe Biden, then the ranking minority member of the Senate Foreign Relations Committee, and begged him not to lay into Bush. Biden agreed that he would grant Bush a mulligan this time.

And just as Bush shunted aside the Kyoto treaty for fear of the economic havoc it would wreak, so too did he announce his administration's intention to walk away from the 1972 Anti-Ballistic Missile Treaty on the grounds that it prevented America from adopting a technologically advanced missile defense system. Bush issued this declaration on the eve of his first trip to Europe in June. BULLY BUSH, read the headline of one German newspaper, and European leaders braced themselves for the arrival of a boorish Texas cowboy.

Instead, Bush had a June wedding with Vladimir Putin.

Falling under the sway of a Russian leader was precisely what Bush had derided Clinton for doing with Boris Yeltsin. And there was little to foreshadow the dour ex-KGB official turning the president's head. But Bush had been sensing a moment for bigness. As Air Force One shuttled from Madrid to Brussels to Göteborg to Warsaw—from one strong ally to hard questions at NATO and EU meetings to another strong ally—all discussion inevitably led to the June 16 apex in Brdo pri Kranju, Slovenia, site of the castle that had once been Josef Tito's summer retreat, where Bush and Putin would meet on neutral ground, and for the very first time.

The first favorable portent came two weeks prior, when the Bush advance team arrived in Slovenia to map out their events. When the

Russian team at last showed up, the White House group braced for multiple rounds of petty bickering, as they knew had been de rigueur during the Cold War days of the first Bush administration.

The Russian advance team studied the plans. Handed them back without objections.

In his press conference with Polish President Aleksander Kwaśniewski the day before his arrival in Slovenia, Bush would not dwell on the sundry opportunities for quarrel between himself and Putin: the ABM treaty, missile defense, NATO enlargement, partnerships with China, arms deals with Iran, violence in Chechnya, and questions involving freedom of the press. Insisted Bush, "The discussion tomorrow . . . will focus on a frame of mind, an attitude."

He added, "The definition of the relationship will evolve over time. But first and foremost, it's got to start with the simple word *friend*."

Bush motorcaded with the president of Slovenia from Brnik Airport to the castle and arrived first. Putin then strode in from a nine-hour flight. The Russian president was shorter and tauter than Bush, and his blue eyes were at least forty degrees cooler than Bush's. He remarked that he had just watched a movie about the Bushes on the plane. "I understand you played rugby," Putin said.

The two men, Condi Rice, and foreign minister Sergei Ivanov retreated to a small room in the castle. The meeting was scheduled to last a half hour.

They started with small talk. The fact that they both had daughters named after each man's mother-in-law. (They agreed that this was proof of skilled diplomacy.) The fact that Bush's dad, like Putin, had worked for a spy agency. (Though the Russian leader seemed to think that this made Poppy, President Ford's CIA director, a bona fide spook like Putin, and Bush gave up on trying to explain otherwise.)

They spoke of NATO, ABM, China, Iran, Chechnya—they had to, because they were big matters . . . and yet, in the scheme of Bush's appetite, small ball. Intractability was part of yesteryear's mind-set. Putin had flattered Bush by referring to him as a "student of history." Now Bush wished to dispense with it.

They discussed energy partnerships in the Caspian Basin. But Bush had an outside-the-box notion. He'd seen something back home in Texas that he wished to share. There were legions of Russian software engineers in Austin, making Dell rich. Shouldn't they be back home in Russia, developing software for Putin's economy?

"Your human capital is going to be the real key to Russia's economy," he said, "if you can open that up and encourage entrepreneurship."

The point registered with Putin. (At the press conference immediately following their meeting, he observed that "we need an additional impulse from our businessmen.")

Bush had been briefed on a trip Putin had taken to Israel, where he had blessed a family cross that his mother had given him. "You know, I found that story very interesting," Bush told him. "You see, President Putin, I think you judge a person on something other than just politics. I think it's important for me and you to look for the depth of a person's soul and character. I was touched by the fact that your mother gave you the cross."

Putin warmed to the subject. He'd nearly lost the cross in a burning building, he said. But a fireman had retrieved it and, as if divining its importance to the Russian president, handed it—and only it—over to Putin.

Bush alighted on this. "President Putin, that's what it's all about," he said. "That's the story of the cross."

Outside the door, Logan Walters eyed his watch. He'd never known his boss to run an hour overtime.

"Let's not get stuck in history," Bush encouraged Putin. "We're making history together." The two leaders, he said, were "young guys. . . . Let's not be Brezhnev and Nixon. Let's be Bush and Putin."

"You should come visit my ranch in Crawford," Bush said. Putin accepted.

Ninety minutes after the two men had greeted each other, they stepped outside to face the press. Bush's opening remarks were charged with optimism. He referred to the former KGB operative as "an honest, straightforward man who loves his country."

Putin then said, "First of all, I wanted to confirm everything that's been said by President Bush when he characterized our meeting." Several in the gathering, including White House aides, began to giggle. The interpreter had a piercing Brooklyn accent and was chewing gum as he translated.

Nonetheless, Bush for once would not descend into the comedic. A reporter had thrown out the question of whether Putin could be trusted. The Russian president dryly responded, "Can we trust Russia? I'm not going to answer that. We could ask the very same question."

Bush lunged. "I will answer the question," he said. "I looked the man in the eye. I found him to be very straightforward and trustworthy. We had a very good dialogue. I was able to get a sense of his soul; a man deeply committed to his country and the best interests of his country. And I appreciated so very much the frank dialogue."

As the press conference came to a close, he punctuated this sentiment: "I said it in Poland, and I'll say it again: Russia is not the enemy of the United States. As a matter of fact, after our meeting today, I'm convinced it can be a strong partner and friend—more so than people could imagine."

Air Force One was wheels-up by seven in the evening. Bush was jazzed on the long flight back. "I just feel that this is the start of something really historic," he told Rice.

Bush wanted it to be so. For this drowsy pace did not suit him, no matter what his critics thought. Yes, he required comfort. Yes, he liked his exercise. Yes, he loved Texas, and contrived ways to spend some fifty days of his first eight months in office esconced in Crawford—the one place in the world where he could stick a key in the ignition and drive, or wander in the woods for two hours, and not have to talk about the budget.

But he was at root a man who craved purpose—a sense of movement, of consequence. And things did not seem especially consequential in the summer of 2001.

On the evening of September 6, after hosting his first state dinner, in honor of Vicente Fox, the two presidents and their wives sat on the Truman Balcony and watched the sky erupt with fireworks.

The following morning began the three-day National Book Festival hosted by Laura—a spinoff of her Texas antecedent, but also the beginning of a week-long messaging push dubbed "Putting Reading First," to revive the languishing No Child Left Behind education initiative. Bush attended some of the festival events, as his schedule was light and a few Texas friends were in town. On Sunday morning, the Bushes hosted a breakfast gathering for the other Texans at the residence. The president milled about in his shirtsleeves. At one point, he ventured down to the South Lawn and, surrounded by Peewee Leaguers, flipped a coin to commemorate the start of the NFL football season.

Back in the residence, Bush stood smiling as he watched his dog Barney wrestle with a chew toy.

The next day, September 10, after a lunch with Australian Prime Minister John Howard, he flew to Florida.

Bush stayed that evening at the Colony Beach & Tennis Resort in Sarasota. At a dinner with Governor Jeb and various other Republican Floridians, Bush washed down his strip steak with a few nonalcoholic beers. He was in bed by ten and up the next morning by six. Bush wanted to jog along the beach, but the Secret Service nixed that and instead drove him to a nearby golf course. Accompanying him on the predawn run was the lanky Bloomberg News reporter Dick Keil, who had been an All-American cross-country runner at the University of Rochester.

"Really? You think?" Bush asked with delight when Keil observed that their pace was in the area of 7:15 a mile. The president had a personal goal that year to shave his running time down to less than 7 minutes a mile. It would be a slow fall, he told Keil—no elections, no looming events . . . a perfect window for Bush to amp up his personal training regimen. As the two ran, they crossed chalk marks that the agents had drawn just that morning to establish his pace. An agent called out the time, and Bush observed with satisfaction that they were maintaining at 7:15.

Four and a half miles later, Bush parted company with the reporter, showered and had breakfast, and then received his daily intelligence briefing. On today's docket was an event at Emma E. Booker Elementary School—a photo op in a classroom full of African American second-graders, followed by a big speech on education funding. Sandy Kress, the Texas Democrat tapped by Bush to lobby for No Child Left Behind on the Hill, brought a chart into Bush's suite to brief him. Kress knew that Bush was fanatical about punctuality, so he raced through the main points.

But Bush was feeling uncharacteristically languid that morning. He started chatting about Texas politics, folks they knew back home. Rove and Bartlett and Secretary of Education Rod Paige lingered in the room. The Boss was having a good time. The event could wait.

Then: "I guess we better go." And so Bush climbed into the limo at 8:35, somewhat behind schedule. The motorcade headed south on Gulf of Mexico Drive, bound for Emma E. Booker Elementary.

Everything back in Washington was as it seemed in Sarasota: exquisite skies, and seemingly nothing going on below them. Though Congress was back from recess—and indeed, Laura was on the Hill, giving remarks on early reading at Ted Kennedy's education subcommittee— no single issue fixated either side of the aisle. With the president traveling that day, the schedule was light at the White House. The usual morning meetings ground on in the West Wing and the Old Executive Office Building. Pete Wehner, a deputy speechwriter, sent over an e-mail at 8:41 to Mike Gerson, who had decided to spend the day at his home in Arlington, drafting a speech for a volunteerism initiative called Communities of Character:

"Very little of note happened. The word from Andy (via Josh) is 'Don't panic' regarding the economy. The economy dominated the discussions, but little new was said. Senior staff should plan to attend at least some of tonight's congressional barbecue. Of relevance to us: the UN dues payment is 'falling apart' on the Hill, and Condi may make some calls.The highlight of the morning: President Bush (41) dropped in the senior staff meeting to say hi."

Word that a plane of some sort had crashed into the North Tower of lower Manhattan's World Trade Center was passed up from junior to senior staffers as a kind of ghoulish curiosity. When Rice learned about it during an NSC meeting, she telephoned Bush, who had just heard about it from Bartlett, who himself had been told by media aide Jill Foley as soon as the motorcade pulled up to Booker Elementary.

"You don't just hit a building like that," Bush mused when Bartlett passed on the news. "What kind of plane was it?"

"We don't know, sir."

Rice didn't know either. But her thinking was that it had to be some kind of freak accident. She and Bush recalled the Lear jet ferrying champion golfer Payne Stewart that flew off course and crashed in South Dakota two years earlier. Bush agreed that it was likely pilot error. "Keep me informed," the president said as he headed into the school.

Rice returned to her meeting in the conference portion of the Situation Room. A few minutes later, Josh Bolten stepped in. She began to introduce the deputy chief of staff to her subordinates.

"No. Come now," said Bolten. But the deputy chief was ever unflappable, and his voice betrayed no sense of calamity. Rice motioned for her deputy, Steve Hadley, to go see what business needed tending to.

In the doorway, Bolten whispered to Hadley, "There's been a second plane. This is an attack."

In Sarasota, Andy Card whispered into the president's right ear, "A second plane hit the second tower. America is under attack."

Bush had been sitting cross-legged in a school chair, listening to children chant out phonics drills—smiling occasionally, saying "Yeah!" and clapping at one point. When he heard Card's words, Bush's head keened slightly, as if in reaction to an electrical surge. His eyes narrowed and lost focus. Card had entered and departed the president's airspace in the span of four seconds. It was as if the words had come from inside his own head. *America is under attack.*

"Everybody get ready to read the title of the story the fast way," the schoolteacher called out.

"The Pet Goat."

Bush kept his arms folded. He was acutely aware of the photographers. Ari Fleischer had been standing at the back of the classroom, scribbling something on a piece of paper. Now the press secretary edged forward slightly and flashed the paper so that Bush could see it: DON'T SAY ANYTHING YET.

It took forty seconds for Bush to pick up his copy of *The Pet Goat.* He opened it, but his gaze wandered—beyond the children, then at them, then off into some unoccupied crease of space. His lips disappeared. He shot a glance at the teacher. She was perfectly unaware, as were the chanting students.

"She played with her goat in her yard."

"Good job. Go on."

He seemed, just then, to relate the chant to what he was holding in his hands. He looked down at the book, nodding in time with the rapping of the teacher's pen.

"But the goat did some things that made the girl's dad mad."

Connecting to the absurdity of the words, he looked at the children. For that fleeting second, Card's words seemed to vaporize.

"Very impressive," Bush said to the children when the drill was over. "Thank you all so much for showing me your reading skills." And he lingered there in the classroom for a few more minutes, complimenting and posing for photos with the children—strangely so, as he'd already held his cool, kept things calm . . . but now stubbornly making some kind of elusive point, or simply not knowing what else to do in the world outside the comfortable little classroom.

An inside line was ringing in Bolten's office on the first floor of the West Wing. It was, of all people, Clinton's former deputy chief of staff Steve Ricchetti. "You know about the procedure, right?" asked Ricchetti, who was aware that his counterpart had been working in the White House for only eight months. "You know where the bunker is?"

Bolten said that he did. He hustled over to the VP's office, where Cheney—having just spoken to Bush—stood with his deputy, Scooter Libby, and Rice, gaping at the replays of the two Boeing 767s roaring literally out of the blue and puncturing the Twin Towers within a seventeen-minute interval. Bolten had been there for barely a minute before two Secret Service agents appeared, hoisted the surprised VP up by his armpits, and proceeded to cart him toward the East Wing. Bolten and Libby followed behind.

Rice returned to the Situation Room. She tried calling Rumsfeld but had no luck. Powell was also unreachable—he was in South America, and, for a horrified moment, Rice wondered: *Is it Colombia he's in? The FARC terrorist guerrillas are over there, who knows if they're involved in all this. . . .* No, she then remembered. He was in Peru.

In a holding room outside the Booker Elementary auditorium, Bush spoke by phone to Cheney and to New York Governor George Pataki. He also placed a call to FBI director Robert Mueller, who had been on the job all of a week. "All right, Bob, this is what we paid you to do," Bush told him. "Let's get on it."

He pulled out a couple of 5 × 8 cards and scribbled some notes. Then he proceeded into the auditorium—escorted by Secret Service agents who were as unaware as Bush that other rogue planes remained in the skies that morning—and nodded to the applause of teachers and students. He stood behind the podium from which he had intended to deliver his No Child Left Behind speech. At his back were various posters extolling reading, designed by the White House advance team.

"Ladies and gentlemen, this is a difficult moment for America," he began. "I unfortunately will be going back to Washington after my remarks. . . . Today we've had a national tragedy. Two airplanes have crashed into the World Trade Center in an apparent terrorist attack on our country."

Bush added that he had spoken to Cheney, Pataki, and Mueller, and that the federal government would render immediate assistance to New York. He vowed "to hunt down and to find the folks who committed this act."

Then he said, "Terrorism against our nation will not stand." To hear that strange echo of eleven years earlier—when George Herbert

Walker Bush responded to Saddam Hussein's invasion of Kuwait by saying, "This aggression will not stand"—was to speculate that this Bush had fallen back on the familiar . . . that, at least for now, he lacked words of his own.

He called for an ever-so-brief moment of silence, then shook a few hands on his way out the door. It was 9:30 AM.

In the bunker, Cheney sat across the table from Secretary of Transportation Norm Mineta, who was talking on the phone to Federal Aviation Administration deputy administrator Monte Belger. An aide to the VP had stepped into the room to inform Cheney that the plane that had been fifty miles outside Washington was now thirty miles away. Then ten miles away. Belger told Mineta that the plane's transponder had been turned off, that the FAA could follow its progress only on the radar screen.

A minute later, Belger said, "Uh-oh. We just lost the target."

"Where do you think you lost it?" asked Mineta.

"Somewhere between Pentagon City and Reagan National Airport."

Just then, a voice cut in: "Mr. Secretary, we just had a confirmed report by an Arlington County police officer that he saw an American Airlines plane going into the Pentagon."

Condi Rice saw the televised image in the Situation Room, which was abuzz with hysterical reports—a car bomb outside the State Department building in Foggy Bottom, a fire near the Washington Monument.

A uniformed division officer ran into the room adjacent to the Oval Office. "You need to evacuate the White House," he told Bush's secretary Ashley Estes and his bodyman, Logan Walters (who hadn't made the trip to Sarasota due to an illness). "There's a plane on its way here."

Next door at the Old Executive Office Building, Secret Service agents galloped down the hallways, calling out, "Take off your shoes and run! Get the fuck out! Run!"

As they sprinted across the North Lawn and out the gates, a single airplane shot across the sky. Those who saw it were terrified. The plane kept going, and so did they.

On her way to the bunker, Rice reached the president, who had learned of the attack on the Pentagon while in the motorcade to the

Sarasota airport. The Secret Service agent accompanying her picked up on what the Boss was saying.

"He can't come back here," the agent insisted.

"Mr. President, you can't come back here," she repeated. "Washington is under attack."

Then she called her aunt and uncle in Birmingham to let them know she was okay, before descending into the Presidential Emergency Operations Center.

"Monte," said Mineta to the FAA deputy, "bring all planes down."

In fact, the FAA's national operations manager, Ben Sliney—whose first day on the job this was—had already ordered all planes to land at once. Belger added that this was "per pilot discretion."

"Fuck pilot discretion! I want these planes down!"

There were 4,546 planes in the air. One of them, United Flight 93, was causing particular concern as it U-turned from its westward passage to San Francisco and now barreled toward Washington. From Air Force One, Bush conferred with Cheney, who wanted to know if he could be granted authorization to shoot down any planes that failed to respond to orders. After repeated attempts to reach his secretary of defense, the president learned that Donald Rumsfeld was outside the Pentagon, assisting in the rescue of co-workers.

After finally getting hold of Rumsfeld and discussing the shootdown procedure with him, Bush called Cheney back. "You bet," he said.

The VP's wife, Lynne Cheney, and his assistant Mary Matalin were now in the bunker as well. Bush told Cheney that he wished to return to Washington now. Cheney insisted that this was a very bad idea. The VP had been involved in government decapitation strategies during the Cold War. Obsessed with the need for continuity, he had already made sure that the third in succession to the presidency, House Speaker Dennis Hastert, be carted off to a secure location.

"Look at that!" someone called out, and everyone in the bunker glanced at the TV screen. It was 9:59. Amid a huff of smoke, the South Tower of the World Trade Center collapsed like an accordion.

A military aide approached Cheney and requested permission to engage Flight 93 with fighter planes. "Yes," the VP said—so calmly that the aide thought Cheney hadn't understood the question. So he asked it a second time, and then a third.

"Yes, engage!" Cheney snapped.

The room got very quiet.

At 10:06, Flight 93 crashed into the emptiness of Shanksville, Pennsylvania. On the phone, Bush asked Cheney, "Did we shoot it down, or did it crash?"

No one in the room knew the answer.

Hadley had made it to the bunker, leaving the Situation Room in the hands of NSC aides Richard Clarke and Frank Miller. The West Wing was largely evacuated now, but there remained a few brave souls—including Andy Card's two assistants—handling the phones in the Sit Room. Miller asked an aide to go quietly around the room, jot down everyone's name and Social Security number, and e-mail the data off-site, so that if the White House was attacked, there would be a record of who perished inside.

Outside the White House, a few staffers made their way to the offices of the *Weekly Standard,* until word reached them that Poppy Bush's former bodyman, Tim McBride, had set up a conference room in the DaimlerChrysler office on 14th and H. Computers and platters of sandwiches and cookies awaited them. Political director Ken Mehlman's manic mind was already racing. *What does Karl need . . .* Mehlman's gift was the ability to divine macro and micro simultaneously. He could structure an avalanche. Two ideas came to him. Mehlman told staff secretary Brad Blakeman and Office of Strategic Initiatives director Barry Jackson to go online and research what if any significance the date September 11 carried in the Muslim world. He also directed them to download newspaper articles describing how Clinton, Bush 41, and Reagan had responded to crises in their presidencies.

Deputy speechwriters Matthew Scully, David Frum, John McConnell, and Matt Rees sat in a separate office at DaimlerChrysler while their boss, Mike Gerson, was stranded on Route 395, where all traffic was at a standstill near the Pentagon. Gerson had been sitting in his parked car, writing on a notepad: *We are at war.*

Frum was the only speechwriter among them who knew much of significance about terrorism. While they worked, a call came in from his wife that their friend, conservative commentator Barbara Olson, had been a passenger on Flight 77.

Concerned about leaving records on a nongovernment hard drive, the four of them did their work on legal pads. On the speakerphone,

Gerson mentioned that he had just spoken with Rice, who wanted to see a particular sentiment in the draft. Scully wrote it in his own words: *We will make no distinction between those who planned the acts and those who tolerated or encouraged the terrorists.*

Logan Walters and Ashley Estes also sat at the conference table. At Mehlman's direction, they scripted a schedule based on how crises had been managed in past presidencies.

The entire schedule would soon go out the window.

On Air Force One, Bush demanded to know whether his wife and daughters were safe. In fact, it had taken more than an hour for agents to escort Barbara to a secure location on campus at Yale, and to ferry Jenna to a room at the Driskill Hotel in Austin. Laura had stayed in Ted Kennedy's office, and then the office of Judd Gregg, for forty-five minutes before the Secret Service moved her and Margaret Spellings to a building in the District. She was badly shaken, worried sick about her daughters and her husband and her mother, and did not wish to see the images on television. But she was safe.

Bush landed at Barksdale Air Force Base in Louisiana. It happened that the base had been conducting a nuclear weapons exercise at the time. Air Force One taxied past forty fully uploaded B-52s. Most of the passengers—including Walters' stand-in, Blake Gottesman, the congressional delegation that had accompanied Bush to Sarasota, and the media—were informed that they were getting off here.

A *Time* magazine reporter was apoplectic to hear that the administration was shutting out the press. "You're panicking!" he yelled at Dan Bartlett. "This is going to go down in history!"

Whatever, thought Bartlett.

An armored vehicle whisked Bush past the bombers toward the operations center, from which he would speak briefly to the nation. "Slow down!" Bush told the driver as they screeched around the bombers. Both he and Rove were seized by the thought that this day would culminate in the president's crashing into his own nuclear arsenal.

At the operations center, Bush gave a two-minute statement. "We will show the world that we will pass this test," he said, enunciating each word with exaggerated earnestness. His seriousness was evident. But the focused, righteous leader had yet to emerge.

In truth, Bush was pissed off—vowing on the plane that he "couldn't wait" to find the enemy and "kick their ass," and in the meantime indignant that he, rather than they, had to be on the run. "Unless they tell me something I haven't heard," he told Cheney on the phone, "this ass is going back to Washington."

When the VP repeated, with patient but enduring forcefulness, that it would be foolhardy for the president to return, Bush snapped, "I'm gonna entertain this continuity-of-government thing a bit longer. But we're going back."

Instead, the plane took off for Offutt Air Force Base in Omaha, Nebraska.

Josh Bolten was going nuts trying to find Karen. The White House needed a Washington face—visual evidence that the government was functioning. After forty-five minutes, Bolten located her picking up her son Robert at the St. Albans School. He arranged for military aides to bring her in.

Karen scribbled notes en route and finalized the draft in the bunker. Then she gave her briefing at the Justice Department press office, since Secret Service agents had closed off the White House to the media. Grim but assuring, Karen ticked off the various emblems of stability. All senior officials were secure and either in Washington or on their way back. Federal assistance was flowing into New York. Though the markets were closed and all flights had been suspended, banks were functioning and the skies were safe again. Both at the beginning and at the end of her statement, Karen referred to "these despicable attacks." Even in crisis, the towering, sharp-eyed lady remained On Message.

At about noon, word reached the Situation Room that an aircraft was heading toward Crawford, Texas. "Is there anyone at the ranch?" Frank Miller asked no one in particular.

Walters had returned from DaimlerChrysler to the Sit Room. "The foreman lives there," he said.

"Can you get a hold of him?" asked Miller.

"How much time does he have?"

"It may already be too late."

Walters reached the ranch's caretaker, Ken Engelbrecht. "Where are you?"

"I'm in my house," Engelbrecht said.

"Get as far away from there as you can."

Miller soon received a call informing him that Combat Air Patrol had been established over the ranch. This struck Miller as a rather drastic defensive maneuver. He tried to reach Hadley in the bunker, but, to his astonishment, there existed no secure line between the two rooms. Miller walked down to the PEOC. Did Hadley think CAP was a good idea over the ranch? No—it seemed excessive to him as well.

Back in the Sit Room, Miller called off Combat Air Patrol . . . only to find out that CAP had not been established to begin with, and that, for that matter, there was no rogue aircraft headed Crawford's way.

Heroism may well have been reborn in America on September 11, 2001. Yet the day would also be marred by appalling haplessness. Though the State and Treasury departments had been evacuated without incident, no agents thought to take charge of the Commerce Department, which housed five thousand employees. Eventually, Secretary Don Evans got tired of waiting for orders and had someone drive him to his home in McLean, where he sat for hours until he finally made contact with the Secret Service.

Meanwhile, the agents who had custody of Laura Bush realized at some point that having the first lady on the top floor of a seven-story building was perhaps not such a hot idea, whereupon they moved her to the basement.

By early afternoon, some forty or fifty individuals had been ushered to the PEOC, which was designed to hold no more than two dozen. Oxygen in the bunker became scarce—so much so that agents kept other senior staffers out of the immediate vicinity of Dick Cheney, the man next in line to succeed the president.

The FAA faxed over to the Situation Room positive identification of the four hijacked airplanes. Two of the four flight numbers were wrong.

And though two of the airplanes' passengers had already been identified as Al Qaeda terrorists by the time Bush arrived at Offutt's strategic command center and conducted his first war council by video conference, the queston was beyond begged: What were known threats to America doing *inside America, on board airplanes and in control of cockpits?*

Answers were already leaking out, courtesy of a few doomed passengers who had managed to dial their cell phones and say goodbye to loved ones on the ground—conveying, amid all the grief and hysteria, the utterly unfathomable:

Box cutters. They'd done all this with box cutters.

Bush got his wish at 4:33 PM. Air Force One went wheels-up and headed east. Soon it was accompanied by a fighter escort on each wingtip. Bush looked out the window. He could see the stubble on the pilot's face. It wasn't like the president to feel fear at such moments— "I'm the kind of guy, my attitude is, if your number is up, it's up, you know?" he would later say—but it was nonetheless an awesome spectacle, seeing his last line of defense hovering just a few yards away. The pilot looked over at his commander in chief and saluted.

Rove pulled his camera out of his pocket and took a picture.

There was perhaps only one other aircraft flying across America at that moment. It was an Air Force carrier, flying deputy chief of staff for operations Joe Hagin back to Washington. Hagin had been in New York that morning planning for the president's forthcoming United Nations visit. After the Twin Towers had been struck, he was shuttled over to Dover Air Force Base in Delaware, where a plane ferried him west toward Offutt—then hooked back toward the District when Hagin learned from Andy Card that Air Force One was leaving Nebraska. Staring out at the empty sky, a dreadful thought came to Hagin: *Shit, we're the only airplane up here. What if some Virginia farmer looks up, thinks we're a terrorist, and fires his deer rifle at us?*

Swooping over the Pentagon in flames, the nation's capital seemingly deserted, heavily armored vehicles barricading the Mall, the White House senior staff experienced something altogether unique in American history: an aerial view of democracy's bastion of power in a state of siege.

Bush descended the stairs of Air Force One at Andrews Air Force Base, climbed into Marine One, and arrived on the South Lawn of the White House shortly before seven in the evening. He walked directly into the Oval Office. Rice, Karen, and counsel Al Gonzales met him there.

"You should go down to the bunker," Rice told him.

"Why would I want to do that?" Bush was tired of cowering.

"Well, for one thing, Mrs. Bush is there," she said.

Bush went down to the bunker. The agents there advised him that he and Laura should plan on sleeping there that evening. Bush took one look at the bed—a pull-out couch from the 1950s.

"I'm not staying in here," he told them.

He addressed the nation that night from the Oval Office at eight thirty. The decision was Bush's to throw out Gerson's "We are at war" verbiage. Tonight was about reassuring the nation, so it would be a Karen kind of speech.

In many ways, it *was* Karen's earlier briefing. The "despicable act," the reminders of hardy volunteers and plucky bureaucracies, all made an encore. Bush recited Psalm 23—"Even though I walk through the valley of the shadow of death, I will fear no evil; for You are with me"—and concluded blandly with, "None of us will ever forget this day. Yet we go forward to defend freedom, and all that is good and just in our world."

So tepid, and even meek, was the address that it was nearly possible to overlook that one tough line of Matthew Scully's that had been salvaged, in modified form: "We will make no distinction between the terrorists who committed these acts and those who harbor them."

Bush then descended to the PEOC for two national security meetings. By ten, he was back in the residence, in bed with his wife and Barney and the cat.

He couldn't sleep. His mind was racing. Presently, he heard the sound of heavy breathing in his doorway. It was a Secret Service agent.

"They're coming!" the agent managed. "We're under attack!"

Bush threw on a T-shirt and running shorts. Laura ("I'm blind, I don't have on my contacts," she would recall) slipped into her bathrobe and fuzzy house slippers. With the dog under one arm and the cat under the other, Bush strode briskly down to the PEOC. Agents stood waiting with weapons drawn.

"What's happening?" he demanded.

There was an unidentified plane racing down the airspace over the Potomac River.

Hagin, Rice, and Card joined the Bushes in the bunker. After a few speechless minutes, word came: The plane was one of theirs.

"Okay," said Bush, and went back to bed.

Laura and the pets accompanied him. Then the others filed through the tunnel. Most of them went home. Rice and Hagin both found beds in the residence.

It was the kind of sleep you slept with one eye open.

"Al Qaeda. It means, 'the base.' "

Bush explained the term to John McConnell on Wednesday morning in the Oval Office. McConnell—the deputy speechwriter for the president, and the VP's chief speechwriter—had never heard of this enemy before. Neither had Mike Gerson, despite having sat in on every single policy meeting hosted for the benefit of George W.

Bush's continuing education from 1999 through 2000. There had been discussion of cyberterrorism, of chemical and biological warfare, and of rogue regimes—including the Taliban government in Afghanistan, which had hosted Al Qaeda's leader, Osama bin Laden, since his expulsion from Sudan in 1996. But never any discussion of bin Laden and his repeated attacks on America.

Not one meeting.

Of course, since taking office, George W. Bush had been briefed frequently on bin Laden's threats. "I'm tired of swatting flies," Condi Rice would tell reporters that he'd said at one point—that Clinton's targeted-bombing retaliations against Al Qaeda activities struck Bush as small ball, bespeaking a feebleness of will that could only embolden the terrorists. But if the president, as his national security adviser had claimed, truly wished to deliver a knockout blow to bin Laden's organization, he did not make it a priority during the summer months of 2001. Instead, the administration focused on missile defense, even as alarming chatter found its way into intelligence reports, hinting of a "spectacular" moment.

Now the reek of fire and demolition hung over downtown Manhattan and Pentagon City. Bin Laden had Bush's attention.

He convened his cabinet Wednesday morning, inviting as well the congressional leadership of both parties. The 9/11 attacks had produced a long list of unintended consequences. A generator was needed to power the New York Stock Exchange—necessitating a wide-load permit as it was transported through Maryland and then by tugboat into the New York Harbor. Running the generator would require a Clean Air Act waiver.

The sealing of the Canadian border meant that imported auto parts could not get through. The automotive industry was therefore contemplating shutting down all production in Michigan.

ATMs all across America were functioning only sporadically.

Building construction had come to a halt, since insurance was now impossible to buy.

The airlines, already economically hobbled, would require a massive federal bailout to avoid bankruptcy. Even so, there was simply no hope that Americans would ever fly again unless the Bush administration demonstrated a commitment to airport security.

At one point, Michigan Congressman David Bonier spoke up. "Mr. President, we have a very large Arab American population in our state," he said. They were fearful of retaliation, Bonier added, and he hoped that the White House would address this fear.

"Dave, you're absolutely correct," Bush replied. "You *should* be concerned about that, because"—and here he glanced over at his secretary of transportation, a Japanese American whose family had been forced into a World War II internment camp—"we don't want what happened to Norm in 1942 to happen again."

Bush was sensing the expansiveness of the damage, but not yet its depth. That appreciation began to develop later in the afternoon, when he visited the Pentagon.

While the president and Rumsfeld stepped through the rubble, an Army major approached Joe Hagin. "I run the morgue team," he told the deputy chief. "My guys have been pulling bodies out of that building for twenty-four hours, and they're in pretty rough shape, feeling awful low. It would sure be nice if they could say hi to the president."

"Major, follow me," said Hagin.

Beside the presidential limo, Bush met them—eight men with masks and yellow gloves and tie-back suits, covered with dust, their bodies sagging and their eyes red. He hugged each of them, and for the first time since the preceding morning in Sarasota, the president began to cry.

"Coming here makes me sad, on the one hand," he said that day at the Pentagon. "It also makes me mad." But if this was—as Bush had inscribed in his diary the evening before—"the Pearl Harbor of the 21st Century," Bush had yet to summon his inner FDR. The emotions and instincts and decisions tugging at him had not coalesced into a persona of wartime leadership. His address to the nation the preceding evening had fallen far short of inspirational. White House staffers were hearing this from friends and opinion leaders, and they were quietly saying it to each other, as Gerson did to Rove that Wednesday evening:

"If people around here think things are going well," the speechwriter told the president's top adviser, "they're wrong."

The blue state of New York needed a visit from its president. Bush knew that. He figured that Sunday would be an appropriate time. Hagin, who planned such operations, argued that such a momentous trip would require the weekend to plan it. He suggested Monday.

But on Thursday morning, September 13, as Bush spoke from his phone in the Oval Office to Governor Pataki and Mayor Rudy Giuliani, he paced behind his desk, seemingly agitated by the distance between where he was and where he was needed. Barely a minute into their conversation, he said, "You've extended me a kind invitation to come to New York City. I accept. I'll be there tomorrow afternoon. . . ."

Bug-eyed, Hagin whispered to Logan Walters, "What did he just say?"

"I think he said he'll be there tomorrow."

Ari Fleischer had allowed a pool of reporters to witness the call. They pummeled the president with questions the moment he hung up. All intelligence agencies had undergone a severe clampdown following the attacks; information was at a premium, and Bush seemed willing, for once, to provide it.

Was it safe to fly? "Yes, I would—if a family member asked whether they should fly, I'd say yes."

How close was he to finding out who was responsible? "First, let me condition the press this way," Bush said. "Any sources and methods of intelligence will remain guarded and secret. . . . It is important as we battle this enemy to conduct ourselves that way."

Would previously recalcitrant countries like Afghanistan and Pakistan cooperate in the War on Terror? Bush replied that Pakistan had offered a pledge of support—"and now we'll just find out what that means, won't we?" He said nothing about Afghanistan.

Then he offered up a thought that had been percolating in his head throughout this nightmare. It was something he had said more than once to his staff and would repeat throughout the weeks, and in the weeks that followed:

"You know, through the tears of sadness, I see an opportunity," he said. "Make no mistake about it, this nation is sad. But we're also tough and resolute. And now is an opportunity to do generations a favor, by coming together and whipping terrorism; hunting it down, finding them, and holding them accountable. The nation must understand, this is now the focus of my administration. We will very much engage in domestic policy, of course. I look forward to working with Congress on a variety of issues. But now that war has been declared on us, we will lead the world to victory."

Then he said it again: "To victory."

Francine Kiefer of the *Christian Science Monitor* asked, "About the prayer day tomorrow, Mr. President. Could you give a sense as to what kind of prayer *you* are thinking, and where your heart is for yourself, as you—"

Bush dismissed the notion: "Well, I don't think about myself right now. I think about the families, the children. . . ."

Then he turned away, and his eyes noticeably glistened. Bartlett shot a glance at Ari. Should they pull the press out?

But Bush got it back together. "I am a loving guy," he said, his voice growing stronger again, "and I am also someone, however, who has got a job to do. And I intend to do it. And this is a terrible moment. But this country will not relent until we have saved ourselves from the terrible tragedy that came upon America."

"Thank you, Mr. President," reporters called out as they were shown the door.

It was building.

"Was it bad?" Bush asked Gerson later in the Oval. He was referring to the show of emotion.

"It was perfect," Gerson assured him—knowing that it was a suck-up kind of thing to say, but he also felt it was the truth.

Bush and Laura had just returned from the Washington hospital that was treating burn victims from the Pentagon. A few of them had been able to speak. They told him what it was like to be half buried in debris. They told him what it was like to run through flames. Now he sat in a chair beside the fireplace where he often sat with guests, except that the other chair was empty.

"My feelings are coming out," he said to his speechwriters.

McConnell wanted to say that he was proud of Bush, that he was praying for him. None of those words would quite roll off of his tongue.

"President Mubarak is on the phone," Ashley Estes informed Bush.

Bush nodded but did not immediately get up. As Scully and McConnell left, they saw the president sitting in his chair, his left hand on the small apple-wood table—the wedding ring tapping quietly against the tabletop, and Bush seeming transfixed by the rhythm, as if it were a clock ticking only for him.

Andy Card said to him, "Do you know about Brad's nephew?"

Bush buzzed his staff secretary Brad Blakeman. "You didn't tell me that your nephew's missing," the president said.

Yes, Blakeman acknowledged quietly. He was a first responder when the planes hit the World Trade Center. The nephew was now somewhere beneath the rubble.

"He may be still alive," Bush reminded him. "Let's hope."

But the matter gnawed at him. He later showed up at Blakeman's desk.

"We're going to find the people who did this," Bush promised his staff secretary. "And they're going to pay."

"We are in the middle hour of our grief," Bush said, reciting McConnell's lovely opener in a pensive cadence as he stood in the Washington National Cathedral early in the afternoon of September 14.

To a nation that had not seen him since his address on the evening of September 11, George W. Bush seemed very much in the aforementioned middle hour. His voice no longer had that high, insistent tone of enforced optimism. He spoke mournfully of "the names"—those belonging to workers at the Pentagon and the World Trade Center; those of the heroes of Flight 93, who, it was now known, had wrested the cockpit from the hijackers, thus saving the intended target, the Capitol; and those of the rescuers, some in uniform and some not. "We will read all these names," Bush pledged. "We will linger over them, and learn their stories, and many Americans will weep."

Sitting before him were members of both parties, cabinet secretaries, former presidents, and candidates—the most powerful men and women in the country, assembled before their leader. The president was here to proclaim a National Day of Prayer and Remembrance. But with memory came resolve, and one could now, at last, hear it in his voice. "This conflict was begun on the timing and terms of others," he said in the otherwise silent cathedral. "It will end in a way, and at an hour, of our choosing."

When Bush finished and took his seat in the pews, his father reached over and patted his hand.

The collection plates were passed. Amid the heaviness, Dan Bartlett watched Alan Greenspan, chairman of the Federal Reserve, search his pockets in vain for cash. Greenspan's wife, Andrea Mitchell of NBC News, opened her purse and bailed him out.

The organ swelled, and the congregation began to sing: *Onward, Christian soldiers . . . marching off to war . . .*

"Stop the car," said Bush. "I'm getting out."

Marine One and the accompanying choppers had just come to a

rest at the Wall Street landing zone and were headed to Ground Zero. But from the window of his limo, Bush had seen them: a small gathering of New York City firemen, covered in ash and concrete dust, standing by the side of the pier to observe the president's arrival.

Wearing a gray windbreaker and slacks, he stepped up to a firefighter who had to be six foot four. Bush's hand disappeared in his. At the point of contact, the big man's face buckled. A large tear trickled down his face, leaving a track through the dust on his cheek.

Bush held the fireman for a very long time.

What awaited him at Ground Zero did not fit the message of Prayer and Remembrance. Bush arrived with a multidenominational group of religious leaders. From the moment they stepped out into the immensity of ruin and heard the thick-voiced chants of "USA! USA! USA!" it was clear that a prayer session was not going to take place.

It was Rove who heard the advance woman crying out that the men wanted to hear from their president—and seeing the crinkle-faced firefighter Bob Beckwith standing atop the hull of a crushed fire engine, Rove galloped over, had Beckwith jump up and down to determine the makeshift platform's stability, and then told him that "someone important" would soon need a hand up, after which the firefighter should make himself scarce.

But it was Bush who, upon being hoisted up to the truck, told Beckwith, "You stay right here," and put his arm around him.

Bush took Beckwith's bullhorn. "Thank you all," he began.

"Get 'em, George!" someone called out.

"I want you all to know—"

"Can't hear you!"

"It doesn't get any louder," Bush called out, and many laughed. Karen watched closely off to the side as the president continued the message: "I want you all to know that America today—that America today is on bended knee in prayer for the people whose lives were lost here. . . ."

The spirit had gone out of the area. *Please*, their faces seemed to say. *Tell us you didn't come all the way to remind us of our grief.* Bush continued, only to hear . . .

"I can't hear you!"

Unslinging his arm from Beckwith's shoulder, Bush seemed slapped awake: "I can hear YOU!"

Sudden, wild applause.

Finding his fervor, Bush jabbed the sooty air with his index finger. "I can hear you! The rest of the world can hear you! And the people—"

At first, he was drowned out by the roars.

"And the people," he repeated, motioning somewhere behind them, "who knocked these buildings down will hear all of us soon!"

The skies exploded with lusty cries—woofing noises, the incessant chant of "USA! USA! USA!" and demands that George get 'em, that he not let them down. . . .

Still, he had one more thing to do there in New York. One more moment of sadness, before he turned hard toward the war that he had not asked for but now fully intended to wage.

Governor Pataki had wanted the president to visit the armory. It was the epicenter of the nation's sorrow, this grim warehouse where a hundred detectives sitting behind folding tables asked the same fruitless questions a hundred times: "So what was he wearing when he went to work at the World Trade Center that morning?" Hagin had visited there. The stark gamut of emotions—shrieking, discordant laughter, sheer expressionlessness—was beyond heartbreaking.

"I'm not about to put the president in here," Hagin declared, instead deciding to create an event at the Javits Center. He told the police and firefighter unions to gather five hundred family members of missing first responders. Hagin said that the president would try to spend twenty minutes with them before he headed off to Camp David for a weekend with his war council.

Bush spent an hour and forty-five minutes with the families. Among them were a boy and a girl, both small and shy, whose mother pushed them toward the president, who kneeled down and said to the boy, who held a piece of paper in his hand:

"Son, would you like me to sign that, so that you can prove to your dad you met me?"

The boy handed over the paper. It was a photograph of his missing father in full uniform.

Bush signed it, the boy burst into tears, and he gathered both children into his arms.

Arlene Howard was the last. She sat alone against a wall, a large woman with a quiet face, queenly in her abjectness as family members stood over her. Her son, a Port Authority policeman, had perished in the rubble not far from there. Bush went to her, leaned down to take her hand.

She placed her son's badge in his hand. It was now his, she said.

He wrapped his fingers around the badge. "We'll get them," he whispered.

Six days later, Bush gave the greatest speech of his presidency.

It was one of the most remarkable team efforts of the Bush White House—a speech that went through a multitude of drafts and was improved by the edits of numerous speechwriters and senior staffers. What made the speech work, what gave it a center and a clarity of purpose, was that the man who delivered it suffered no ambiguity as to where he stood or what he wished to convey. For nine days he had been reflective, and angry, and emotionally overwhelmed—and, in his briefings and war council meetings, deeply, searingly curious. The psychic journey all America had taken, from peace and prosperity to war and instability, was now manifest in him.

Gerson, McConnell, and Scully were told to begin work on the speech Monday morning, the seventeenth, just after Bush had returned from his weekend at Camp David. Karen further informed Gerson that the president would be expecting a draft that evening. The three speechwriters sat at McConnell's computer in a high-ceilinged office in the OEOB. In keeping with the man, Bush's speechwriters often strove for big, at times grandiose themes. The overreaching of generational "callings" and "awakenings" brought to mind a man who would be king, if only a proper kingdom could be found. Here, though, was a *purpose*. No self-conscious embellishing was required.

Karen had fed questions—*Who is this enemy? Why do they hate us?*—to NSC counterterrorism expert Dick Clarke, who fired back data on the Taliban. The White House's inside soccer mom had an ear for the familiar. She liked the idea of comparing Al Qaeda to the Mafia. She seized upon the notion that in Afghanistan, someone could be arrested for watching *Gone with the Wind*. The latter image seemed discordant and didn't make the cut, but the Mafia allusion did. (Though Bush himself insisted on modifying Karen's initial construction: *Al Qaeda is to Arabs as the Mafia is to Italians*. "Isn't that kind of a slight ethnic insult?" he observed.)

Rove's memo emphasized both the righteousness of America's response and the expectation that this was not an overnight proposition: "Expect not instantaneous action but a long sustained struggle. . . . There's a reason the civilized world is rallying to America's side. They understand that if such terror goes unanswered here, they could well be the next to understand its horror. Terrorism's corrosive power will not just bring down buildings but the authority of governments built on democratic values."

But Rove's major contribution was to the setting. Bush's speech in the Oval Office on the evening of 9/11 was a failure both of content and of venue. Bush didn't do well sitting at a desk, starting at the teleprompter. He was a man of physicality who got pumped up in front of crowds. Rove believed that this speech ought to be delivered before a joint session of Congress. House Speaker Denny Hastert said that Congress would be delighted to host the president, but throughout the week he pestered Andy Card for advance notice so that security could have adequate preparation time.

"You tell him we're not certain yet," Bush informed Card. "The president of the United States will come when he decides, and I assume he'll be ready."

Powell and his deputy, Richard Armitage, had been told by Rice to prepare a list of ultimatums to the Taliban regime. Knowing a blank check when they saw one, the two men decided not to limit the demands to handing over Osama bin Laden. They added: *Release all foreign nationals whom you have unjustly imprisoned. Protect foreign journalists, aid workers, and diplomats in your country. Close every terrorist training camp in your country. Give the United States inspection access to those camps. Turn over every member of Al Qaeda.*

Rumsfeld and others at the Pentagon had suggested that the speech evoke the grim eventuality of terrorists procuring weapons of mass destruction from rogue regimes. Bush personally rejected the inclusion. He said that Americans were already jumpy and there was no need to scare them further.

Bush also nixed a quote from FDR that Gerson had brought in. "I don't want to quote anyone!" he insisted. "I want to lead! I want to be the guy they quote!"

He told his speechwriters that week, "Time is going to pass, and people are going to think that this has gone away. But I want them to know that I am going to be thinking about this every morning when I wake up, for the rest of my presidency."

The speechwriters decided that this sentiment had to go into the speech. What they came up with—"I will not yield; I will not rest; I will not relent in waging this struggle for freedom and security for the American people"—didn't sit well with Bush at first. He didn't like negative constructions. Americans wanted to know what he *would* be doing, not what he wouldn't. (Somehow the line survived his doubts, and after it received some of the evening's most intense applause, Bush grinned and told his deputies, "Okay, you got me on that one.")

One other line provoked internal controversy: "Americans are asking: What is expected of us? I ask you to live your lives, and hug your children."

It was a Karen line, of course. The speechwriters found the hugging bit too Hallmarky. "I don't know what the problem is—it's very nice!" Karen insisted. Bush read it aloud one day in the Oval. The speechwriters mumbled their misgivings. Karen would not give ground.

"We'll keep it," said Bush.

He did his first read-throughs the day before the speech, on Wednesday, September 19, in the theater, in his jogging sweats. Bush was in a jocular mood. Those who did not know him might have found this levity bizarre or even unbecoming. But Bush was pacing himself, "husbanding his resources" as his speechwriters liked to say. At his first utterance of "Al Qaeda," he overpronounced the last word, a cacophony of hard consonants and wayward vowels.

"That's how the briefers pronounce it," he protested as some in the audience snickered.

"I don't think you have to pronounce it in Arabic," suggested Rice.

But on the morning of September 20, Bush was wearing his suit in the theater, and he was plenty serious. Near the end of the speech, he declared, "And I will carry this." In previous read-throughs, he had held up his Dasani water bottle. This time, Bush held aloft the policeman's badge of Arlene Howard's son George.

At 4:15 that day, Bush gave a final read-through. Logan Walters then approached him. Prime Minister Tony Blair—who would attend tonight's speech but was currently bogged down in traffic after attending a memorial service in New York—would arrive late. The president had more time to practice his speech, if that's what he wished.

Bush thought for a moment. "No," he then said. "I'm ready."

Then he headed upstairs and took a nap.

"We've got a crisis," Midland accountant Robert McCleskey informed the president that day.

Bush braced himself. "Jenna's registration tag has expired," McCleskey finished.

*   *   *

He strode into the Capitol at nine o'clock that evening. For all the swelling applause from both sides of the aisle, those viewing George W. Bush both in person and at home on television could be forgiven their anxiety. For the jury was still out on this man. The image of him was diffuse, incomplete, at times contradictory. *Was* he a uniter? *Was* he a leader? *Was* he the man for this moment?

Only this much was certain: Today, at least, America did not want to see him fail.

From the opening syllables, Bush was in full command of the room, and of the text laid before him: "In the normal course of events, presidents come to this chamber to report on the state of the union. Tonight, no such report is needed. It has already been delivered by the American people."

In a calm, unhurried voice, he invoked the name of Todd Beamer, one of the heroes of Flight 93, whose widow, Lisa, sat in the gallery. He spoke of rescuers, of bipartisan acclamation, and of the waves of sympathy throughout the world. "Thank you for coming, friend," he said as he nodded to Blair, seated beside Laura Bush.

"Americans have many questions tonight," he continued. "Americans are asking: Who attacked our country?" Bush described Al Qaeda, incorporating Karen's Mafia analogy, ticking off radical Islam's deleterious effects on Afghanistan, and then read off Powell and Armitage's list of ultimatums to the Taliban. "These demands are not open to negotiation or discussion," Bush said. "The Taliban must act, and act immediately. They will hand over the terrorists, or they will share in their fate."

Then, as John Kennedy had addressed the Cuban people during his Cuban missile crisis speech, Bush said, "I also want to speak tonight directly to Muslims throughout the world. We respect your faith." In fact, said Bush, "The terrorists are traitors to their own faith—trying, in effect, to hijack Islam itself." Their piety was a false idol, Bush said, cloud cover for an extremism less kindred to Islam than to Nazism. "And they will follow that path all the way to where it ends," promised Bush, "in history's unmarked grave of discarded lies."

After describing how the nature of the enemy would require a different kind of war—sometimes highly covert, at other times plodding and bloody—Bush then pivoted, addressing those countries known to have harbored Al Qaeda in the past. "Every nation, in every region, now has a decision to make," he said, his eyes narrowing into slits.

Then he issued his famous binary choice: "Either you are with us, or you are with the terrorists." The applause that followed was the first of the night to appear two-voiced—raucousness from the hawks, tentative and somewhat abashed from the doves.

Then, throwing ideology to the wind, Bush announced the creation of a new cabinet-level position, director of the Office of Homeland Security, to be filled by former governor of Pennsylvania Tom Ridge. But, he reminded his audience, "This is not, however, just America's fight." He recited Rove's line: "Terror, unanswered, can not only bring down buildings—it can threaten the stability of legitimate governments." He then strayed from the text for the first time: "And you know what? We're not going to allow it."

Bush said, "Americans are asking: What is expected of us? I ask you to live your lives, and hug your children." The sentiment was exquisite—Karen had been right.

He saluted America's ultimate patriots: Governor Pataki and Mayor Giuliani. (Though undoubtedly the wild applause was intended for Giuliani, whose courage and pitch-perfect articulations throughout 9/11 were irreplicable, certainly by the dour Pataki.) He pledged to "rebuild New York City"—and further, he vowed that "this will not be an age of terror. This will be an age of liberty, here and across the world."

All the same, he noted, "Great harm has been done to us. We have suffered great loss. And in our grief and anger we have found our mission and our moment."

Here Bush coupled his administration with America. Both now had a purpose, and he expounded on it in unvarnished terms: "Freedom and fear are at war. The advance of human freedom—the great achievement of our time, and the great hope of every time—now depends on us. Our nation—this generation—will lift a dark threat of violence from our people and our future. We will rally the world to this cause by our efforts, by our courage. We will not tire, we will not falter, and we will not fail."

Brandishing his talisman, the badge of fallen policeman George Howard, Bush now personalized this oath: "I will not yield; I will not rest; I will not relent in waging this struggle for freedom and security for the American people."

He laid down a final marker of spiritual certainty: "Freedom and fear, justice and cruelty, have always been at war; and we know that God is not neutral between them."

Applause detonated for the singular man behind the podium. Democratic Senate Majority Leader Tom Daschle reached out and hugged him.

But that was nothing.

October 30, 2001, Yankee Stadium. He wore a blue New York City Fire Department windbreaker, and underneath it a bulletproof vest. The vest was what worried him. He had thrown out the first pitch on opening day, April 6, 2001, at Milwaukee's Miller Park, bragging to players beforehand that he might be tempted to throw a split-finger fastball, or "some big breaking stuff." Instead, to his horror, he'd done just as the old man had done in the Astrodome fifteen years ago, with George W. right there in the pricey seats, bearing witness: bounced the sucker several feet in front of home plate.

He'd blamed it on the boots he wore. Still, Bush was lucky: It was a minor media market and the stakes were low, his presidency was young, and no one was rooting for him to fail. And later that year at the College World Series, he wore shoes with better traction and got off a decent pitch. This, though, was the World Series. This was the home of the New York Yankees. Big stage, tough crowd. That was daunting any year.

But this was seven weeks after September 11, 2001. The president of the United States, a marked man, was going to stand in the middle of a stadium, alone.

"I'll bet you ten thousand dollars," said Bush's personal accountant, Robert McCleskey, "you throw it in the dirt."

Bush got there early. He threw warm-ups in the batting cage with a friendly old clubhouse manager. In the tunnel, he encountered the great Yankee shortstop Derek Jeter.

"Hey, Prez," said Jeter. "Are you gonna throw it from the mound?"

"What do you think?" Bush asked.

"Yeah. Be a man. Throw it from the mound."

"Okay, I will."

After beginning to walk away, Jeter turned back around. "Just don't bounce it," Jeter advised the president. "They'll boo you."

When his name was called, he strolled to the mound as the crowd of fifty-seven thousand cheered. The cheering did not stop. For a moment, Bush could feel his heart hammering against his bulletproof vest. He stood on the pitching rubber, letting the acclamation wash over him. He held up his thumb. What it meant was that he was there—he and they knew it now: The city, the nation, would go forward.

He turned to face the catcher, 60.6 feet away. A compact wind-up . . . and then, with the seams of the baseball twirling, a near-perfect strike.

"USA! USA! USA! USA!"

They would prevail—that was what it meant.

"That was Yankee Stadium!" Bush told Josh Bolten later, still flushed with amazement. "That was New York City! *Those people didn't even vote for me!* And to hear them chanting like that . . ."

New Hampshire, Florida—they no longer mattered.

That was New York City.

Message: They cared.

And now it was a different ball game.

PART THREE

DARK CITY ON A HILL

7

NIGHTMARE SCENARIO

"History begins today," Deputy Secretary of State Richard Armitage informed Pakistani intelligence director Mahmoud Ahmad after serving him tea.

"Today" was September 12, 2001. Mahmoud had been ruminating aloud on Pakistan's difficult history, but Armitage didn't want to hear it. The only salient feature of Pakistan's history was its support of the Taliban. *Tell your boss he's either with us or against us,* Colin Powell's bald, hulking lieutenant growled. Mahmoud couldn't believe Armitage's rudeness and left in a huff. But he conveyed the message.

And on November 10, Bush met with the president of Pakistan, General Pervez Musharraf, in the New York residence of UN Ambassador John Negroponte. While they sat, U.S.-led Coalition forces were obliterating the front lines of the Taliban in Musharraf's neighboring country, Afghanistan. Kabul would fall to the Coalition in two days. This was what being *against us* looked like.

Already, Musharraf had acquiesced to a list of nonnegotiable matters that Powell and Armitage had drawn up demanding that Pakistan end all ties with the Taliban and Al Qaeda. Now Bush pressed him to address the radical teachings in Pakistan's Islamic schools known as *madrassas*. With the stick came carrots: assurances that Afghanistan's feared Northern Alliance would not be running that country, and the promise of $1 billion in emergency economic aid to Pakistan.

That evening, Musharraf faced the TV cameras with Bush standing just behind him. He told the world, "Let me right away say that Pakistan has taken the considered decision to be a part of the Coalition, to be with the United States, to fight terrorism in all its forms wherever it lives."

Still, the *madrassas* in Pakistan would remain open.

Seventeen days later, on November 27, the president of Yemen, Ali Abdullah Saleh, stepped into the Oval Office for the very first time. Bush welcomed him with words more or less like Armitage's: *You're either with us or against us. And if you're with us, we expect results.*

The pint-size, mustachioed leader of Osama bin Laden's ancestral homeland was no pushover. He'd been Yemen's strongman for twenty-three years. Critics of Saleh were routinely harassed and jailed. He enjoyed wearing his ceremonial *jambiya* dagger, and at a G-8 summit he would horrify Secret Service agents by unsheathing it and wagging its curled blade in the airspace occupied by Bush and several other world leaders.

But now Kabul had fallen, and Saleh had heard reports that America might make Yemen, as he would put it, "a second Afghanistan." After all, Yemen had been the site of Al Qaeda's last successful strike. On October 12, 2000, a skiff in the port of Aden had detonated alongside the USS *Cole*, killing seventeen sailors. Saleh's government had obstructed the FBI's investigation of the *Cole* bombing; the masterminds of the attack were still on the prowl. Neither Clinton nor Bush had made Yemen pay for its dereliction. That could change very quickly.

So the savvy Yemeni came prepared to deal. Bush wanted greater cooperation in the *Cole* investigation and Al Qaeda assets frozen. Saleh wanted aid much as Musharraf had received. Bush had already pledged $400 million to Yemen. Now Saleh was talking about funding for intelligence gathering and new weapons systems. Andy Card watched the Yemeni leader make his pitch and thought with bemusement, *The bazaar's open and Saleh's ready to shop.*

Bush didn't make any further promises. But as he took in the diminutive Muslim leader's tangle of rhetoric—the assurances of support, the reminder of Yemen's poverty, the hope that America would not obsess over terrorism at the expense of pressing issues like the plight of the Palestinians—Bush knew that this would be the new soundtrack of his life. Yemen would be *with us*, yes. As would Pakistan, Saudi Arabia, Egypt, Turkey, and Russia. They would all be *with us*. Only as much as necessary, and at times not even that much, and always for a price.

In fighting this "different kind of war" against a "different kind of enemy," Bush would have to learn to be satisfied with a different kind of alliance. It went against his grain, this dysclarity. "I don't do nuance," he would say—or, when Condi Rice employed the term to a visiting dignitary, Bush would feel the need to add, with arid disdain: "*Nuance* is a word that we use in foreign policy." (Having seen the grimacing reaction to that word, Armitage learned to use *fact* or *problem* or *hurdle*—anything but *nuance*.) His nuance detector was especially keen when reading through speech drafts that had been worked over by staffers who saw it as their duty to obscure policy with verbal balancing acts. Bush would read out such a line with a contemptuous lilt in a voice, adding, "What the hell does that mean? Who wants to own up to it?"

Well, Mr. President, the unlucky staffer would say, *in terms of how we've always dealt with the issue—*

"I want it out. We make the point plainly or we don't make it at all."

Enforcing plainness on the outside world was the tricky part.

In the days after September 11, 2001, when Bush's admiring speechwriters sat together in the Old Executive Office Building and imagined the man whose impulsiveness and awkward diction they would recast in clean, assertive prose, the persona that they decided on was that of a big brother. He was dutiful and he was protective. He led by example. His vision was unmottled by pubescent tremors. There would be manful clarity to his every word and deed.

It did not occur to Mike Gerson, Matthew Scully, and John McConnell—all younger siblings themselves—to ascertain whether this was an accurate characterization of their boss. Was George W. Bush a role model to Jeb, Marvin, Neil, and Doro? Did his peers at Andover, Yale, and Harvard fall in line behind him? How had the voting public and the oil community of Midland judged his leadership capabilities? Would even Texans have regarded him as presidential material had his last name been anything but Bush?

The evidence was as stark as the language his speechwriters would assign to him: Bush had struck almost no one in his prepresidential past as an archetypal "big brother," much less as big brother to the free world.

Something, then, had changed. For after 9/11, George W. Bush filled the arena. All the man's undersized, self-conscious ways—the smirk, the reedy defensiveness, the exaggerated imperiousness of his executive stroll—had collapsed into this new persona, which seemed in fact not to be a persona but instead a natural habitat, waiting for his ownership all this time. He was a war president now, and perfectly at ease with the role. Anyone could see that. His tutors, Cheney and Rice, now stood back. He didn't need their direction anymore. It was as if the long-whirring gears in his impatient corpus had finally been jarred into place by 9/11, precisely at the time when America most needed strong leadership.

Bush became that leader, seemingly overnight. Whatever he asked for, Congress now gave him. Security measures for airports. A massive bailout for America's crippled airlines. Another $42 billion in tax cuts. And the Patriot Act, approved by a 98–1 vote in the Senate—the kind of terrorism-surveillance legislation that a weak president could never have shepherded through Capitol Hill.

The man who had lost the popular vote eleven months prior now had an approval rating of 90 percent. He'd seen the look in Vladimir Putin's eyes when the Russian leader first walked into the Oval Office. "My God," Putin had uttered. That office conferred immense authority, and now Bush had the clear mandate to wield it. It was his view, as Rice would later tell a visitor, that "this is a time when the U.S. has unparalleled power and you can try and sit on it and husband it and use a little bit here and a little bit there . . . or you can try and make big strategic plays that will fundamentally alter things in the way that the U.S. did after 1947."

Bush had been reading former Secretary of State Dean Acheson's memoir, *Present at the Creation*. Both Rice and he admired how Truman had spent the political capital afforded him by victory in World War II, merging power with Wilsonian ideals—"dragging it across the finish line," as Rice would say. Bush had the very same ambitions: *Spend the capital now. You get more from spending it.*

"Through our tears, we see opportunity," Bush continued to declare. But he also saw darkening skies. In the wake of 9/11, America was alert yet also soft, its chagrined intelligence officials still trying to piece together the most devastating attack ever on U.S. soil. The White House braced for a deadly encore, knowing Al Qaeda's tendency to go back for seconds. Bush began his mornings sifting through reams of unfiltered intelligence. In later months, and lasting throughout his presidency, he would receive a formal Terrorist Threat Matrix—prepared in part by FBI Director Robert Mueller, wholly separate from his Presidential Daily Briefing. Becoming, as one national security aide would say, "in a sense a desk officer," Bush would begin each morning with nerve-jangling scenarios and maddening chatter. Pakistani scientists, radiological bombs, Al Qaeda with nuclear capability, a biological scare in which several Americans had supposedly been infected, discussion of attack sites all over America—each episode producing spasmodic deployments of National Guard troops, bomb-sniffing dogs, and FBI agents. Having banned racial profiling earlier in the year, White House and Justice Department officials quietly went to work rewriting the language to allow for greater scrutiny of Arab and Muslim suspects. Meanwhile, to the gratitude of late-night TV comics, Cheney spent much of the latter part of October in an undisclosed facility with his wife, Lynne, surfacing now and then to rumble about bin Laden's determination to "decapitate" the U.S. government.

On October 4, 2001, Bush gave a speech to employees at the State Department. He spoke of the early victories in the War on Terror. The U.S. Treasury had seized bank accounts believed to be connected to Al Qaeda. More than 150 terrorists had been arrested worldwide. Countries continued to join the Coalition and "accept assignments," as Bush put it. Over and over, Bush pledged during the speech that good would spring from this evil.

Yet he teared up early in the speech during an innocuous moment of thanking "those of you who have worked extra long hours . . ." Something was weighing on Bush, and Ari Fleischer learned what it was when the motorcade returned them to the South Lawn. Bush motioned for his press secretary to follow him into the Oval Office.

A Boca Raton tabloid photo editor had checked in to a Florida hospital yesterday, Bush told Fleischer. *Anthrax.* The veil of resoluteness fell away from the president. His shoulders were hunched. Fleischer had never seen him so upset. Neither man said it aloud—neither had to: This was it, the dreaded second wave.

That afternoon, Fleischer brought Health and Human Services Secretary Tommy Thompson to the press briefing, where the latter assured reporters that the Florida anthrax incident was just "an isolated case. There's no evidence of terrorism. . . ." Eleven days later, a letter containing anthrax spores reached the Capitol office of Tom Daschle. Within the next two weeks, more than a dozen other contaminated letters were received at either the offices or the mailing sites of ABC, CBS, NBC, the Justice Department, the State Department, Governor George Pataki, numerous senators, and the White House.

Most of the envelopes also contained a note dated 09–11–01. Said several such notes: *Death to America. Death to Israel. Allah is Great.*

The crudely lettered envelopes hardly echoed the sophistication of the 9/11 plot. Still, Bush along with Rice and her deputy Steve Hadley, Powell and his deputy Armitage, and others in the administration assumed that a link had to exist. Fully two months passed before the White House concluded publicly that the anthrax case was likely a domestic operation, albeit one with an unknown perpetrator.

On the morning of November 12, American Airlines Flight 587 took off from JFK bound for the Dominican Republic, only to fall from the sky and crash in a neighborhood in Queens, killing all 260 on board. Fleischer's statement that day captured the White House's abjectness: "We have not ruled anything in; we have not ruled anything out."

It was in this state of anxious confusion that Bush and his team rethought the forthcoming State of the Union address. With the fall of the Taliban and the triumphant emergence of Hamid Karzai as a West-friendly leader of Afghanistan, the impulse had been to focus on democratic liberties, and specifically on women's rights. But before Christmas, Bush told Gerson and Rice that he wanted that aspect truncated and an emphasis placed on the dawning nightmare scenario—namely, that the terrorists whose chatter was giving the White House fits would actually get their hands on weapons of mass destruction, courtesy of nations hostile to the United States.

The phrase *axis of evil*—inspired by speechwriter David Frum and refined by Gerson—curiously set off no alarms among a message-savvy administration. No one, from Bush on down, thought it to be anything other than a catchy way of describing the relationship between terrorists and three rogue nations that Bush called out by name: North Korea, Iran, and, most expressively, Iraq. Bush and Rice saw it as a deft reframing of the War on Terror, now that the elusive bin Laden (who went unmentioned in the address) had vanished through the rugged creases of Tora Bora. Still, they and Gerson were certain that the headline grabber would be the speech's call for Muslim nations to observe "the nonnegotiable demands of human dignity: the rule of law; limits on the power of the state; respect for women; private property; free speech; equal justice; and religious tolerance." So convinced was Rice that this passage would make waves that she telephoned Saudi Ambassador Prince Bandar in advance and said, "Bandar, there are going to be things in this speech that may be hard for you. Don't get worried that we're trying to come after you tomorrow."

Instead, "axis of evil" got all the ink, setting off worries that Bush was now aiming his executive howitzer at Iraq, Iran, and North Korea. Administration officials began to leak reassuring qualifiers to the media, which infuriated Bush. "No backing off," he ordered Fleischer. To Rice he said, "Go out there and fix this," and in a speech before the Conservative Political Action Committee that Rove had lined up for her, she continued the tough talk. For his part, three days after the State of the Union address, Bush seized on a reporter's question during a brief availability with the visiting king of Jordan to say, "All the three countries I mentioned are now on notice that we intend to take their development of weapons of mass destruction very seriously."

Bush was not of a mind to be upbraided. As he put it in the State of the Union address, "our nation is at war, our economy is in recession, and the civilized world faces unprecedented dangers." The onus to lead America through this unquiet moment fell singularly on him. Equivocation, nuance—some other leader, some other time. That you're-either-with-us-or-against-us steeliness wasn't just reserved for Presidents Musharraf and Saleh. One early evening in October 2001, Bush sent for House Republican leaders Denny Hastert, Tom DeLay, and Dick Armey, who were holding up his airport security bill on the grounds that it didn't stipulate that baggage screening be privatized. On the Truman Balcony, Bush laid into them. "Why are you obstructing our efforts?" he demanded. "This is a time to be supporting your president!"

The flush of post-9/11 bipartisan good feelings embodied in Daschle's hugging Bush at the conclusion of his September 20 speech were fast wilting in the hothouse climate of the president's certitude. After signing No Child Left Behind into law in January 2002, the White House slashed its funding by $90 million a month later, prompting a livid Ted Kennedy and George Miller to hold a press conference on February 12 and all but call Bush a liar. The weekly White House breakfasts with congressional leaders largely found Bush talking rather than asking or listening. Attendees who felt short-changed by the president's seeming intransigence were that much more inclined to chafe at Bush's frequent jibes: *Don't you want more than just that yogurt, Tom? Denny, you eat all that, you're going to have to spend all day on the treadmill!*

It didn't take long for the emblems of terror to insinuate themselves into the political arena. In November, the conservative Family Research Council took out a newspaper ad saying, "What do Saddam Hussein and Senate Majority Leader Tom Daschle have in common? Neither man wants America to drill for oil in Alaska's Arctic National Wildlife Refuge." When asked by Tim Russert on *Meet the Press* to repudiate the sideswipe, VP Cheney sidestepped: "Well, I'm not responsible for that ad."

What the Bush White House *was* responsible for was a masterful if sharp-elbowed pirouette on the subject of a cabinet-level Department of Homeland Security. The idea to elevate Tom Ridge's White House office to higher status had been pushed by Democratic Senator Joe Lieberman since October. Bush, Cheney, and others in the White House had little appetite for creating a new bureaucratic superstructure.

But by April 2002 that had changed. Andy Card and four lieutenants began to hold periodic clandestine meetings in the bunker, sketching out an *über*-agency that would swallow up components of virtually every other cabinet department. Even as Card's "Gang of Five" enlarged to include Hagin and Bolten, they kept their discussions to the bunker, fearful of the outrage that would ensue if word leaked out to Capitol Hill, to K Street lobbyists, and, most of all, to turf-conscious cabinet secretaries. And even as they ramped up planning, Calio (who by May was in the loop) was doing all he could to discourage similar legislation being offered by Lieberman and several other senators, including Republican Arlen Specter. The ruse was timed to end the day after the White House's annual congressional picnic. That evening, June 5—a mere six days after Ridge had declared publicly that he would advise Bush to veto Lieberman's proposal—hundreds of elected officials gathered on the South Lawn and ate barbecue, absolutely clueless as to the about-face that would be sprung on them the following evening, in a presidential address to the nation.

Further to the adage that sometimes it's better to be lucky than good, White House political director Ken Mehlman hadn't anticipated that the Democrats would turn on the proposal that one of their own had first promulgated. Mehlman had intended to follow Rove's playbook and make the 2002 midterm elections about national security (rather than, say, the foundering economy). But when the Democrats balked at Bush's version of Lieberman's proposal because its protections for public-employee unions were weak, Mehlman saw a

particularly delicious opportunity. Calio pulled back from his persuasions. *Let 'em do it to themselves,* he thought.

And so Mehlman snatched the Department of Homeland Security
issue away from its inventors and used it as a cudgel against them. One
of the Lieberman bill's cosponsors was Senator Max Cleland of Georgia. Cleland was a Vietnam vet who had lost both legs and an arm in
the war. He figured that his war credentials indemnified him against
charges that he might be soft on national security issues. He figured
wrong.

"Georgians deserve to know—all Americans deserve to know—why
Max Cleland is more concerned with protecting federal bureaucracy,
rules, and regulations than protecting a department that can respond
effectively to future threats of terrorism," thundered his Republican
opponent Saxby Chambliss, a former lawyer and congressman who
himself had never served in combat. A Chambliss ad offered up the
images of bin Laden and Saddam while suggesting that Cleland lacked
"the courage to lead."

Cleland and other Democrats sputtered that the Republicans were
impugning the triple amputee's patriotism. But the DHS issue was
working in Georgia, in South Dakota, in Missouri—it was the gift that
kept on giving, second only to the presence of George W. Bush, who
relentlessly campaigned on behalf of Chambliss and scores of other
Republicans throughout the fall of 2002. Bush had his post-9/11 capital, and he was spending it to get more. Exhibiting his gift for appear-
ing above the Rovecraft of political brawls, he said of senatorial
candidate John Thune in Aberdeen, South Dakota, on the evening of
October 31, "He doesn't get caught up in all the nasty rhetoric that
tends to divide our nation's capital, that rhetoric which sends bad signals to many of our citizenry." Yet, later in the stump speech, he
assailed "some senators" for stalling the homeland security bill.

From South Dakota Bush flew to South Bend, Indiana, where he
told another crowd, "I went to Congress and asked them to help join
me in creating a Department of Homeland Security." But, he
lamented, "it's stuck in the Senate. See, it got stuck in the Senate
before they went home to campaign." Then to a rally in West Virginia, where Bush repeated this sad state of affairs—Democrats seemingly more interested in politics than in protecting our nation with a
Department of Homeland Security thought up by the president himself, who explained the common sense of combining some one hundred agencies involved in protecting America under one umbrella

agency with such folksy conviction that one could never have imagined Bush having fought such a measure only a short time ago.

And then, in the week to come, Pennsylvania, Kentucky, Tennessee, Georgia, Florida, Illinois, Minnesota, Missouri, Arkansas, Iowa. His denunciation of the Democrat-controlled Senate now all but twinned them with Al Qaeda: "We're under threats from an enemy which hates us, and yet they're trying to prevent me and future presidents from being able to do the job."

"They're more interested in special interests, which dominate the dialogue in Washington, D.C., than they are in protecting the American people."

Finally, on the evening of November 4, in Dallas, he managed one last burst of incredulity: "Here we are with an enemy lurking out there, and the bill got stuck in the Senate because some senators want to take away power from the presidency!"—before retiring to Crawford, where he would cast his ballot the following morning.

That day, November 5, 2002, the Republicans retook the Senate, in no small measure due to the frontal role played by the party leader, who was more than content to let the election be a referendum on him. It might be said that the last vestiges of post-9/11 bipartisanship effectively ended that evening. If that reality vexed yesteryear's uniter-not-a-divider, he didn't let it show. He'd spent his capital, and now his party controlled all branches of government.

And anyway, war was on his mind.

On September 12, 2001, while waves of sympathy for America poured in from all over the globe—even from Libya, Iran, and Palestine—one foreign leader stood alone in his inability to contain his glee. "Notwithstanding the conflicting human feelings about what happened in America yesterday," said Saddam Hussein while conferring with Iraq's minister of military industrialization, "America is reaping the thorns sown by its rulers in the world. Those thorns have not only bloodied the feet and the hearts of many, but also the eyes of people shedding tears on their dead whose souls have been reaped by America."

That statement found its way to a number of desks in the White House. The man behind the desk at the Oval Office was unsurprised. His familial hatred of Saddam needed no stoking. Two years after George H. W. Bush drove the Iraqi Republican Army out of Kuwait in 1991, sixteen men in Kuwait City were arrested and charged with attempting to assassinate the visiting ex-president with a 180-pound car bomb determined to have been assembled by Iraqi intelligence agents. Having failed to kill his nemesis, Saddam contented himself with installing a mosaic of Poppy's face—complete with the slogan "Bush Is Criminal"—on the floor of Baghdad's Al Rashid Hotel, where customers could step on it all day long.

On the campaign trail in 2000, the younger Bush became animated when the subject of Iraq's dictator came up. "I'm just as frustrated as many Americans are that Saddam Hussein still lives," he told PBS's Jim Lehrer during the South Carolina primary. "I will tell you this: If we catch him developing weapons of mass destruction in any way, shape, or form, I'll deal with him in a way that he won't like."

"Like what—bomb him?" pressed Lehrer.

"Well, it could be one option. He just needs to know that he'll be dealt with in a firm way."

Lehrer had asked Bush whether he had supported his father's decision not to remove Saddam from power. It was a question that back in 1998 Condi Rice had predicted would emerge in the campaign. "We better talk through that now, not later," she had said to the governor, who, she would later claim, responded, "No, they did the right thing at the time." Indeed, he echoed that sentiment to Lehrer. And during an interview with a reporter in the summer of 1998, George W. Bush went a step further, speaking with eerie if ironic prescience:

"You *cannot* lead a divided state," he said that afternoon. "That was my problem with Richard Nixon. He divided the country. The leader's job is to unite. George Bush united the country for Desert Storm. Desert Storm is gonna be his legacy. Not only he united the country, but the amazing feat was, *he united the WORLD!*

"But," he concluded with an offhand shrug, "I understand short-term history is never objective."

Yet, that very year, the governor told a family friend, "Dad made a mistake not going into Iraq when he had an approval rating in the nineties. If I'm ever in that situation, I'll use it—I'll spend my political capital."

This was the difference between the father and the son. The latter saw opportunity, even—maybe especially—through tears, and lunged at it. The former was famously prudent. He played small ball. And now Saddam was alive and well, stiff-arming the weapons inspectors, hailing the attack on America.

These were two men spoiling for a fight.

8

DRUMBEATS

The conviction that Saddam Hussein was an imminent threat to America and therefore necessitated removal by force began as a kind of communicable agent to which some in the administration had great resistance and others not. Its host bodies belonged to, among others, Vice President Dick Cheney; his chief of staff, I. Lewis "Scooter" Libby; Deputy Secretary of Defense Paul Wolfowitz; and Douglas J. Feith, undersecretary of defense for policy. The agent resided in these four men, and in lesser hosts, well before September 11. But after the attack on America, the contagion swept through the Beltway and insinuated itself into the minds of many—including the White House national security adviser and the president of the United States.

The virus was hardly without its molecular logic. It was not simply that Saddam was a brutal despot. On a good day, a pre-9/11 day, Saddam was a malignant presence. In 1988, in an ostentatious display of his chemical weapons program, he had trained mustard and nerve gases on Iraq's Kurds, killing thousands. In 1990, he invaded a neighboring country, Kuwait. A year later, during Desert Storm, Saddam without provocation fired thirty-nine Scud missiles into Israel in a failed effort to draw that country into the war. When weapons inspectors descended on Iraq following the Gulf War, they uncovered evidence of a twenty-five-year-old nuclear weapons program that might well have brought Saddam to the brink of nuclear capability. Three years later, in 1994, the inspectors discovered Iraq's plans for biological warfare. Four years after that, Saddam booted the inspectors out of Iraq for good. He continued to defy UN resolutions demanding that inspections resume. As

Bush contended in his Axis of Evil speech, "This is a regime that has something to hide from the civilized world."

In the winter following 9/11, the NSC drafted its National Security Strategy, and Iraq did not figure in the document—at all. Still, the virus had changed. It overtook the lives of its inhabitants—producing fevers that spiked and did not ebb. *Iraq and Al Qaeda . . . Al Qaeda and Iraq.* There'd been contact, hadn't there? Whether operational or just a wary eyeballing between religious extremists and secular strongmen, whether Saddam even knew of such meetings (*but didn't he know everything taking place in his country?*), this was known: Iraq supported terrorists, for Poppy's secretary of state had put them on the list in 1990. (The list of state sponsors also included Libya, Cuba, Sudan, North Korea, Syria, and Iran.) Saddam had cut $25,000 checks to widows of Palestinian suicide bombers—*terrorists!*

The fever produced visions not wholly confirmable by reality. *But wasn't that the point?* Poor George Tenet galloping from the White House to the Justice Department to the State Department to the Pentagon throughout the summer of 2001, the CIA director ranting like Nietzsche's fool with the lantern: "It's coming, I don't know where and how . . ." *And we waited—didn't take it to the enemy, had to wait for the facts, 2,819 dead. . . .*

Powell and Armitage thought the Al Qaeda connection was specious. Cheney did not, but his greater point was this: *If you wait for intelligence to drive policy, you will have waited too long.* As the elder Bush's secretary of defense during the Gulf War, Cheney had cast his faith with intelligence reports predicting that Saddam was perhaps eight or ten years away from owning nuclear weaponry. *Try one or two years!* (Which, like a fisherman's tall tale, the VP would eventually exaggerate as "perhaps within a year," and later, "less than a year away.") Condi Rice picked up on the axiom, and throughout 2002 she would make on-background comments to reporters like this one: "I've been in this business a long time and people always underestimate the time—they rarely overestimate the time. If we're wrong and we had four or five or six years before he was a serious WMD threat, then we just win early. If you're wrong, then we wake up in two or three years and this bloody tyrant has a nuclear weapon and is brandishing it in the most volatile region in the world. So which of those chances do you want to take?"

The wildest hallucination spurred by the contagion after 9/11—that Saddam was behind the attacks—came and went like the fever dream it was. But what could not be dispelled was the nightmare scenario: *If the terrorists could do this with airplanes, think of what they could do with weapons of mass destruction.* And if the intelligence was at this moment far from conclusive, and in the absence of same, suggestive to certain skeptics of a Batman comic book plot—the Joker and the Riddler join forces!—Bush's kinetic nature would not entertain the lawyerly gaming of an airtight case. These were "evildoers," after all. The enemy and its intentions were known. The axis between them? Less known. But as Bush warned in the Axis of Evil speech, "time is not on our side. I will not wait on events, while dangers gather."

Just as the Bush doctrine—"We will make no distinction between the terrorists who committed these acts and those who harbor them"— epitomized his predilection for clarity, so did this corollary of preemption manifest George W. Bush's restive boldness. Still, he did in fact wait on events. Fourteen months would pass between Bush's public conflation of Saddam with terror and the U.S. invasion of Iraq. "We'll be deliberate," Bush had promised, and he was true to his word. He and his lieutenants waited on Congress, on the United Nations, on the midterm election results, on his military commanders, and even on Saddam Hussein.

Bush waited. But the fever persisted, and rather than dwindle against the president's indomitable optimism—"Through our tears, we see opportunity"—the two forces settled in hospitably together, strains of alarmism and idealism occupying a leader whose words reflected, in the Axis of Evil address, a doubled resolve:

"We can't stop short. If we stop now—leaving terror camps intact and terror states unchecked—our sense of security would be false and temporary. History has called America and our allies to action, and it is both our responsibility and our privilege to fight freedom's fight."

In February 2002, at a chiefs-of-mission conference in Washington, D.C., U.S. ambassadors to Middle Eastern nations sat in a conference room and speculated aloud as to whether Iraq was likely to be invaded. Richard Jones, America's ambassador to Kuwait, was seized by an awful premonition. "I hope we avoid a Vietnam situation," he worried aloud, "where the American people feel like they weren't told in advance what we're getting into. We'll be in there at least five years."

"Five years?" erupted one of the other diplomats. Such a continued presence would be unsustainable, she argued. "Within two years, there'll be an insurgency! Don't you know Iraq's history?"

"Well," interjected the meeting's moderator, Bill Burns, "that's exactly why we would never go at this alone."

The diplomats agreed: To avoid another Vietnam-style quagmire, an invasion of Iraq would require solid international backing.

Would it require congressional backing?

Cheney, a former congressmen himself (and therefore, Powell and Armitage believed, contemptuously familiar with its workings), was aware of the stakes. What if Bush sought authorization for force, and Congress voted not to grant it? Such a scenario had nearly occurred in the first Gulf War—it took Jim Baker going to Geneva one last time and failing to achieve peaceful resolution before the Senate capitulated and gave George H. W. Bush the green light by a narrow (52–47) margin. Cheney had been against congressional authorization back then but came later to believe that seeking it had helped solidify public support.

The Senate Foreign Relations Committee, then chaired by Democat Joe Biden, had conducted a two-day hearing on Iraq on July 31 and August 1, during the Senate's last week before recess. Emblematic of the partisan divide of that year, Biden's committee spent those two days deeply absorbed in the witness testimony of scholars, Iraqi exiles, diplomats, and weapons inspectors . . . and though Bush had shaken Biden's hand and said, "I really appreciate your holding these hearings, Mr. Chairman," the day before they commenced, in fact the White House paid almost no attention to what was being said. What mattered was the vote.

And, as Ken Mehlman made it clear: "We need to get them on record before the election."

To prod them into passing a resolution authorizing the president to use force against Iraq, a series of intelligence briefings was conducted by the White House's Office of Legislative Affairs during the waning summer days of 2002. An aggressive whip program identified those leaning but not committed, those who needed more information, and those who might sway others. Some congressmen were brought into the Situation Room or Roosevelt Room and briefed by Tenet or his deputy, John McLaughlin, under Rice's watchful eye. Others were led to Room 407 in the Capitol. Grainy aerial photographs and aluminum tubes were submitted for their inspection. Nick Calio and his deputy, David Hobbs, sat in the room and marveled at the legislative branch's lack of inquisitiveness during these uniformly noncontentious get-togethers.

One who did resist was House Majority Leader Dick Armey, a

folksy but intellectual conservative who distrusted mob passions driving the cry for invasion. "I don't believe that America will justifiably make an unprovoked attack on another nation," Armey told a reporter on August 8. "It would not be consistent with what we have been as a nation or what we should be as a nation."

Armey was among the eighteen congressional leaders whom Bush hosted at the White House on September 4. Said the latter to the former, somewhat sourly, "I really would appreciate it if you would not talk about this point of view in public, until you've had the full briefings I've had."

The majority leader attended more than one intelligence briefing in Room 407 but was not particularly swayed. It was then that Dick Cheney paid a call and summoned Armey to his office in the West Wing.

"When you hear the whole story, you'll agree with me," the VP promised. Cheney then traced the history: the gross underestimations pre–Gulf War, the technological advances since that time such that WMDs could be miniaturized into a suitcase, the likelihood that Saddam would use Al Qaeda as a delivery system, the impossible task faced by inspectors—"You'll never find the stuff until you get in there and clean out everything else. . . ."

The VP wasted none of the time on rosy talk of ridding Iraqis of their dictator or of installing a fountainhead of democracy in the Middle East. He was all about imminent threat. Cheney and Armey leaned over a coffee table and stared at photographs of a supposed centrifuge tube. *That could be an irrigation pipe for all I know*, thought Armey.

"You're going to get mired down there," Armey persisted.

Cheney shook his head. "We have great information," he said. "They're going to welcome us. It'll be like the American army going through the streets of Paris. They're sitting there ready to form a new government. The people will be so happy with their freedoms that we'll probably back ourselves out of there within a month or two."

It didn't sound right to Armey. Still, Dick Cheney had credibility with him. They had been through this before, in 1991, when then-Secretary Cheney had worked over Armey—doubtful then as now, but the Texas congressman had been swayed by Cheney's promise of a battle plan featuring overwhelming force so as to minimize harm to the troops. He'd given Cheney his vote back then, and both had been vindicated.

Back at his office, Armey brooded over it for a while. *I'm going to vote for the damn thing anyway*, the majority leader finally decided. In particular, the likelihood that Saddam was using Al Qaeda as a delivery system had made a decisive impression on him.

"Does he have dangerous assets?" Dick Armey would ask during his floor speech before casting his vote. Then, answering his own question: "More so than we thought."

The summer months were intense in Crawford as Bush and his lieutenants wrangled over diplomatic options, military strategy, whether to seek authorization from Congress, and how the administration would make its case for war, if it came to that. But nothing was leaking out from the inner circle. One day in early September, *New York Times* reporter Elisabeth Bumiller called Andy Card at his vacation home in Maine to find out just what they were scheming.

A thoroughly honest fellow, Card could, when the mood struck him, be cajoled into saying exactly what was on his mind, however imprudent it might be. Thinking to himself, *Look, it's the summer, everyone's on vacation, you've got the B-team in the White House media pool, the David Broder types aren't filing any more columns till after the recess,* the chief of staff told Bumiller, "From a marketing point of view, you don't introduce new products in August."

When the *Times* published its story, Card read the quote and had to ask himself, *What are you, an idiot?* Colleagues wondered the same thing. But the president never said a word about it to his chief.

It wasn't Bush's idea to plead his case before the United Nations. "You know, of course I want to have international support," he told Rice and Powell one evening in August as the three dined together at the residence. "I *loved* building the coalition in Afghanistan." But, added the man who so disdained surprises, he was wary of what the French, the Russians, and the Germans had in store for him.

Just as much, he detested what the UN had come to embody. It was all about *process.* As if what counted wasn't action but instead the act of talking, with the desired outcome being promises to talk again and again . . . endless navel-gazing, while dangers gathered.

But during dinner that night with Bush and Rice, Powell suggested another paradigm for a UN speech—and for going after Saddam. The secretary of state warned the president that if he invaded Iraq, "you'll be the proud owner of the hopes and aspirations of 25 million Iraqis. *And* you become the government! You're *it*!" Under such a scenario, Powell said, Bush would be tying down perhaps 40 percent of the Army for the next several years. "It's going to remove a lot of your military flexibility. It's going to be hugely expensive. And, Mr. President, it's going to suck the political oxygen out of the environment for the rest of your presidency." (Powell would later contend, and Richard Armitage would confirm, that contrary to reports it was Armitage and not Powell who employed the term "Pottery Barn Rule" for breaking and therefore buying Iraq. Powell later wrote a somewhat miffed Pottery Barn to explain this.)

Powell had a solution. "The offended party is not us," he said. "It's the UN. You've got to take it to the UN." It was a no-lose proposition, said Powell. Through a new resolution, the UN might actually be able to force Saddam to resubmit to weapons inspectors. If that didn't work, then going to the UN would help Bush generate support for a military coalition.

"Go to the UN," he told Bush, "and *challenge* the United Nations. Tell them: This is not about us and Iraq. This is a challenge to the international community. Sixteen resolutions. Twelve years of diplomacy." *Appeal to their pride as leaders.*

But, Powell warned, there was a catch: "It might be possible for Iraq to satisfy this resolution. And if they satisfy this resolution, you have to be prepared to accept not a regime change, but a changed regime."

This was not the preferred scenario for Bush, and it showed. The president had, by August 2002, already decided that nothing short of regime change would do. He nonetheless saw the merit to exhausting diplomatic options, if only as a public relations exercise. "The American people gotta know that diplomacy was tried, and vigorously tried," he would say. And further: "One thing people don't realize is unlike the U.S., where the president can feel free to make policy *without* UN approval, there are other countries that really need UN approval for them to act. . . . Our key partners—Tony Blair of Great Britain, Aznar [of Spain], Berlusconi [of Italy], John Howard [of Australia]—they're all saying, 'We need to do this at the UN, give diplomacy a chance.' "

When Bush agreed to go to the UN, Powell thought it meant that Bush agreed as well to accept a "changed regime." The secretary later used that very phrase at a press forum—putting it out there, hoping that others would hold Bush to it.

For the annual September meeting of UN delegates in New York, Gerson had proposed a speech expounding further on democratization and the "nonnegotiable demands of human dignity." He brought an outline with him into the Oval Office.

"No, we're gonna talk about Iraq," Bush told him.

Rice could see what was juicing the boss. She added a historical flourish. *Think of the League of Nations*, she suggested to the president. After all, this wasn't a case of Saddam outwitting the international community. This was the UN simply letting Iraq get away with the flouting of one resolution after the next. The time had come for world leaders to choose. Would they enforce order? Or would they descend into irrelevancy as the League of Nations had, while dangers gathered in Nazi Germany?

Bush liked the idea. The post-9/11 starkness of good versus evil was, to him, a throwback. During what had figured to be a perfunctory chat with the prime minister of Estonia in the White House, Bush had launched into his spiel on Saddam's evil intentions when the prime minister interrupted him: "You don't have to tell me about Iraq. In 1938, the great democracies did not act, and my people lived in bondage for the next fifty years. You don't have to tell me about dealing with tyranny."

The speech went through a multitude of rewrites, all the way until September 11, 2002, the night before he was to give the address. At issue was the question of whether Bush should request another resolution from the UN Security Council demanding that Saddam resubmit to weapons inspections. Powell was for another resolution, Cheney against.

In the green room at the UN building on the morning of September 12, Powell phoned Armitage. "Who's that?" called out Bush as he was getting powder applied to his face. When Powell told him, Bush called out his nickname for the brawny deputy secretary: "Hey, Tiny!"

Powell murmured quietly to Armitage, "It's in."

The line in which Bush requested a resolution from the UN was in fact in the final draft of the speech. But that final draft hadn't been loaded into the teleprompter. While Powell sat in the audience, while Armitage sat at his State Department, and while Rice and Hadley watched from the West Wing—each of them following along the final draft—Bush came to the line, "My nation will work with the UN Security Council to meet our common challenges." The president then went on: "If Iraq's regime defies us again . . ."

Powell gasped. Hadley sat upright in his chair and put a hand on Rice. Armitage all but lost control of his bodily functions. *He left out the resolution sentence!*

Then Bush himself realized the omission. A sentence later, he ad-libbed: "We will work with the UN Security Council for the necessary resolutions."

Nice catch, thought Armitage. Powell exhaled. Rice and Hadley were relieved as well—though later they fretted among themselves: *He said "resolutions"—plural. We need to clean that up.* They decided not to—hoping that no one would notice the incorrect formulation, and no one did.

What *was* noticed was the frigid reception the president's address received. Bush had expected no less. He began the speech by acknowledging the anniversary of 9/11, and then reminded the delegates of the UN Security Council's original purpose: "so that unlike the League of Nations, our deliberations would be more than talk, our resolutions will be more than wishes." And the speech's conclusion offered one of Bush's patented binary choices: "We must choose between a world of fear and a world of progress. We cannot stand by and do nothing while dangers gather."

But in the meat of the speech, Bush got personal. "All the world now faces a test," he said, "and the United Nations a difficult and defining moment. Are Security Council resolutions to be honored and enforced, or cast aside without consequence? Will the United Nations serve the purpose of its founding, or will it be irrelevant?"

Rather than clap after this searing line, a single cell phone went off in the audience, as if taunting Bush's famous aversion to such interruptions. As it developed, one single line in the twenty-five-minute speech received applause: "As a symbol of our commitment to human dignity, the United States will return to UNESCO." Bush's tribute to the nations that had joined America's War on Terror was met with silence. So was his ingratiating pledge that his government "stands committed to an independent and democratic Palestine, living side by side with Israel in peace and security." The audience didn't respond.

"For a guy who's used to clapping and cheering, dead silence is interesting," Bush would later muse. As he recited, in plodding, almost lawyerly fashion, Iraq's long history of promise breaking, he made a point of staring into the stony faces of Iraq's representatives, and those of other scowling delegates. And their reaction fueled him—they didn't care about the facts, and that to Bush was the point. He *wanted* to make them uncomfortable! He *wanted* them to be offended! Calling them on their complicity—they *needed* to feel their honor stung.

Hell, they ought to be thanking him! "I did the UN a favor when I went and gave my speech September the twelfth of last year," he told a handful of reporters in an off-the-record session the following January. "You know, I joke and say, 'You know, I came from a part of the world where there's more bumper stickers saying GET THE US OUT OF THE UN than GOD BLESS AMERICA.' And here I am, standing up in front of the UN, saying, 'You can either be the UN or the League of Nations. Take your pick. And we want you to be a strong United Nations.' "

Bush thought he was doing the UN a favor by shaming it. It didn't occur to him, as he hammered away at the delegates' consciences, that this might not feel at all like a favor—a mighty, fabulously privileged country telling lowly nations how and when they must act. It didn't occur to him that these nations might already have felt enough condescension from the world's last great superpower; that process, to countries that had little else, *did* matter; that though they bore no love for Saddam Hussein, in many ways they identified more with him than with this all-powerful man standing behind the podium. It seemed not to occur to Bush what it would really be like to be on the receiving end of his lecture—not as the wealthy, strong, unconditionally loved George W. Bush, but as a man blessed by none of these characteristics.

It didn't occur to Bush to step outside his own skin, because he seldom did that. This was his skin, he was comfortable inside it, and inside it was the only way he knew how to be. In any event, the diplomats seated there weren't his audience. "When the president of the United States walks in and gives a pretty powerful speech in front of a world body, the message to Saddam Hussein should've been, 'This guy's serious,' " Bush later said. "And I don't believe he took me seriously. I don't. I think it's more of the same, in his mind. And I tried hard to make him understand that one way or the other, we were going to deal with the threat."

Inside his presidential limo after the speech, he told the man accompanying him, Afghanistan's Hamid Karzai, "That was like speaking to a wax museum."

But he also called Gerson that day and said, "I *really* liked giving that speech."

That was September 12. The following month, a spree of sniper attacks in the Washington, D.C., area once again threw the administration into a panic as intelligence officials scrambled for leads, convinced that the shootings were the work of Al Qaeda. On October 10, the House of Representatives passed a resolution authorizing the president to use force against Iraq by a vote of 296–133. The next day, the Senate followed suit by a 77–23 vote count. Yet by August the ramp-up to war had begun, quietly but furiously—four months before Tenet assured Bush, with others present, that the case for Saddam being in possession of WMDs was a "slam dunk."

In the middle of the Kuwaiti desert, the world's biggest helipad and a runway to accommodate C-130s were constructed. A portable deepwater pier and a landing ramp for L-Cat catamarans were installed in the Gulf. A pipeline for fueling sorties was attached to a refinery south of Kuwait City and extended some thirty miles to the camouflaged hamlets of Camps Virginia, New York, New Jersey, Pennsylvania, and Connecticut, all situated less than fifty miles from the Iraq border. Troops began to fill the tents. Calls from the White House went out to allies throughout the Middle East and Europe. War and postwar plans circulated throughout the West Wing, the Pentagon, and the State Department. The four-stars on the ground and the national security aides in the White House all looked at the same heat graphs. By April, temperatures in Iraq would exceed one hundred degrees. The invasion, if there was to be one, would have to begin by March at the latest.

(Condi Rice said this explicitly to Republican Senator Chuck Hagel: "We've got to get in there before it gets too hot," she told Hagel in November. "We've got to get this done within a window."

Hagel couldn't believe what he was hearing. "Wait—you've already committed to this war?" he demanded. And though Rice tried to mollify him, Hagel was convinced that the toothpaste was already out of the tube.)

Bush was preparing to go into Iraq with little or no support, if need be. Cheney was the chief caretaker of the fever—having gone way out on a limb in an August 26 speech before the Veterans of Foreign Wars: "Simply stated, there is no doubt that Saddam Hussein now has weapons of mass destruction."

"What the hell is going on here?" Chuck Hagel hollered on the phone to Powell the next day. "You guys say you're not going to war—*you're going to war!*"

And though Rice had gently admonished Cheney that such a categorical claim might create "a problem for the president"—resulting in a second, less apocalyptic speech by the VP—by October the fever possessed Bush as well. At a speech in Cincinnati that month, the president quoted a weapons inspector, saying, "Saddam Hussein is a

homicidal dictator who is addicted to weapons of mass destruction."
For the first but hardly the last time, he unveiled an eerie image that
Rice had formulated: "Facing clear evidence of peril, we cannot wait
for the final proof—the smoking gun—that could come in the form of
a mushroom cloud."

In the Cincinnati address—"the speech that nobody listened to," he
later remarked, other than perhaps a few conservative commentators
and "my mother"—Bush for the first time began to lay out a case for
a Saddam–Al Qaeda connection. It was not a formidable marshaling of
evidence. Both actors hated us, said the president. Saddam had celebrated the 9/11 attacks. A senior Al Qaeda member had received
medical treatment in Baghdad. Others were taking refuge in Iraq.
Bush referred to "high-level contacts that go back a decade"—not
adding that members of his own administration, particularly in the
State Department, viewed this intelligence with great skepticism.

On the campaign trail for fellow Republicans, the president didn't
bother with the irksome details. "We know that he's had connections with Al Qaeda," he told a crowd in Tampa on the evening of
November 2.

The next morning, in Springfield, Illinois, Bush pushed the connection further: "He is a man who would likely team up with Al Qaeda."

Later that day, at a Minnesota rally: "This is a man who has had
contacts with Al Qaeda. This is a man who poses a serious threat in
many forms—but catch this form: He's the kind of guy that would
love nothing more than to train terrorists and provide arms to terrorists so they could attack his worst enemy and leave no fingerprints."

And then on to Sioux Falls, South Dakota: "He can't stand America. He can't stand some of our closest friends. And not only that: He
is—would like nothing better than to hook up with one of these
shadowy terrorist networks like Al Qaeda, provide some weapons
and training to them, let them come and do his dirty work, and we
wouldn't be able to see his fingerprints on his action."

And the following day in Arkansas: "He's had contacts with Al
Qaeda. Imagine a scenario where an Al Qaeda–type organization
uses Iraq as an arsenal, a place to get weapons, a place to be trained to
use the weapons. Saddam Hussein could use surrogates to come and
attack people he hates."

And finally, at his last stop, in Dallas: "This is a man who has got
connections with Al Qaeda."

Bush wasn't relying on intelligence to buttress his claims of

Saddam's dark fantasies of plotting attacks on America with Al Qaeda, or of direct contact with Al Qaeda. For no such intelligence existed.

Nor was there intelligence documenting the existence of a WMD stockpile in Iraq. Rice's deputy, Steve Hadley, indicated to a colleague discomfort that the administration was going so far out on a limb with such unsupported claims. But there was no stopping Bush's momentum. At each of these campaign stops, he stated it categorically, with only the slightest variations from his phraseology in Dallas: "This is a man who told the world he wouldn't have weapons of mass destruction, promised he wouldn't have them. He's got them."

Forty-seven days after that final, unequivocal utterance, Bush sat in the Oval Office with Rice, Card, Tenet, and McLaughlin. Reversing his own certitude, he admitted to those in the room that evidence of Saddam's weapons of mass destruction was less than persuasive.

"It's a slam dunk," Tenet assured the president.

And that, as Card would remember, was *"the* confirmation."

Tenet was not alone. Few voices, either in the administration or on Capitol Hill, questioned Saddam's possession of WMDs. Why else would he behave like a man with something to hide?

Senate Foreign Relations Committee chairman Joe Biden certainly shared this belief. He and fellow committee member Hagel had boldly snuck across the border into the Kurdish region of northern Iraq in November 2002. Both men returned to the States convinced of the need for Saddam's removal. But Biden was squeamish about the feeble international support Bush had mustered and worried that the White House had little understanding of what it might face in Iraq. Above all, he thought the administration's case for immediate invasion was anemic.

Chairman Biden picked up the phone and called his old friend Colin Powell not long before Powell would be making the case for immediate regime change to the UN on February 5, 2003. "Look, just stick to what we know, okay, Colin?" he told the secretary of state. None of that crazy shit about Saddam buying uranium from Africa that Bush had mentioned in his January 27 State of the Union address.

"Joe," Powell sighed, "someday when you're retired and I'm retired, I'll tell you about all the pressure I've been put under over here."

There is no commodity in the world more valuable than the president's time. After 9/11, it became even more scarce. Cabinet secretaries and policy advisers outside the foreign-affairs apparatus found themselves at a further remove. Press conferences and one-on-one interviews with Bush had gone the way of the South Carolina primary. Bush would beckon select members of Congress to the Oval—but only when he needed them, and almost never to solicit a dissenting point of view.

Hour-long sessions between the president and private citizens were especially rare. So it was an unusual moment on the afternoon of January 10, 2003, when three Iraqi exiles were shepherded into the Oval Office. Such gatherings of Iraqis had frequently taken place in the White House over the past year. But none of them had been granted an audience with Bush, until now.

The three participants had been vetted by the NSC and preinterviewed by Rice. They were Kanan Makiya, a professor at Brandeis and chronicler of the Baath Party's atrocities; Hatem Mukhlis, a Sunni Muslim surgeon and cofounder of the Iraq National Movement; and Rend Franke, director of the Iraq Foundation. None of them had been living inside his or her native country for decades. The State Department did not find their views particularly authoritative. By no coincidence, Rice, Cheney, Card, Fleischer, and Zalmay Khalilzad had been invited to join the meeting . . . but no one from State had.

Bush welcomed his visitors. As was typical, he began the talk with his own thoughts. Though Secretary Powell would return to the UN next month, implicit in the president's language was that war was inevitable. Saddam's heart "is of stone," he said.

The president wanted to hear their personal stories. Mukhlis's was especially moving—his father, also a doctor, had been ordered killed by Saddam.

"What reaction do you expect from the Iraqis to the entry of U.S. forces in their cities?" Bush wanted to know.

"The Iraqis will welcome the U.S. forces with flowers and sweets when they come in," volunteered Makiya. That had been the case in 1991, he said—people were on their rooftops, cheering at the pilots who were bombing their cities. The other two agreed that American troops would face immediate jubilation.

Bush was ready to believe this. He and Rice had discussed what the Coalition forces had confronted in Afghanistan, a country with no democratic tradition whatsoever. The Afghans responded immediately to their liberation. They played music. They sent their daughters to school. As Rice had reminded a reporter, "Afghanistan is just an example of the effect that we tend to forget time and time again. We saw it with Milosevic, too. When people are freed of these regimes, they're actually more than happy to be liberated."

What would happen in Iraq, Bush predicted to a reporter, would be "the same we did in Afghanistan—it's a blueprint, it's a model."

But, Bush pressed the three exiles: Would Iraqis feel so warm if their country sustained serious damage during the invasion?

Serious damage wouldn't be necessary, said one of them, for the simple reason that "the regime will be destroyed with the first blow."

Well, said Bush, "we're planning for the worst." But, he added, "I pledge to the people of Iraq that the U.S. Army itself will rebuild every power station or installation that might be damaged during the military operations." America wouldn't abandon Iraq—unlike "the situation in 1991," he said, referring to his father's failure to protect the Iraqi people from a vengeful Saddam. There would be, in essence, two armies: the first to defeat the regime, the second to rebuild the country.

Rice chimed in assurances. The Army would bring in doctors, engineers, and technicians. Wartime preparations were keenly focused on this matter, she said.

Makiya gushed about "the importance of this new pledge that we have not heard before."

Bush had another important question for the exiles. He knew that Iraq was riven with ethnic and religious conflict. "Will these differences turn into hatred, leading to civil conflicts and more disasters for Iraq?" he wanted to know.

All three said the same thing: This hatred had been spawned by Saddam's regime, which pitted tribe against tribe. With a flowering democracy and wise leadership, they said, persistent animosity would be unlikely.

The three exiles differed on how long it would take to stand up a full-fledged democratic government. And while Mukhlis strongly believed that the new government should emerge from within Iraq, the other two were just as emphatic that the Iraqi opposition in exile should play a key role, à la Karzai in Afghanistan. (When Makiya made a point of criticizing State and the CIA for failing to support the exile groups, Bush asked Rice, "Is this true?" She didn't deny it, Khalilzad confirmed it, and Cheney observed dryly that there were "differences" in the administration.)

But Franke, Mukhlis, and Makiya all agreed without qualification:

Iraq would greet American forces with enthusiasm. Ethnic and religious tensions would dissolve with the collapse of Saddam's regime. And democracy would spring forth with little effort—particularly in light of Bush's commitment to rebuild the country.

Rice, Card, and Fleischer could all see it: The meeting had a significant impact on the Boss.

Eighteen days later, Bush explained to a group of American conservative thinkers how hospitable the soon-to-be-invaded country would be to a post-Saddam way of life.

"It's important for the world to see that first of all, Iraq is a sophisticated society with about $16 billion of income," Bush told them in the Oval Office. "The degree of difficulty compared to Afghanistan in terms of the reconstruction effort, or emerging from dictatorship, is, like, infinitesimal.

"I mean," he went on, "Afghanistan has *zero*. Nothing. Karen Hughes just came back from there. She said it's like a giant windstorm has swept through there and kind of sandblasted everything. And there's no food and there's no way to sustain life."

By contrast, Bush said, "Iraq is a sophisticated society. And it's a society that can emerge and show the Muslim world that it's possible to have peace on its borders without rallying the extremists. And the other thing that will happen will be, there will be less exportation of terror out of Iraq—which will provide more comfort and stability for a country like Israel, which, frankly, will make, in my judgment, easier for us to achieve a peace in the Palestinian-Israel issue."

Through tears, he saw opportunity. Great opportunity.

But he was not blind to the consequences.

Andy Card had been his dad's deputy chief of staff during the Gulf War. He had traveled with 41 to meet with American families whose sons had been killed during the hostilities. He told Bush about these experiences. *This is going to be part of your job*, the chief of staff informed the president. "It's going to be hard."

Bush knew where he had to turn.

It didn't come naturally, talking about his faith. Bushes tended not to boast of their devoutness. As a gubernatorial candidate, and later as governor, he never spoke publicly of his days teaching Sunday school in Dallas. He and Laura read the Bible daily, and they spoke to the girls about their Christian faith. And even though by 1996 Bush was a vocal proponent of government support for faith-based initiatives, he largely restricted his own articulation of faith to praying before his meals.

On November 3, 1996, Bush spoke to an Austin Presbyterian congregation at the behest of one of its elders, Karen Hughes. "I usually don't address churches or religious organizations," he acknowledged in his speech that Sunday. "I worry about the political world adopting the religious world. I think of the candidates who say, 'Vote for me, I am the most religious.' Or, 'I walk closer to God than old so-and-so.' How contradictory to the teachings of the Lord."

Said Bush that day, "I have worries. Worries about dragging my wife into a fishbowl and worries about the happiness of our twin teenagers. I have moments of doubt, moments of pride, and moments of hope. Yet my faith helps me a lot. I have a sense of calm because I do believe in the Bible when it implores: 'Thy will be done.' I guess it is the Presbyterian in me that says if it is meant to be, it is meant to be. There is something very assuring in the belief that there is a higher being and a divine plan."

Seven years later, on the eve of sending his fellow countrymen off to kill and possibly be killed, George W. Bush tried to explain to a group that belief was his beacon, not his almighty spear. "I would never justify my faith to make a difficult decision on war and peace," he told them. "I would use my faith to help guide me personally and provide the strength I need as an individual."

On March 19, 2003, seventeen months after sending troops into Afghanistan, George W. Bush again gave the order to invade a country. Later that morning, he walked with his dog Spot but otherwise alone on the circle of the South Lawn. During the past several weeks, Laura had seen him taking the very same stroll with his dog, and she knew that Iraq was what he was thinking about. ("I would say that we didn't talk about it that much, really," she would recall. "The way that we find comfort in out marriage is just by being together and our routine—getting in bed, our books and our animals around us. It's not a lot of conversation. It's much more a physical being close to each other.")

This time, he prayed as he walked. The expression he wore was not that of a believer liberated by his faith, but rather of a man burdened by his mortal journey and beseeching God for a light that was slow to shine.

9

The Grid

"Why can't we generate more electricity?" Bush demanded in the fall of 2003. "Why, after all these months, is there still just eight hours of electricity in Baghdad?"

George W. Bush, the war president, had prepared himself for a difficult war. He and his subordinates assumed that Saddam would unleash biological weapons on American troops. They anticipated that the dictator would set his oil fields aflame. They believed that he would use his citizenry as human shields. They readied allied nations in the region against the prospect of missiles or worse being launched in their direction. They braced for the likelihood of a humanitarian crisis in the wake of prolonged conflict—millions of starving refugees who would be fed and sheltered in tents across the desert. ("We spent *hours* talking about refugee flows and hunger, or what happens if Baghdad becomes a fortress," the president would recall.) And Bush resigned himself to knowing that he would soon be holding in his arms the weeping mothers of soldiers he had sent off to die in Operation Enduring Freedom.

It never once occurred to the president that he would spend much time in fretful consideration of Iraq's electrical grid. Nor did Deputy Secretary of Defense Paul Wolfowitz envision being forced to dwell on so arcane a matter. Nor did National Security Adviser Condoleezza Rice. Nor did her deputy, Steve Hadley. Nor did General David Petraeus of the 101st Airborne. That bringing electricity to Iraq would become part of each's job description seemed to fly in the face

191

of how the Bush administration perceived the land it had liberated in three shock-and-awe weeks.

Everything in the prewar intelligence made Iraq sound much more like an Arab cousin of America than like the country the U.S.-led Coalition had previously liberated, Afghanistan. Of all the Middle Eastern nations, Iraq was the most educated. Bush's three Iraqi visitors to the Oval Office in January 2003 were far from the only ones to say it: Iraq was a fertile field for democracy and a market economy. All it needed were a few well-meaning gardeners.

And so the first postinvasion wave of American manpower to Iraq, on May 9, 2003, consisted of self-styled governance specialists bent on filling the void left by Saddam with an independent judiciary, a flourishing press, a sturdy currency, and the foundation for a resilient democracy. Some of those who filed out of the C-17s at Baghdad International Airport that day were Iraqi exiles with designs on this or that ministry post. Others were young Americans undaunted by their ignorance of the region and determined to implement the president's strategic vision for Iraq.

What they amounted to was, as one of them would later observe, "a deployment of policymakers."

The president said nothing whatsoever about policymakers on May 1, 2003, when he stood aboard the USS *Abraham Lincoln*—although if he had, no one would have noticed it anyway, since the theatrics of that event would loom in the months and even years to come, long after the message of Bush's words had been forgotten.

There was a certain justice to that eventuality, since giving a speech had not been uppermost in the White House's mind. Shortly after the statue of Saddam Hussein in central Baghdad had been toppled and ceremonially pummeled by the locals, Bush declared his desire to visit the troops, perhaps at a military base, and express his appreciation. The operational details were farmed out, as always, to Joe Hagin—who, like all advance men, was at bottom a storyteller. Casting about for a logistically suitable event location that would convey a resonant message, he happened upon the *Lincoln*, an aircraft carrier that had endured a deployment at sea longer than any other vessel since the Vietnam War yet had not suffered a single fatality. The *Lincoln* had seen action during both the invasion of Afghanistan and Operation Iraqi Freedom, then had left the Gulf for Pearl Harbor, and would thereafter make its way south across the Pacific Ocean to

San Diego, where it would at last come into port on the second day of May. Hagin made his pitch to Card and Bartlett. They went for it. Only then did it occur to the communications shop to build a speech into the event.

Gerson, when he erred, erred on the side of historical weightiness. He walked into the speechwriters' office in the OEOB one morning in late April with a marked-up copy of MacArthur's 1945 address aboard the USS *Missouri* during the surrender ceremonies following the nuclear bombings of Hiroshima and Nagasaki. *Today the guns are silent. A great tragedy has ended. A great victory has been won. . . .* Powell and Rumsfeld shared few things in common, but one of them was a wariness of speechwriters' tendency to overreach for dramatic effect. Rumsfeld (and Karen Hughes, who disdained bellicosity) took a heavy pen to Gerson's initial draft, minimizing what the SecDef saw as "an implication of finality."

Still, what survived the many edits was among Bush's loftiest addresses. "Admiral Kelly, Captain Card, officers and sailors of the USS *Lincoln*, my fellow Americans," it began, "major combat operations in Iraq have ended. In the battle of Iraq, the United States and our allies have prevailed." And it ended with a biblical touch that was both light-handed and unabashedly pretentious—courtesy of speechwriter (and eventual Office of Strategic Initiatives director) Pete Wehner, to whom Gerson often turned for scripture references: *To the captives, "Come out"; and to those in darkness, "Be free."*

The speech was hardly exuberant. In sending up the cause of America's War on Terror, it acknowledged that Iraq was but a "battle" in this ongoing war ("We've removed an ally of Al Qaeda," it offhandedly stated), that "our mission continues," that there remained "difficult work to do in Iraq." Still, the victor's buoyancy was abundant. The speech evoked images of the morally unambiguous Second World War. It immortalized the "strength and kindness and goodwill" of the U.S. military. It heralded "the arrival of a new era" in which "new tactics and precision weapons" could "achieve military objectives without directing violence against civilians."

Above all, it embraced the justness of the fight in marbled yet ultimately Bushian sentiment: "In the images of celebrating Iraqis, we have also seen the ageless appeal of human freedom. Decades of lies and intimidation could not make the Iraqi people love their oppressors or desire their own enslavement. Men and women in every culture need liberty like they need food and water and air. Everywhere that freedom arrives, humanity rejoices; and everywhere that freedom stirs, let tyrants fear."

These were the words. But they became secondary the moment Joe Hagin told his boss, "You're going to have to board the carrier by air. Are you comfortable going out there on a tactical plane?"

Hagin saw a twinkle in Bush's eye. *He's gonna want to fly it*, the deputy chief of staff thought.

In the White House swimming pool, Bush and Andy Card went through the water-rescue routines, looking somewhat like addled seniors as they splashed about in their inflatable vests. The Secret Service hated the whole idea. POTUS in a dinky S-3B Viking, landing on a moving vessel in the middle of the Pacific? Jeez, why didn't they just parachute him into downtown Baghdad? And who would be piloting the S-3B? "Joe," implored one of the security boys, "you've been in meetings where the big corporate CEOs get in front of the president and get totally tongue-tied. I mean, this pilot may have all the combat experience in the world, but still . . ."

Hagin flew out ahead on a cargo plane to San Diego and met with the pilots at a naval station. They were unflappable, ice in their veins. These men weren't going to freak out about flying Bush.

"You think he might want to fly it?" one of them asked Hagin.

"I'm sure he would," he replied.

Scott Sforza flew out to the USS *Lincoln* five days before the speech. Sforza was the White House's in-house producer. A lean, bookish former protégé of ABC's Ted Koppel, Sforza's job was distinctly postmodern: to maximize the theatrical value of presidential events. He had built a pullout stage inside a train during a 2000 campaign swing. He had barged an armada of stage lights across New York Harbor so as to set the Statue of Liberty aglow behind Bush during his address on the one-year anniversary of September 11. But Sforza had never before staged an event on a moving target.

At Pearl Harbor, Sforza loaded onto the *Lincoln* crates of HMI lights from the White House communications inventory, along with the standard podium and a state-of-the-art rotary marine antenna that could lock on to a satellite signal while in motion. For the next couple of days, he and the sailors on board diagrammed where the S-3Bs would be positioned and when the aircraft platforms would be moved. Sforza tested the satellite at sea. He studied the variance of the sunlight, the glare off the ocean, and how these would be factored in to the choreography of the ship's inalterable schedule.

In the course of his labors, Sforza became quite taken with the crew. When they mentioned to the White House aide that they would like to emblazon the stage with a banner reading MISSION ACCOMPLISHED so as to send up a victorious signal to their families and Navy buddies, Sforza loved the spirit of it and was effusive in his pitch to Fleischer, Bartlett, and the others. By conference call, they mused among themselves: Could the slogan backfire? But Fleischer reminded the others that the press had been haranguing Bush to declare an end to major combat operations for weeks now. The press shop gave Sforza the green light.

Sforza had the MISSION ACCOMPLISHED banner designed by a private vendor, with a slick red-white-and-blue background. It was unfurled and pinned alongside the carrier, directly behind where the president would give his nationally televised speech on the evening of May 1.

Bush soared away from the North Island Naval Air Station that morning, headed for the aircraft carrier at sea. He wore a green flight suit and a white helmet and sat in the S-3Bs copilot seat, beside the pilot and in front of a copilot and a Secret Service agent. It wasn't long into the flight before the pilot asked Bush if he would like the joystick. He hadn't piloted since his days in the Guard.

The Viking was much more sophisticated than the planes he used to fly. He steered straight, nothing fancy. From his window he could see the accompanying S-3B. Andy Card was in the copilot's seat with the joystick in his hand. With his free hand, Card signaled a thumbs-up to Bush.

He surrendered the controls so that the pilot could land—a spectacular visual, the Viking cutting across the pale spring sky and dropping down onto the four-and-a-half-acre deck of the mighty USS *Lincoln*, with its five thousand inhabitants cheering wildly as their commander in chief stepped out of the plane with his helmet cradled under his arm, the crinkled eyes and gray-flecked hair and form-fitting flight suit summoning a Paul Newmanesque virility . . . while Hagin and Sforza gaped at this, their best event ever, and Gerson stood on deck as well, contemplating the words of the pilot who had flown him over: "All we've been eating for months and months is chicken. I swear, I'll never eat chicken again, unless it's at home or at a Hooter's."

Gerson's words would be summoned that evening, when Bush shucked his flight suit and stood behind the podium to declare the end of major combat operations and victory in "the battle of Iraq." But in the ensuing weeks and months, all of his MacArthur-channeling prose would be lost, swallowed up by those two words screaming out from behind Bush's ramrod frame. (Rumsfeld learned of the banner only after the fact and was not pleased. The final draft of the speech, he would say, "was properly calibrated. But the sign left the opposite impression, and that was unfortunate.")

Perhaps no one took it harder than Scott Sforza, who *knew the truth!* The banner—it was for the troops! And everyone was saying that the White House was announcing "mission accomplished"! When anyone could plainly see in the text, plainly hear the president say it: *We have difficult work to do in Iraq.*

And anyway, no one in the media bothered to call Sforza and find out what the facts were. This was what so galled him. Because Sforza had worked with the great ones, Koppel and Brinkley and Roone Arledge, back in the day when reporters weren't hired just for their looks. It was quite a somber epiphany for the man who had spent the past week adjusting lights and divining camera angles and dressing up crew members in matching colors. . . .

The media—they just don't pay attention to facts the way they used to.

Amid all the flourish and braggadocio, one plain, factual line in the very first paragraph of the speech escaped comment: "And now our Coalition is engaged in securing and reconstructing that country."

Securing and reconstructing Iraq was now the mission. To the Iraqis, who had seen America vanquish Saddam's heralded army in three short weeks, this new mission would surely be accomplished with similar dispatch.

And so they waited throughout the year of Saddam's defeat. And they waited the following year. And the year after that. And the year after that.

Robyn McGuckin was a USAID worker with a master's degree in agricultural engineering. Randall Richardson was a lieutenant colonel in the Army with a civil engineering background. Stephen Browning was an Army Corps of Engineers officer who had led the Corps' Urban Search and Rescue operations at Ground Zero after 9/11. Nick Horne was a British computer nerd who happened to be working in Jordan during the invasion of Iraq and took a taxi down to Baghdad after the war was over, looking for a job.

These four men and women who spearheaded the reconstruction of

Iraq's electricity grid did not have an electrical engineering degree among them. Yet they were of sufficient technical knowledge to comprehend what they saw as they toured the sector in the late spring of 2003.

It was a disaster. Every power substation had been plundered. Doorknobs, light fixtures, furniture, windows—gone. All the wires had been yanked out of the walls. As jarring as the spectacle was, the reconstruction team wasn't thoroughly surprised. All around the world, TV viewers had watched as looters raided Iraq's national museum. Seventeen ministry buildings had been torched. Hospitals had been stripped of their mattresses. As Rumsfeld had observed with characteristic equanimity, "Freedom's untidy, and free people are free to make mistakes and commit crimes and do bad things."

But *untidy* was too merciful a term for the state of Iraq's power plants. They were literally held together with duct tape and baling wire. Mismatched parts dangled haphazardly. Such plants always required scheduled maintenances, but obviously war had prevented a maintenance period for the spring. What the reconstruction team saw, however, were plants that hadn't been serviced for years. For the most part, the electrical generators hadn't had any maintenance since 1993 except when they broke down. The team mordantly wondered aloud: *And the Coalition thought they were doing us a FAVOR not targeting the infrastructure?*

The country's plants were operating at only 40 percent of installed capacity. Whole swaths of Iraq were getting little or no electricity—partly as Saddam's means of punishing particular factions, but also as a crude rationing policy. *Shit*, thought Randy Richardson as he eyeballed the rickety and primitive assemblages. *It's a miracle they've got power here at all.*

Word of Iraq's pathetic electrical grid made its way up to Washington. Rice and Hadley were speechless. Who knew?

Yet these things were knowable. War planners were well aware that Iraq's power stations had been targeted to devastating effect during the first Gulf War. Every major station had been hit. In the intervening twelve years, UN sanctions had kept spare parts and technical assistance out of the country. Any engineer could, if asked, have deduced what effect this would have on even a highly modernized generating system. And any military tactician could, if asked, have predicted that Saddam would do as he did on the eve of war—namely, ratchet up Iraq's military-industrial machine, which would only further strain the power grid. (Three significant boilers exploded as a result.)

The CIA had largely failed at embedding agents in Saddam's regime. But covert action wasn't required to determine the woeful state of electricity in Iraq. They didn't need spies; just interviewing the UN Development Program officials would've told them that infrastructure supplies hadn't made it across the border in years. Nor did they need secret documents—only an Iraqi newspaper, with its daily publishing of scheduled blackouts throughout the nation.

The Defense Intelligence Agency—which was, of course, under Rumsfeld's aegis—in fact produced reams of infrastructure-related analysis for the Joint Warfare Analysis Center. That agency in turn furnished a technical model to Central Command so that Tommy Franks's bombers could target select units of Iraq's electrical grid without doing lasting damage. That same intelligence spelled out with "exquisite understanding" (as one top-level analyst put it) the frailties in Iraq's power supply. But CENTCOM was focused on storming Baghdad, not restoring electrical lines. The thought apparently never occurred to anyone in the Pentagon that the DIA's infrastructure data might be useful after Baghdad fell.

The State Department had in fact looked into the matter of Iraq's infrastructure when one of its officials, Tom Warrick, oversaw the Future of Iraq Project throughout the latter part of 2002 and early 2003. One of the project's subcommittees focused on electricity. Its numbers were way off, it outlined no strategy, and when Warrick himself briefed an NSC executive steering group on the topic, his droning presentation made no mention whatsoever of the grid's state of disrepair.

Nonetheless, the Future of Iraq report correctly speculated that demand for electricity in Iraq already greatly exceeded supply, and that the costs for meeting demand would run into the billions. No other document containing those forecasts was circulating. At a postwar planning session at Fort McNair, in Washington, D.C., a month before the invasion, Tom Warrick was on hand to lend his expertise. This delighted retired Lt. General Jay Garner, whom Rumsfeld had selected to oversee the Office for Reconstruction and Humanitarian Assistance in Iraq. Stephen Browning, who would advise several of the Iraqi ministries, gravitated to Warrick during the first day of the "rock drill" (so named to reflect the goal of leaving no stone unturned).

Later, Garner pulled Browning aside. The general looked rather sour as he recited orders he'd just been given from the Pentagon. "We are not supposed to engage with the State Department in general, and Tom Warrick in particular," Garner informed Browning.

So Browning and the rest arrived in Iraq thoroughly unprepared for what they now faced. Frantically, they began to pull documents off the Internet.

Things were a mess but all was not lost by May 12, 2003, when Ambassador Lewis Paul Bremer III rode into Baghdad on a red carpet of self-regard as "the president's man." In fact, it was difficult to say just whose man the head of the Coalition Provisional Authority was. Rumsfeld told Bremer that he was Bush's hand-picked envoy to Iraq. Bush later told Jay Garner that it was Rumsfeld who had picked Garner's replacement. Rumsfeld would insist to reporter Bob Woodward that former Secretary of State George Shultz had offered up Bremer's name, while Shultz would assert to Woodward that this was not so.

As it would develop, Bremer was Bremer's man—ignoring the NSC and State, scorning the Army command in Baghdad, checking in now and then with the Pentagon, and grabbing face time with the president whenever possible . . . but as much his own boss as a federal employee could be. There was a determined optimism to the man, and to his young American subordinates. He worked like a dog, and his ambitions for the Iraqi people were perhaps greater than those that they had for themselves. In this desert he saw the makings of a democratic oasis. And in himself Jerry (as his friends called him) Bremer seemed to see a touch of Douglas MacArthur. No one, not even those who found him arrogant and micromanagerial, questioned his fearlessness.

Bremer's first edict directed at the electricity sector was to promote "equalization"—meaning, to spread out the power supply across the country more equitably. It was a shrewd way of currying favor with Shiites in the south and Kurds in the north, whom Saddam had kept literally in the dark for years, and whom Bremer now wanted to buy into the nascent Iraq Governing Council. It also allowed Bremer to sidestep the somber issue of Iraq's power supply. Now he could, and repeatedly would, claim that under the provisional government, "more Iraqis were receiving electricity" than ever before . . . which was not the same thing as there being more electricity in Iraq.

"This is a huge mistake," Stephen Browning warned Bremer. In recognizing that the electricity grid was the most ominous of all the postwar challenges, Bremer had relieved Browning from his advisory responsibilities to the health, transportation, and communications sectors. Now Browning was to devote all his attention to electricity.

And so Bremer's new electricity adviser had this to say about equalization: "The battle of Iraq is going to be fought in Baghdad. It's the center of everything. If you cut their power in half by giving it to the rural areas, you'll lose the center of mass."

Bremer heard him out. Then he said, "It's too late to change it now."

He's not going to say he made a mistake, Browning thought.

Nor was Bremer going to say that equalization was merely, as they would say back at the White House, "aspirational." In fact, the generators were far too unreliable to provide regularly scheduled service anyway. And even when ordered to transfer power from one region to another, Ministry of Electricity employees routinely accepted bribes—or acquiesced at gunpoint—to keep the juice flowing. The CPA never issued a single report to determine whether the substations were doing as Bremer had ordered. Equalization worked—but only as a communications strategy. It was something nice to tell the Kurds and the Shiites, and the folks back home . . . until the Baghdad-centric media went nuts over the city's severely diminished power supply, ultimately forcing Bremer to reverse policy in 2004.

By the time of Bremer's arrival in May, Iraq was generating 2,200–2,800 megawatts of power a day, according to his advisers' estimates. Bremer's goal was to restore Iraq's electricity to prewar levels. He dispatched Garner's electricity adviser, Peter Gibson—a well-meaning but profoundly overmatched Army Corps of Engineers official—to discuss this matter with the electricity team.

"What's the strategy?" Nick Horne asked Gibson.

"There isn't one," Gibson admitted.

Stephen Browning asked the same question and received the same answer. "I don't understand this, Pete," he said. "You've made a promise to Ambassador Bremer that you'll increase power to prewar levels—and *you've got no plan?* Where's your budget for this?"

Gibson said that he had no budget, either.

Browning and Horne informed Bremer that despite his stated intention to generate more power, it wasn't going to happen, because there simply wasn't a plan for doing so. Incredulous, Bremer stammered, "That's totally unacceptable."

Bremer went to USAID workers Robyn McGuckin and Dick Dumford. Restoring electricity to prewar levels was the highest priority, he told them. Assuming that they had all the money and staff they needed, how quickly could they meet that goal? McGuckin and Dumford saw this as some kind of figurative "blue sky" exercise. Surely Bremer wasn't going to take their estimates as gospel.

Browning, Horne, McGuckin, Dumford, Randy Richardson, and a few others convened a conference at the convention center across the street from Al Rashid Hotel. Every plant manager in Iraq showed up. Most of them had never met before, though they'd faced many of the same problems for years—not only medieval equipment, but also the stress of complying with the dictates of Saddam, who never hesitated to send his goons over to a plant if an outage occurred in one of his favored regions.

For two days the managers sat and listed both the spare parts they needed and the ones they didn't but had anyway. The United Nations Development Programme officials rattled off the parts stored in Jordan, Turkey, and Syria. The Iraqi engineers sketched out each's respective plant from memory. They estimated how much power they'd been able to produce at peak periods and for how many hours. For Stephen Browning, whom Bremer had appointed senior adviser to the Ministry of Electricity, it was like watching an elephant attempt to pick up a safety pin with its trunk. But the conference was enormously useful, and from it, Robyn McGuckin and Dick Dumford were able to produce a kind of master plan, which Browning then walked over to Jerry Bremer.

"We need to put a goal out there and execute it," the CPA envoy said.

"I think we can get to 4,200 megawatts of power generation by the end of September," said Browning.

"Is that the best you can do?"

Well, confessed Browning, the prewar level was 4,400 megawatts. But he hated to advertise that number. Browning regarded 4,400 as a "stretch goal."

The next day, Bremer's office announced that Iraq would be served with 4,400 megawatts of electricity by October 1, 2003.

The 4400 Project, as it came to be known, resembled a playoff game in which a team facing elimination pulls out all the stops—keeping its best athletes on the field from beginning to end, hosing them down and numbing them with painkillers, throwing the entire playbook at the opposition—without any real hope for sustaining the effort beyond this single contest. But Bremer and the White House didn't believe they had a choice in the matter. By midsummer 2003, no one would have thought to unfurl a banner declaring "mission accomplished." Saddam's legendary weapons of mass destruction hadn't been located. The dictator himself remained at large (though his two malevolent sons, Uday and Qusay, had been gunned down by U.S. troops in Mosul on July 22). No Hamid Karzai–like unifying presence had emerged from the fractured country. Instead, the American-led Coalition had attempted to fill the void. Springtime's liberators had become an occupying force—one still under attack by shape-shifting pockets of foes who wore no uniform and fought with crude explosive devices rather than missiles. Postwar Iraq was becoming an increasingly dangerous and dysfunctional place. Good news was hard to come by. Bush's goal—"securing and reconstructing that country"—was far easier said than done, if it would be done at all.

A victory was badly needed.

The electricity team couldn't believe that Bremer was foisting this crazy goal on them with less than two months to pull it off. Why the hell hadn't he and Garner taken the problem seriously sooner? From June to August, a total of six hundred transmission towers had been bombed to the ground by thieves who then proceeded to dig up the transmission lines with back hoes, melt them down, and sell the metal across the border in Iran. (The trafficking became so brisk that the region saw a distinct dip in the market price of copper and aluminum.) Much of the transmission-line looting took place in the south, in a region governed by British forces. The Brits had rules of engagement that bordered on pacifism. They weren't cops; they weren't here to shoot civilians. And so a vandal could walk right past them with an armload of stolen goods, and unless he opened fire, the Brits would not stand in the way.

When informed of all the looting, Bremer invariably replied, *Security's not my area. Go talk to General Sanchez.* Bremer was stating a fact. Another fact was this: The looting during this period would double, perhaps even triple, the cost of rebuilding Iraq's power sector.

Still, the ambassador had laid down the law. They had to get to 4,400 megawatts by October 1. And so the race was on. Every military unit in Iraq surrendered two engineers to the project. Iraq's Oil for Food coffers were raided to pay for new equipment. A $200 million

GE generator was convoyed into the country under the kind of heavy guard reserved for heads of state, since all it would take was one well-placed bullet to destroy its frail circuitry. Parts flowed in from across the borders. When the part for one particularly antiquated plant couldn't be found among the inventory, the sector's main contractor, Bechtel, did some research and at last located a replacement—in a vacuum-tube museum.

"We're going to see peaks and valleys," Browning reminded Bremer, who seemed to understand that the power supply would not follow an orderly trajectory. There would be scheduled shutdowns as parts were installed. There would be lootings and human bungles. This was Iraq. The ambassador maybe hadn't gotten it when he first rolled into town. But three months into the mission, he got it now.

It was the White House that didn't get it. During the weekly secure video teleconferences, Browning and Bremer were hammered by Rice, Hadley, and others: *Why is the power going down, not up?* And there was always a reason, albeit an aggravating one. There'd been a fire at the thermal plant near Basra. Or a malfunction at the Mosul dam. A substation manager had thrown the switch at the wrong time, causing a regional blackout. The transmission lines from Basra to Baghdad had been cut again—whether by common looters, or by tribal powers who wanted to keep the electricity in the south, or by some more malevolent force seeking to create instability wherever it could. . . .

What the CPA team didn't get was that the president had become engaged.

"I want to know what's happening with the electricity," Bush asked Andy Card.

The chief of staff didn't quite finish the explanation.

"What do you *mean*, they took down another tower!"

Each plant pushed and pushed. It took the perky can-doers of the CPA a while to adjust to the work habits of the Ministry of Electricity's employees. (And to round them up. The first deployment of Americans arrived to find all the ministries "totally gutted," as one of them would recall. "We were literally out on the streets collecting people, saying, 'Hey, did you used to work in this building? Who was your supervisor?' ") There were about thirty-eight thousand of them on the ministry's payroll. Many of these people never materialized. Some of them were dead and their paychecks had been collected by relatives for years. The majority of those who did show up for work spent their days quietly drinking tea. Under Saddam's reign, government workers received a salary simply for being there. To do actual work, bonuses were supplied. Ministry employees accepted bribes without the slightest shame.

Despite what the three Iraqi exiles suggested to Bush in the Oval Office in January 2003, Iraq was not a country hardwired for entrepreneurship, but rather a socialist nation. A major from the First Marine Division named Ben Connable wrote a widely circulated analysis of the cultural divide separating the liberators from the liberated. Its title: *Marines Are From Mars, Iraqis Are From Venus.*

Stephen Browning distrusted such stereotypes. Many of his coworkers in the CPA—even those he regarded as political hacks, of which there were several—were well intentioned. But it ill served their mission to view Iraq's needs through the rosy prism of the American experience. Revolutionizing the Iraqi stock exchange, publishing a glossy monthly magazine that lavishly propagandized the "new Iraq," funding a nonsmoking campaign . . . *Iraqis didn't give a damn about these things.*

But Browning had discovered a way to make Iraqis give a damn about the 4400 Project. Appealing to their sense of pride, he realized, yielded extraordinary results. Bremer's electricity czar urged the plant managers, who in turn urged their ministry employees, to see the project as something to benefit their families, their communities, and their nation. Every evening around midnight, while Dick Dumford put together the power accumulations to send over to Washington, the men at the plants cheered the numbers they'd generated that day.

On October 9, CPA administrator Bremer convened a press conference in Baghdad. "Six months ago," he announced with barely contained glee, "the entire country of Iraq could generate a bare 300 megawatts of electricity. Monday, October 6, power generation hit 4,518 megawatts, exceeding the prewar average."

It being that kind of a day, Bremer permitted himself a reckless boast: "If we get the funding that the president has requested in his emergency budget," he said, "we expect to produce enough electricity for all Iraqis to have electrical service twenty-four hours daily— something essential to their hopes for the future."

Later, the Coalition put more conservative numbers to Bremer's pledge. By June 2004, Iraq would supply 6,000 megawatts of electrical power—provided Congress gave Bush the $18.4 billion emergency funding he had requested to spur the reconstruction of Iraq.

The money came. But the 6,000 megawatts never did.

Not by June 2004.
Or by 2005.
Or 2006.
Or 2007.

Bremer disdained what he called the micromanagerial "8,000-mile screwdriver" that Washington kept thrusting into his eighteen-to-twenty-hour days of audible calling. The man in the White House who wielded that screwdriver was Frank Miller.

Miller was neither an engineer nor a technician. He'd spent the better part of three decades immersed in national security policymaking. Miller had served seven secretaries of defense. He considered himself a protégé of the first Bush's SecDef, Dick Cheney. Miller's official title by 2003 was Special Assistant to the President and Senior Adviser for Defense Policy and Arms Control on the National Security Policy—Washington gobbledygook that essentially meant: *Monster Portfolio.* Though his expertise lay in nuclear-proliferation issues, Miller was the kind of bureaucratic zen master whose skill sets were easily transferrable to whatever the task force or interagency group du jour happened to be. His coolheadedness was evidenced on September 11, 2001, when Miller commanded the White House Situation Room throughout the day while his superiors remained in the bunker.

People with Frank Miller's platinum-status résumé weren't supposed to be spending their time obsessing over Iraq's power supply. The last time someone at the NSC had freelanced so extensively in another nation's internal affairs was in 1986, when Oliver North was running guns to Iran and then funneling the profits to Nicaragua's Contras. Miller wasn't playing cowboy—he was promoting established policy, not inventing a new one as North had. Still, his reluctant, somewhat desperate micromanagement of the Coalition's reconstruction effort ran counter to both NSC history and Bush's Harvard MBA playbook.

To get from 4,400 megawatts to 6,000, Miller figured there was an obvious solution: increasing Iraq's power-generation capability. Bechtel, the recipient of a $1 billion contract in September, was installing new gas turbines and rehabbing old plants all over Iraq. A ninety-person Army Corps of Engineers task force dropped down into Baghdad to assist. Of Bush's $18.4 billion supplemental request, the biggest chunk, $5.6 billion, went to the electricity sector. The Republican administration was doing what the GOP frequently accused

Democrats of—"throwing money at the problem"—and it wasn't even a domestic problem.

Why, then, with all this money and all this new generating capacity, are we still showing only 4,400 goddamn megawatts? Miller wondered.

The answers seemed calculated to flummox a forward-leaning White House. After reaching Bremer's stated goal on October 5, the plants underwent their scheduled maintenance, causing the power supply to plummet. To keep the grid from cratering would require more such shutdowns, not fewer. In other words: The 4400 Project had been but a brief fireworks display—an illusion, an empty campaign boast.

But that wasn't the worst of it. Iraq's plants ran largely on light fuels. It never occurred to anyone at the White House, including Frank Miller, that this might be an issue. After all, didn't Iraq possess the world's second-largest supply of oil? The problem (which, of course, the prewar intellligence had failed to reveal) was that the refineries were as wretched as the power plants. Crude oil was therefore in abundance, while refined fuel was scarce—even more so after the war, when a pent-up demand for automobiles in Iraq resulted in hordes of self-styled used-car dealers heading across the unsecured borders. In a year's time, *one million* more autos materialized in Iraq. Suddenly, the country experienced an intense gas shortage. With no small measure of chagrin—since Wolfowitz and others had claimed that Iraq could pay for its reconstruction through its immense petroleum reserves—the Coalition began to spend $250 million a month importing oil from Kuwait and Turkey.

Can't generate more power because we're spending all this money to SHUT THE PLANTS DOWN?! Can't fuel the plants because there's NOT ENOUGH OIL IN IRAQ?!

Miller dreaded facing these questions.

He received daily color-coded charts from the electricity team in Baghdad. The cities listed in green received more than twelve hours of power daily; those in yellow, eight to twelve hours; those in red, less than eight hours. Showing the charts to Hadley and Rice—who in turn passed them on to Bush—was not the happiest part of Miller's day.

Scowling at the chart, Rice told Miller, "This is unacceptable."

Miller didn't disagree.

The Coalition continued to scratch around for electrical power wherever it could be found. Bush 41's old chief of staff, John Sununu, had formed a consulting firm and was looking to run a transmission line from Kuwait to supply 200 megawatts of power to Khor az-Zubayr in southern Iraq. Relishing their upper hand, the Kuwaiti royalty insisted on an obnoxiously high tariff. Sununu's deal never came to fruition.

The Turks were willing to tie in and provide 170 megawatts—though not before trying to jack up the price at the last minute. The power from the southern Turkish town of Silopi would benefit only Kurdistan, which was already green on Miller's chart. *But hell*, he thought, *we'll take it wherever we can get it.*

That meant doing business with two nations that had hostile relations to the United States: Syria and Iran. Both countries had long been supplying power to Iraq under Saddam's regime. In the months after the statue of Saddam was toppled, visiting congressmen would invariably ask a member of the electricity team, "We're not still doing business with Iran or Syria, are we?"

To which Randy Richardson had the correct reply: "Sir, we have no formal contract with either nation."

Instead, they had gentlemen's agreements. With Iran, the quiet negotiations began in 2003; the intertie became operational late the following year. And on September 3, 2003, several Syrian officials were airlifted by Black Hawk helicopters into Mosul to formalize an agreement whereby that city would be supplied with about 70 megawatts of power in exchange for barrels of crude oil. An elaborate signing ceremony took place in a restaurant along the Tigris River. Before it did, however, the Syrians also tried to welch on the terms of the agreement.

The resourceful commander of the 101st Airborne, Major General David Petraeus, put an end to the haggling. "Look, we're already getting the electricity from you," he said. "Now, I'm gonna turn on the oil. You can let it run into the sand for all I care."

From Washington, Miller, Rice, and Hadley watched glumly as George W. Bush's stark line in the sand—*We will make no distinction between the terrorists and those that harbor them*—went ablur. For the sake of Iraq's power grid, America was now doing business with state sponsors of terror.

Or trying to, at least. USAID had ordered a massive Siemens generator that was shipped into Jordan, where it would commence a tortuous overland journey into Iraq. That was the plan. But it was stymied at a bridge dam near the Syrian border. The generator was too heavy to allow passage, Syrian officials insisted.

"What the hell's going on?" Miller demanded over the phone to AID officials.

They replied that Bechtel was negotiating with the Syrians.

Weeks passed. "Break it down and send it across piece by piece," snapped Miller.

Can't be done, was the reply.

The generator sat in the desert for a few more weeks.

"Just order a new one and send it by boat upriver," Miller suggested.

That wasn't possible, either.

Frank Miller was about to explode. During this saga, U.S. Ambassador to Iraq John Negroponte happened to be visiting Washington. He found Miller and Hadley in the Sit Room.

"Frank," Negroponte said, not without sympathy, "why are you in the White House focusing on some goddamn lousy generator? You're way too senior to be looking at this."

"It's not the generator," Miller snapped. "The generator's the tip of the iceberg. Haven't you heard the word on the street? *These guys can go to the moon. If they wanted to, they could give us electricity.*"

The Siemens generator arrived at its destination in Iraq two years later.

One day in the fall of 2003, an official at General Electric, Nancy Dorn, called Miller. "We're going to have to pull our team out of Baghdad," she said. "We're getting nothing done."

"Why?" asked Miller, though he could guess.

"The chief contractors and the guys running the mixing trucks live on one side of Baghdad," said Dorn, "and they're tired of getting shot at on their way to the site on the other side of Baghdad."

Miller had an idea: "Why don't we throw up some tents—have them live on site?" he suggested.

Dorn agreed to the fix, and GE's workers returned to their project. Still, a fix is all it was. It was far from a solution to the one X-factor bedeviling not only the electricity effort but every other postwar activity.

Iraq, well after Bush declared major combat operations completed, remained a war zone.

That thudding reality did not hit home until August 19, 2003, when a truck bomb blasted a hole in Baghdad's UN headquarters, leaving seventeen dead. Earlier that month, bombs had ripped through the Jordanian embassy and water and oil pipelines. The perpetrators were not looters or Baathist dead-enders as before. They were guerrilla cells—many of them streaming in from across the borders, some bearing ties to Al Qaeda.

The face of this burgeoning threat was far from distinct. After a who-is-the-enemy briefing by the CIA in the West Wing, Cheney wryly turned to a fellow participant and said, "You just heard: We don't have any idea."

As Bush would later acknowledge, "The idea of [Al Qaeda lieutenant Abu Musab Al-] Zarqawi fomenting sectarian violence—he was successful in doing that, which is something we didn't spend a lot of time planning for. We planned for what happens if Saddam and his people dug into Baghdad."

Of course, in meetings such as the January 10, 2003, Oval Office session with the three Iraqi exiles, what Bush had been told was that the source of sectarian strife was Saddam Hussein—which, he would say, made perfect sense to him: "Absolutely, in order to create a sense of need for a strong central state and to keep people off balance." Bush therefore believed that taking out Saddam, "and the idea of people being in a position to kind of be free, the universality-of-freedom concept," would minimize any possibility of postwar violence in Iraq. Instead, as Rumsfeld would later observe, "You end up with 25–28 million Iraqis who are liberated from Saddam's oppressive regime—and in the process you take away the mechanism that was maintaining order through repression."

He nonetheless remained undaunted by this new development. In a brief press availability in the Roosevelt Room after announcing his global AIDS initiative, Bush took a question on the signs of disquiet in Iraq. "There are some who feel like that the conditions are such that they can attack us there," Bush said. "My answer is, bring 'em on. We've got the force necessary to deal with the security situation."

Ari Fleischer anxiously sidled up to Bush after the event. "Mr. President," he beseeched, "can you imagine how that would sound to a mother who just lost her son in Iraq?"

The president hadn't thought of that. "I was just trying to express my confidence in our military," he said.

The military needed more than Bush's confidence. Signs of a growing insurgency had appeared as far back as early April, just after Saddam's statue fell. The electricity team could see the wave of violence gather intensity. Transmission-tower sabotages were becoming more cunning and deadly. Ministry of Electricity workers were increasingly threatened: a station manager kidnapped for months, another manager shot dead on the front steps of his home. Convoys carrying spare parts were falling prey to ambushes en route to the power plants.

Nonetheless, the period between April and August 2003 had been one of relative calm. And, to a person, the electricity team would look back wistfully at that four-month window of opportunity when, instead of quick fixes to achieve an illusory triumph of 4,400 megawatts, lasting changes to the grid could've been accomplished. Durable steam turbines could have replaced the combustion turbines fueled by diesel. The power plants could have been retrofitted to run on natural gas. That long-voiced sentiment in fact had a friend in high places—Bob Zoellick, the U.S. trade representative, who would argue the case for natural gas to the NSC in 2004. Everyone in the Situation Room loved Zoellick's idea—until they learned that the retrofitting would take two or more years. The White House needed a solution *now*.

And so there was no solution at all.

The lootings and violence got worse and worse. Bremer voiced his concerns separately to Bush and Rumsfeld in the fall of 2003: *We're making a mistake if we think the police we're training are going to be ready by the spring*. They weren't ready, as the CPA envoy had warned, and by the spring of 2004, contractors were ordering their employees not to show up at work. That April, a generator bound for Basra suffered a month-long delivery delay by barging it across the Gulf rather than the direct overland route through Najaf, where the convoy units feared they would be waylaid by extremists. A month later, a Russian craftsman was shot to death and two others were kidnapped outside a Baghdad power plant.

Seeing a major fiasco on their hands, CPA and USAID proceeded to divert over a fifth of the electricity sector's $5.6 billion to pay for protection. Much of the money went to reconstituting Saddam's old Electrical Power Security Service under the auspices of the Ministry of Electricity. But the EPSS proved to be suspiciously ineffectual. Its commanding officer, despite his modest salary, drove a shiny BMW that he proudly parked in front of the ministry building.

They also resorted to bribery. The oft-looted transmission lines ran through remote desert lands controlled by tribes that had been paid handsomely by Saddam for their loyalty. The CPA tried the same approach. Bechtel put tribal leaders on their payroll as "consultants." Coalition forces bought off sheiks with cash—until the lootings continued and a new Iraqi would show up with hand outstretched, claiming that *he* in fact was the sheik.

Every time Stephen Browning met with Bremer to discuss the foundering electricity effort, the subject inevitably returned to the hazards out in the field. "We simply don't have enough troops on the ground," Browning would say, over and over. Occasionally, Bremer would murmur his agreement—though adding, as any good soldier would, that they had a mission to perform regardless.

In fact, Bremer had been worried about the eroding security situation for some time. "I'd never say this publicly," Bremer had confided to one of his top aides all the way back in the summer of 2003. "But we need more troops."

Not only did he never say it publicly: On July 20, 2003, Bremer went on *Meet the Press* and stated the opposite point of view: "I think the military commanders are confident we have enough troops on the ground, and I accept that analysis."

Those commanders had not been consulted by Bremer when he issued Coalition Provisional Authority Number One on May 23, 2003, which disbanded the entire Iraqi military. Nor, for that matter, had the president. ("Well, the policy was to keep the army intact," Bush later said, adding, "Didn't happen.") The White House had assumed that half of the three hundred thousand troops needed to occupy postwar Iraq would be home-grown. Bush himself had signed off on this assumption following a briefing on this subject a week before the invasion. But Bremer learned, on his arrival, that the Iraqi military had (as Hadley would elegantly put it) "melted away" anyway. They had not reported to their barracks as ordered. Then again, there were no barracks to report to—the buildings had been destroyed by looters.

More worrisome to Bremer and the White House were widespread fears among Shiites that the Americans had cooked up a deal with the Sunnis to return them to power. Signs of a possible Shiite uprising could collapse every postwar arrangement. "Iraq is on a knife edge," Steve Hadley told Mike Gerson in April. The CPA administrator therefore felt it necessary to demonstrate a commitment to a new Iraq. And so rather than attempt to reconstitute the Iraqi military, he formally disbanded it. The White House permitted Bremer to do so. No one—Rice, Hadley, Cheney, Rumsfeld, or Powell—

contacted the president and said, *Maybe we should consider calling the Iraqi soldiers back.*

This and CPA Order Number Two, purging the four upper strata of Baathists from public-sector employment, amounted to total reversals of Bush-approved policy and were met with horror by the electricity team. *Surely Bremer's not that stupid,* thought Nick Horne. Browning and others in the CPA voiced their objections to Bremer. "This isn't open for discussion," the ambassador said flatly. "Your job is to execute."

Bremer knew that his infrastructure team had come to rely on senior civil servants from the Baathist regime. Exceptions would be made, he promised. Bremer would later insist that his two orders were wildly popular among Iraqis. The electricity team saw nothing but strong sentiment to the contrary. It was bad enough that the reconstruction efforts couldn't move forward without the kind of additional troop strength that a reconstituted Iraqi army could have brought. The more profound injury was to the Coalition's image among Iraqis. The U.S. military had dropped thousands of leaflets promising the Iraqi army that they would remain employed after the invasion. Now those former soldiers—hundreds of thousands of them—were unemployed, armed, and angry. It was, Stephen Browning and others on the electricity team thought, not exactly a recipe for stability.

And it was of a piece with Iraq's growing suspicion of its liberators. Even CPA members not involved in the electricity sector heard the common refrain: *If you really wanted to give us more electricity, you could.* That the streets of Baghdad did not erupt in riots over the glacial pace of the reconstruction could perhaps be interpreted as a vote of confidence in the Coalition. Most, however, viewed it as evidence of a corrosive cynicism. "You're such bad occupiers," one of Bremer's lieutenants, Meghan O'Sullivan, frequently heard Iraqis say. O'Sullivan had to agree. Back in Washington, Frank Miller and Steve Hadley could only shake their heads. The White House and Congress had thrown billions of dollars into the electricity sector. (Though due in large part to convoluted federal regulations on contracting, of the $18.4 billion appropriated for Iraq, only $400 million—$265 million on security and the rest on reconstruction—had actually been spent by the time Bremer's team left Baghdad in June 2004.) And yet by the fall of 2006, Iraq's power supply would hover at 4,800 megawatts—barely more than the prewar level of 4,400, and far short of Bremer's goal of

6,000 megawatts by 2004. It made no sense to Miller and Hadley. Neither man could muster an explanation.

And the Iraqis had long since stopped waiting for one. By 2004, they were taking matters into their own hands. Some bribed Ministry of Electricity workers into supplying them with power. Others managed to pirate some juice by tying bricks to electrical wires and heaving them over power lines. The ones with money bought portable generators—which ran on diesel, which exacerbated the fuel shortage, which diminished the national power supply. . . .

10

THANKSGIVING

"Do you still want to go?" Andy Card asked the president on the evening of October 16, 2003.

"Yeah, I want to do it," said Bush.

They were on Air Force One, bound for Tokyo. The chief of staff left the president and sat beside his deputy, Joe Hagin. "The president wants to go to Baghdad," Card told him.

Hagin spent most of the long flight contemplating the logistics. *If they know we're coming, they're going to take a shot at us*, he thought. *Thanksgiving's when we ought to do it. The press'll be relaxed—they won't expect it. And it'll be easier to sneak him out of Crawford.*

Condi Rice was also on board for the trip to Asia. Hagin ran his idea by her, Card, and the boss. On the flight back, he discussed it with the pilot of Air Force One. "You could do it, from Andrews," the pilot said, "but not Crawford." Which wasn't what Hagin wanted to hear—but, as an old advance man, he was accustomed to obstacles.

Over the coming days, Hagin would write a scenario on a notepad, then draw an arrow: *If we do this, who has to know we're doing it?* The less it got out, the better—and it was amazing, really, how few needed to be in the loop. The director of the military office. The Secret Service agent in charge of the detail, his deputy, and their two bosses. The director of advance, Greg Jenkins. Lt. Colonel Greg Huffman, who would accompany Jenkins on the advance trip to Baghdad. The air crew. For weeks, no one else would have a clue.

On a flight to London about ten days before the secret trip, Hagin found himself standing next to Bush in the hall of Air Force One. The president edged closer to him. "Are we really gonna be able to do this?" he asked.

Bush's voice was freighted with concern. Was this a dumb idea that could trigger a crisis? Would the troops be endangered by his visit?

Hagin himself began to have doubts. But he didn't voice them.

Thanksgiving meant that most of the White House's A team would be on vacation. Hagin didn't think it was worth the risk to tell them, *Uh, look, don't make any plans for the holidays, okay?* In Crawford on the morning of Wednesday, November 26, Hagin individually brought deputy trip director Steve Atkiss, deputy White House photographer Tina Hager, and deputy press secretary Claire Buchan into his double-wide trailer to clue them in.

Hager thought she was going to be fired. She was relieved when Hagin instead said quietly, "You have to swear to me that you won't breathe a word of this to anybody, because all of our lives depend on it."

Atkiss managed to suppress a groan when Hagin informed him, "You can't cancel any plans. You can't call anyone." He'd been invited to a turkey dinner at his girlfriend's parents' house in Dallas. (The following evening, Atkiss would hear her holiday message on his voice mail: *You asshole! The least you could've done was call!*)

Hagin summoned Buchan only after she had just finished telling the press at the morning briefing, "The president will be spending Thanksgiving at his ranch here in Crawford, Texas. . . . Menu will be a traditional Thanksgiving dinner, including free range turkey, turkey cornbread dressing, chipotle sweet potatoes, mash potatoes, asparagus, Texas grapefruit, toasted walnuts, and green salad—that's all one item—pumpkin pie, and Prairie Chapel pecan pie made with pecans from the president's ranch."

By midday, Bartlett showed up in Crawford and pulled *Washington Post* writer Mike Allen aside, while Hagin did the same with Bloomberg's Dick Keil. The latter had brought along his black pug, Buddyroo. *Jesus, a dog! You plan for weeks, you think you've thought of everything. . . . Shit!* Keil assured Hagin that he'd leave the dog with someone, make up a story about a sick relative in Dallas.

Atkiss informed the five press photographers. Each of them was skilled at perpetrating gags and was certain that this was a setup. Only when Bartlett and Blake Gottesman (Logan Walters's replacement as Bush's personal aide) drove up with Hagin in the back alley of a Waco hotel and told the photographers to get in did a collective expression of *holy shit* cross their faces.

At the ranch, Bush and Rice climbed into the back of a red SUV driven by a Secret Service agent. The president wore a windbreaker and a baseball cap. The agents who waved the SUV through the gate didn't notice who he was. On Interstate 35, the vehicle got stuck in traffic, and Rice laughed at her boss, who hated any kind of waiting but hadn't experienced an actual traffic jam since he had first been assigned Secret Service detail back in 1999.

They boarded Air Force One. On the flight to Andrews Air Force Base, Bush scribbled a draft of the remarks he would make in Baghdad, with Bartlett and Rice and Hagin offering a few suggestions. After finishing a page, Bush handed it to Gottesman, who typed and printed it out. After two edits, Bush pronounced it a speech. A few minutes later, they landed at Andrews, where they picked up a Fox TV crew.

The flight was timed to land Bush in Baghdad around dusk, when the unmistakable billboard that was Air Force One would be at least partially obscured. Somewhere approaching the coast of England, the pilot crew picked up a conversation from the air traffic control center. A German airliner with a British pilot had spotted them in the sky.

"Is that Air Force One?" the pilot inquired.

The air traffic controller looked at the data on his computer screen. "No, it's a Gulfstream Five," he replied.

The Air Force One pilot headed back to the cabin to inform Hagin. "Oh, shit," gasped the deputy chief. While everyone else on the plane slept, Hagin stared at his phone and his BlackBerry, waiting for any word from the Sit Room's senior duty officer, who was monitoring all the wire services and news channels worldwide in case word of their trip leaked, at which point Hagin would give the order to turn the plane around.

It had rained earlier that day in Baghdad. Dusty mist swirled in the air, rendering Air Force One invisible as it landed on the airstrip. The Special Forces detail on the ground had been told that they would be greeting a VIP. Their eyes became huge when they saw who it was. Bush climbed into an armored SUV with General Rick Sanchez. The corridor from the airport to the Green Zone was dark; Coalition firepower was everywhere. The drive seemed much longer than the seven or eight minutes it took.

Bush wore a denim shirt and jeans. Someone handed him a First Armored Division windbreaker, which he promptly put on. Walking through the back door of the mess hall, he encountered Jerry Bremer. "Welcome to Free Iraq, Mr. President," said the CPA administrator. Bush hugged him.

The First Armored Division troops under the tent had been led to believe that they would be treated to a USO show. Sanchez strode to the podium and asked Bremer to read the president's Thanksgiving declaration. Seeing a moment for drama, Bremer said, "Thank you, General. But by tradition, the most senior U.S. government representative present should read it. Is there a representative more senior than me in the room?"

When the commander in chief materialized from behind the curtain, a momentary gasp filled the room. Then came a roar—deafening, exuberant, boots pounding on tables and chairs. Tears streamed down their faces. Bush began to cry as well.

"Shit," said Hagin to Atkiss through tears of his own, "I don't know if he's gonna be able to speak."

But Bush composed himself, and for a few minutes he stood behind the podium, giving thanks to the troops and reminding them of the justness of their cause. When Bush concluded to a final wave of applause, Hagin and Greg Jenkins tried to lead him to a table where he would eat dinner with a few members of the First AD.

Bush refused. "I want to serve these guys," he said.

He had his Thanksgiving dinner on the plane with Bartlett and Hagin and the advance team. Six minutes after takeoff, the press was given the okay to file their stories. Reporters were given access to the plane's air-to-ground phones. Steve Atkiss transmitted the photographs and the pool report on his laptop. An audio feed was piped in of a reporter in Baghdad breathlessly saying, *We can now confirm—the president is in Baghdad!*

It was incredible, all that power pumping out information aboard Air Force One.

Somewhere below them, there was a country—liberated, but still dark.

PART FOUR

A CHOICE, NOT A REFERENDUM

11

THE ONE-LEGGED RUNNER

"I did *not* come here to negotiate!"

Bush pounded his fist on the table of the Roosevelt Room. It was October 14, 2003, and the president was meeting with a number of Republican and moderate Democratic senators to discuss a seemingly benign subject: Should the $18.6 billion supplemental dedicated to the rebuilding of Iraq be paid for by a grant, or should the fund be considered a loan to be repaid to America later? Bush had staked out a position thoroughly counter to conservative orthodoxy—namely, that Iraq shouldn't be saddled with the costs of its own reconstruction. There was an altruistic whiff to this gesture, redolent of America's benevolent occupation of Japan.

But there was a calculating subtext to Bush's embrace of a grant. The only possible way Iraq could repay the multibillion-dollar debt would be through oil revenues. Unfortunately, Iraq's refineries were as much of a mess as its electrical plants. And, as with its transmission towers, the oil pipelines were under siege by insurgents. The attacks abated only when the infrastructure was down. As soon as new pipelines were built, the bombings resumed. Rumsfeld's commanders refused to accept securing the oil infrastructure as part of their mission in Iraq. *Other priorities*, they told the CPA—and indeed, the military had its hands full.

In any event, a large-scale Coalition effort to ramp up oil production would heighten the suspicion that America's dark motive for invading Iraq was to plunder Saddam's oil fields. Everyone in the CPA, from Jerry Bremer on down, was sensitized to this

perception—which was why Bremer ignored the advice of his subordinates and insisted that the Coalition not play any role in the area of
oil exploration, despite the $250 million monthly cost of importing oil
to meet Iraq's growing energy demands. *And* it was why Bush was now
insisting that America pick up the tab for Iraq's reconstruction. Today
in the Roosevelt Room, he and Senator John McCain said to the
other senators what Bush dared not say in public: A loan rather than
a grant would send the signal that America had gone into Iraq for the
sake of oil profits.

Senator Arlen Specter had a big problem with all this. The moderate Republican from Pennsylvania reminded Bush: *Didn't the UN
resolution anticipate that Iraqi oil would help underwrite the reconstruction
costs?*

"I did *not* come here to negotiate!"

An astonished silence swept the room. Bush's lips disappeared. His
hand remained fisted on the table.

Somewhat more meekly, Specter waded back in: *Look, we're just following what the UN—*

BAM! "Did I make myself clear?!" Bush hollered as his fist came
down again.

"Well, I didn't come here to negotiate either," retorted Lindsey
Graham, himself visibly annoyed. The scrawny South Carolina
Republican faced down Bush's indignation and continued, "Let me tell
you why I'm gonna vote against you, Mr. President. I'm not worried
about pleasing people who think we went to Iraq for oil. They're nuts!
I *am* worried about people back home paying the bill."

The folks he represented, Graham reminded Bush, were hurting.
Textile mills were closing; jobs were being outsourced. "Mr. President,
this thing's turning," he warned. "People are beginning to wonder
how many lives we're gonna lose and how much money we're gonna
spend. It's beginning to lose its flavor, the War on Terror. And if the
American people feel like they're being taken advantage of, you're
gonna lose their trust."

Bush cooled down. Some left the meeting cowed by Bush. Specter
reversed his opposition, blandly remarking later that the president had
been quite "passionate." Texas Senator Kay Bailey Hutchison, who
had introduced the amendment in question, ended up voting against
her own legislation. But Lindsey Graham didn't budge. Nor did
Saxby Chambliss—who, like Graham, had been elected to the Senate
the year before in no small measure due to Bush's relentless campaign-

ing on his behalf. Their fidelity to the war president had been cultlike only a few months earlier. Within that span of time, the gallantry and the glory of the mission in Iraq had begun to wither against the psychic grind of war. Not even the capturing of Saddam in a spider hole outside Tikrit on December 14, 2003, could change the growing restiveness. Despite Bush's unequivocal claims that Saddam possessed weapons of mass destruction, the Iraq Survey Group had failed to find them. On January 28, 2004, the ISG's director, David Kay, testified before the Senate Armed Services Committee that no such weapons existed.

The hopeful notion that Iraq would follow the political model of Afghanistan and discover within its ranks an Iraqi Hamid Karzai had proved to be illusory. For some time, Cheney, Pentagon assistant secretary Doug Feith, and a number of Capitol Hill Republicans had insisted to Bush that such a leader already existed: Ahmad Chalabi, the supple and well-connected director of the Iraqi National Congress. The CIA had long thought Chalabi was a liar. His outlandish claims that a liberated Iraq would surely recognize Israel and would welcome permanent U.S. military bases on its land soured Powell and Armitage on him as well. Armitage began to wonder how the INC was spending the millions of dollars that State had been funneling to it. When Chalabi was unable to produce receipts, Powell's deputy ordered an audit. While the State Department's inspector general, Clark Kent Ervin, was proceeding with the investigation, he received a call from a Chalabi friend. Would Ervin like to come to dinner at the home of journalist Christopher Hitchens and meet Chalabi? the caller wanted to know.

The inspector general thanked Chalabi's friend, adding that dining with the subject of his audit probably wouldn't be a good idea. But when a member of Vice President Cheney's staff called Ervin and asked to be "briefed" on the findings of the Chalabi audit, the inspector general gave in.

Chalabi had friends in high places, not all of them bastions of neoconservatism. McCain had been a longtime supporter of his INC. The *New York Times* reporter Judith Miller relied on him—to her detriment, as it would turn out—as a background source. Left-leaning publications like *Vanity Fair* and *GQ* had credulously trumpeted the inevitability of his ascent to power in post-Saddam Iraq. Despite the fact that Chalabi had never managed to woo Rumsfeld—"I think I met the guy once," the SecDef offhandedly told his press secretary, Torie

Clarke—he nonetheless had achieved sufficient clout in the Pentagon that in April 2003, a C-130 had deposited him and a few hundred exiles in military garb into the south Iraq city of Nasiriyah. This was the closest Chalabi would come to emulating Karzai, who himself had reentered Afghanistan in September 2001 to do battle with the Taliban. Alas, the able Pashtun politician had proved himself to be no fighter and required rescue by the U.S. Army. Chalabi was similarly ineffectual on the battlefield, and eventually he migrated from Nasiriyah to Baghdad, where he hijacked Bremer's de-Baathification apparatus and began to purge workers from public service with a wholesale crudeness that outraged Iraqis and embarrassed Bremer.

The wily Chalabi had parlayed his influence into a seat at the table of the Iraqi Governing Council. But Bush remained a skeptic. He preferred the idea of Iraqis, not Beltway inhabitants, selecting their leader. Plus, he had met the slick, Western-educated neocon It boy, and the odor Chalabi gave off was not to Bush's liking. NSC strategic planning coordinator Robert Blackwill said as much to Chalabi in the early months of 2004, when it appeared that the latter might try to obstruct the UN's participation in the shaping of Iraq's interim government.

"You're at an intersection with the president and the administration here, Dr. Chalabi," Blackwill warned during a one-on-one meeting in Baghdad. "And if you oppose the UN in an advisory role in the political process, you're not going to have the same relationship."

"Please convey to the president," assured Chalabi, "that I would do nothing to undermine what he wishes to accomplish in Iraq."

Whereupon Ahmad Chalabi returned to the Governing Council and attempted to organize a revolt against the UN's involvement.

"What was Chalabi doing sitting behind Laura last night at the State of the Union?" Bush inquired to a roomful of staffers on January 21, 2004.

No one replied—including Dick Cheney and Andy Card, the two men who had influence over such things—and Bush let the matter drop. Iraq was properly on his mind, but last night's speech in the Capitol was also an attempt to assure Americans that the president remained engaged in domestic matters as well. And so he proposed $23 million for a school drug-testing program. He proposed a grab bag of educational measures under the rubric Jobs for the Twenty-first Century. He proposed that federal funding for abstinence programs be doubled. He proposed that athletics be rid of steroids. He proposed that faith-based charities be eligible for federal grants. He proposed that the sanctity of marriage be defended. He proposed a $300 million "prisoner reentry initiative." And he proposed, to the scantest of applause from fellow Republicans, a temporary worker program for illegal immigrants.

In lavishing on Congress these sundry proposals, Bush the incumbent aspirant sounded precisely like Clinton circa 1996 with his election-mode paeans to the "vital center" such as school uniforms and . . . defending the sanctity of marriage. "A litany of little-ball," Bush sighed to his speechwriters. The address was widely regarded as a dud, and perhaps it would have gotten worse reviews had not Rove and Bartlett argued against including an initiative to revitalize NASA. In a speech earlier that month, the president, seeking to channel JFK, pledged to send astronauts to Mars. Coming at a time when the nation felt the heavy burden of Iraq, the space initiative seemed whimsical in the extreme.

Bartlett recognized this when his brother phoned him from Bridgeview, Texas, and said, "All right, let me get this straight. I'm going down to the coffee shop with my boys and I'm defending you on war, on taxes . . . but what the *hell* is Mars?"

There was no changing the subject. As a war president, George W. Bush had found, as he put it, his mission and his moment. But Colin Powell had issued fair warning that night over dinner: *And, Mr. President, it's gonna suck the political oxygen out of the environment for the rest of your presidency.*

Bush had listened, had professed to understand the consequences. Now he had to live with them. That "major combat operations in Iraq have ended" was, by 2004, thoroughly beside the point. Far more American troops had been killed since that "Mission Accomplished" moment than before it. The mission—to rid the world of menace in Iraq—was far from accomplished, and the toll it exacted was there for him to see, every time he visited a wounded soldier or the families of the fallen.

No one can force a president to make such visits. But, as Andy Card had warned him, this was part of a commander in chief's job description, and Bush did not run from it. The task became a part of his routine whenever his travels took him near a military hospital. Because such moments couldn't be a perfunctory meet-and-greet, but instead had to last as much as twenty minutes for each family, the visits taxed his schedule. They also sapped Bush of his emotional reserves, such that the staff knew not to schedule a major public event for him afterward. He invariably cried during such encounters; and though, as some staffers would theorize, Bush's ability to emote freely enabled him to carry on untormented, the spectacle of maimed young men and women, and of sobbing mothers, would scar anyone's heart.

Sometimes Card joined his boss; sometimes a warm body from the press shop stood nearby. Joe Hagin nearly always accompanied Bush—though really, this was a lonely moment, the man who sent Americans into harm's way now confronting the grimness of that act. It was hard for others to appreciate this. Later, in the summer of 2004, Bush was conducting a final run-through of his convention speech, in a suite at the Waldorf-Astoria, in the presence of Rice, Karen Hughes, Card, Rove, Gerson, and Ed Gillespie. He came to an emotionally charged part at the end of the speech in which he acknowledged the somberness of these visits: "I've held the children of the fallen who are told their dad or mom is a hero, but would rather just have their mom or dad."

Karen and Rice both began to cry when he read the line—or tried to read it: Bush was starting to cry as well. Gillespie whispered to Gerson, "Do we really have to say this line?"

When Gerson spoke up and said, "Mr. President, it's very important that we say this line to show that we understand what's going on," Bush angrily cut him off.

"*We* don't have to say this line," he snapped. "*I* have to say this line."

To the wounded, he asked where they were from and what they liked to do. When it seemed the thing to do, he would crack a joke. Without fail, he thanked them for their service and told them that they made him proud. Often, they told their president that they would like to go back to combat again. Bush would try not to choke up as he indicated that they had already served enough.

To those who had lost a son or a daughter, he could offer no levity. Bush hugged them and wept with them. Occasionally, a family would refuse at the last minute to see the man who had prosecuted this lethal war. Or they would get in his face: "You killed my son! How could you?"

"Your son gave his life for his country," was all he could say in reply. Or: "Your son was a hero."

Far more often, they thanked him: *Our son died for something he believed in.* And this was both a humbling and an emboldening thing to hear—though perhaps not as much as the most common refrain of all, usually spoken with searing eye contact:

Don't let my son die in vain.

Bush visited the wounded at Walter Reed Army Medical Center for the first time on January 17, 2003. The day before his arrival, members of the White House advance dropped in to canvass Ward 57, which housed soldiers who had been seriously injured while serving in Afghanistan. The advance team wanted to know how they felt about the president paying them a visit—and if the patients bore some grudge against Bush, to please say so now. The advance men also offered to arrange for haircuts, in case they were interested.

The Secret Service and bomb-sniffing dogs were the first to arrive the next morning. Then came the familiar voice in the corridor, accompanied by the laughter of nurses. The president and the first lady stepped inside a room. "Hey, Sergeant, how you doing?" asked Bush.

"Doing very well, sir," said Staff Sgt. Michael McNaughton from the 769th Engineer Battalion of the Louisiana National Guard. McNaughton's voice was thick from morphine, and he couldn't salute because his right hand was heavily bandaged. The major damage had been to his right leg, which had been amputated. McNaughton had signed up for the National Guard three months after 9/11. They flew him to Afghanistan in the spring of 2002. In Bagul, he used a case of Coke and Snickers bars to bribe a warlord into letting his unit sweep the area for land mines. One day outside Bagram Air Force Base, he stepped on something, then heard what that something was, and in an instant knew that his right foot was gone. Two weeks later, he was lying in a hospital bed, missing two fingers and one leg, doped up and with his hair freshly cut, meeting with the president of the United States.

Laura smiled and introduced herself to McNaughton's wife, Kim, whose look of stricken amazement the Bushes were accustomed to seeing. Bush knew Kim's name, knew McNaughton's unit. Both McNaughton and his buddy in the room, Sgt. Dave Silva, said that they lived in Louisiana. Grinning, Bush said, "Y'all are just one state away from being Texans."

Bush looked at the hand-drawn American flag on the wall. McNaughton said that his son had made it. The sergeant saw Bush's eyes take in the stuffed reindeer on the shelf. "If I was able, I'd get it out of here," McNaughton said with embarrassment.

The wounded soldier then said, "I'm proud to have served."

Bush put his hand on the thirty-one-year-old man's shoulder. "I'm proud of you," he said.

"At least now I'll get to watch sports," said McNaughton.

Bush asked him what sports he liked. Football and NASCAR, said the Louisianan. "And I like to run," added the man with no right leg.

The president wanted to hear more about this. McNaughton said that he ran both for distance and for speed—half marathons, and two-milers at an eleven-minute clip.

Bush considered this. Then: "You gonna run again?"

"I don't know," said the soldier. "I'd like to. They give me a wooden leg, I'll run on it."

"You call me when you get better. I want to run with you. I want to see if you can hang with me."

Then Bush left. But a few minutes later, he popped his head in the door.

"Don't forget to call me," he told McNaughton. "We'll run at the White House."

Fifteen months later, after bone-spur surgery and the installation of a new suction socket, Michael McNaughton stood on the South Lawn with his prosthetic leg. Bush strolled up in dark sweats with the collar flipped up.

"Do you want to stretch, Sarge?" he asked.

"No, I'm ready," said McNaughton.

It was raining and the footing was not particularly good on the pathway. McNaughton wore shorts, and as they ran Bush kept glancing at his artificial leg, onto which an American flag had been laminated near the thigh. "Do you sleep with it on?" the president asked.

"Do you sleep with your shoes on?" replied McNaughton.

Barney was quite riled by the visitor with the strange leg. "Mr. President, if he gets too close, I'll have to kick your dog," the soldier warned.

Toward the end, McNaughton was tempted to sprint. But Bush's doctor had specifically forbidden this, and the rain was getting nastier. They slowed to a walk short of a mile. McNaughton wasn't winded. He'd trained for this. In time, he'd be doing half marathons again.

"I'd like to go back overseas," he told Bush.

The president shook his head. "You did your job admirably," he said. "It's someone else's turn."

Bush's eyes began to fill with tears. "I can't tell you how proud I am of what you did then," he managed. He struggled to get out the words: "And of what you're doing now."

Then: "Do you want to go to the exercise room?"

They were together for two hours, the commander in chief and his wounded soldier. Sixteen days earlier, four American security guards had been waylaid, killed, burned, and strung up in the city of Fallujah. Eleven days from now, *60 Minutes* would broadcast equally ghastly images of Iraqis being humiliated and brutalized in the Abu Ghraib prison.

Today, no one bothered Bush. This was what mattered.

12

"You Know Where I Stand"

The campaign to reelect George W. Bush began less than two months after he took the oath of office. In March 2001, Bush's pollster, Matthew Dowd, sent over to Rove a rather startling graph. From 1976 through 2000, Dowd had found, the percentage of swing voters—those who weren't wedded to either party and tended to make up their minds late in the campaign—had declined steadily, election by election, from 22 percent of the electorate to 7 percent. Partisanship and polarization were now the insurmountable realities. There no longer existed much of a "gettable middle." And so it followed: There was no longer any point of moving *toward* the center. That, of course, had been the premise behind Bush's I'm-a-uniter-not-a-divider campaign of 2000. What Dowd had found was that the political rationale for Compassionate Conservatism no longer existed.

Instead, Dowd argued to Rove, "It's about *motivation* rather than *persuasion*. We maximize the number of Republicans on election day, and we win."

The Dowd graph had a profound impact on Rove's thinking. He road-tested the theory in 2002, eager to determine whether the seismic trauma of 9/11 had somehow softened party allegiances. Instead, the midterm results validated Matthew Dowd's findings in a big way: Even though the Republicans had cumulatively lost the undecided vote, they'd won overall by 4 percentage points. How? By focusing on the "new" swing votes: the occasional voter rather than the undecided.

Rove wasn't the only one in the White House making early plans for Bush's reelection campaign. Bush himself had not forgotten the

230

awful train wreck of his father's experience and wanted to get a jump on avoiding such an occurrence. By early 2002, he and Rove began to confer on how to build a successful reelection model. They decided to drop the project in Dowd's lap. "You can't tell anybody about this," Rove told Dowd when he reached him in Austin.

For two weeks, Matthew Dowd quietly shuttled from one presidential library to the next. He spent a day in College Station, Texas, reliving the 1992 debacle through 41's campaign documents. He flew to Ann Arbor and, with Gerald Ford's permission, scoured through the ex-president's 1976 records. After Rove placed a call to Nancy Reagan—who, in her persistent effort to protect Ronnie's image, insisted that the White House provide her with copies of whatever Dowd had uncovered—the pollster traveled to Reagan's library in Simi Valley. There was, of course, no point in approaching the Clintonistas to gain access to the 1996 records at Little Rock. Offsetting that loss was the fact that Jim Baker's library at Rice University in Houston was a gold mine: 41's longtime adviser had been intimately involved in every Republican presidential campaign since 1976.

Dowd produced a report in April that contained suggestions great and small relating to agenda setting, meeting scheduling, and memo dispersing. But the most salient conclusion boiled down to this: The worst reelection campaigns (Ford in '76, Bush in '92) were those in which practically anyone from the White House could and did meddle in the campaign. The best reelection campaign (Reagan in '84, set up by Baker) had a strictly defined pipeline from the White House to the campaign.

It went without saying that Karl Rove would be at the White House end of the pipeline. He and Bush decided in the spring of 2002 who would be at the other end, as the president's campaign manager: It had to be Mehlman.

There wasn't even a second choice. When Rove plucked him from the Hill in 1999 to see if he could make something happen for Bush in Iowa, thirty-two-year-old Ken Mehlman darted off to the Midwest like a crazed jackal and in seven weeks assembled an Amway-style pyramid of volunteers that delivered Bush a victory in the Ames straw poll despite having entered the contest later than every other Republican candidate. During the course of his efforts, Mehlman adopted a stray dog that had followed him one day while he was jogging. He brought it to the local animal shelter, only to receive a call later that the mutt was about to be put to death. Mehlman retrieved it, named the dog W, and kept it at the Iowa office—all the way up until the landlord evicted the Bush operation for keeping a pet on the premises.

He was Rove's protégé, his hyperactive little brother—that was the reductive version, and it was a measure of Ken Mehlman's self-assurance that he never felt the need to dispel it. They shared the geeky vocabulary of the hopelessly obsessed operative: metrics, seventy-two-hour canvassing, viral marketing strategies, more skin on the ground, team leaders, microtargets. . . . And they were both undisputed Bush men, their separate and distinct histories rendered irrelevant by servitude to the highest office in the land.

Rove was from the slashing school of Lee Atwater: wily itinerant kingmakers in search of that one indomitable king. Mehlman had never met Atwater. The tug he felt to George W. Bush was deeper than ambition could account for. To Mehlman, the better insult to hurl at an opponent wasn't that he was a liberal, but rather that he was a politician, a believer in nothing except self-preservation. He had beliefs, and he liked that Bush did as well. Mehlman was a Jewish kid from Baltimore; his grandfather had been a member of the NAACP. He graduated from Harvard Law School in the same class as Senator Barack Obama. And though the two didn't hang out much back then—Obama gravitated to the law-review brainiacs, while Mehlman was more at home with the goobers who stayed up all night chugging beer and listening to Pink Floyd—they were close enough that Mehlman took Obama out for dinner in late 2004, just after the former was designated the head of the Republican National Committee and the latter had achieved overnight-sensation status within the Democratic Party as the newly elected U.S. Senator from Illinois. Obama's inspiring trajectory meant more to Mehlman than his party affiliation . . . though it was Ken Mehlman's abiding belief that *his* party, the party of Lincoln, could and must overcome its race-baiting southern-strategy past and be the kind of party that a Barack Obama would want to be a part of. Mehlman believed that Bush, the Compassionate Conservative, harbored similar yearnings.

He had not spent Rove's many years of grooming on the GOP's glad-handing fields, and it showed. The cherubic Rove had achieved a made man's swagger; when he wisecracked, he could be sure that laughter would ensue. Mehlman was twitchy, with a blurting cadence and a starved, almost cornered-beast aspect to his long face. But appearances deceived: Mehlman was fundamentally secure, while

Rove was anything but. In many ways, he was an improved version of his mentor: insanely focused, not a minute wasted on hazing some imagined foe, so prone to hiccuping arcane data that fellow campaign aides referred to him as Rain Man (after the autistic savant in the movie of the same name), insistent on accountability while equally uninterested in micromanaging, challenging but humane to his staff, and seemingly willing to let others hog the credit. That last factor was major. Mehlman was not a threat to Karl Rove. His turf was Turdblossom's turf, in the end, and Mehlman was okay with that. Ordinarily, a campaign manager would insist on face time with his client. In this case, Rove would be—*needed* to be—the conduit to Bush.

What Mehlman insisted on, and got, was this: *I'm in charge of who works in the campaign, and any major decision in the campaign needs my authorization.* He wasn't going to let his Arlington headquarters become a dumping ground for failed GOP hacks. Nor would it be permissible for some West Wing Junior Birdman to call up Mehlman's office and harass one of his deputies. He would deal with Rove or Bartlett or Card or the VP or Bush. No one else need call Arlington.

Florida, Ohio, Iowa, Minnesota, Wisconsin, New Mexico—this was Ken Mehlman's taut map of America. By the end of 2002, he'd visited each battleground state, meeting with each's governor and strategic and communications and finance gurus. "I want to know everything *you* know," he'd say. And with that left-hander's tilt, he'd bore in: "I want to suck all the knowledge out of your brain—have it in *my* brain. I want to know *every* ad you ran, *every* voter group you targeted. . . ."

And what he learned—well, an ordinary person wouldn't care. But you won elections by caring about the fact that Ohio wasn't just about the three *C*s (Cleveland, Cincinnati, Columbus) anymore, but also the Toledo media market and the clusters amassing in the so-called exurbs a full forty-five-minute drive from where the Democrats were lavishing their attention. You won by caring that in Florida, the moderate I-4 corridor wasn't the only object of desire, but also the burgeoning Panhandle to the southwest and the increasing Republican densities around Jacksonville to the northeast. You won by caring that African Americans in St. Louis and Detroit were responding to the urban radio ads about gay marriage. You won by caring that when a Hispanic focus group in Las Vegas was tested on abortion, the men's backs noticeably stiffened on the matter of parental notification:

I'm the head of the household, you're telling me what MY daughter can or can't do. . . .

You won, Ken Mehlman knew, not just by adhering to the Matthew Dowd graph and energizing the Republican base . . . but by hitting *every* target, micro or macro, wherever you could throw skin on the ground. Because—as Mehlman, Dowd, McKinnon, Stuart Stevens, and others on the campaign staff acknowledged with dark snickers— it wasn't 2000 anymore, when the backstage slogan was: *Things have never been better. Vote for change.*

Now it was 2004, with a fittingly bleak inner-circle encapsulation: *Things have never been worse. Stay the course.*

"This election is a choice—not a referendum."

Mehlman and the others said it over and over throughout 2004, with a startling lack of abashment. Implicit in this assertion was the recognition that if the public were to vote purely on the merits of the president's first-term performance, he would likely be excused from further service. The war in Iraq was now officially unpopular. The economy was performing poorly. And the year began with the release of two books by former Bush administration officials—Treasury Secretary Paul O'Neill and NSC counterterrorism adviser Richard Clarke—that cast the president as an edgy, incurious, insulated executive whom, given a choice, voters would surely disapprove of . . .

. . . Depending, of course, *on* the choice.

In May 2003, Rove, Bartlett, and Dowd huddled in the West Wing to discuss for the first time the growing field of Democratic presidential candidates. Dowd said that the guy he'd most like to face was the junior senator from Massachusetts, John Kerry. Back when Dowd was working with moderate Democratic Senator Lloyd Bentsen, he had met Kerry at a DNC fund-raiser and found him to be a first-class jerk—self-important, obnoxious to his staff. Voters would see right through this man.

John Edwards was another matter. The youthful and charismatic first-term senator from North Carolina possessed not only Bush's sunniness but a moving life story (son of a mill worker, avenging lawyer for the downtrodden, father of a teenager who died in a car accident) and the next-generation aura of a JFK. Dowd couldn't figure out how to go after a guy like Edwards.

Rove could. *Two words: predatory lawyer.* Plus, Edwards was freshfaced to a fault. Dowd's deputy on the campaign, Sara Taylor, had been running focus groups on the candidates. Their conclusion of John Edwards was: *He'd make a great mayor.*

Rove's worry, shared by Bartlett, was Dick Gephardt. Sure, the veteran Missouri congressman was a hardy perennial oozing unexcitement. But Gephardt could energize the unions. Bartlett remarked that Gephardt was solid, blue collar, Middle America, pro-war—and this wasn't his first rodeo, having given Michael Dukakis a tough fight during the 1988 campaign.

On one score the three Bush deputies could agree: It would be a sweet, sweet thing if Howard Dean were to get the nomination. Oh, how the oppo dudes salivated! Their file on the Vermont governor was at least twice as thick as those on Dean's rivals. His ever-shifting stance on same-sex unions, the way he'd jacked up Medicaid participation rates in his state . . . and, as Sara Taylor's focus group testing showed, the man positively scared voters.

By the fall of 2003, Mehlman had matched each candidate with a "red team" of Republican operatives on the periphery of the campaign who wanted to make themselves useful: Mary Matalin, Charlie Black, Linda DiVall, Alex Castellanos, Vin Weber. . . . By November, Howard Dean was surging ahead and his was the sexy red team to be on. But then Dean and Gephardt proceeded to cut each other up in Iowa over Medicare. On the night of his surprise defeat in the Iowa caucus, Dean self-immolated before a national television audience, hollering out each upcoming primary state—"New Hampshire! South Carolina! Michigan! Virginia!"—and punching his fist in the air like a deranged wrestling fan. The RNC's oppo dudes sighed, sealed away the Dean file.

The subject of their attention, Iowa's victor, was now John Kerry.

"The other party's nomination battle is still playing out," Bush declared at a Republican fund-raiser on the evening of February 23, 2004. With a sly half-grin, he continued: "The candidates are an interesting group, with diverse opinions: for tax cuts and against them; for NAFTA and against NAFTA; for the Patriot Act and against the Patriot Act; in favor of liberating Iraq and opposed to it. And that's just one senator from Massachusetts."

Less than two weeks later, at another fund-raiser, just after the aforementioned senator from Massachusetts had effectively sewn up the nomination, Bush twisted the knife just a bit. "Last Tuesday I placed a call to Senator Kerry," he said with evident amusement. "I told him I was looking forward to a spirited campaign and I congratulated him on his victory. It's going to be an interesting debate on the issues. My opponent has spent two decades in Washington and he's built up quite a record. In fact, Senator Kerry has been in Washington long enough to take both sides on just about every issue."

Sitting presidents ordinarily waited until convention time before deigning to acknowledge their presumptive opponent. But after weeks of discussion between the White House and Arlington, the consensus was that they couldn't afford to wait. Kerry needed to be defined *now*. And everyone would pitch in, including Bush.

How to define him? That, too, had been the subject of vigorous argument. It was ever the temptation to sum up Kerry as a Taxachusetts Liberal in the manner of Dukakis and Ted Kennedy. But, as Mehlman pointed out, liberalism wasn't quite the bogeyman of old, thanks to Clinton's welfare reform and other such triangulations. Besides, the campaign manager said, in an intensely polarized nation, deriding the Democrat as a liberal meant locking in 46 percent of the electorate for Kerry. If you called him weak and indecisive, however, you got both the nonliberals and the centrists who preferred strong leaders.

And so the Flip-Flopper.

The setup for the flip-flop came on two fronts. The first salvo was delivered by Ed Gillespie, the head of the Republican National Committee, at the RNC winter meeting on January 28, 2004. In his speech, Gillespie rattled off every missile Kerry had ever voted against, every budget cut for defense and intelligence he had promoted. The idea was to goad Kerry into contradicting his legislative record by protesting that he was in fact a megahawk. Gillespie and Mehlman had absolutely no doubt that Kerry would take the bait. They watched how he couldn't let any taunt by Dean go unrefuted during the primary debates. Kerry protested too much—it was what insecure men did.

The second line of attack was more atmospheric. To turn a referendum on George W. Bush into a choice, it wasn't quite enough to malign John Kerry as a flip-flopper. The Bush campaign also had to evoke a world in which flip-flopping leadership would prove apocalyptic. This was where Mark McKinnon came in. The admaker walked into the Yellow Room of the residence one day in February 2004 with a DVD of the rollout ad campaign. Bush, Laura, Rove, Bartlett, Cheney, and Card sat expectantly as McKinnon played the first spot.

It was plenty dark: images of a smoldering Ground Zero, a tattered flag, headlines signaling the cratering of the stock market.

"President Bush," the ad intoned at the end. "Steady leadership in times of change."

No one in the room applauded. Even for hard-bitten politicos like Rove and Card, the message was a little . . . bleak. Bush told McKinnon that he'd have to talk it over with Laura.

The ad began airing in the first week of March. Several families of 9/11 victims expressed outrage that the images of tragedy had been exploited for the purposes of a political campaign. "I respectfully, completely disagree," Karen Hughes said the morning the ads hit the airwaves—sitting in a chair beside a bromeliad she'd bought at a grocery store the night before. The ad's imagery, she suggested, was "a reminder of our shared experience as a nation."

It was also a reminder of the world that a flip-flopper would inherit, if elected.

Kerry ambled into the trap with comic timing. From the way he thrust his thumb skyward at moments that didn't call for brio, to his painful insistence that he loved NASCAR, seemingly everything he said and did reinforced his inauthenticity. When *GQ* magazine reporter Michael Hainey innocently asked him a prosaic rock-and-roll question—whom did he prefer, the Beatles or the Rolling Stones—Kerry refused, once again, to take a stance.

But the steel jaws that awaited Kerry were in Huntington, West Virginia. He visited there on March 16, intending to shore up his foreign-policy credentials by striding into the auditorium of Marshall University with a cluster of war veterans. Of course, Rove, Mehlman, and Coddy Johnson had snatched West Virginia away from the slumbering Democrats in 2000. They weren't about to cede it back. And so, four hours before Kerry's arrival, Sara Taylor and McKinnon's assistant Ashley Connor hastily produced and threw on the air in local markets a TV ad showing Kerry declaring "No" on the Senate floor to the $87 billion supplemental package that would fund military efforts in Iraq.

This was a rabbit that John Kerry could not let go unchased. Standing before the audience with microphone in hand, he explained that the Iraq bill should have been funded with the help of other nations— or by repealing Bush's tax cuts for the wealthy, which in fact Kerry had proposed in an amendment . . . all of which was to say, and Kerry said it: "I actually did vote for the $87 billion before I voted against it."

When Ken Mehlman learned of Kerry's words, he nearly burst into song. It was his happiest day of the campaign. Mehlman didn't have to say a word to McKinnon. The new ad containing Kerry's immortal words would be up and running forty-eight hours after he uttered them.

Six months later, Kerry explained the $87 billion flip-flop remark to ABC's Diane Sawyer: "I had one of those inarticulate moments late in the evening when I was dead tired in the primaries, and I didn't say something very clearly." The Bush campaign helpfully corrected Kerry later: He'd committed his gaffe at around one in the afternoon, not in the evening.

(During the campaign, a Duke political scientist named Peter Feaver would brief both sides on a study he had helped conduct regarding public opinion in wartime. Feaver pointed out to a Kerry campaign staffer that though opinion trends favored the commander in chief, there was in fact a kind of "sweet spot" for the senator: oppose the war, but be *for* victory. Or in this case, vote against authorization for use of force and vote for funding the troops . . . which, of course, was the opposite of what Kerry had done.

"That fucking vote," sighed the Kerry staffer.)

In a way, Kerry laid his own trap.

He had famously served in Vietnam, braving enemy fire while commanding a group of Swift Boats in the Mekong Delta. This, Kerry and other Democrats believed, indemnified him against charges of dovishness, and Sara Taylor saw focus groups respond warmly to Kerry's many war medals. Mehlman wasn't buying it. Lawyers like him would refer to Kerry's military service as an "attractive nuisance": seemingly desirable, but in the end, creating more problems than it solved. For every time the senator boasted of his expertise in national security matters, the subject *became* national security. Bush the war president was going to win that subject, hands down. What the campaign staff feared was a John Kerry who harped on domestic issues as Clinton had done in 1992—who camped out in the electorally crucial but economically bedraggled state of Ohio, and who bashed Bush on jobs and health care at every turn.

But that John Kerry never emerged. He stuck to the turf where Bush was strongest—and where, for that matter, the flip-flop charge continued to dog him. In 1971, Kerry the war-hero-turned-war-protester had joined a number of veterans in tossing their war medals over a fence during a demonstration at the Capitol. Later in life, Kerry the politician admitted that the medals he'd chunked were someone else's—that in fact he'd never claimed otherwise.

"How can you throw away somebody else's medals and pretend they're yours?" Karen asked in exasperation after studying her briefing book on Kerry. On its face, the act seemed the height of phoniness.

But there was a greater height, which the RNC oppo dudes discovered: Kerry *had* in fact claimed once on TV that the thrown medals were his. The Republicans peddled the footage to ABC, which aired it, prompting Kerry to thunder that the network was "doing the bidding of the Republican National Committee." Still, the words and acts were his, and they spoke for themselves.

What they said was: flip-flop.

In Kerry's zeal to promote his own valor, he fatally stirred up a hornet's nest. Kerry authorized the biographer Douglas Brinkley to memorialize his wartime experiences in the book *Tour of Duty*, which was published during the primary season. While playing up Kerry's exploits, the book took a harsh swipe at the search-and-destroy tactics of retired Admiral Roy F. Hoffmann. Hoffmann, who had spoken kindly of Kerry's heroism in the past, was offended by this depiction of him and decided to fight back. He contacted other veterans who had served with Kerry. On August 5, a week after Kerry and his running mate John Edwards had been anointed at the Democratic National Convention, a group led by Hoffmann calling itself Swift Boat Veterans for Truth began airing ads in major markets throughout the nation.

The crisply produced commercials brandished black-and-white images of one middle-aged Vietnam vet after the next staring somberly into the camera and speaking in unadorned declarative sentences: *I served with John Kerry. . . . John Kerry has not been honest about what happened in Vietnam. . . . I know John Kerry is lying about his first Purple Heart because I treated him for that injury. . . . His account of what happened and what actually happened are the difference between night and day. . . . When the chips were down, you could not count on John Kerry. . . . He dishonored his country—he most certainly did. . . . John Kerry cannot be trusted.*

The Bush campaign had been notified at least a day beforehand that the ads would be broadcast and made no efforts to intervene. New Swift Boat commercials followed; each was pilloried for its misleading innuendo. But just as he had four years ago when Vietnam vets attacked John McCain, Bush remained silent on the subject—and so, oddly, did Kerry, whose top strategists, Bob Shrum and Mary Beth Cahill, maintained that to rebut the charges would be to dignify them. Throughout early August, Kerry received calls from anxious friends begging that he not take the Swift Boat attacks lying down. Nearly three weeks passed before he finally heeded them. By then, what little momentum Kerry had accrued from the convention and his pick of Edwards had completely disappeared.

The Swift Boat campaign was that much deadlier for Kerry's insistence that he be viewed as America's Soldier. "I'm John Kerry, and I'm reporting for duty," the senator had declared at the beginning of his acceptance speech on July 29, saluting crisply for effect. The day before, several admirals and generals had lined up on the same stage to indicate their support for the Democrat.

Russ Schriefer, the program director for the upcoming Republican National Convention in New York, sat in front of his television and counted the number of military commanders the Democrats had amassed for the occasion. Twelve.

We are going to bury this guy, Schriefer thought.

"We are in the process of turning this convention into a TV show," Schriefer proudly wrote in a memo to the GOP program committee in late July. "Shorter segments, more graphics, faster pacing . . ."

They'd done this sort of thing at the 2000 convention. And although it drew snickers for its "We Are the World" parade of racially diverse speakers (when virtually every GOP delegate on the convention floor was as white as a refrigerator), that convention laid the groundwork for what Schriefer had in mind for 2004. Meaning: The fewer politicians speaking, the better. The more episodic, the better. For inspiration, Schriefer was ignoring every past convention and instead turning to Broadway plays, variety shows, Fox news segments—things people actually watched. There was only one point to any of this: to give the nominee a postconvention bounce in the polls. Kerry's convention in Boston had added a scant two points' worth of momentum. Schriefer wasn't going to let that happen to Bush in New York.

Schriefer, McKinnon, convention manager Bill Harris, and the other planners let their imaginations run wild. Olympic stars, a Miss America, the Boys Choir of Harlem, more country-western crooners

January 20, 2001: President-elect George W. Bush and Laura Bush are received by President Bill Clinton and Hillary Clinton on Inaugural day. Candidate Bush had repeatedly pledged to "restore honor and dignity to the White House," an implicit swipe at his predecessor. (White House photo by Eric Draper)

Karl Christian Rove. His title—senior adviser to the president— was, like Rove himself, a triumph of the opaque. (White House photo by Eric Draper)

The post-9/11 president, cheered by New Yorkers while throwing out the first pitch at Yankee Stadium before Game 3 of the World Series, October 30, 2001. "Be a man. Throw it from the mound," Yankees star Derek Jeter had advised Bush. (White House photo by Eric Draper)

The boss and his two counselors, fellow Texans Dan Bartlett and Karen Hughes, aboard Air Force One on November 27, 2002. Emboldened by the midterms and the War President's high approval rating, Hughes and Bartlett had little difficulty instilling "message discipline"—for a while, at least. (White House photo by Eric Draper)

Bush and national security adviser Condoleezza Rice conferring at Crawford ten weeks before the invasion of Iraq. Formerly a Great Powers Realist, Rice fell in the sway of Bush's worldview, confessing to a friend, "It's not *my* exercising influence over *him*. *I'm* internalizing *his* world." (White House photo by Eric Draper)

March 19, 2003: in the West Wing office of Condi Rice, press secretary Ari Fleischer, chief of staff Andy Card, Bartlett, Hughes, and Rice follow the news coverage of Operation Iraqi Freedom. (White House photo by Tina Hager)

Chief speechwriter Michael Gerson presenting a draft of the 2004 State of the Union address to Bush with Rice looking on. Uncommonly powerful for a White House scribe, Gerson became the author of the president's intellectual and moral framework—though this particular speech fell flat, derided by Bush himself as a "litany of Little Ball." (White House photo by Eric Draper)

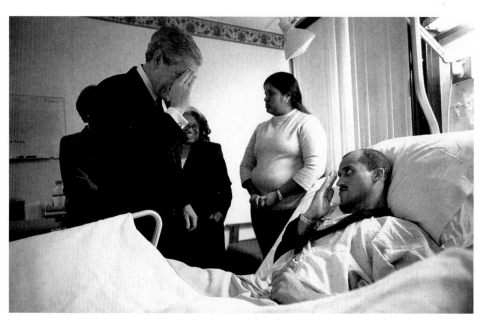

Taking a break from the 2004 campaign trail, Bush visits wounded U.S. Army Staff Sergeant Santiago Frias of Bronx, New York, at Walter Reed Medical Center. Recalling the pleas of grieving parents—*Don't let my son die in vain*—Bush would say, "I often hear those voices. I really do." (White House photo by Eric Draper)

Vice President Dick Cheney during debate prep with his staff at the VP's Naval Observatory residence, October 1, 2004. After Bush's disastrous showing against John Kerry in their first debate, it fell to Cheney to stop the bleeding in his showdown with John Edwards. (White House photo by David Bohrer)

The president and first lady on Inaugural Night 2005. Never one for the dance floor, Bush nonetheless had a spring in his step after delivering his audacious "Freedom Agenda" earlier that day. (White House photo by Susan Sterner)

"I've got political capital, and I intend to spend it." Bush on his politically risky and ultimately doomed Social Security "Conversation" tour, February 4, 2005. (White House photo by Eric Draper)

Being deputy chief of staff in charge of operations meant, for Joe Hagin, "the care and feeding of the president"—including clearing brush for Bush's biking paths. (White House photo by Eric Draper)

Harriet Miers was many things to the president—staff secretary, deputy chief of staff in charge of policy, White House counsel and leading West Wing workaholic—but as a Supreme Court nominee, a nonstarter. (White House photo by Eric Draper)

Bush announcing the replacement of Andy Card with Josh Bolten as his chief of staff, March 28, 2006. A "Bolten bounce" ensued, but only briefly, as Bush's approval numbers settled into the mid-thirties. (White House photo by David Bohrer)

The more detractors called for the dismissal of Secretary of Defense Donald Rumsfeld, the more Bush dug in his heels. By the time Rumsfeld stepped down, Baghdad was in chaos and Congress had fallen to the Democrats.
(White House photo by Paul Morse)

Leading, though with few followers:
the Cyclist in Chief undeterred.
(White House photo by Paul Morse)

than they could possibly need—these were the staples, the givens. How about: a video clip of Poppy Bush parachuting out of a plane. (Done—with the Van Halen song "Jump" wailing in the background.) Another video of the Bush girls lampooning their dad. (McKinnon was on the case.) The program directors commissioned a send-up of the iconic Reagan. (What came back was cheerless and amateurish; they picked up a premade substitute.) They tried to find an "appropriate" rapper. (Couldn't make it happen.) They fantasized about an event at Yankee Stadium. (No way to fill the place.) Negotiations with Aerosmith broke down. Kelsey Grammer, star of the TV show *Frasier*, sent his last-minute apologies—he and his wife had to fly overseas to adopt a baby. Toby Keith had a conflict. Kenny Chesney was in, couldn't wait to do it—until the week before the convention, when Coca-Cola offered him a million bucks to play for an event in Atlanta.

On the evening of Monday, August 30, John McCain took the stage. His place in Bushworld remained a precarious thing. Since the day of their rote embrace in Pittsburgh four years earlier ("I endorse Governor Bush. I endorse Governor Bush. I endorse . . ."), a wariness attended their alliance. Both men were two-sided—McCain's good soldier and hot-tempered maverick, Bush's confident leader and defensive eldest-son-of-a-famous-man—and in each other's presence those sides tended to make revolving-door appearances. During the Philadelphia convention of 2000, Bush's people kept McCain off prime time until McCain showed up in town and began to stage events of his own. The senator was then added to the billing, prompting McCain's spokesman Todd Harris to say with a smirk, "We are, of course, honored to accept this last-minute invitation."

After Philadelphia, the senator and the governor campaigned together by train in California. It astounded the McCain camp when Bush refused to get out at a particular stop because there were too many protesters outside the train. "Keep going," Bush had ordered, and all the window shades were drawn as the train resumed locomotion. This wasn't the Straight Talk Express anymore. Then again, McCain's vehicle had run off the rails months ago.

Barely a week into Bush's presidency, he and McCain were back to bickering about campaign finance reform. Before Jim Jeffords switched parties in May, Tom Daschle visited McCain at his ranch outside Sedona, Arizona, to see if perhaps he could make an honest Democrat out of him. Depending on which staff one believed, Daschle either came very close to succeeding or never had a chance to begin with. Nonetheless, the flirtation did not go unnoticed by the White House.

September 11 put Bush and McCain back on the same page. But when the president signed the campaign reform package in 2002, he pointedly did so without a ceremony that would have given the architect, McCain, his due. And when John Kerry pleaded with McCain, throughout the early summer of 2004, to be his running mate—asking more than once, sometimes late in the evening, begging his Republican colleague to at least think about it—McCain's refusal seemed, as with the Daschle gambit, almost a little too polite . . . as if McCain rather enjoyed the agony that this was putting Bush through. As half-assed as McCain had been about quashing both overtures, he was equally prompt and emphatic in excoriating the Swift Boat ads that attacked his fellow Vietnam vet, and he called on the Bush campaign to join his denunciation. To some, the stiffness in the Bush-McCain relationship was perfectly embodied by their first event together in four years, at Fort Lewis on June 18, 2004. At that campaign rally, Bush reached for McCain, who responded by hugging the incumbent as one might embrace a porcupine . . . although McCain aides later pointed out that McCain's injuries from Hanoi had left him unable to fully extend his arms.

McCain had shown up at Fort Lewis at the behest of Rove, who had made the request in a phone call to McCain's strategist John Weaver. This, in and of itself, was a noteworthy event. Rove was anything but a McCain fan. As the keeper of all betrayals to Bush, he cunningly used his access to remind his boss of every slight or act of grandstanding that McCain had committed at the president's expense. By the same token, Weaver seldom missed an opportunity to condemn the real or imagined acts of Rove—who, Weaver maintained, had damaged his consulting business in Texas and slandered him by spreading bizarre stories casting Weaver as some kind of deviant.

There seemed no end to this medieval feud—until one day in the spring of 2004, when Mark McKinnon received a call from Weaver, with whom he had remained on good terms despite McKinnon's friendship with Rove. Weaver spoke of his recent bout with leukemia. The near-death experience had produced an epiphany, Weaver said: "I've been carrying a lot of baggage, and this is one I'd like to unload."

McKinnon visited Rove's office on the second floor of the West

Wing a day later. "Weaver would like to talk to you about burying the hatchet," he said.

Five seconds passed before Rove tentatively replied, "Okay . . ."

McKinnon suggested that the three of them get together at his apartment four blocks from the White House. Weaver was fine with that. Rove wasn't. He preferred a venue with an easier exit. They agreed on the Caribou Coffee at Pennsylvania Avenue and 17th Street.

And so one May morning at about ten thirty, the three Texas politicos convened. The small talk between them was clumsy until Weaver began to talk about his leukemia and asked Rove about his wife, Darby, who had also survived a cancer scare.

"You know, John, there are a lot of things that happen in life that you can't go back and change," Rove said quietly. "But if I could, I would."

Weaver nodded. "Well, that's water under the bridge," he said. "Let's talk about the future." Then he brought up McCain, who was unaware of this meeting—but who, Weaver believed, would happily assist with the reelect. "I certainly don't want it to be because of our relationship that he wouldn't be asked to go out there for the president."

McKinnon's heart stopped. A familiar face materialized outside the window: NBC's Norah O'Donnell, who covered the White House, was now staring straight at the news scoop of the week. She waved at Weaver, glanced briefly at McKinnon and Rove, and then kept walking.

"Well, given our conversation," Rove concluded, "let me get back to you." The two rivals shook hands.

"Guess where I've been," Weaver told McCain in the Russell Senate Office Building. "I've just been talking to Karl Rove."

"Holy shit," said the senator.

About a week later, Rove called Weaver. Would McCain be willing to join the president at Fort Lewis and later in Reno?

"All you had to do was ask," Weaver affirmed.

Thus did McCain hit the road for what would be the first of twenty or so campaign swings in the service of the Bush campaign—entertaining Mehlman and other accompanying staffers, though somewhat at the expense of Bush spokesman Scott Stanzel, whom McCain nicknamed Staff Scum. And tonight, August 30, John McCain kicked off the Republican convention with a twenty-minute salute to George

W. Bush. "President Bush deserves not only our support," he unambiguously declared that night, "but our admiration."

McCain's appearance was only one of several signal moments that week in New York. The city's iconic mayor, Rudy Giuliani, went on twenty minutes longer than his designated time slot. But no one was going to complain, considering that Giuliani's presence implicitly gave the Bush campaign permission to be in New York, shamelessly working the War on Terror theme. California Governor Arnold Schwarzenegger refused Russ Schriefer's pleas to enter the stage on a Harley. "Ah-nuhld" more than made up for it, however, with an exquisite performance on Tuesday in which the Austrian émigré, bodybuilder, and star of Hollywood's *The Terminator* preached the virtues of political unity even as he chided Democrats for being "economy girly-men." The headliner of that evening, Laura Bush, couldn't match The Governor's timing. Nor did she have to: Her sole mission Tuesday night was to soothe viewers only just now coming down from the spectacle of Kerry's eccentric wife, Teresa, a few weeks before.

Between Schwarzenegger and Laura, the twins had also graced the stage that evening. Their five-minute duet was not quite riveting in the manner of Kerry's older, more poised daughters at the Democratic affair. Karen's script for Jenna and Barbara came off like a painful talent-show skit. (Addressing Grandmother Bar, Jenna said, "Gammy, we love you dearly, but you're just not very hip. She thinks *Sex and the City* is something married people do, but never talk about.") And yet their giggly demeanor reinforced the notion of Bush Authenticity: They were unvarnished, familiar, one of us. Where the Kerrys seemed (as Ed Gillespie and other Bush operatives helpfully suggested) . . . *French.*

Jenna and Barbara's turn on the stage marked the formal beginning of their contribution to the Bush reelection campaign. The preceding Christmas, the twins had announced to their dad that they wanted to help out. "Barbara and Jenna decided I was going to lose," he would recall. "They started listening to all the polls. And felt terrible about that, and said, 'We want to be involved in the campaign.' . . . Basically saying, 'If you're gonna lose'—they didn't put it that way, but you could tell that's what they meant—'we want it to be said that we tried our little bit, did our little part as hard as we could in order to prevent this from happening, because we love you.' "

Bush was completely floored. To say that his girls had been politically disengaged didn't quite cover it. His decision in 1993 to run for governor had robbed them of their normalcy. They expressed their displeasure by refusing to ride in the 1995 inaugural parade.

Of course, being the governor's daughter was not without its perks. And in any event, Bush's authority as chief executive of Texas had not conferred on him additional parenting powers, as the governor himself acknowledged with a feeble grin to an aide while driving together one weekend morning from the mansion to Crawford: "Should I be nervous that my daughter was just coming in as I was going out?"

Still, it had been a source of disappointment to Bush that the girls' participation in his political career had been limited to putting out a few yard signs in New Hampshire. It elated him, then, to hear the twins express interest in joining the 2004 campaign. They signed on for their first ever interview—a safe one, conducted by an old family friend, Julia Reed for *Vogue*. (The piece turned out to be a glorified caption for the photo spread of the girls—originally decked out in long white gowns, suggestive of a debutante's coming out, until the White House nixed the fashion choice.) "Things will change after this," a White House staffer warned the twins. But things did not. They did no further interviews and campaigned for their father only in thoroughly controlled settings. At one huge rally, Bush walked onstage to thunderous applause and saw Barbara on the side of the stage, weeping. "The energy—it just overwhelmed her," he remembered.

He told them, during their tour of America aboard Air Force One and Marine One and luxury buses, "This is the camping trip I never took you on."

What Bush would say in his speech had been a source of great internal angst. The rigor of the first term had left voters beaten. Scaring voters about the War on Terror had been the easy part and was by no means enough to build a speech on. There had to be a feeling of newness, of possibility. Deliberately, then, the White House had held back on any policy initiatives throughout the summer—saving them for the convention speech as a kind of second State of the Union address. All of which unsettled Bush's counselor, Dan Bartlett. There wouldn't be any rollout for any of these initiatives. What if they went over like the lead balloons of Mars and the guest worker program? What if the boss tanked in front of the biggest television audience of the year?

Bartlett need not have worried. Bush's extravagant promises on the evening of Thursday, September 2—doubling the number of participants in federally funded job training programs; providing every poor county in America with its own health center; building seven million low-cost homes within the next decade—would go thoroughly unremembered. The night was all about Choice, Not Referendum.

"You know where I stand," Bush said not once but twice as he stood in the round of the audience, on a special stage designed by Bartlett's crafty deputy Scott Sforza. By now, he had given numerous "biggest speech of your life"s. He took his time (unlike Kerry, who had begun to sweat profusely in apparent fear that the networks would cut him off before he concluded his speech), luxuriating in the raptness of his audience, and teasing from them a chorus of *flip-flop! flip-flop!* when he recited his opponent's $87 billion gem. Bemusement then vanished from his voice as he repeated Kerry's charge that America's "coalition of the willing" in Iraq amounted to a "coalition of the coerced and the bribed." In brittle, scolding tones, Bush said, "That would be nations like Great Britain, Poland, Italy, Japan, the Netherlands, Denmark, El Salvador, Australia, and others—allies that deserve the respect of all Americans, not the scorn of a politician."

Having belittled Kerry, Bush proceeded to work the other side of the Choice. "You may have noticed I have a few flaws, too," he acknowledged. "People sometimes have to correct my English. I knew I had a problem when Arnold Schwarzenegger started doing it. Some folks look at me and see a certain swagger—which in Texas is calling 'walking.' Now and then I come across as a little too blunt—and for that," he said as his eyes set on his mother in the balcony, "we can all thank the white-haired lady sitting right up there."

Two days after Bush's speech, a CNN-Gallup poll showed him ahead of Kerry, 52–41. He had received a staggering 13-point bounce from the convention.

13

ASK PRESIDENT BUSH

"See, I'm here in Lima [Ohio] asking for the vote."

"We're in your state asking for the vote. . . ."

"Not only am I asking for the vote . . ."

"I'm traveling the country asking for the vote."

"So I'm here asking for the vote, see."

"It's a lost concept in American politics," Bush liked to tell his aides, going back to his first gubernatorial campaign. "Politicians have lost the art of asking for the vote. You've literally got to *ask* for it."

Bush saw himself as different from his father, who at times seemed self-conscious on the campaign trail, and from Reagan and Clinton, who basked unashamedly in the adulation. He believed there ought to be a measure of humility—a recognition, not unlike prayer, that a higher power's will would be done.

At the same time, Bush required comfort. He wasn't about to throw himself at the feet of the rabble and risk being jeered. Humility he could do; humiliation, not.

During the month of June, friends and staffers had reported to Karen Hughes that the president didn't seem to enjoy himself very much when he spoke from the podium at campaign events. It was important to talk about the War on Terror. But the genial, teasing candidate whom Iowans and South Carolinians had found so appealing four years ago had been replaced by a strident doomsayer. The following month, at a strategy meeting organized by Mehlman, Karen reported this. "We've got to remind people why they like George W. Bush," she told the others. "We've got to show the person *we* know."

When the others agreed, Karen went to the boss. What she told Bush was what half of him wanted to hear and what the other half dreaded: He would need to break out of the bubble and expose himself to the electorate. "You've got a difficult, demanding job," she told him. "But if you want to keep it another four years, we need to put you in settings to show them the person you are."

Bush was reluctant. He knew how polarized it was out there. He didn't want to be subjected to protesters. Karen assured him that they would find a way to satisfy the potentially conflicting urges of "asking for the vote" while avoiding a discomfiting response.

The format they arrived at would guarantee both lively TV clips and thoroughly innocuous contact with those from whom Bush would ask for the vote. Ask President Bush, the events were called—unoriginally, since Poppy had hosted similar gatherings in 1988 under the heading, Meet George Bush. Using an all-access stage in the round not unlike the one Brian Montgomery had conceived for One on One with Governor Bush during the 2000 South Carolina primary, the president would be within intimate reach of the audience as he roved about in his denim shirt, mike in hand, his restless physicality a virile message of its own. On the same stage would sit three or more Regular Citizens carefully chosen from the local Republican organization under the guidance of the RNC: a first-time homeowner who had benefited from a Bush-era housing loan; a small businessman appreciative of Bush's tax cuts; a small-town doctor about to be driven into early retirement by junk lawsuits; a faith-based "social entrepreneur"; and so on.

Bush would engage in folksy, joshing dialogue with these Regular Citizens—unrehearsed, strictly speaking, except that the campaign staff had chosen them on the basis of their stories, which sounded remarkably similar to the stories told by Regular Citizens in the last town Bush had visited. With the nimbleness of a country lawyer, Bush would pose a leading question: "So did you add employees this year?" And then, upon receiving the answer—"We've added three new employees this year"—he would wheel to the crowd and explain the moral: "Here's what's happening in America: Small businesses are adding employees all across the country!"

Or, after hearing from a Regular Citizen named Steve who revealed that the Bush tax cuts had eased his tax burden: "See, he saved eighteen hundred dollars. And in '04 he saved twenty-two hundred dollars. Now, I know that doesn't sound like a lot to the budgeters in Washington, D.C. But here's a fellow whose wife is working, and he's gone back to school, and I expect that four thousand came in handy over the last two years. Didn't it?"

"Yes, definitely," Steve gushed, and the crowd applauded.

"Good job," Bush would tell the blushing Regular Citizens after they'd done their piece. Or, "Appreciate you coming, buddy."

During these colloquies, the distance between Regular Citizen and Leader of the Free World seemed to vaporize. Now he was just George W., hamming it up, freely mangling his syntax. Invoking Bar whenever possible: "Listen to your mom. I'm still listening to mine." Praising a revered profession ("Thank you for teaching") and smirking at a reviled one ("Legal term. You and I aren't lawyers."). And, inevitably, contrasting his virtuous plainness with the amoral nuance of John Kerry: "He said, well, I actually did vote for the $87 billion before I voted against it. That's not the way they talk in this part of Ohio, I don't think."

There was a meta aspect to these show-ups, a shared knowledge that this was in fact a packaged event—and ol' George's 'fessing up to the charade made him that much more *one of us*, a victim himself of the whole political farce. "I know there's a lot of cameras over there," he apologized to a stay-at-home mom in Derry, New Hampshire. In Fond du Lac, Wisconsin, Bush interrupted a rambling female participant by saying, "We haven't rehearsed this too well." As the audience guffawed, Bush elaborated: "She's doing the fox trot and I'm doing the twist. Anyway, they still do the twist? I know, a little odd." The more corn he laid on, the further from the Beltway he seemed.

Then Bush would open up the floor to questions from the audience. And these questions were also unrehearsed. But they came from men and women who had been run through a subtle yet rigid gauntlet of indoctrination patented by Ken Mehlman. To get a ticket to Ask President Bush, one had to make a request to the local Republican headquarters. It wasn't enough to pass the eyeball inspection, however. In return for the coveted ticket, the recipient had to agree to work as a volunteer for the local Bush campaign chapter. By that point, the audience member was thoroughly invested, and hardly of the mind to ask a question that would throw the president off stride.

"I was just wondering what your favorite book is, because I'd like to read it."

"Do you like being president?"

"How do we get our friends in the media back there to report the positive, good things going on in Iraq?"

"What kinds of pets do you have in the White House?"

"[I]t breaks my heart when I see all the soldiers in Afghanistan and Iraq doing fantastic things, as you mentioned when you initially came out here—they come home, they put the television on, and they just see horrible news of what's going on, a completely different perspective of what they have done during their tour of duty. What can I do as an American citizen to show my appreciation?"

"Do you think you can beat John Kerry?"

"After you are elected in 2004, what will your memoirs say about you, what will the title be, and what will the main theme say?"

"What can all of us here do to help you and Dick Cheney be sure to be reelected?"

"What is your biggest fear with, if you'll excuse me, a Kerry administration?"

Some of the questions, though never hostile, were poignant. Were we taking adequate care of veterans' families? Were learning-disabled children covered under No Child Left Behind? Would Bush "take on health care the same way you've taken on Iraq"? Would he reinstitute the draft? What were his views on renewable energy sources? When would Osama bin Laden be captured?

"Appreciate the question," Bush would invariably answer, and then proceed into a lengthy, digressive reply as he wandered the stage. To the grubby, desultory bunch in the rafters with their laptops and tape recorders, the answers were familiar. But folks in towns like Sedalia, Fond du Lac, and Perrysburg, Ohio, had never seen a president up close before, much less one who took their questions and offered expansive replies. The facts that there was no opportunity for a follow-up question and there seemed to be not a single undecided voter amid the throngs (or, for that matter, a single dark-skinned face) were of no consequence. Their president had taken time out from his busy schedule to drop in for a chat . . . and, well, he seemed just like one of them.

Some of the questions posed at Ask President Bush were not even questions at all. Many simply wished to say that they were praying for Bush. In Lima, Ohio, a man stood up and said, "I'm a lifetime member of the National Rifle Association. And Mr. Kerry and Edwards have got F minuses, and they said you're the only man."

In Kutztown, Pennsylvania, a voice hollered out, "Come visit our farm!"

In Sedalia, Missouri, a self-professed Christian woman exclaimed, "I am definitely impressed that you've been chosen for this time."

The woman added, much as a mother would, "And finally, I don't want you to worry about those weapons of mass destruction. They're going to find them. They're there."

It was in this atmosphere of breezy flesh pressing and deferential banter that George W. Bush was led, like a lamb to the slaughter, in to the first presidential debate.

He had prepared for it. Bush always prepared. He never failed to devour the briefing books that the propeller-heads assembled. But it was one thing to spit out factoids, another to engage in an intellectual brawl on a playing field that was mercilessly level.

His staff had worried about him in 2000. After several good prep sessions, he melted down not long before the first debate against Gore. Bush was exhausted from the campaign trail, and, to make matters worse, they'd decided to hold this prep session in the evening, as the actual debates would be. The governor didn't like working at night.

To simulate the debate setting, they decided not to hold this session in the dinky bunkhouse with the exercise equipment on his Crawford spread. Instead, they chose a small country church nearby. Rove and Judd Gregg (who played Gore in the preps) went in a different car. Upon arriving at the church, they wondered where everyone else was . . . until Rove's cell phone rang, and it was the governor, chewing out Rove, who'd taken a wrong turn, gone to an entirely different church in an entirely different town. . . .

Bush was cranky. And Gregg—whose effete Gore-isms were so grating that when he'd first performed them back in 1996, while prepping Dole's running mate Jack Kemp for the VP debate, Kemp shot the bird at Gregg and stormed off the stage—was doing his thing, nagging and baiting, violating Bush's airspace, demanding that he sign this or that pledge, just bein' Al . . . except that Bush started getting nasty, and Karen stepped in and abruptly called an end to the session.

Don Evans and Stuart Stevens walked outside the church to relieve themselves. "This is bad," Evans muttered as they stood in a meadow. "How fucked do you think we are?"

Bush had been saved that first debate by Gore's audible sighs of exasperation and Victorian layers of facial makeup. Thereafter, Bush held his own against the pugnacious VP, whose trophy case included the heads of Kemp and Ross Perot and Bill Bradley . . . but who came off as a canned orator and a bully. Karen had expertly ratcheted down media expectations, as she had in 1994 against Ann Richards. Bush the underdog showed up, didn't drool or declare war on China, and that was good enough.

Now he was the incumbent president, riding high in the polls and on a tide of good feelings from his Ask President Bush love-ins. Continuing the tradition of low expectations, the brooding Dowd made a half-convincing show of pessimism to the press, proclaiming John Kerry "the best debater since Cicero." Bush wasn't intimidated. But within his camp, there was sufficient respect for Kerry and institutional knowledge of Bush's foibles that they decided, well before the convention, to bring in outside help.

Rove had met Liberty University debate coach Brett O'Donnell while giving the commencement address on the Reverend Jerry Falwell's campus in May. Rove later sent over hundreds of hours of taped debates for O'Donnell to analyze. The debate coach wrote reports assessing the past performances of Bush, Kerry, Cheney, and Edwards and sent them over to Mehlman—who read them, promptly put Brett O'Donnell on the campaign's payroll, and summoned him to Arlington in August.

O'Donnell had never before consulted for a campaign. He would therefore have had no way of knowing how unusual it was to face an audience of the Bush team's heaviest hitters: Mehlman, Rove, Karen, Bartlett, Dowd, McKinnon, Mark Wallace (an attorney who with McKinnon would conduct the debate negotiations), campaign communications director Nicolle Devenish, and Bush's two policy briefers for the debates, Tevi Troy and Gary Edson. Rove introduced O'Donnell to the others and urged him to help himself to the platters of Red Hot & Blue barbecue sitting on the conference table.

O'Donnell told the gathering that their boss was at his best when he stuck to simple themes, as he had in 1994 against Richards. But Kerry would be a stronger opponent than Gore, he warned. The senator was agile on his feet, particularly at turning an opponent's remark back against him.

"The format of the debates matters greatly," said O'Donnell. They should avoid any kind of event where Kerry could directly engage the president. Gore had beaten Bush in their town hall debate, he asserted.

Several people in the room openly disagreed—Bush had clearly won, they said. "We were just playing for a tie then," Rove allowed.

"Format matters," O'Donnell maintained. In the primary debates, Kerry frequently ignored the bell and ran on after the time limit. He suggested that the negotiators insist on a timing light, perhaps even an audible signal, so that Kerry would be seen as a rule breaker.

"The president is such a play-by-the-rules type of guy that he expects everyone else to be the same way," Karen observed. And when the opponent crossed the line, she added, Bush tended to complain about it, to the point of sounding whiny.

He's got to get over that, said O'Donnell. Let the viewers make their own judgment. And in the meantime, he told McKinnon and Wallace, insist on hard-and-fast time limits. And if there's got to be a town hall gathering, make it the middle debate—don't let it be the last thing voters remember about Bush.

There was another significant matter that O'Donnell felt he should bring up. He'd analyzed Bush's "nonverbal characteristics." Against Richards, Bush's posture was bad. Against Mauro in '98, he sneered repeatedly. Against Gore, he slumped during their seated debate, and at times he winced. "Nonverbal is big," O'Donnell warned. When he asked them to recall some of the most electrifying moments of debates past, several in the room brought up the 1988 vice presidential debate, when Lloyd Bentsen seared Dan Quayle with his "You're no Jack Kennedy" retort. It was a stiletto line, but just as memorable was Quayle's little-boy-lost expression. Bush should be apprised of his tendencies, and the negotiators should insist that there be no rear cameras to reveal his slouching, nor a split-screen view of both candidates to show Bush's reactions to Kerry's words.

O'Donnell could tell that he was getting through to McKinnon, Rove, and Mehlman. But Edson, the policy guy, was skeptical about this emphasis on style and format. He clearly thought that substance was all that mattered.

The debate coach had a couple of additional suggestions. First, he thought it might be a good idea for Bush to do a final debate prep in front of a live audience, with an immediate evaluation to follow. The idea drew snickers. The president was a busy man—and anyway, O'Donnell was told, the objective at this point was to make Bush feel comfortable. Suggestions could come at some later point.

Finally, Brett O'Donnell proposed that he attend the prep sessions himself. He could show the president what he meant about the nonverbal stuff.

"You don't want to," McKinnon advised him with a smile. "It'd be a bad idea."

Ten days before the first debate, Bush concluded his final Ask President Bush in Derry, New Hampshire. The last question posed to him was by a retired naval officer, and it was in fact not a question at all: "My heartfelt prayer to you, sir, is stay the course and win the election in '04."

"Thank you, sir," Bush replied. Then he said, "I can't conclude on a better note. Thank you all for coming. God bless." Having thus endured the inquisition of the voting public, the president returned to his bubble.

That same day, opposing campaign managers Ken Mehlman and Mary Beth Cahill signed their names to a Memorandum of Understanding regarding the debates. Much of O'Donnell's advice had been heeded. The candidates couldn't pose questions to each other or attempt to extract pledges. The moderator would verbally alert a candidate when his time had elapsed, and a timing light would be illuminated. The rear camera could be focused only on the moderator. And the town hall format, while unavoidable, had been scheduled for the second of three debates.

One other suggestion by O'Donnell had made it into the memorandum: "There will be no TV cutaways to any candidate who is not responding to a question while another candidate is answering a question. . . ." But both sides knew that it would be up to the networks to enforce this rule, and likely they would refuse to do so.

A couple of days before the first debate—the subject of which was national security, Bush's strong suit—the president engaged in a rigorous prep session at Crawford. Karen, McKinnon, and others thought he was fabulous. The forty $8 \times 5\frac{1}{2}$-inch flashcards he carried with him had been thoroughly digested. They fired questions at him, and Bush tossed the answers back with swaggering elan. Judd Gregg was there to play Kerry, and he continually went after Bush. Bush enjoyed Gregg's antics but assured those present, "He's not gonna attack. He's gonna try to look presidential."

So delighted were the staffers with Bush's knowledge of the facts—and with his evident state of comfort—that no one insisted on a ninety-minute replication of the debate format. Nor did anyone pass on to Bush the admonition of Brett O'Donnell: *Nonverbal is big.* Bush was feeling it. No one wanted to belly flop into his punch bowl.

After the debate prep, Bush and McKinnon went for a bike ride in the clawing heat. Both men rode until they could no longer move their legs. At the time, it felt cathartic.

"Do you believe you could do a better job than President Bush in preventing another 9/11-type terrorist attack against the United States?"

"Yes, I do," replied John Kerry to the first question of the night posed by moderator Jim Lehrer in the University of Miami arena. Kerry digressed to thank the moderator, the university, the debate commission, and the president. Then he continued: "I'll never give a veto to any country over our security. But I also know how to lead those alliances. The president has left them in shatters across the globe, and we're now 90 percent of the casualties and 90 percent of the costs. I think that's wrong, and I think we can do better . . ."

Bush listened. Or tried to. And tried, but failed, to conceal his reaction, which was, for all the world to see: *Who the hell does this asshole think he is?* Getting up in the grill of the president of the United States—for four years it hadn't happened, not even close, no one did this to him, Rove and Bartlett and Card and Cheney and Rice always knew when to draw back, Hagin and McKinnon and Harriet Miers doted on him like kindly grandparents, even Army-brat Karen, who had left the White House in '02 and come back for the campaign in August, didn't lay into him like this, and he'd held one-fifth as many press conferences as his dad and half as many as Nixon because he didn't *have* to submit to their obnoxious grilling, he was chief executive. . . . He was commander in chief, saluted by obedient men and women, and coming off a convention so dazzling that he could still see the whirling confetti, could still hear the chants of *FOUR MORE YEARS! FOUR MORE YEARS!* harmonizing with the fervent cheers of those good people in Sedalia and Fond du Lac and Derry. . . . Now he stood alone—just a candidate, or worse, a sitting president with a record to attack, a sitting duck with a stupid red buzzer on his podium telling him he couldn't go on as long as he damn well pleased, and it was ordinarily his bedtime, besides which he'd spent the morning touring Florida by helicopter to view hurricane damage and right now the tank was feeling perilously unfull . . . and Kerry: No one said he'd be this good, they'd been saying the guy sucked, well he wasn't sucking at all, he was concise, decisive, presidential—*and* going straight after the President of the United States. . . .

His lips screwed themselves into a rubbery fist. The muscles around his eyes knotted. Karen and Bartlett knew that look: It meant that the president was done hearing this crap. Except that now he couldn't cut in. He had to take it.

Backstage in the staff holding room, Bartlett and Karen saw their boss's expression on the monitors, because the networks had ignored the cutaway rule and placed Bush on a split screen beside Kerry, so that all of America could watch the president react with haughty indignation to the challenger's words.

"I think we've got a problem," Karen told Bartlett.

She said the same thing to Nicolle Devenish, who didn't know what Karen was talking about—Devenish had been listening while typing on the computer and hadn't looked up.

One of the staffers in a different holding room was listening to the debate on the radio and called Judd Gregg to say: *Aren't we KICKING ASS?* "No, we're not," Gregg murmured in reply. "The visual here is not good."

Bartlett walked back into the media-spin room rolling his eyes in dismay. "How bad do you think it is?" he asked Ed Gillespie.

"I think it's bad," admitted Gillespie. "But we'll survive it."

Sitting in the audience, watching Kerry issue his crisp answers while Bush glared and smirked and then repeated, "It's hard," about Iraq as if the words were an ever-twitching nerve, Brett O'Donnell—who had studied footage of every single presidential debate since Kennedy–Nixon in 1960—believed he was witnessing the most comprehensive beating in the history of the American presidency.

"What do you think?" Bush asked Joe Hagin as soon as it was over.

"You were great!" Hagin assured him.

He learned otherwise, late that evening, on Air Force One.

It fell, as always, to Karen to tell him. "They're going to report that you lost the debate," she said.

Bush was astonished. "Why?" he asked.

"You looked mad."

"I wasn't mad! Tell them that!"

"I can't. Because you *did* look mad. You looked defensive."

Bush turned to Bartlett, who affirmed that this was so.

"Oh, y'all are blowing it out of proportion," the president insisted.

Bartlett decided to tread a step further into the valley of the shadow of death. "Can we show you how many times—the looks?" he ventured.

And so Bush sat in his Air Force One suite and watched himself on television acting pissed off—and got pissed off at Bartlett for making him watch himself.

Mehlman saw a glumness settle into Bush's face. He'd screwed up—he knew it now.

It was warm in Miami. But it felt like New Hampshire.

Bush's collosal lead over Kerry had collapsed like a soufflé. He was now down by three points.

Cheney would have to stop the bleeding.

His opponent in the October 5 vice presidential debate, John Edwards, hadn't been Kerry's first choice. (McCain was.) Edwards could accept that—the vice presidency hadn't been *his* first choice, either. But once it became clear that the nomination would belong to the senator from Massachusetts—a man of patrician bloodlines who didn't know a mill town from a Miller Lite—Edwards campaigned so vigorously for the second-tier post that it would have embarrassed both men and their party to turn him away. Kerry's running mate offered a number of cosmetic virtues. He projected youth (Mehlman dubbed him Breck Girl), his children were adorable, and his wife, Elizabeth, was a savvy operator with the media.

Chiefly, however, the smooth southerner was on the ticket for two reasons. The first was to deliver Kerry a red state—any red state, just one would do, perhaps for example his own. The second reason was to leverage his prowess as Killer of the Courtroom by beating Dick Cheney in the debate.

The Bush camp knew that the former scenario wasn't likely. Edwards had begun his run for the presidency after serving only four years in public office. That kind of seething ambition rubbed North Carolinians the wrong way. Bush was more popular in that state than its own senator was.

As for Edwards's rhetorical skills—well, the auditorium at Case Western Reserve University in Cleveland, Ohio, wasn't a courtroom. As a senator, Edwards wasn't one for detailed briefings, or details of any kind. Colleagues who had seen great promise in him, like John McCain and Joe Biden, gradually grew disillusioned. They observed that Edwards's incuriosity surpassed that of Bush—who at least read history books and who had never argued, as John Edwards had in the summer of 2002, that the best reason for invading Iraq was Saddam's nuclear weapons program . . . a program that, as it turned out, never existed.

Nonetheless, Edwards remained a handsome, clever-tongued ally of the man who'd just clocked Bush in Miami. And Cheney? He remained a politician of unsurpassingly high negative approval ratings . . . but also one of great guile and caution. So in the summer he retreated to the bunker—or rather, to his ranch in Jackson Hole, Wyoming, where he prepared as if John Edwards were the second coming of Clarence Darrow, Daniel Webster, and Atticus Finch combined.

Cheney's unflappable bearing was the product of hard work. For the 2000 VP debate against Joe Lieberman, he faced an uphill battle: He knew almost nothing about Governor Bush's record, and in the debate preps the former Halliburton executive had the unfortunate tendency to refer to that scandal-plagued corporation as "we." Cheney nonetheless thoroughly disarmed Lieberman in that debate, to the point where it seemed hardly a debate at all, but instead a collegial dis-agreement between old Beltway warhorses.

The VP's camp—which included Stuart Stevens, press secretary Steve Schmidt, and Edwards's stand-in, Congressman Rob Portman, but at its core consisted of Cheney's two daughters and his wife, Lynne—had no illusions that Edwards would be as docile. At the same time, Cheney thought Lieberman was a serious candidate. He could not find it within himself to respect John Edwards. Unlike the Bush preps, Cheney's run-throughs were always timed to coincide with the debate format. The VP wasn't terribly familiar with the domestic side of the ledger, and it rattled him whenever he looked up during a reply and saw Lynne's sour expression. (Liz, the elder daughter, even-tually moved her mom out of her dad's field of vision.) But Cheney studied demonically for the event at Case Western. He knew that vice-presidential debates were supposed to be inconsequential. He knew that no one cast his ballot solely on the basis of the number two guy.

He'd also seen Bush's debate, seen the numbers go south.

October 5 would not be inconsequential.

Edwards came out slugging that night. "Mr. Vice President, you are still not being straight with the American people," he said in response to Cheney's first answer, regarding the supposed Al Qaeda–Saddam Hussein connection. The North Carolina senator was fiery and direct. Cheney was unruffled and equally direct.

It didn't take long, however, for the VP to reveal his two-pronged strategy: make Kerry and Edwards look like flip-floppers and cast Edwards as an unserious slickster. When Edwards said of Iraq's cost to America, "We're at $200 billion and counting," Cheney brought out the blade: "With regard to the cost, it wasn't $200 billion. You probably weren't there to vote for that, but the $120 billion is, in fact, what has been allocated to Iraq."

Every attempt by Edwards to establish consistency in Kerry's record was met by that immovable monotone: "Your rhetoric, Senator, would be a lot more credible if there was a record to back it up." And: "Well, Gwen [Ifill, the debate's moderator], I think the record speaks for itself. These are two individuals who have been for the war when the headlines were good, and against it when their poll ratings were bad."

The debate was halfway over when Cheney pounced. The topic was Halliburton—or it was, until the VP said, "The reason they keep trying to attack Halliburton is because they want to obscure their own record. And, Senator, frankly, you have a record in the Senate that's not very distinguished. You've missed thirty-three out of thirty-six meetings of the Judiciary Committee, almost 70 percent of the meetings of the Intelligence Committee. You've missed a lot of key votes on tax policy, on energy, on Medicare reform. Your hometown newspaper has taken to calling you Senator Gone. You've got one of the worst attendance records in the United States Senate.

"Now, in my capacity as vice president," he went on, "I am president of the Senate, the presiding officer. I'm up in the Senate most Tuesdays when they're in session. The first time I ever met you was when you walked on the stage tonight."

There was a strange noise in the audience—or was it the implied sound of catastrophic silence? Of course, Edwards had missed votes and meetings because he'd been on the campaign trail for most of 2003 and 2004. And, as it developed, he and Cheney had met at least once before, or at least were photographed together, on Capitol Hill—but at a prayer breakfast.

Still, Cheney had seized upon an emblematic truth. And that look on John Edwards's face—gaping, eyes wide below the foppish hairdo—was not only emblematic but all too familiar: *You're no Jack Kennedy.*

The bleeding had stopped.

*   *   *

Bush righted himself, more or less—bedazzling no one, and indeed in the second debate exhibiting a scarecrowish posture on a town hall stage in St. Louis where the crowd had not been stacked in his favor as it had in other Missouri towns a month beforehand. But he reined in the testiness, while Kerry began to wear on the viewer. By the end of the third and final debate in Tempe on October 13, it was clear that the senator from Massachusetts deserved coronation as Debater in Chief—leaving unanswered: *Could* he lead? *Did* voters know where he stood? *Was* there really any substance to buttress his continual droning declaration of *I haaave a plaaaan*? Just what did he mean when he said that preemptive military action had to be done "in a way that passes the test, that passes the global test"? And what did it say about Kerry and Edwards that each of them felt the need during the debates to remind TV viewers that Dick Cheney had a gay daughter? Given a choice, not a referendum . . .

Still, the president hardly emerged from the debates with the wind at his back. Despite the triumphalism of the convention and the blissful cruise control of Ask President Bush, it had not been an easy summer for the Bush campaign. Mehlman's ground team in Florida awakened in August to the sick realization that the liberal groups ACT and MoveOn were dumping hordes of skin on the ground in that crucial state. The other key state in 2004, Ohio, remained an economic disaster. Every time Mehlman felt he could step back and regard his massive volunteer organization as one would a fine new automobile, along came Donald Rumsfeld with some brutally tone-deaf aphorism about Iraq—"Stuff happens"—to puncture the tires.

Karen and Rove were fighting even worse than they had in 2000. "Karl decides where we go; I decide what we say," was the Message Disciplinarian's reductionist description, but the division of labor was not quite so neat. Karen's predilection for intruding into a long-planned scheme and tearing it up at the last minute was wearing thin among her colleagues. Her instincts, though highly respected, were not unerring: The new slogan she had contrived—"We're turning a corner, and we can't turn back!"—registered as a dud and was soon abandoned. By the fall, Nicolle Devenish was commissioned by Mehlman and Bartlett to ride Air Force One primarily for the purpose of keeping Rove and Karen's warring to a minimum.

For Bush, the frantic pace of the campaign combined with the demands of the Oval Office were beating him down. He functioned best when Laura was with him, but the campaign often needed her for separate events. He was exercising less, eating junk food, gaining weight, complaining of being overscheduled. This was hardly 1994's "campaign of joy," or the cakewalk of '98—or even 2000, when he had the governorship to fall back on and could tell himself and others, *I don't need this.*

Could he say that now?

Bush was determined, as always, to view his prospects optimistically, in defiance of the facts at hand. Back in the Abu Ghraib–benighted days of May 2004, he convened a meeting in the residence with Laura, Card, Rove, Bartlett, Mehlman, Devenish, Dowd, Mc-Kinnon, and Gillespie for a campaign update. After thanking everyone for their hard work, Bush then said, "Our numbers are right at where Reagan's were at this point in 1984. So that means we're headed for a big victory . . . What, Matty?"

Dowd's expression was one of total bewilderment.

"I'm sorry, sir?"

"That look on your face."

"It's just that—well, Mr. President, it's just not true," Dowd said. "Our numbers are nowhere near Reagan's. We're like twelve to fourteen points off of his. I mean, we're ahead slightly. But we're in the margin of error. And if we win, it won't be a big victory. It'll be like two or three points."

If they won? Bush was momentarily speechless. Then: "KARL!"

"Well," Rove stammered, "if you take a look at all the historical data, average things out . . ." The others in the room had seen Rove's dissembling act before. So had Bush, and after a few moments, he interrupted Rove and moved on with the meeting—grassroots updates from Mehlman, media buys from McKinnon—thereby dispensing with Rove's pseudoscience, but also with Dowd's gloomy forecast.

At times the optimism frayed and he took out his stresses on his favorite punching bag, Rove. "Why are you saying 'flex time' *and* 'comp time'?" Bush snapped at him one day aboard Air Force One, referring to the two alternative overtime-pay methods for businesses Bush was now advocating. "Which one do you mean? Are they different, or aren't they?"

And Rove reddened, blubbery lips quivering: "I . . . uh . . ."

"You don't know what the hell you're talking about!"

"I'll, uh, make some calls, sir."

Instead, he went off to yell at a reporter.

At other times, Bush pounded on the CIA staffers who gave him his

Presidential Daily Briefing. There were continual threat warnings that summer and fall—and, as well, ongoing covert assessments of the dangers in Iraq and the occupation's unpopularity among the locals there. Many of these reports were finding their way into the press, to Bush's fury. At one point he growled at a CIA briefer, "Since whatever you tell me in the PDB is in the *New York Times* two or three days later, why don't we just cut out this middle stage? Just give it directly to the *Times* and I'll find out about it in my morning press briefing."

There were, of course, lovely moments as well. While reposing in Kennebunkport, he received his PDBs in 41's study, with Poppy present—always silent, the former president content with his ongoing role as supportive father—and 43 would respond in kind by reacting to an item about China with a measured "Well, I know *you* won't agree with this, because it's kind of rough on your friends in Beijing, but . . ."

The party's rising stars were rallying to their chief. McCain traveled with him to Nevada and Oregon. Giuliani flew along to Colorado, Iowa, and Wisconsin. Schwarzenegger joined him in Ohio. (Though the governor's operatives requested that White House staffers not ask him for autographs.) The crowds at the rallies were uncanny, buoying the creature hidden beneath the regular-guy architecture who flourished when the masses fell in behind him. On Air Force One that fall, an aide just had to ask his boss: How did he manage to confront the monotony of these dreadful campaign events?

Bush smiled and said, "It's not hard, when thirty thousand people are chanting your name."

At times it felt like that; and at others—like when he sat on the plane shaking his head in disgust as two Republican senators, Chuck Hagel and Dick Lugar, criticized his Iraq policy on a Sunday talk show—it felt like 1992, when all the rats scurried from his dad's foundering campaign. A president was not so in control, after all. Hurricanes in Florida—did Governor Jeb and FEMA have the recovery under wraps? Michael Moore's new celluloid indictment of the Bush administration, *Fahrenheit 9/11*, was shrill, factually shabby . . . and breaking box-office records for a documentary. Meanwhile, insurgents were roiling Iraq—and "Damn it, why can't they find that out?" he would snap to no one in particular as he waited helplessly for more briefing information, which would arrive too late for his approval, and only a few days before it would be digested by readers of the *Times* and regurgitated by John Kerry.

It was now October, the month of surprises. In September,

60 Minutes had taken its best shot at Bush, instead shooting itself in the foot with an exposé of Bush's "missing days" in the National Guard, using documents that were discredited within days of their airing. Now the program, in collaboration with the *Times*, was offering a fresh hell—namely, 380 tons of weapons in Iraq that the Coalition had failed to guard and that were now missing.

For what felt like much longer than a moment, the campaign reeled. Kerry was crowing that the missing weapons cache was the latest evidence of Bush's faulty judgment. Bartlett could only watch with growing nausea as the Pentagon fumbled the response. But Mehlman was strangely delighted. Kerry's spokesman Mike McCurry had vowed that their campaign's "closing argument" would be on health care and the economy. Yet here was Kerry, chasing another rabbit—and to Bush's benefit, Mehlman believed. As Dowd put it to Ed Gillespie, "I'd rather be on a bad national-security story than a bad economic story."

The Friday morning before Election Day, Bush was campaigning in Manchester, New Hampshire, when a call came in to Condi Rice as she sat in the holding room. Her mouth fell open as she listened. "Bin Laden has released *another tape?*" she managed.

Al Qaeda's fugitive leader had not been heard from in over a year. Now a new videotape of him had made its way to Al Jazeera, which had dutifully aired it. Bin Laden's taped monologues were never short on self-reverence and denunciations of America. But this video seemed intent on engineering Bush's defeat. He made mocking reference to Bush reading *My Pet Goat* while the Twin Towers smoldered.

That evening, as the campaign concluded the day in Columbus, an aide brought up the bin Laden tape to Rove as they rode in the back of the support car to their hotel. "This has the feel of something," Rove said—slowly, as if still completing the calculation—"that's not gonna hurt us at all."

1 4

"Stand with Me"

"We're leaving it all on the field," Bush declared, for the thousandth time, on Monday, November 1.

Today was the final, mad marathon: seven events, six states, nineteen hours. From their overnight stop in Cincinnati, they choppered to a rally at an air hangar in Wilmington, Ohio. While Air Force One flew to Pittsburgh, Laura split off to two separate rallies in hopes of cutting in to Kerry's female vote. Bush spent the leg in his airborne office talking baseball with Red Sox pitcher Curt Schilling, who had jilted the campaign the previous week—variously citing medical concerns over his injured leg and misgivings about issuing an endorsement—but now was proud to introduce Bush to the throngs.

In Pittsburgh, Bush talked about steel mills, fair trade, and lower taxes. In Milwaukee—a city he was visiting for the thirteenth time this year, and where Kerry's plane would be landing any minute now—Bush relied on Choice, Not Referendum: "Ultimately the election comes down to, who do you trust?"

Laura rejoined him in Iowa, a state that had swung Gore's way in 2000. "If you're a Democrat who thinks your party has swung too far to the left, I ask you to come stand with me," Bush said. "If you're a minority . . . and if you are tired of your vote being taken for granted . . . I ask you to come stand with me."

Joe Hagin stood at the side of the stage and found himself choking up. He'd always loved the "come stand with me" rallying cry. Today, though, it carried a double meaning. The vast majority of those on board for this final stretch—Hagin, Bartlett, Karen, Rove, Rice,

McKinnon, Gerson, Devenish, Gottesman, Brett Kavanaugh, Scott McClellan, head of advance Todd Beyer, assistant press secretary Josh Deckard—had been standing with the president since 2000 or before. And none more so than Andy Card's deputy chief, an unmarried man with no kids who literally stood by Bush every time he left the White House. It was almost hard to remember what the other life had been like, before Joe Hagin made a life out of standing with George W. Bush.

On the flight from Albquerque to Dallas, they succumbed to nostalgia. Sitting in the Air Force One conference room—now thoroughly trashed with campaign detritus, including a sign Rove had picked up in Iowa that read FREE KITTENS and taped to the wall—the staffers began to exchange Bush campaign chestnuts from years past: *Honor and decency to the White House, so—help—me—GOD! Si no puedes leer, no puedes realizar tus sueños! Is our children learning?*

Bush ambled in, grinning at what he'd overheard, and contributed a few one-liners of his own. Someone put in a request for Devenish to do her Teresa Heinz Kerry imitation, which she fulfilled in wicked deadpan. The boss sat with young Deckard and challenged him to a game of gin rummy. "Uh, I might have to pipe in 'Hail to the Chief,' in case you forget who's supposed to win," Gottesman warned Deckard. There was no need: Bush annihilated the kid, while at the same table two other games of gin were in progress—Rice versus Jenna, Devenish versus Beyer—and staff secretary Kavanaugh read through the Dallas speech and eradicated any mention of Kerry, as it was decided that this, the last hurrah in front of a Texas crowd, should be all about sentimentality.

"You know what?" Bush said to those in the conference room. "I was thinking about it—when we get to Dallas, I want you guys standing behind me onstage when I speak."

When a few of them laughed, Bush protested, "No, no, I'm serious. I want you guys standing behind me."

Amid moans of gratitude, the president's eyes flooded. Perhaps, someone gently suggested, it might not be so good an idea. Perhaps "somebody" would get choked up. And so instead, Bush walked around the table, offering his hand, hugging, head bowed as he said, "Thank you. Really. Sincerely. Thank you."

They touched down in Dallas and motorcaded to Southern Methodist University, Laura's alma mater. The gym was sweltering, impossibly packed. The first lady wore red. Seemingly impervious to the day's tortured zigzag, her eyes were brilliant as she held the president's hand.

Joe Hagin stood off to the side. He could see, standing in the foreground of the electric crowd, two young women hollering as they held up a sign. It was the twins, Jenna and Barbara. The sign read: HAGIN ROCKS!

Past midnight, the staff disembarked from the motorcade and filed into the choppers that would convey them to Crawford or Waco. Rove stood on the helipad and consulted his BlackBerry. After reading his e-mails, he looked up at Gerson.

"We're winning," he told the speechwriter.

"Tomorrow's gonna be a big day," the president said by way of good night as he and Laura disappeared inside the house at Crawford.

Inside the senior staff trailer, Rove thought about the e-mail he had read on the helipad. Yes, as he'd told Gerson, they were winning. But the margin of the tracking poll was razor thin: two to three up in Ohio, dead even in Florida. He decided to call Mehlman.

"I think we need to do both states tomorrow," the campaign manager told him.

Rove agreed. Air Force One was already headed for Columbus in the morning. "We'll look for a place to stop in Florida," he said and hung up.

It was one in the morning, but Hagin was still awake in the trailer. Rove talked to him about the need for a rendezvous in Florida. "You can do it—you can make it happen," he told the chief of operations.

"I don't know," muttered Hagin. It was two o'clock on the east coast. A plane would have to airlift a motorcade of armored cars into Florida. He tried calling one of his advance men, but the latter's cell phone had died. Beyer wasn't picking up his phone. Finally, Hagin located a Secret Service agent who dealt with car–plane logistics. The armored cars awaiting them in Columbus could be moved to Florida, the agent said. Getting a second fleet at this hour . . . well . . .

At two in the morning, Hagin said to Rove, "I don't think we can hit it."

"Let's forget it," Bush's senior adviser said. "I think we'll be okay in Florida anyway."

Just to be sure, he ran the scenario by Mehlman. "One stop is all we can do," Rove said. "You make the call."

"We gotta do Ohio," said Mehlman.

On Tuesday, November 2, 2004, at seven in the morning, the president cast his ballot in the Crawford, Texas, fire station. Rove, standing outside the voting booth, felt his cell phone buzz and flipped it open.

"You're on live television right now," Ed Gillespie told Rove.

Not missing a beat, Rove exclaimed, loud enough for the TV mikes to pick him up, "Wow! That's great! These numbers are even higher than we expected!"

Bush emerged from the booth waving—though not well rested, and already the media had begun to dissect his absence of ebullience. In fact, he felt good. And he was about to feel better, after placing two calls on the way from Crawford to the Waco airstrip.

The first was to Matthew Dowd. "What do you think, Matty?" he asked.

Dowd was congenitally incapable of rosiness. "I think you'll win by three," the strategist said.

"Well, I'm a five-point man," Bush proclaimed.

"Well, Mr. President, I hope you're right. But I think it's gonna be three."

"Okay, okay."

Then he placed his second call before stepping out of the limo and trudging across the muddy loading zone with socks over his shoes. Aboard Air Force One, Bush spoke to the staff with barely restrained excitement. "I just talked to Jeb," the president said. "Jeb said everything's going to be fine in Florida."

Reacting to their relieved faces, Bush reminded them, "Jeb's a pretty dour guy. You're not gonna get happy talk from Jeb Bush. And Jeb is some kind of fired up."

After the final stop in Columbus, Air Force One headed for home. Bush walked up and down the aisles, thanking his staff again. "I've done everything I can do," he said.

At around that same time, Sara Taylor received the first exit polls. Because she was rather fair-skinned, Mehlman and Dowd could not immediately detect the blood vanishing from her cheeks.

"These can't be right," Mehlman said as he looked at the numbers.

Dowd retreated to his office. He refused to speak to anyone.

Taylor called Rove.

The plane was descending when Rove's cell phone rang. He left the others in the conference room and headed to the senior staff cabin. Bartlett followed and sat next to him. Rove heard the words *not good,* but then they went through clouds and he lost the call.

Rove called her back. Karen was now in the cabin. Rice and Bush also joined them, looking over Rove's shoulder as he tried to write down the tallies on a piece of paper against his knee—except that his hand was shaking, perhaps only because of the turbulence. . . . Bartlett reached over and held down the paper as Rove scribbled.

South Carolina—tied. Virginia—down 1. Pennsylvania—down 17 . . .

"That Pennsylvania number is wrong," Rove said.

"Absolutely," said Sara Taylor.

He hung up. Then he looked at the others, who had been staring at the piece of paper.

Karen gasped, "That doesn't make any sense—losing *Virginia?*"

For the first time all year, Bush looked utterly defeated. "I'm really surprised," he said. "But it is what it is."

Then he said, "Look, if it is what it is, we'll deal with it. But I don't believe it. We've been here before." With that, Bush retreated to his cabin, to give Laura the news.

After they had landed, Bartlett met his wife, Allyson, and drove to the polling station two blocks from their house in Chevy Chase. "So I guess we'll move back to Austin," Bartlett began. "After that—I don't know. . . ."

His wife's eyes narrowed, and Bartlett then realized what she was thinking. Back on election night of 2000, he'd sung the same tune—taken Allyson aside, told her, *I want to prepare you for a long night—it's over. . . .*

"I'm tired of hearing you say we're going to lose," she said. "I didn't believe you then and I'm not going to believe you now."

Seeking solace, Bush called Mehlman in Arlington. The conversation was patched in to the White House, where Poppy was anxiously awaiting news.

"I don't believe them," Mehlman said of the numbers. "The sampling can't be right."

"Why not?"

"Look at Pennsylvania," Mehlman said. Conservative Lancaster County was showing record turnout. "Unless there's a lot of Amish voting for Kerry, you can't have that kind of turnout and lose the state by seventeen," he said.

Bush was hugely relieved. Mehlman wasn't one of those staffers who told the president only what he wanted to hear . . . like McKinnon, whom Bush reached back at his apartment, just to add another voice to the chorus.

"You believe these numbers?" he asked his media adviser.

McKinnon, fighting off a deep gloom, nonetheless knew his role. "Hell no!"

Karen had checked in to the Hay-Adams Hotel a couple of blocks from the White House. Sleep did not come as she thrashed in bed, thinking, *What did we miss?* Followed by: *We are NOT going to lose Virginia!*

Bartlett called her. "Karl says there's some problems with these numbers," he said.

But both of them were thinking the same thing. Even if there *were* some problems, they couldn't possibly account for the totality of the margin. Karen brought up the need to draft a concession speech.

"Mike's already given some thought to it," said Bartlett.

Karen was already preparing herself. *We've got to be gracious*, she thought.

Rove was not feeling gracious. Sitting in his office on the second floor of the West Wing, he combed through the stacks of exit-poll data. None of them made any sense. *Losing the white male vote in Florida?* It hadn't happened to a Republican since Goldwater. Bush had just called, having spoken to Jeb, who didn't at all believe they were down in his state.

Rice and Office of Legislative Affairs director David Hobbs appeared in his doorway. It was going to be like this all night, he knew. This was Rove's night, for better or for worse.

"My gut is, we take Florida and Ohio, and we win," he told them. Then he excused himself to take a shower next door in the Old Executive Office Building.

When Rove returned, Rice, Andy Card, and Hagin were all in his office, waiting for his next words of encouragement.

*   *   *

Nicolle Devenish entered Dowd's office to find him in a more or less fetal position, with the hood of his sweatshirt pulled over his head. "Matthew, you've got to come down and talk to the media. Not seeing you is totally making them think that we think we've lost."

From beneath the hood: "I've not going down. I'm not going down."

Sara Taylor went in his place. She'd gotten the cross-tabs at 5:00 PM. In Florida, Bush was receiving more than 50 percent of the Hispanic vote. No way they could lose the state under such a scenario. Turnout in the Ohio exurbs was huge, exceeding expectations. Taylor passed this on to the media downstairs. "You should wait for the actuals," she warned them.

The first actuals were from Kentucky and came in at 6:30. Dowd saw them. "The exits don't match," he said, and Lazarus-like he sprang out of his office and down the stairs to where the media had gathered.

No one seemed terribly swayed by the Kentucky numbers. But Dowd had his groove back. "The next one you're gonna see is South Carolina," he predicted. "We'll go from a tie to us winning by fifteen or sixteen."

On his way out of the building, he said to the reporters, "Cheer up, everyone. You're covering the winning campaign."

He walked briskly down the street to the Irish pub where a number of staffers had intended to host a postelection celebration but were now in the throes of a wake—including McKinnon, who sat at the bar, wearing a shirt that said BOWLING FOR BUSH and muttering, "It could be a landslide for Kerry."

Dowd spun McKinnon around on his bar stool. "Fuck, these exit polls are so screwed up!" he said. "Did you see North Carolina? This is fucking amazing. This is why they need to do away with the exits and go back to the way they used to."

Then, in a louder voice, the strategist said, "Okay, everyone listen. Here's the deal. I think things are gonna be fine. . . ."

Rove was trying to tell the networks the same thing, but they weren't buying it. "We can't be losing white men in Florida!" he yelled into the phone receiver. "*It can't happen!*"

Well, the reporters would say, *let us check with the newsroom.* And then they would call back Rove with the words of wisdom their editors had imparted: *We believe Kerry may have succeeded in changing the nature of the electorate.*

"The nature of—look at New Hampshire," Rove said, trying to stay rational. "If you take all of the polls from last week in New Hampshire and average them together, we're down one. Then there's the unde-cideds—about four. So *give* those to Kerry. Say we're down five. *We're not down nineteen like the exits say, for God's sake!*"

Interesting. Let us check again. . . . Uh, the feeling here is that all the undecideds are breaking decisively for John Kerry, and George W. Bush is hemorrhaging his base.

"GIVE THEM *ALL* THE UNDECIDEDS!" Rove couldn't believe it. Had every news organization in America been drinking MoveOn.org's Kool-Aid? Or were they so spellbound by the ghastly margins of the exit polls that they simply couldn't fathom an entirely opposite conclusion?

Or—Rove wasn't permitted to utter it aloud, but he thought it, over and over: *Oh, God, what if I'm wrong?*

He'd relocated to the residence dining room. His assistants Susan Ralston and Israel Hernandez, along with Kavanaugh and his wife, Ashley, sat in front of computers and telephones, with five plasma TV screens arrayed against a wall. Occasionally he would head back over to the Roosevelt Room in the West Wing, where senior staffers and cabinet officers were sitting around look-ing vaguely suicidal and reacting to Rove's cheery assurances as if he'd claimed to have seen Elvis astride a unicorn. But his main fixation was here in the dining room. In front of him sat a computer with a map of the the United States on the screen. He would hit the state of Florida, then hit a county. When he saw the new numbers in that county, he would call them out to the former political-science major sitting at the end of the table: "Condi, Duval County's at 57.8!" And then he would cross-refer the number Rice had scribbled down against what they'd gotten in Duval in 2000, and what they'd pro-jected for 2004.

And they were way ahead.

And by 8:30 that evening, the world outside the White House and the Arlington headquarters began to see what Rove was seeing: a tidal wave dwindling, then slowly coming back, regathering in Florida not only along the I-4 corridor but even in the three-county killing fields of Broward and Palm Beach and Dade. . . . By 9:30 Eastern Time they had Florida, had it legit, and so attention turned else-where. Mehlman had positioned lawyers in each of the fifty states—forty alone in New Mexico, which Rove was convinced had been illegally snatched from Bush in 2000. Both there and in Iowa, the Dems had put on a ferocious early-voting drive, which had freaked Rove out. But Mehlman had insisted that *THEIR early voters would be voting on Election Day anyway. WE'RE targeting occasionals to vote early. All they're doing is cannibalizing their own Election Day turnout. We're bringing in new voters—like the exurbanites who drive forty-five minutes to and from work and don't have time to vote. They're voting! They're ours! Have faith in the plan!*

Mehlman was right: Iowa and New Mexico, both of which had gone to Gore in 2000, were now swinging back into the red column. Yes, momentum was shifting, and now the brainiac exit pollsters were said to be "readjusting their data" . . . But the media, having ridden this bronco in 2000, was not about to jump off early—especially when it came to Ohio, which was being played by the talking heads as 2004's Florida.

Which was bullshit, Rove and Mehlman were telling the nets. *Hey, don't just look at Warren and Cuyahoga Counties! Look at the huge raw turnout in the Southwest! Look at the far Northwest—Wood, Enry, Allen, Fulton, Defiance—and look along the river, Washington and Athens, where a Democrat's gotta run well, and it ain't happening!* But now it was well after midnight, and a game of network chicken, of reverse scoopery, was in the works. None of them wanted to go through the double backflips of 2000 again.

At 1:10 AM, Bartlett's cell rang—and Rove, thoroughly in whirling dervish mode, snatched it up. "Can I speak to Dan Bartlett?" came the familiar voice. "This is Dave Gregory."

To the NBC reporter, Rove asked sweetly, "Will he know who you are?"

Ten minutes later, Senator Pete Domenici called Rove. "New Mexico is won," he intoned.

Five minutes after that, he got word that Iowa was in the bag as well.

Then, at 1:37 AM: *The four big Nevada counties are coming in. Nevada is won.*

Which left Ohio.

"The election that won't end," Bush had sighed in the residence dining room—and that was at 11:30 PM.

He'd gone back to his bedroom around two but wasn't able to sleep. Ordinarily, Bush was a master at husbanding his resources.

He'd taken a nap shortly before giving his historic September 20, 2001, speech before the Joint Session of Congress. And he was utterly whipped—had slept only four hours the night before, after that nineteen-hour death march from Cincinnati to Crawford.

But tonight he wanted to hear, definitively, where he stood.

Who could sleep? Laura's friend Nancy Weiss, in one of the guest bedrooms, had been told by Laura to sleep with her clothes on, in the event that they had to dash over to the Reagan Center to declare victory in the middle of the night. . . . This was nuts, and Bush proceeded to call Rove every few minutes, demanding, "Why the hell won't they call it?"

He's going insane, Rove thought, and realized that the problem was that no one on the ground in Ohio was communicating that the situation was stable there—no fraud, no funny business, just a nice clean victory. Ken Blackwell, the secretary of state, was bungling the message. "Where's Portman? Find Portman," Rove hollered. Hagin eventually tracked down Bush's favorite Ohio congressman in a Columbus hotel, woke him up, and instructed him to go find the press and deliver a suitable declaration, which Portman did.

Bush had finally passed out by 4:00. Card was calling Mary Beth Cahill, making no progress—while Edwards had marched out of the darkness to vow that every ballot in Ohio would be counted. At 4:20 AM, Rove was screaming to Tim Russert and Tom Brokaw of NBC, who calmly replied, "What's the harm in waiting a day?"

"They're gettin' lawyers on the plane! Democrats are on the TV! We cain't let 'em do this to us again!" roared Bush's old Dallas friend Jim Francis—persuading Rove and Card that Bush should be sent out there to the Reagan Center to declare victory before the Democrats snatched it away.

But Bartlett, gesturing to the five plasma screens, hollered back, "Can *anybody* show me what America's seen that shows me that we won this fucker?"

Karen had been sleeping on the floor, along with Mary Matalin. She said that Bartlett had it right.

Bartlett called Arlington using two phones: to Dowd, who had the numbers; and to Devenish, who'd been working a back channel with Kerry's press secretary Mike McCurry and had been told, "Look, I'm not going to walk out in my boxer shorts and go into John Kerry's room and talk to him about conceding. He's going to do the right thing, he knows he's lost, and he'll concede in the morning."

"Are we comfortable we won this?" Bartlett asked Dowd and Devenish. Both said yes. Bartlett then phoned upstairs.

Bush asked Laura what she thought. *You can wait*, she said.

Bartlett's boss told him that there was no need to declare victory tonight. Instead, Karen typed up a statement and handed it to Andy Card, who was driven to the Reagan Center, where he told those still gathered that victory was imminent . . . but that John Kerry would be given time to do the right thing.

At five in the morning, Rove called Mehlman to tell him that he was leaving the White House and heading home. "What are you going to do?" he asked the campaign manager.

"Go running," Mehlman said.

Mehlman would remember that 5:30 AM run through the streets of Arlington as one gigantic endorphin rush.

Rove would not remember his drive back to Chevy Chase.

At the time of Rove's phone call to Mehlman, Sara Taylor and eleven other campaign staffers—press secretaries, lawyers, field directors—flew from Washington to Columbus, Ohio, braced to reprise the battle of Florida 2000. They arrived at a Republican lawyer's office at around eight in the morning. Without preamble, they began strategizing. Ballot-counting monitors, press conferences, demonstrations . . .

They were ready to go, and at eleven in the morning Bush said he was tired of waiting, too. "I'm gonna go exercise," he said to Bartlett and Rove and Karen in the Oval after waiting ninety minutes for Kerry to call. . . . But somehow they got on a tangent, perhaps a little punch-drunk from the night before, and Bush was still standing in the Oval ten minutes later when the call at last came . . .

. . . And then it really seemed so simple. "You're a good man," Bush said to John Kerry.

He would remain president.

And not long after the hugging and the crying, Bush began to feel it, the swelling of excitement. "We gonna have fun in the next term," he promised Bartlett. "We're gonna have a blast. And at the end, we'll load up Air Force One and go to the 2008 Olympics!"

Bartlett hadn't planned to stick around quite until then. But, he told his wife, he had to give the boss at least one more year.

And anyway, Bush promised it would be fun.

PART FIVE

COMEUPPANCE

15

EIGHT-YEAR MEN

One cold Saturday morning in January 2005, the leader of the free world went for a ride on his bicycle.

No warm-ups, no stretching, no ramp-up. Just hammering from the start—that's how he always did it, even now at age fifty-eight. The five men lagging behind were much younger than Bush. He sped along the blacktop of the Secret Service Academy in Beltsville, Maryland. Then off-road, parallel to a small creek, skittering across rocks already damp from predawn flurries. Head to ankle in Lycra, cycling shoes clipped into the pedals of the Trek mountain bike, heaving out sweat and vapor from his mask, he cut an odd, postmodern bedouin-like figure in this blustery dreamscape. Now and then he mustered the wind to indulge in a little towel-snapping banter: "Here comes the hill, boys! Let's go, now!" And when he couldn't hear any reply, he eased up a bit, not wanting to drop the others altogether. Just showing them who's The Man—that was sufficient.

He had been chafing in anticipation of this moment. Obsessed with it, really—badgering young Blake Gottesman throughout the week: *Is M-Cat coming along?* ("M-Cat" being McKinnon.) *What's the weather gonna be like? Freezing? When are they saying it'll snow?* ("They" being the meteorologists Gottesman was harassing at the president's behest.)

Eighteen degrees. Bush was more than fine with it. Lungs seizing up and nostrils gushing? Now that's *adventure*! He used to run along Town Lake as governor in the middle of the day, when the Austin sun fell on you like a vault. When he was an oilman, he used to spend the lunch hour jogging from the Y through the residential streets of Midland at an insane clip, sweating off the previous night's toxins. "George likes to do things to excess"—that was the assessment of Laura, who just didn't *get* competition. Which was in fact part and parcel of her unconflicted beauty, but still . . . She'd be indoors at the Crawford ranch, curled up with a novel, while Bush was swaggering about in his denims, goading his Yankee aides into the ranks of the Hundred Degree Club. Clearing brush all morning till they sagged against the trees, drenched and panting. *Then* whipping along the trails.

But *this* ride—commencing shortly after seven in the morning on January 22, 2005, two days after being inaugurated to a second term as president of the United States of America—was about so much more than the obvious compulsions. It was about more than burning a thousand calories in eighty minutes. (A thousand calories—that was Bush's crazed baseline, though even more so now, after having picked up twelve pounds along the campaign trail.) It was about more than making girlymen out of two Secret Service agents, two White House photographers, and a media guru. It was about more than holding his own against arctic conditions, and indeed besting the elements by making it to the finish line before nine when, according to Gottesman's meteorologists, the snow would start to fall. Beating the damn snow—that was classic Bush, upping the ante wherever possible. But it didn't account for the frenzy of his pace.

This was about *release.*

One by one, Bush muttered into their ears, "Are you an eight-year man?"

Hmm . . . As Laura had dryly remarked to a friend, "Eight years is a *hell* of a long time." Still: Cheney, Bartlett, Card, Hagin, Rice, and Hadley were in. Rove was more in than ever: He would now be running the various White House policy councils in addition to his other intergalactic affairs. Gerson hadn't intended to stick around. But when the president offered the chief speechwriter an actual policy portfolio—AIDS and culture-of-life issues on the domestic side, democratization and human rights on the foreign side—Gerson couldn't say no.

Josh Bolten, Harriet Miers, Alberto Gonzales, and Scott McClellan were in. Clay Johnson, now Bolten's deputy at OMB, would remain in the service of his Andover chum. Margaret Spellings named her price for staying in Washington—becoming secretary of education—

and Bush met it. Ken Mehlman accepted Bush's request to take over the Republican National Committee. Sara Taylor took her mentor Mehlman's place as White House political director. Nicolle Devenish moved up to Bartlett's former post as communications director.

Karen (due to homesickness) and Larry Lindsey (involuntarily) had departed in 2002, Joe Allbaugh (DHS-related disgruntlement) and Ari Fleischer (burnout) in 2003, Don Evans (with regrets, but putting family first) at the end of '04. Otherwise, every single significant figure who had been with Bush since the 2000 campaign was still with him now.

And why not? Having endured New Hampshire and Florida and 9/11 and the reelect—and now, seeing the boss hopped up on adrenaline and Megabig Ideas—how could they just cash in their chips? No: It was time to spend them, after coming down from what Matthew Dowd's postelection memo termed "a historic victory," one in which Bush had received "the most votes by any presidential candidate in history." (Unmentioned in Dowd's memo was that Kerry had won the *second* most votes ever.)

Three days after the election, Pete Wehner, Rove's new Strategic Initiatives director, circulated a memo of his own, assessing what he soberly termed "The Most Important Election in Our Lifetime." Bush, Wehner declared, "is one of history's Consequential Presidents. . . . In foreign policy President Bush has earned the title as one of history's Great Liberators—and in domestic policy he will be seen as one of its Great Reformers. This instinct to seize the moment and to shape history—to 'swing for the fences,' in the words of the columnist Ron Brownstein—is fundamental to who George W. Bush is. His first term was enormously eventful—and tremendously successful. But there is much, much more, that remains to be done. And now this good man has a mandate to claim, and a nation to govern."

Leave all *this*?

"Hobbsy, you've *got* to stay one more year," Bush implored his Legislative Affairs director David Hobbs as he wrapped an arm around the latter's neck and led him around the room. Bush's lips were close to Hobbsy's ear, the voice seductive: "I've got a lot of political capital, I'm gonna spend it, and you're gonna want to be there. . . ."

Hobbs had an eight-month-old baby at home. He got back to the president later and told him that as much as he loved his job and appreciated Bush's entreaties . . .

Bush didn't react well. He ignored Hobbs for the next few days. *Four years of fourteen-hour days in the White House—now I'm frozen out,* Hobbs thought despondently. Later, however, the president hunted down his Lege Dude after a bill-signing ceremony. This time, he put his arm around the other man's shoulder.

As they walked together, the president said, "David, I don't want you to feel bad about your decision. You've done a great job, I'm very grateful, and you've got to be a father first and foremost. A couple years from now, we'll be having a cigar at my library, and we'll be laughing about how you woke me up at four in the morning on the Medicare vote."

Hobbs would never forget that: Bush just in from London, jet-lagged out of his mind, Hobbsy on the Hill terrified of calling him . . . but the vote on the prescription drug bill had gone on for more than two hours now, they were still down, and he knew some House members were going to require a little presidential jawboning. "Hey, Hobbsy, how's it goin'?" came the sleepy voice, and then the Office of Legislative Affairs director proceeded to pass the phone around, and one by one Bush broke them and carried the day. . . . He wouldn't forget that moment, or this one, when David Hobbs decided to be a family man instead of an eight-year man, and Bush wished him all the best for doing so.

Two prominent cabinet officials were not asked whether they were eight-year men.

Even before his confirmation by the Senate, Attorney General John Ashcroft had been the Bush administration's lightning rod—an unanticipated burden for Bush, who barely knew the man. Rove, however, had worked for the former Missouri governor and U.S. senator in past election cycles. He understood that social conservatives revered the evangelical Christian and pressed Bush to consider him. When it became clear that Bush's first choice for the post, former Montana Governor Marc Racicot, couldn't even afford plane tickets to the inaugural, much less four more years as a government employee, Rove—who had sent personnel director Clay Johnson a memo underscoring the need in the cabinet for a "movement conser-vative"—seized the moment, even going so far as to pick Ashcroft up at the Austin airport and smuggle him unseen into the Omni Hotel for his interview with the president-elect.

That Ashcroft continually attracted dust-ups with civil libertarians wasn't what made him, in Bush's eyes, a four-year man. The AG had a knack for showing up on Sunday-morning talk shows and announcing policy that was not for him to roll out. The Sunday after 9/11, Ashcroft appeared on *Meet the Press* to describe his version of the Patriot Act without running it through the White House policy apparatus. Josh Bolten called Ashcroft on the carpet and was assured that such freelancing would not occur again.

But it did recur, and the problem wasn't so much Ashcroft as his two deputies, David Ayres and David Israelite—the Davids, as they were commonly known—who had come up with Ashcroft from Missouri and had great ambitions for their boss. Ashcroft in turn relied heavily on his Davids, and he seemed genuinely unaware of just how greatly the hotdogging they had prescribed for him was upsetting the White House. The terrorist threats announced by Ashcroft were always more dire, and the alleged terrorist arrests always more game-changing, than the original reports had been before the Davids took the editing pens to them. What Ashcroft's deputies had failed to recognize was that by building their own island fiefdom at Justice, it became that much easier to send Ashcroft adrift.

The split with Colin Powell was far messier. The secretary of state was a celebrity, with entrenched loyalties on both sides of the aisle and, for that matter, among the media, to which Powell and Deputy Armitage leaked information and opinions with great vigor (and to Bush's annoyance). Don Rumsfeld didn't enjoy the same pull with the press, but the battles that counted were the ones in the White House, where he had a powerful ally in Dick Cheney and a talent for winning over Bush.

Powell did not lose all his battles. Over Cheney and Rumsfeld's objections, he persuaded Bush to maintain a peacekeeping force in Bosnia. He persuaded Bush to address the UN in September 2002. And when Rumsfeld asserted that the United States should limit its role in Darfur's growing humanitarian crisis, Powell argued forcefully that America should put its money where its mouth is, and Bush concurred. But the internecine warfare between State and Pentagon wore Powell down. Nothing was too small for the SecDef: During a routine attaché review, Rumsfeld himself pored over the personnel structure of each of the United States' 150 embassies, directing that this or that individual be relocated. The many instances of turf grabbing on Rumsfeld's part were wearying enough, but barely half of it. For a former wrestler, Rumsfeld also displayed a talent for psychological warfare—for example, his tendency to answer questions with questions (Why Is There Air questions, as Doug Feith called them), or simply not to answer at all. Powell couldn't believe it when, on September 13, 2001, Bush convened his war cabinet to ask whether the United States should attack Afghanistan or perhaps even Iraq . . . and when it came Rumsfeld's turn, the SecDef said softly, "I need to think about this." He took a pass!

Such episodes drove Powell nuts. But it was not a silly thing, this dysfunctionality between the two secretaries. Their inability to communicate had harmful consequences. When Armitage first visited Iraq a few months after the fall of Saddam, he heard a worrisome refrain from the commanders on the ground. Armitage reported this to his boss, Colin Powell: *They're telling me we need more troops.*

Powell's reply was emphatic. "Be careful," he said. "If they're not going to say it up the food chain, then it's not our place."

By 2004, Powell and Rumsfeld were sitting at the same table during NSC meetings but not so much as glancing in each other's direction. Bush seemed to enjoy such rivalries—in his mind, the other model was his dad's, in which chief of staff Sununu hoarded all the power and controlled all access to the president. Nonetheless, the total breakdown between State and Pentagon necessitated someone's departure.

For Bush, it was simultaneously a complicated matter and yet not a hard call. From the very beginning, Powell's immense popularity had required a counterweight. At Cheney's suggestion, Bush slotted the VP's old friend and Nixon-era employer Rumsfeld for that role. Doing so went against the family grain. In Rummy's first tour as SecDef, during the Ford administration, it was believed by George H. W. Bush that Rumsfeld had recommended Poppy to Ford as CIA director instead of VP, which badly damaged Poppy's prospects for a presidential run in 1980. "All I'm going to say to you is, you know what he did to your daddy," Jim Baker warned Bush as the two men discussed prospective defense secretary candidates. But Bush wasn't especially intimidated by Rumsfeld. In the end, it came down to a question of which ego was more important—that of the father, an ex-president, or of the son, the president here and now.

Though Bush the Compassionate Conservative seemed more in alignment with the rock star Powell rather than the retro Rumsfeld, he found that he had more in common with the latter. Unlike Powell and Armitage, Rummy didn't fight his battles in the media, nor did he ever utter a syllable that could be intrepreted as disloyal to the president.

Bush rather enjoyed Rumsfeld's cussedness and the manner in which he cheerfully tormented the press. The two men shared a penchant for Big Ideas—and indeed, then-Governor Bush had gotten to know Rumsfeld when the latter briefed him on missile defense in January 1998. Rumsfeld would later tell his lieutenants that if you wanted the president's support for an initiative, it was always best to frame it as a "Big New Thing." Colin Powell never came into the Oval Office with Big New Things. He was captivated by *process*, by the ongoing rather than by the transformative.

Therein lay the ultimate Rumsfeldian jujitsu: seventy-one-year-old Beltway warhorse though he was, Rummy had refashioned himself as a maverick—against which fifty-eight-year-old Powell, the well-liked African American, came off as the Establishment.

It was telling that Bush replaced Ashcroft and Powell with unflagging loyalists. Alberto Gonzales was not anybody's idea of a brilliant legal mind. But he was a successful one, and Bush loved his story: Born in San Antonio to parents who lacked a high school education (and who were likely illegal immigrants), he attended Texas public schools and went on to Harvard Law. After that, Gonzales's ascent had been inextricably linked to Bush's. He did not have any Davids standing between him and the president.

Anyone who knew Condoleezza Rice and followed her laserlike trajectory could not have been surprised to see her ascend to the post of secretary of state. She was brilliant and charming—and, as the only daughter of an intellectual who was also a football coach, she early on cultivated the demeanor by which she would impress powerful men: first professors, then chancellors, then power brokers like George Shultz and Brent Scowcroft, then two presidents named Bush.

During interviews with reporters throughout the summer of 2002, she emphasized her closeness to the boss. "I've known President Bush for quite a long time," she would say. Or, "my relationship with the president goes back a long ways, a very personal relationship." In fact, the relationship did *not* go back a long way—certainly not like Cheney's with Rumsfeld or Rove's with Bush: They'd first met in '95, renewed their acquaintanceship at Shultz's house in April '98, and in August of that year officially bonded during a two-day stretch on a boat in Kennebunkport, where the governor and the Stanford provost fished and talked about foreign policy.

Still, it was, as she said, "a very personal relationship." On more than one level, Rice valued her access to the president and endeavored to maintain it at all costs. As national security adviser, she saw her role as that of facilitator rather than opinion leader. Explicitly she instructed her deputy Steve Hadley, who in turn instructed the other staffers: *We're not going to run the NSC like Brent Scowcroft and Sandy Berger did—we're not going to weaken the cabinet secretaries, we're not set up to make policy.* . . . There was much to recommend this model—or there would have been, had Rumsfeld actually used Rice as a conduit, rather than testily informing her, "I report to the president of the United States." But just as much, this modest interpretation of her duties ensured that Condoleezza Rice would be Bush's information broker and sounding board, rather than the person who incessantly ruffled his feathers with opinions that he did not share.

Rice became a constant presence at Camp David, at Crawford, and at White House social functions. The bloggers made great sport of her supposed Freudian slip when Rice accidentally referred to Bush as "my husband." She had never married, which as a rule sent Beltway tongues to clucking. In fact, Condi Rice didn't lack for companionship. Aside from the Bushes, and the other White House women like Karen Hughes and Harriet Miers, with whom she dined, there were the former football players she dated, the African American women who convened regularly at her Watergate apartment to drink wine and talk about everything except, please, the War on Terror . . . plus music to play on the grand piano her parents had bought her when she was fifteen, football games to watch, books (never fiction!) to read, church to attend, shoe stores to raid. She harbored no maternal yearnings, having once told a journalist, "Children and I are not the happiest combination. I like them when they're eighteen and college bound." Anyway, perhaps she was fated never to wed, for as she asserted once to a close friend, there were few African American males who could cope with a woman of her stature.

Bush certainly could cope (though he was white, and taken). His affections for the opposite sex were uncomplicated and, at times, demonstrably humane. As an oil entrepreneur in Midland, Bush employed a female bookkeeper whose baby had difficulties with day care, so the boss told her one day, "Why don't we set up a nursery and have him stay here?" Which was not exactly commonplace in Midland, Texas, circa 1979, and it rather tickled Bush to be so pioneering. He could be heard boasting on the phone to Evans, "Yeah, we're gonna have a nursery up here!"

On another occasion, in 1986, a recently divorced Mexican American woman in Midland approached Bush and told him that, rather than rely on another man's livelihood, she wanted to start a business of her own. She had in mind a *maquiladora*—a factory just across the border that manufactured cheap goods—but the regulations were forbiddingly complicated. Bush was taken by her pluck. He placed a call to Washington—specifically to the White House Office of Vice President George H. W. Bush—and within weeks the woman had the papers for her *maquiladora*.

Though raised by a stay-at-home mom and married to one as well, Bush was hardly averse either to strong-willed women (exhibit A: Bar) or to ones with careers. Still, the working women in his life such as Karen Hughes and Margaret Spellings were also mothers. Hesitantly but deliberately, Bush had put his ambitions ahead of his family. No woman in his life had ever done the same for herself. He had little experience with career-driven women, and occasionally he would disarm a female reporter with the pointed query: "How come you don't have kids?"

But Condoleezza Rice was an unusual breed of female careerist, one whose training was to be focused and dispassionate. "You never cede control of your own ability to be successful to something called racism," she once told a journalist. "That would be a complete rejection of the way that I was raised, or the way that my parents taught me to think about things." Amid the brutality of Birmingham, Alabama, in the 1960s, her schoolteacher mother and minister father shut out the world, instead drilling young Condi on etiquette in the Tots & Tea Club the Rices taught at home: *Set the knife and spoon on the right side of the table. . . . Wait until everyone is served before you begin to eat. . . .* Profoundly gifted—she had learned how to read sheet music at age three—Rice also never let her passions get the better of her judgment. By her teenage years, the concert pianist had sensibly concluded on her own that she would not likely achieve distinction as a musician, so she took up Russian instead.

It was Rice's destiny to succeed, but it was not her way to be daring. She found her opposite in George W. Bush. As a woman of caution and linearity, she admired the governor's instinctual feel for issues—and, as she would tell others, there was a presence to him that the TV cameras failed to capture. Coming from an academic background, it struck her that Bush wasn't the type to sit through lectures—he was restless, tending to cut through someone's bloviations . . . he was "interactive." Her swoon for him was such that she announced her resignation from Stanford in December 1998, making herself available for a presidential candidacy that had not yet been officially determined. She shared with Bush an absurdist sense of humor—*Austin Powers* cracked her up—though she never joined him in the Dr. Evil mimicry, as it was never her habit to play the clown . . . or, for that matter, to speak of looking into Vladimir Putin's soul: that was *not* how one dealt with the Russians! But Bush did, and Condi Rice came to believe that relations between the two countries took a historic leap that day in June 2001 when Bush dared to say what was in his heart.

Her respect for Bush only deepened after 9/11. "People don't understand," she told a close friend during that period. "It's not *my* exercising influence over *him*. I'm internalizing *his* world." His moral clarity became her moral clarity. It was striking to hear this woman, so often teased by Bush for speaking of *nuance*, now telling reporters, "I suppose there are people who like more nuance. But I think we're being successful with the style that the president has. . . . Nuance isn't always good when you're talking about terror and bad regimes— nuance is not a good thing."

Two days after the election, Bush collared Mike Gerson. "I just want to make sure you're going to stay to help me on the inaugural," he said.

Gerson was so fidgety that he would chew on pens until they broke open in his mouth. (Though he was accustomed to Bush inflicting his will on him. It had been this way since their first meeting at a Washington hotel in January 1999, when the governor narrowed his eyes and said, "This isn't an interview. I want you to move to Texas. I want you to work on my announcement speech, my convention speech, and my inaugural.") "Sure, I'll do that," managed the speechwriter.

"I've been giving it a lot of thought," continued the president. "I want it to be the Freedom Speech."

This delighted Gerson. Lincoln's "with malice toward none" masterwork notwithstanding, second inaugural addresses tended to be gaseous, instantly forgettable things. The Freedom Speech would be anything but forgettable. This Gerson knew as he shambled from the cabinet room to his office on the second floor of the West Wing— already lost in that intellectual muddle of titillation and torture. *Freedom. Purest expression of the Bush Doctrine—no, of his thinking. Of what he thinks his presidency is about . . . The culmination. We've been talking about it since, um, September 20, 2001, okay. The West Point speech, Axis of Evil speech, National Endowment for Democracy speech . . . But no—more than that. Bigger. The CULTURE of freedom. The ECONOMY of freedom. What America is.*

Later in November, Bush summoned Gerson and Bartlett to the Oval. They went over Gerson's outline of the inaugural. Good concept, well organized for the most part. What it lacked was . . . well, what did freedom *look* like?

Gerson wanted to avoid further evocations of 9/11—smoke and tears and lines in the sand. He brought up the Cold War imagery of inaugurals past: a city upon a hill. Watchmen on the wall. Beaconlike, citadellike. Too static. Needed something *active*.

"A prairie fire!" Bush said.

Gerson took the idea over to his deputy John McConnell's office in the Old Executive Office Building. They tossed out the "prairie" modifier—a little, dare it be said, *too* Texas—but "fire" would work splendidly. Gerson and McConnell began riffing on the first of twenty drafts. Ever mindful of Bush's severe editing pen. Short sentences, direct language (forget about adjectives!), no downbeat thoughts. *Never begin a sentence with the word* it. (Who knows where he got this stuff—he told Karen that one of his most memorable courses at Yale had been History of American Oratory—but the truth was, Bush made them better writers. And he did his best editing during read-throughs. Frowning at the murky prose: "C'mon, boys, we're losing altitude here.")

Still, this was the inaugural address. A certain grandiosity, a historical sweep, was called for. And so the speechwriters imagined a leader's monologue, prefacing the journey yet to come with a nod to the vista of an era past: "After the shipwreck of communism came years of relative quiet, years of repose, years of sabbatical. And then there came a day of fire."

Fire! But later in their draft, they doubled back with the image: "By our efforts, we have lit a fire as well—a fire in the minds of men. It warms those who feel its power; it burns those who fight its progress. And one day this untamed fire of freedom will reach the darkest corners of our world."

It worked!

Draft three made the rounds on January 3, 2005. Bartlett, Rove, Rice, Cheney, and Rumsfeld all weighed in. Karen, ever fearful of alarming soccer moms, cautioned Bartlett, "Fighting fire with fire— that could lead to a conflagration. We'd better think this through."

So it went during this, the postelection preinaugural interregnum—a period of relative inactivity, with West Wingers scattering for the holidays, so that the great white beehive on Pennsylvania Avenue scarcely buzzed beyond the droning of the scribes and Bush's own leisurely pre-term rounds. Nominating fresh secretaries for Agriculture, Veterans Affairs, Health and Human Services, and Energy. Giving pep talks to wounded veterans. Teasing the White House press corps about their unpretty faces. Sending his VP off to Afghanistan to grace the troops with that patented Cheney charm. Lighting the National Christmas Tree. Doling out Presidental Medals of Freedom. Clearing brush in Crawford. All in all, a season of blessings and replenishment, auguring a season of dynamism . . . though already there were portents, ripe for dark soothsaying, about a second term that would veer wildly from the intended script.

Such as: On the evening of December 10, 2004, former New York City Police Commissioner Bernard Kerik withdrew his name for consideration as director of the Department of Homeland Security— busted for not paying taxes on his maid, for extramarital affairs, and for a sexual harassment lawsuit, all of which had failed to come up in White House background checks.

Such as: On the morning of December 17, forty-year-old Mike Gerson suffered a heart attack.

Such as: On December 26, the Indian Ocean erupted with a tsunami of biblical force, killing some 187,000 inhabitants of South and Southeast Asia—to which the president responded with an address from his Crawford retreat fully three days later, and with an aid package criticized for its stinginess.

But only a killjoy would dwell on such things, during such a time as this.

On January 20, 2005, a proper coronation was made. Snow draped the nation's capital that Thursday noon as the forty-third president swore anew to preserve, protect, and defend the Constitution of the United States. The man standing on the west flank of the Capitol with his left hand on a family Bible and his right hand raised Caesarlike at eye level, with family and friend and even foe haloed around him—this man was a bit grayer now, perhaps (the campaign doughnuts notwithstanding) harder as well. He had entered office as a six-year governor without a mandate or anything resembling useful foreign-policy experience. Now he was a battle-tested commander in chief who had gained a majority of the popular vote for precisely that reason. You could still say that he was wrong for the job, but no longer that he was too small for it. He was now a man of executive gravitas . . . and by now, no one doubted that he had something to say.

He said this:

"There is only one force of history that can break the reign of hatred and resentment, and expose the pretensions of tyrants, and reward the hopes of the decent and tolerant, and that is the force of human freedom. . . . So it is the policy of the United States to seek and support the growth of democratic movements and institutions in every nation and culture, with the ultimate goal of ending tyranny in our world."

The Freedom Speech, and the Freedom Agenda from which it sprang, was thematically kindred to Bill Clinton's internationalist aims of spreading democracy through the expansion of world markets. And it seemed a defiant repudiation of candidate Bush's own words during the 2000 campaign, when he said disapprovingly of Al Gore, "He believes in nation building." What was this, if not that? But the president offered no equivocation. There had come "a day of fire," not of America's choosing. Bush was simply reciting a timeless verity in Gersonian prose: "Freedom is the permanent hope of mankind, the hunger in dark places, the longing of the soul."

And, as Gerson had predicted, the address elicited intense reaction. "Bold." "Eloquent." "Ambitious." "Startling." "Idealistic." Even the surlier assessments reflected that a chord had been struck. Henry Kissinger confided to an acquaintance that he was "appalled." And Pat Buchanan, ever given to understatement, narrowed his eyes into cobralike slits and intoned, "These words will be thrown back at Bush and will haunt him as long as he lives."

But from the other side of the world came a made-to-order valida-tion of the expanded Bush Doctrine. Three days after the inaugural address, the voice of Abu Musab Al-Zarqawi, the Jordanian terrorist bedeviling Coalition forces in Iraq, appeared on a website with this message: "We have declared a fierce war on this evil principle of democracy and those who follow this wrong ideology."

The world's most aggressive terrorist was now on record opposing democracy. Both sides now acknowledged the bright line between them. And so all those who had spent the last four years chiding Bush for his stubborn simplemindedness, for his "I don't do nuance" and his "You are either with us or against us" and his "You know where I stand"—what, really, did those naysayers have to say for themselves now?

One of those naysayers was Colin Powell. He was still Bush's titular secretary of state by Inauguration Day but received a copy of the address only the day before it was given. *Oh boy*, he mused. *We've got a lot of friends who are gonna be saying: Who do you think you are? You're telling ME, the king of Saudi Arabia, who's had a very successful run for two hundred years with this royal family, that the Americans actually think we'd be better off with an ELECTION in Saudi Arabia? Do they KNOW who'd be elected? What are they THINKING?!*

(Powell would have a similar reaction after reading the text of Condi Rice's speech in Cairo on June 21, 2005: "We should all look to a future when every government respects the will of its citizens—because the ideal of democracy is universal. For sixty years, my country, the United States, pursued stability at the expense of democracy in this region here in the Middle East—and we achieved neither. Now, we are taking a different course. We are supporting the democratic aspirations of all people." *Wow*, he thought. *For sixty years, we pursued stability at the expense of democracy and achieved neither—in that one phrase, she crapped on eight presidents! Including 41!* Powell's last six months in office had been devoted to walking back from this post-9/11 fever for democratization. In January 2005, he'd gone to Morocco to meet with twenty-six other nations in a Forum for the Future. At the gathering, Powell had emphasized the word *reform*. Other nations could buy into that. It was incremental. It was executable. It wasn't bellicose. And yes, it "pursued stability"—and *stability*, as 41's old Secretary of State Jim Baker would say, should not be a dirty word.)

Anyway, Powell figured, it was Condi's mess now. She got to be the eight-year man.

16

Big Ball, Long Bomb

Bush had been a little nervous about the inaugural, understandably. "It's the speech of your life, you know," Bartlett would remind him—an inside joke: So far, he'd had about fifteen to twenty speeches of your life. Now, though, with the wind suddenly at his back, with no races left to run and the Republican majority united behind their fearless party leader . . . well, there were no excuses, were there? So the competing force was just his own mortal limits.

After the final read-through of the address the day before Inauguration Day, he left the family theater and strode through the corridor of the East Wing. Though he'd taken this route a thousand times, a permanent fixture caught his eye, and he stopped. It was a model displaying the West Wing in its various configurations since the days of Jefferson. Bush stood in the hallway, not so much studying the model as transfixed by it—or rather, by the notion, staggering to anyone who knew him from boyhood, that he was now in that model somewhere, custodian of its majesty.

The speechwriter John McConnell strolled up. "Are you starting to feel the history?" he asked his boss.

Bush half smiled by way of reply. Then Andy Card caught up, handed him the daily schedule. Scowling at it, he stepped into the residential elevator.

None of them would say that he had changed per se. Immalleability—*You know where I stand*—was Bush's iconic feature, just as Reagan's was his legendary sunniness. The demands of the Oval Office, the terrorists, war, and now 51 percent of the popular vote had left no dent on the man. His teleology was as rigid and reliable as that of a chair. So, at least, went the view, which he did nothing to dismiss.

And yet they couldn't help but notice . . . something different. Perhaps a week or two after the Inauguration Day of January 20, 2005, when Bush stood under snowy skies and talked about the fire of freedom, Gerson was sitting with Karen Hughes in his office in the West Wing and talking about the address. "The thing that struck me," Gerson told her, "was this man we've known for so long—he now *completely* fills the office that he holds."

"That's amazing!" said Karen. "That's exactly what I thought, too." Though in fact she had considered the spectacle not in spatial terms but through the familiar Bushian paradigm of *comfortableness*. She had never seen Bush so *comfortable* than behind the podium that day; "the mantle of the presidency," she would later say, "rested *comfortably* on him." Her son Robert had been standing next to her during the address and had expressed the very same thing.

And the president's old Midland buddy Joe O'Neill—who, along with his wife, Jan, had introduced Bush to Laura twenty-eight years earlier—also detected a "much higher comfort level" when he visited Washington during the inaugural festivities. Experience didn't fully explain it, O'Neill thought. This was about *legitimacy*. Lacking an unassailable mandate, well, there'd been a defensive sort of brashness before. What Joe O'Neill now saw in its place was self-assurance.

Detractors were coming around to seeing this as well. When Bush and Cheney together met with the 9/11 Commission in August 2004, the committee's Democrats fully expected to see the president defer to the VP and in all other ways live up to his meager stereotype. They were startled to see Bush thoroughly dominate the interview, while "Cheney spoke 5 percent of the time," the commission's chairman, Philip Zelikow, would recall.

Bush's confidence had become a kinetic, devouring force. To sell him on an idea, aides were now learning, the best approach was to tell the president, *This is going to be a really tough decision.* The tougher it was, the more alluring the invitation.

But in contemplating these developments, one could not stray too far, into an abyss that presupposed the world's most powerful man to be a pliable, evolving organism. One had to draw back from the brink and remind oneself: Bush was now self-assured—not that he hadn't been sure of himself before. He now completely filled the office—

which wasn't to suggest that he'd been undersized before. He thrived on hard choices—and always had. He'd never been so comfortable—though really, the presidency had never caused him discomfort in the past.

HE HAD NOT CHANGED!

Only the rest of the world had.

A month after his reelection, Bush summoned two Republicans and two Democrats to the Oval Office to tell them what he had in mind for the next term.

That the president intended to throw his newly acquired weight into Social Security reform wasn't a surprise. He'd been talking about doing so for the past couple of weeks. And Rove had signaled as much some months earlier, during a phone conversation with one of the Democrats present, Senator Max Baucus. The Montana moderate who had faithfully delivered Bush the swing votes for the first two rounds of tax cuts and Medicare prescription drugs had complained to Rove that Bush's third round of tax cuts made no sense, given the swelling deficit and Congress's inability to pay for entitlement programs like Medicare and Social Security.

"Well, whoever the president's going to be next year, he's going to have to deal with entitlements," Rove had told Baucus back then. "And if it's us, we're gonna deal with them."

Good, said Baucus. *Because Medicare's going bankrupt in 2012.*

Rove disagreed. The real problem, he told the senator, was Social Security.

Which struck Baucus at the time as nonsensical—Social Security was solvent till 2042—until it dawned on him that solvency wasn't what was preoccupying Bush and Rove. This was about privatizing the New Deal.

When Bush told the four congressmen in the Oval Office that he intended to push for personal accounts, the ranking Democrat on the House Ways and Means Committee, Charlie Rangel, erupted. "This is crazy," he said. Besides, Rangel added, "Why should I play when *he*"—gesturing to the Republican chairman, Bill Thomas—"won't tell me when the meetings are?"

Thomas routinely shut the Democratic leadership out of his conferences—they weren't going to be swayed anyway—and he made no apologies for this now. Ignoring Rangel's rant, the Ways and Means chairman told Bush that he would support private accounts for Social

Security—except why not use the opportunity to pitch, for example, pension reform as well?

Thomas was looking for a grand solution to all problems related to entitlements. For once, Bush found an idea too Big for his liking. He insisted that they stay focused on Social Security for now.

The other congressman in the room, Senate Finance Committee chairman Charles Grassley, was going to support his party leader no matter what. "It's the right thing to do, Mr. President," he said. "But this is a big fight. Are you sure you want to do this big fight first?"

Baucus expanded on Grassley's concerns. "I'll work with you, Mr. President," he said. "But I can't sell privatization to my caucus. Why don't you form a commission on entitlements—pull everything together. . . ."

"No more commissions," Bush said emphatically. "This is what the people want. I've got political capital, and I intend to spend it."

Later, Baucus phoned Andy Card. The ranking Democrat on the Senate Finance Committee had spoken with a few of his colleagues. Privatization wouldn't fly, he told the chief of staff. It was fine to talk about making Social Security solvent. But personal accounts wouldn't do that. Financing such accounts would add trillions of dollars to the national debt. Could Baucus please have a private conversation with the president to explain this to him?

No, said Card curtly. "This is where we're going." Card saw what this was about. Back when Tom Daschle was Senate minority leader, the White House could deal with Baucus, since Baucus and Daschle couldn't even be in the same room together. But Daschle had been defeated in November. The new minority leader was Baucus's friend Harry Reid from Nevada. Baucus wasn't going to cross Reid the way he used to buck Daschle. Card saw little point in trying.

He figured that they didn't need Baucus anyway. No Child Left Behind, tax cuts, the Patriot Act, Homeland Security, authorization to invade Iraq, Medicare prescription drugs, supplemental war funding— the White House had always gotten what it wanted. And that was before November 2004. Bush was stronger than ever.

Bush had already given three State of the Union addresses, and they weren't really his thing. Interminable in length, delivered near his bedtime hour . . . and all about small ball. George W. Bush's disdain for small ball was personal—or deeper than that: Small ball was like a pathogen to which his immune system provided no defense. "Govern-

ment should do a few things, and do them right." He'd said it a million times over the course of his political career. That was the kind of
government Bush believed in, perhaps because that's the kind of man
Bush was. "If you've got fifty goals," the governor once lectured the
Texas Education Agency, "you've got *no* goals." Which was both reasonable and illogical, but underlying the point was this: George W.
Bush with fifty goals—unimaginable. Be a good servant to the Lord,
be a good father and husband, be a leader. . . . The list ended there. Al
Gore, the pedantic Ozone Man, could tick off a hundred goals. Kerry
could tick off fifty iterations of the same goal. Bush could do only a
few things, and apparently that was sufficient.

The White House was full of, and indeed required, small-ball
players, ever tinkering with the molecular structure of their boss's
hulking Vision Thing. Good for them. "Everything's important,"
Bush would say, meaning it sincerely. (Harriet Miers, for years a
member of Bush's inner circle, lived for small ball.) But on that small-
ball playing field, Bush wasn't just a hapless Gulliver bested by Lil-
liputians. No, the consequences were existential: He, and the reason
for him, receded altogether.

"A leader sets priorities—he doesn't just list," then-Governor Bush
had said to an aide after they'd watched a Clinton State of the Union
speech. A little something for everyone, appeasements aplenty—it all
bespoke 42's tragic lack of discipline, his eagerness to be
loved. . . . Bush grew up knowing he was loved. His needs were therefore quite different. He needed to be the quarterback. He needed to
throw the big ball, and to throw it long. Give him those things—and
then cheer, boo, break his leg. He would die contentedly on that field.

Social Security. That was the big ball he would heave on February
2, 2005.

Bracketing Bush's inaugural address, each political party hosted a
bicameral caucus. In early January, the Republicans gathered at the
posh West Virginia resort The Greenbrier. At the end of the day's
three meetings, the president dropped in for an off-the-record chat.
He talked about the progress in Iraq and about the need to rein in federal spending. The Republicans in the audience cheered and laughed
loudly. They had kicked ass in November. Levity came easily—until
Bush changed the subject to Social Security.

Make no mistake, he told them: This was going to be his top
domestic priority. Bush said that he was depending on Congress to

move quickly. "Before long," he reminded them, "I'm going to be quacking like a duck."

Bush saw worried faces in the audience. He acknowledged that overhauling the hoary third rail was not going to be pleasant business. But, he added yet again, "I've got political capital, and now I'm going to spend it."

A few weeks later, the Democrats gathered in the Rayburn House Building. Reid and the new House minority leader, Nancy Pelosi, presided, or attempted to. Things fell apart in a hurry. The conference room erupted in anguished yells. *What the hell do we stand for? Where the hell are we going? Do we even know how the hell to WIN anymore?*

Members were bitter, accusatory, frustrated. Any visitor could see it: This was a lost and splintered tribe.

What could possibly galvanize them?

Bush had long hankered for Social Security private accounts. He'd been touting them going back to his 1978 race—before mandatory testing in schools, before tort reform, before juvenile justice reform, certainly before nation building in the Middle East. In the pre–Bush Republican days, he was a Reagan Republican, openly skeptical that the government could do anything better than the entrepreneur. Why *shouldn't* an individual have the option to invest his hard-earned wages in a higher-performing retirement fund?

He talked about it in 1978. He talked about it in 1998 to the Hoover Institution sages at George Shultz's house, pledging to them, "I'm going to spend the political capital necessary" to reform Social Security. He talked about it in 2000 against Gore. He talked about it in 2001, when he formed a Social Security advisory commission—bipartisan in composition, except that every single one of the appointees happened to be an advocate of personal accounts. (And Bush's plan had been to spend 2002 enacting into law his commission's reform package. But Josh Bolten told Bush's Social Security advisers that it would have to wait: Neither Congress nor the public could handle the War on Terror, Iraq, *and* an additional major issue.) He talked about it during the 2002 midterms. He talked about it in the 2004 State of the Union address. He talked about it in his nomination acceptance speech. And he talked about it throughout the reelect as an essential component to the Ownership Society—gripping that dreaded third rail time and again . . . and here he still was, impervious to its lethal voltage. . . .

But more than that: The third rail *illuminated him*—and he in turn viewed himself as Social Security's beacon of hope. For as he proudly told a few commentators in the White House in early 2003, "It used to be that people would never talk about the issue. I happen to think my speech in, I can remember where I gave it—Cucamonga Ranch, California [in early 2000]—I think it helped define the election. I do. I think it was a very important issue. I think it spoke to a lot of people. And it's an issue that for years was demagogued because people were frightened of it."

Far from electrocuting him, Bush truly believed that the third rail had helped put him over the top in 2000. And in 2004. As Bush told his staffers, he had littered the campaign trail with references to Social Security personal accounts—"going all the way back to Cucamonga Ranch," Bush invariably reminded them, such that the words *Cucamonga Ranch* came, in the West Wing, to achieve some kind of epochal significance, like a latter Bronze Age. . . . Why, he'd *pounded* the damned issue, had been reelected, and thus one could only conclude . . .

No one told him otherwise. No one in the White House reminded the president that the election had been framed as a Choice, Not a Referendum, the Steady Leadership versus the Flip-Flopping Windsurfer—that McKinnon's ad campaign had begun with images of the World Trade Center in ruins and ended with packs of roaming terrorist-wolves; that the Mehlman-Dowd mantra had been *If it's about national security, we win*; that Bush had given a million campaign speeches on Iraq and not a single one devoted to fixing Social Security; that the thunderous chants of *USA! USA! USA!* were always about America's military might, and not once in response to a presidential call for personal accounts. . . .

Instead, all the eight-year men agreed with Bush: Social Security reform was not only what he should do, it was what the voters had elected him to do. And so, really, it was his obligation.

Plus, there was all that political capital. He *had* to spend it.

And he couldn't wait to start! Well before the official rollout of his February 2 State of the Union address, Bush was a one-man hyping machine. His own experts had reported that the Social Security trust fund would not run out until 2041, after which it would still pay beneficiaries some 70 percent of what it had promised. Nonetheless: "the crisis is now," Bush intoned in December. And a few weeks later: "If you're twenty years old, in your midtwenties, and you're beginning

to work, I want you to think about a Social Security system that will be
flat bust, bankrupt, unless the United States Congress has got the willingness to act now."

By "act now," Bush explained to a group of reporters on January 13,
"I would like to get it done in the first five months of this year." The
reporters were speechless. It took Bush five months to pass a *tax cut*!
How was he going to get Congress to pass in five months an institution that hadn't been *grazed* in twenty-two years?

In fact, they were figuring that out, back at the White House.
Card had called a meeting to discuss rollout strategy. Josh Bolten at
the Office of Management and Budget argued that they should put
out a legislative package. *Write out exactly what we want. Then let one of
the think tanks drop it in Frist's and Hastert's laps so they can put their
names at the top of it and act like they're the authors. Do the directive tem-
plate. Let's not go the organic route. We did that with No Child Left Behind
and it took us nearly a year—and that was education.*

Bolten had the backing of the other policy guys, like John Cogan,
who thought that Bush's spelling out exactly what he wanted was the
best way to show leadership. Some of them worried that Republicans
on the Hill, who had begged the White House not to push Social
Security during the midterm year of 2002, were just playing rope-a-
dope and were never going to get around to crafting their own legislation. Tom DeLay, Tom Reynolds, Tom Davis—the House Toms all
broke out in hives at the very mention of the third rail. But in the end,
the propeller-heads got trumped by Rove and the staff of the Office of
Legislative Affairs. Their view was: *Don't give the Democrats something to shoot at. Just lay out the principles, like we did with No Child Left
Behind and Medicare. Give Congress some ownership.*

Andy Card let Rove do it his way.

During one of his rounds on the Hill just before the State of the
Union address, Rove dropped in on Max Baucus. "I can't get you one
Democratic vote on private accounts," the latter warned Rove. Revise
the benefits formula, put together a Social Security–Medicare reform
package—he'd bring people over for that kind of stuff. But it wasn't
going to happen for Bush's pet project.

"You're wrong," Rove replied. "There'll be people who *have* to
come on this."

They were supposed to be all business, these prespeech read-throughs
in the residence theater. Even wearing his jogging suit on a Sunday

afternoon, Bush wouldn't brook laxity. "Karl? No editing remarks. Today's about organization." Or in later read-throughs, after he'd had enough of all the rhetorical fiddling and wished to concentrate on delivery: "Okay, this is *not* an edit session." Thus did Rove, Bartlett, Miers, national security adviser Steve Hadley, and the speechwriters sit in the theater chairs and balance, as ever, the care and the feeding of the president.

And yet, by the final read-throughs, the atmosphere also recalled game day in the locker room, with all the unspoken confidence that ass would soon be kicked. How else to explain the boss's reaction after someone in the audience carefully suggested, "Mr. President, I think you're going to trip up on the word *subsistence*."

All sound was sucked out of the room. The man behind the podium finally reacted with his assymetrical semisneer. And then with:

"Why don't you get a betting pool started, then?"

Then Bush recited, with exaggerated tenderness, "Sub-SIS-tence . . . Sub-SISTENCE. SUBSISTENCE."

Over a dozen times in all, before dryly concluding, "I wouldn't worry."

(The speechwriters removed the word from the final draft anyway.)

Everyone felt great about the speech. "Now *that's* an applause line," someone would invariably call out during the read-throughs, until the final tally of such lines came to seventy. Bill McGurn—brought in to relieve Gerson of the day-to-day writing functions so that the latter could spend his time less stressfully, luxuriating in Big Ideas on the first floor of the West Wing—had done an exemplary job of knitting together the disparate threads supplied by others through-out the White House. Among these was Rove's familiar ideological refrain, "We must update institutions that were created to meet the needs of an earlier time." And never complete without Karen's homey touch: "Our generation has been blessed . . . by our parents' sacrifice. Now, as we see a little gray in the mirror—or a lot of gray . . ."

Bush delivered it on the evening of February 2, 2005. One certainly could not say that it was slight. Nor could one say that it was poorly received. In all, there were sixty-five applause lines, just shy of the pro-jection. The night's punditry was not belittling, as it had been the pre-ceding year. And the next day's airwaves were not cluttered with talk of casualties in Iraq, as had been the case in 2004. Instead, the address was bookended by serendipity: the dramatic voter turnout in the Iraqi elections the evening before, and the spontaneous embrace at the end of the speech between an Iraqi woman whose father had been assassinated by Saddam Hussein and a Texas woman whose Marine son had perished in the assault on Fallujah.

Yet, The Hug, as it came to be called, was not intended to be the evening's high point. And in a curious way, that glorious, unscripted personification of Freedom also typified the twin themes of uncommon luck and cheated triumph that would gallop through George W. Bush's presidency side by side. For it did not pass unnoticed by Bush, or by others in his senior staff, that a line intended to be met with *thunderous* applause—"I welcome the bipartisan enthusiasm for spending discipline"—instead received no applause at all. And when the president stood before the federal government's legislative branch and reminded them that Social Security must be saved for the sake of future generations, saying, "[I]t should not be a small matter to the United States Congress," only one hand, the Republican hand, clapped . . . while the Democrats sat there like a tribe of deaf-mutes, staring back at him with predatory smiles.

This was stupefying to him. Bush, freshly reelected and newly mandated, believed now was the time to tackle something Big. Instead—and he just had to say it aloud that evening following the speech, as he and Rove and Laura rode the residence elevator to the diplomatic reception:

"They don't even think there's a *problem!*"

Such a simple, simple thing. And they couldn't see it.

The day after his State of the Union address, Bush traveled to Max Baucus's state to talk to its citizens about Social Security. He neglected, however, to tell Baucus, who learned of Bush's upcoming visit from the Associated Press.

Less than four hours before the president's arrival in Great Falls, Baucus staged a rally of his own in that city—one in which he ferociously attacked Bush's plan to "privatize" Social Security. From there he drove to the airport, where he offered this measured greeting to the arriving president: "We can solve this thing. Right now, it's not happening."

Bush offered some mollifying words to his swing senator during the Social Security event. "We have worked a lot together in four years," he told the crowd as he gestured to Baucus. "And I appreciate working with you, Max. It's been a lot of fun. We got more work to do."

But Baucus was in a lethal stew—observing, as he sat behind the president, how the Bush people had stuck him onstage way in the back, and planted the newly elected Democratic governor Brian Schweitzer in the audience. . . . Tax cuts, prescription drug care—all the crap Maxie had to take from his Caucus in exchange for working with the White House, and *he has to learn about the president coming to his state to talk about Social Security from the AP?*

Baucus notified Senate minority leader Harry Reid that this was jihad, and he would be happy to lead it.

A month after Bush test-drove his message into Great Falls, he officially hit the road with a "60 Cities in 60 Days" tour to educate the public about the need to reform Social Security. In conjunction with Bush's barnstorming, the White House and Republican leadership were putting the heat on congressmen to do the same—to get out there and proselytize their constituents.

Two very different experiences were had.

For the president, Rove revived 2004's Ask President Bush format. The events were exquisitely manicured, from the all-access stage to the Office of Public Liaison–selected Ordinary Citizens who recited their testimonials to the carefully controlled distribution of audience tickets. Bush sat on his stool and spewed forth the corn. He talked about that locale's great commonsense people and he expressed his regrets that Laura couldn't make the trip and he extolled the remarkable progress being made in Afghanistan and Iraq. And once the crowd was properly warmed up, he launched into the crisis that Social Security was in—never failing to first stipulate that "Franklin Roosevelt did a good thing by setting up a safety net for seniors. And I applaud him for that."

And having graced FDR with his flattery, he would turn to the others onstage. They were old people dependent on Social Security or young people who expected one day to be dependent themselves. Beyond establishing these basic facts, there was not much else for them to say. Bush would rib them about their age, thank them, and then continue with his sales pitch about personal accounts while they sat on stools beside him, fulfilling their role as mute and homey props. Because no archenemy was cited at these "Conversations"—no terrorists, no flip-floppers—the only real drama attendant to them was that Ordinary Citizens were getting to meet the president. Still, Bush entered and exited on a wave of sustained applause, with every reason to believe that he was winning over the American public. "The issue's beginning to permeate," he declared during a Conversation in Cedar Rapids, perched on a stool in his impermeable bubble.

The Republican congressmen hosting *their* town hall meetings were not so protected. They, unlike the president, actually had to meet the skeptical public—not a hand-picked Greek chorus, but the ones whose votes they would be asking for in a scant year's time. And what they encountered was jolting: picketers, street rallies, senior citizens battering them with hostile questions. Bruised and reeling, the Republicans returned to the Beltway, murmuring among themselves: *SOMEONE is well organized, and it ain't us.*

It was the AFL-CIO, which threatened the business community with shareholder lawsuits. It was MoveOn.org and Campaign for America's Future. It was the mighty AARP, which had agreed in 2003 to join the White House in a Social Security "education campaign" but reversed field by the end of the year and was now financing an aggressive ad campaign depicting images of crumbling houses as a vivid warning of what Bush would do to its 35 million members' treasured safety net.

And it was a group called Americans United to Protect Social Security—begun by Max Baucus's chief of staff Jim Messina and run out of Harry Reid's Senate offices, with satellite offices in twenty-nine states. Every time a Republican surfaced to call a town hall meeting, Americans United dispatched picketers and staged rallies. And every time a moderate started to wobble, Americans United put the fear of God in them: *Do you really want your local TV stations showing footage of you being booed and picketed for taking away the safety net of senior citizens and further enriching Bush's Wall Street cronies?*

Meanwhile, Rove was having difficulty fulfilling his boast to Baucus that he would find Democrats who would "have to come on this." Kent Conrad vigorously agreed, "This has to happen," but he would only venture to the precipice before getting whacked back by Americans United. Ben Nelson of Nebraska had promised to be "open"— but the man Bush called Nelly (much to Nelson's annoyance) simply couldn't be the first defector, not a year before his 2006 reelection. Joe Lieberman seemed at times promising. But no sooner had he declared, "I want to be part of this discussion," than Reid tightened the screws, and Lieberman went zombielike on Rove, incanting, "To me, the main goal is solvency. . . ." Which, of course, personal accounts did nothing to address.

Dianne Feinstein was leaning the White House's way, ever so

slightly: The California Democrat was fashioning a bill to put a Social Security commission together . . . and though Bush had snapped to Baucus, "No more commissions," this looked like an opening, an invitation. . . . Then Baucus collared her on the floor: *Drop this bill. You cannot do this.*

"Max," Feinstein protested, "I'm trying to be responsible."

Screw responsible. We are WINNING this.

Tom Carper, Mary Landrieu, Mark Pryor . . . every moderate on Rove's list had drifted away. *And* the northeastern Mod Squad— Republicans Lincoln Chafee of Rhode Island and Olympia Snowe and Susan Collins of Maine—had said no to private accounts as well. Lacking Baucus to bring in the moderates as he had in the past, Rove's only hope was that Bush's tour could turn the public, who would then pressure the Democrats.

But even as Bush carried on with his cross-country joshing and cajoling, the presidential bubble had begun to rattle. The protesters were becoming harder for his advance men to circumnavigate. The resourceful stagecraftsman Scott Sforza fought to keep up with the steep arc of the public-opinion curve—changing the event banner from STRENGTHENING SOCIAL SECURITY to a more reassuring PROTECTING OUR SENIORS . . . and then, in a sign of growing defensiveness, to KEEPING OUR PROMISE TO OUR SENIORS.

By the end of May, when George W. Bush completed his sixty-day swing, polls indicated that his Social Security initiative was less popular than when he had begun it . . . and Bush himself was less popular as well.

Now the White House was hinting that it was willing to cut a deal, perhaps even take privatization off the table, as Grassley had been begging them to do for months now. But the Democrats smelled a bait-and-switch—after all, the president was still carrying on about the virtues of personal accounts. Even as Republicans quietly pleaded with the White House for an exit strategy, the Democrats began to press for a vote. This was no longer Bush's pet cause. Now it was theirs: They'd held together, the Republicans were crawfishing, the White House had badly overreached, Rove the Architect had constructed a house of cards . . . and now here was an issue with legs, one to run on in 2006, how the Republicans tried to screw with America's time-honored safety net, and so *let's get them on record, put it to a vote NOW!*

Frist and Hastert wouldn't let the bleeding become an all-out hemorrhage. Both the Senate and the House mounted a full retreat. By the end of June, after five months of flailing, Social Security reform had writhed its last . . . and rising from its corpus was a fully resuscitated Democratic Party.

Even in the initiative's death throes, the president and his lieutenants would not go quietly. By standing on principle, they contended, Bush had changed forever the debate on Social Security. Hereafter, the Democrats would be seen as obstructionists and would pay for their cowardice in the polls. And the president would be back with this issue, make no mistake. This was the White House's refrain throughout the summer of 2005.

If any of this was true at the time, none of it would prove to be true by November 7, 2006.

17

HECK OF A JOB

One sweltering summer day in August 2005, the leader of the free world went for a ride on his bicycle.

It was coming up on a hundred degrees in Crawford, and he was loving it. Loving how the younger guys melted. Loving how he waxed even the Secret Service's "track unit" of agents who were put on this detail specifically to keep up with the old man. Loving how invariably someone would crash into a tree and fall to the ground, inspiring the catcall, "YARD SALE!" (Sometimes that someone was he—and the SS boys caravaning after him in their Suburban and amphibious vehicles would be scurrying to help him up in a matter of seconds, or else he'd smirk and say, "Y'all enjoying your AC?") Loving how the Yard Sales upped the stakes, turning a civilized fitness activity into mortal combat from which one agent emerged with a broken rib, McKinnon with a separated shoulder, Don Evans with a broken collarbone, and Bush himself with a bad gash on the back of his leg trying to make it up a steep incline, which thereafter became known as Achilles Hill. (Though let it be remembered: Bush warded off Dr. Tubb, saying, "Just bandage it up, but I'm gonna do whatever it takes to finish my ride.")

Loving how he could sustain a heart rate of 140 to 175 for ninety minutes—something he could never do when he was running—while regularly checking his calorie burn, relishing the metrics: 1,000 calories, 1,200, sometimes 1,500 . . . Loving the pain, seeking it out. (The banter between him and the agents: "Where you find sympathy around here?" "In the dictionary, sir.") Absolutely geared to the *men-*

305

tality of the sport: grinding, pushing, meeting resistance head-on. Quitting only when the hurt consumed him. And loving the feeling that, even in this solitary pastime, he was ahead of the curve, among the first Baby Boomers with failing joints to give up the jogging track for the cycle. . . . Even now, *he was setting an example—he was leading*.

He'd just come back from the Tamarack Resort in Donnelly, Idaho. Usually Bush stayed at such luxury retreats only for Laura's sake—she liked that sort of stuff—but Hagin had informed him that the advance guys had scoped out a number of riding prospects, and, well, Tamarack featured some really stellar biking trails. Single-track trails, which he'd never done before. And man! The double tracks at Crawford were fast but essentially jeep roads, not a narrow cut that whipped you through dense forests and challenged your reflexes as well as your stamina. Imagine the Yard Sales on *these*! Before they had even returned to Crawford from Idaho, Hagin (who in addition to his many White House duties served as the ranch's adjunct foreman) put out the word to the SS detail: *Forget about clearing brush. We're spending the rest of August building the perfect single track*.

The advance guys and Secret Service devoted inordinate energy to satisfying Bush's need for biking trails. They would descend on a town a couple of days before his arrival, focusing on secluded hotels away from downtown, properties that they could fully take over, and ones with the kinds of trails the boss would find challenging. Which "track unit" agents would be available, how to get the bikes out there . . . a whole new layer of logistical complications. No one questioned the importance of the biking. (Though at least one of his top aides would question its *primacy*: "What kind of male," this adviser would wonder aloud, "obsesses over his bike riding time, other than Lance Armstrong or a twelve-year-old boy?") As Bush himself told a group of journalists he'd taken for a bike ride on his ranch, "I think the people want the president to be in a position to make good, crisp decisions and to stay healthy." The president didn't drink, didn't cheat, it was a time of war, he needed the outlet—they *wanted* him, dear God, to have his release.

So, upon Bush's return from Idaho, the agents got out their Weed Eaters and their rakes and proceeded to clear new trails for the president to ride on.

"Find me a ranch," Bush had ordered a Texas developer and politician named Byron Cook during the summer of 1998, after the governor had cashed out his share of the Texas Rangers. Bush gave Cook the broad outline: He liked to fish, he liked to run, and he liked privacy. (Bush had no interest in horses, for riding or otherwise.) What Cook found for him was the old Engelbrecht spread near the north-central Texas town of Crawford—1,583 acres bordered on the east by the Bosque River, encompassing as well a stretch of Middle Bosque Creek, with a magnificent box canyon affording excellent sunset views, obscured Indian mounds, and a vast bottomland of prickly-pear cactus. The Engelbrechts had run cattle and at one time owned a sizable hog operation. Bush was a city boy; he knew nothing about such things. The old barns and pig sheds would soon be hauled off. To appease the twins, Bush had a swimming pool constructed—he called it the Whining Pool—and a fish tank he stocked with largemouth bass. Laura designed an eco-friendly ranch house. The Putins and Foxes had been there, along with a dozen other world leaders, including Colombian President Álvaro Uribe just a couple of weeks earlier. Bush loved to show off the vistas, rattle off the dozen or so varieties of indigenous trees. Often they hosted barbecues for their Texas friends. When the hour got too late for Bush's taste, he would gather the dishes, wash them himself, and then announce, "Y'all lock up," before departing for his bedroom. The twins had celebrated their twenty-first birthdays there, with a raucous bash of Yalies and Texans, featuring a frozen-margarita machine that Bush had opposed, to no avail. (Though the father got his revenge at seven the next morning when he drove past the tents where the revelers were asleep and repeatedly blasted the horn.)

This was now his one permanent home. Armed guards would man its perimeters until the day he died. Convoys of Secret Service agents followed him wherever he walked or rode. It was still not quite what an ordinary person would call privacy. But he could get out, and the cameras could not see him, and by now he had come to regard the men with the earplugs as semivisible necessities, like seat belts or telephone poles.

And anyway, they helped him build his bike trails.

This was Bush's fiftieth trip to the ranch since his inauguration. His intention was to stay there five weeks. It was, of course, billed as a working vacation, with ten Air Force One day trips scheduled, on top of the usual routine of intelligence briefings and strategizing of the months ahead. Still and all, heavy lifting would not be the order of the day for the president. Bartlett, Rove, Rice, Card, Devenish, and Bolten were all on separate holidays. The media's B-team was holed up in Waco. Lance Armstrong was coming to Crawford for a bike ride and a dip in the Whining Pool, followed by lunch. Life was good.

It had not been quite the year his grand addresses had foretold. On January 20, Bush had inaugurated the Freedom Agenda. For a moment there, it appeared to have taken hold. Free elections had been held in Iraq. Thousands of freedom-loving Lebanese had taken to the streets of Beirut demanding Syria's withdrawal from their country. In Egypt, President Hosni Mubarak freed his chief political opponent after Rice canceled a visit to Cairo in the wake of the opponent's jailing.

Alas, Mubarak jailed the opponent again, and Hamas staged an even bigger counterrally in Beirut, and Iraq remained a land of raging violence . . . while the other two Axis of Evil nations, North Korea and Iran, ramped up their nuclear programs unchecked. When Bush traveled to Slovakia in February and criticized Putin for eroding the democratic institutions in his country, Bush's Russian soulmate didn't back down, instead wisecracking that at least *he* wasn't installed by an electoral college over the popular will.

The Ownership Society heralded in his State of the Union address hadn't gone as planned, either. Gas prices were soaring. Interest rates were climbing. The five months of wasted effort on Social Security meant that immigration and tax code reform would be put off until the fall.

Two other unforeseen melodramas were further dimming the triumphalism of the ruling majority. While Bush was risking his political capital and his party's robust health on personal accounts, a forty-one-year-old woman named Terri Schiavo lay in a vegetative state in a Pinellas Park, Florida, hospice. Contending that she would not wish to live this way, Schiavo's husband obtained a court order to have her feeding tube removed. Her parents appealed the matter, and instantly their protests became a cause célèbre among social conservatives, including the governor of Florida, Jeb Bush.

When Congress responded to the heat in late March by passing emergency legislation to grant federal courts the authority to hear the Schiavo case, Bush happened to be reposing in Crawford. Explaining that the president "ought to err on the side of life," he interrupted his vacation, was whisked back to Washington on Air Force One, signed the Schiavo bill, and then returned to Crawford.

For a moment, things seemed fine. A week later, Bush's numbers dropped from 52 to 45, an apparent expression of Americans appalled by the notion of the president and Congress meddling in the private affairs of a family. Meanwhile, the federal courts ruled that Bush had, indeed, erred by overstepping. The feeding tube stayed out, Terri Schiavo's fifteen-year coma came to an end, and the White House took great pains to avoid discussing the matter further.

The other melodrama involved scandal. A Republican lobbyist named Jack Abramoff had been indicted for allegedly bilking Indian tribes. His sundry associations threatened to reach into the office of Rove, whose assistant once worked for Abramoff. But this was a minor concern, a fear of being slimed, compared to the serious legal matter involving former CIA operative Valerie Plame.

Plame's husband, a retired ambassador named Joseph Wilson, had been sent by the administration to Niger in 2002 to determine whether Saddam's government had attempted to obtain uranium from that country. Wilson found that such a transaction had not occurred. He was therefore stunned to hear Bush declare in his 2003 State of the Union address, "The British government has learned that Saddam Hussein recently sought significant quantities of uranium from Africa."

Wilson assailed the White House's credibility in a *New York Times* op-ed piece. Shortly after that, his wife's CIA identity was leaked (by Richard Armitage, as it turned out) in Robert Novak's column. A special prosecutor was named, and Karl Rove was soon brought in for questioning. Though that shoe would not drop for months, the implications of the Plame case cast a long shadow. Rove had assured Bush that he had known nothing about Wilson's wife. When Bush learned otherwise, he hit the roof. But Rove kept his job, while his lawyers worked to stave off a federal indictment.

It had been a very strange year, but far from unproductive. Just before leaving for Crawford, Bush signed the Central American Free Trade Agreement, largely on a party-line vote. Major transportation and energy bills had also been passed in a prerecess flurry of activity. The unexpected resignation in July of Sandra Day O'Connor from the Supreme Court had presented Bush with a huge opportunity to replace the swing jurist with a reliable conservative vote. His nominee, a U.S. Court of Appeals judge and Beltway lifer named John Roberts, had a distinguished if at times politically overheated legal paper trail. Roberts's confirmation was as close to a sure thing as could be forecast in so polarized a climate.

Along the way, Bush had shed the fat he'd accumulated during the reelect. He now weighed 191.6 pounds, and his physical rated him "superior." And that was *before* these five weeks of grinding the pedals under triple-digit temperatures.

Life was indeed good. But it could become less good in a hurry. Bartlett had seen the numbers. For all the postelection swagger, they'd found no traction on any single initiative. The rising gas prices and the surging toll in Iraq were sapping the public will. For the first time since the invasion, the number of Americans polled who approved of the war had dropped to beneath 40.

And besides: There was a developing story elsewhere in Crawford—a sad-faced forty-eight-year-old woman named Cindy Sheehan, whose son Casey had died in Iraq the year before, and who had encamped in the town, demanding an opportunity to tell Bush, face-to-face, to bring the troops home now.

On its face, it seemed a quintessential August story, a space filler. But the Army specialist's mother was neither shrill nor slick. Sheehan had in fact met with Bush two months prior, with other bereaved families at Fort Lewis, Washington, and her depiction of the president was not flattering: He tried to force levity, he didn't know Casey's name, and he repeatedly referred to her as "Mom," which she found disrespectful. Bored by the daily nonevents at Crawford's "Western White House," the press corps had been venturing out to Camp Casey, the growing shantytown abutting Bush's property. The Sheehan story had legs.

In Bartlett's communications shop, serious consideration was given to the idea of the president meeting with Cindy Sheehan. Hagin thought it would set a bad precedent: *Come to Crawford, camp out, wave a few signs . . . and meet the president!* Plus, he'd seen the photos of Bush's first encounter of Sheehan—the hugging, the evident warmth. Yes, he'd called her Mom. Bush did that a lot. He meant it as a term of endearment. Every other grieving mother had apparently taken it that way.

Nonetheless, they couldn't let the Sheehan controversy fester. So on the afternoon of Saturday, August 6, an advance guy mingled at Camp Casey, waiting until the cameras were gone, at about four thirty or so, before speaking into his mike—at which point Hagin and Steve Hadley drove up in a sedan, with Hadley's detail in a car behind them.

She and her sister were sitting on the side of the road in folding chairs. A half-dozen supporters stood nearby and glared at the White House officials as they introduced themselves. Cindy Sheehan said that she was glad to see them but still did not intend to leave until the president gave her an audience.

Hadley spoke to her about her son's valor, about the justness of the fight in Iraq. He wanted her to know about the progress.

"I just know—you all are nice and intelligent people, and I know you don't believe all of that," she said.

For forty-five minutes they talked in circles. Finally, Hagin said, "Look, we're not here to try to convince you. But there's one thing I want you to know. And that's that he truly does care about every soldier who is over there, and every family who has lost a loved one. I'm the guy who goes to most of these meetings. And I know, there's not a doubt in my mind. . . ."

"No he doesn't," Cindy Sheehan said quietly. "That's just not true."

She thanked them for coming. And she remained where she was, at Camp Casey beside Bush's ranch, for the rest of August.

Bush saw her a few days later, through the window of his limo, as he drove by in a fifteen-car caravan to a Republican fund-raiser at the nearby Broken Spoke Ranch. She looked pretty much like any other protester. There'd even been a few outside the Tamarack Resort in Idaho. It came with the job, he was beginning to realize. His dad had had them. Reagan had, too.

So there was nothing in particular to feel, seeing a bunch of people on the side of the road holding up signs and yelling. Bush was paid to consider their loss, but not to dwell on it.

Cindy Sheehan's son had done his job. Bush was doing his.

That afternoon at the Broken Spoke Ranch, he raised over $2 million for the Republican National Committee. Bush returned the way he had come two hours later. Cindy Sheehan was still standing there, and the motorcade once again drove past her.

Until the hurricane devastated the city, Bush had not been to New Orleans since January 15, 2004. That day happened to be Martin Luther King Day, and the year happened to be an election year. And because Rove liked to roll out policies in conjunction with the president's State of the Union address, he decided to target MLK's birthday as an opportunity for Bush to launch the faith-based initiative put in place by executive order when Congress refused to legislate it.

Rove asked Jim Towey, the White House director of the Office of Faith-Based and Community Initiatives, to find a suitable African American venue for Martin Luther King Day. Since the president was going to conclude that afternoon with a wreath-laying ceremony at

King's grave in Atlanta, Rove was angling for an additional locale in the South. New Orleans—*Bingo, we can squeeze in a fund-raiser lunch-eon. . . .* Towey's staff did its research and found a perfect spot. The Union Bethel African Methodist Episcopal Church, adjacent to the projects of east New Orleans, had served the low-income neighborhood for nearly 140 years. The church delivered food, paid medical and housing bills, offered day-care services, and in every meaningful way served as the conscience of that community. Union Bethel had the city's largest African American membership on December 14, 1961, when Dr. King came to town and was not permitted to host a speech at the municipal auditorium. King gave his speech at Union Bethel instead—and what came of that episode were new laws allowing blacks to congregate in public places. Karl Rove could not have scripted it better.

Towey called the church's pastor, the Reverend Thomas Brown Jr. He warned that Brown would probably take some heat in the black community for hosting a Republican president who had received all of 9 percent of the African American vote in 2000. The Reverend thought he had better clear the matter with his bishop—whose initial reaction had been the same as Brown's: "President? *What* president?"

But Bishop Hennings's second reaction also echoed that of the pastor: "Let us not be stupid here. We may not agree with him on a lot of issues, but he *is* the president."

The day before the president came to visit, Reverend Brown's staff spent hours calling its members, asking them for their Social Security numbers and dates of birth and urging them to come to church on Thursday morning. Meanwhile, one of Union Bethel's most active members, a young woman named Tenisha Stevens, received a call from the White House. Tenisha was informed that she had been selected to be a member of the USA Freedom Corps. Tenisha asked what that meant.

You show up at the airport and get your picture taken shaking the president's hand right after he deplanes, Tenisha was informed. She agreed to be enlisted in the USA Freedom Corps.

At about ten the next morning, Tenisha Stevens stood on the tarmac of Louis Armstrong International Airport and fulfilled her duties. Bush put his arm around her for the camera, thanked her for her spirit of volunteerism, and climbed into his limo. Tenisha followed behind the motorcade in a white van.

Union Bethel ordinarily held twelve hundred congregants. This day, close to two thousand had managed to squeeze in. The vast majority of them were Democrats. They'd talked among themselves: *Why is he coming to OUR church? Why on Martin Luther King's birthday?* But they trusted their pastor—and besides, this was the *president of the United States . . . in THEIR church . . .* and he seemed so likable, not at all the man of privilege or the white fish squirming nervously in a black sea. He called the Reverend's wife by her name, their son by his nickname (Benjy). He called out Tenisha Stevens from the congregation—"Thank you for being a soldier in the great army of compassion here in America."

With the church choir serving as his backdrop, he referred to addiction as an affliction "of the heart"—and he spoke of his own addiction, alcohol. Then he declared that "the government should not fear faith-based programs" like ones "right here in this church." The president invoked the dreaded D-word. The government, he said, "discriminated against faith-based programs. It's the truth. How does it happen that way? Well, oftentimes, a faith-based program that applies [to the] federal government says, I want to help, and they say, fine, you can help, but take the cross down from the wall, take off the Star of David, take down the crescent. And my answer to that is: How can you be a faith-based program if you can't practice your faith? It seems to be a contradiction in terms."

So here was the president, evangelizing—"changing a culture"—*in THEIR church!* He mingled, shook hands. Then the big men in earplugs steered him out the door, through an ungodly swarm of TV cameras and boom mikes that would broadcast this moment—*THEIR moment! THEIR church!*—throughout the nation . . . while the motorcade whizzed off, ferrying the president to the fund-raiser Rove had arranged, near Lee Circle, where a crowd was burning Bush's likeness in effigy. . . .

Reverend Brown and Tenisha Stevens and their church family were *so* proud. Proud not only to relive it through the images on TV and in the papers but to learn at the end of July that the White House's Office of Faith-Based and Community Initiatives had awarded Union Bethel three hundred thousand dollars over a three-year period to mentor children of incarcerated parents. A true blessing, and it took the sting out of the Reverend's losing his quest to be bishop that summer. (Towey's prediction was right: The general conference of the Reverend's host church had endorsed Kerry, implicitly denouncing Reverend Brown for hosting Bush at his church. *What else could I do?*

He's our president. Give honor, said Brown, quoting scripture, but they turned a deaf ear.) Union Bethel had done so much without the government's help . . . but *now*, this gift would take them to the next level. And there would be another level after that one. The president's visit represented the turning of a corner. The Reverend wrote Jim Towey: *Bring him back again, let us build on this—we have an OPPOR-TUNITY here, first Dr. King and then the president, let us keep going . . .*

They felt this way at Union Bethel, a tingling sense of possibility, all the way up until the storm blew in.

Reverend Brown gave his sermon on Sunday, August 28, to only a few dozen members. Many of them had already loaded their cars. He'd called nearly all the seniors the day before and insisted that they leave town immediately. His wife wasn't pleased that they were sticking around to give one more service. *The Lord gave you five good senses—now USE 'em!* But the Reverend insisted on this last blessing, adding, *The Lord will provide.*

"Based on the reports that are coming in, this is going to be *the* storm," he said from the pulpit. "And Jesus will not be walking on water to come to us."

They bowed their heads in prayer: *Deliver our city from the storm, O God, and watch over your children here at Union Bethel. . . .* They sang a last hymn, hugged one another, and agreed that it had been a good service. Outside, it was a brilliant August morning. Nothing in the sky foretold malevolence. Some got into their cars to head for Mississippi or Texas. Others said they were going home to ride it out—unaware that in the coming minutes, their mayor, Ray Nagin, would order a mandatory evacuation of New Orleans. They all agreed to be back at church by the middle of the week.

"See you Wednesday," they sang out to one another.

Wednesday never came.

Those who made it out did not have it easy. Even with the contraflow, traffic along Interstate 10 was not moving. The ninety-minute drive to Baton Rouge took eleven hours. But make it they did, a few hours before the rain commenced. The storm churned westward, felling trees and cascading garbage through the streets, causing power outages everywhere.

By Monday at noon the skies were miraculously clear again. Still, it was a day for sitting indoors in front of the television—staring at the continuing visual of the city they had left behind, images that in no way comported with the lovely weather that day. The news stations kept airing footage of the levees along 17th Street and the Industrial Canal. Water was sloshing over them . . . though by midafternoon it had become a barreling deluge, and the commentators were no longer saying "overtopping." They were saying "breached." Lake Pontchartrain had slammed through the levees. New Orleans was drowning.

And those from Union Bethel who had decided to ride it out learned this the hard way. Three of the members stayed in their houses on the east side of town. The water crashed through the windows, and they couldn't get out, and they died under water. A few others scrambled up to their rooftops, where they stayed for more than a day in the broiling sun with no water, croaking out to strangers in boats. One of the church's senior members, ninety-year-old Rita Steele, made it to the expressway but there lost all resolve. She sat on the side of the road for three days and nights, until someone came along and asked if she needed help.

Still others from the church had come to recognize the direness a day too late, and had no means of transportation out of the city, and therefore joined the ten thousand encamped in the Superdome. One of them was a woman who couldn't swim. She'd held on to a daughter who could, and who paddled through the wretched water until they saw a bridge, and climbed up onto it and staggered to the Dome—deliverance to a reeking slum without food or bathroom facilities for three days. And only then did they board buses, leaving New Orleans and all that they had for the unfamiliar: Atlanta, Memphis, Jackson, Dallas, Washington, San Diego, Los Angeles, New Hampshire . . .

And those were the members whose whereabouts were known. At least a hundred of the congregants were never heard from again. Had they consciously given up on New Orleans, or were they adrift in America—or maybe still nearby—or were they at the bottom of Lake Pontchartrain. . . . It had been disintegrated and scattered, this Union Bethel Church family that had provided such a pleasing backdrop to President Bush's faith-based initiative nineteen months earlier. As burst the levees, so burst they.

But the Reverend Thomas Brown Jr. would not believe this. He did not accept it, even after he drove in from his temporary refuge in Mississippi on September 9 and saw the church for the first time since the storm. Its stained glass windows were gutted, the walls had buckled, and the third floor had collapsed. *Lord, what are we gonna do here?* the

Reverend thought miserably as he waded through two and a half feet of water. There was no way Union Bethel's insurance would cover even half of the damage. Yes, it was a historic church—but there were other historic churches that had sustained damage, on top of tens of thousands of homes, and bridges and roads and schools . . .

. . . And yet, Reverend Brown remembered, this place was special. For the president had been here. *To OUR church*. And the president had spoken of partnerships between the federal government and churches such as Union Bethel. And—now the Reverend's mind was racing—because the city was in such distress, the community so battered . . . well, surely the president could see that this church, whose efforts he had praised so effusively, was now needed more than ever. Surely *now* was the time to build—or *rebuild . . . surely* help would come to Union Bethel, and with that help the church would remind the city and the outside world not only that great men had once spoken here but that after the applause and the photographs they had returned—they had brought hope.

He didn't realize how much he was thinking like Bush when the notion took hold: *This church represents an OPPORTUNITY.* And through his tears, Reverend Brown saw that opportunity, and believed that the president would, too.

On Sunday, August 28, just as the Reverend was concluding his last service at Union Bethel, Bush went for a bike ride at his ranch.

As always, he rode hard. But he took great pride in pointing out to the Austin guests who rode with him the new single tracks that had been freshly cleared for their pleasure. The morning was hot, and after about eighty minutes on the trails, Bush was gassed. He and his friends then stripped down and dived into the Whining Pool. Bush floated on the water, commenting on the beauty of the day. After about a half hour, he excused himself, saying that he had a call to take.

He joined Joe Hagin in the Crawford guesthouse and participated in a secure video teleconference to discuss Hurricane Katrina's impending arrival in New Orleans. For days now, Bush had been receiving briefings from Hagin and Steve Atkiss, both of whom were participating in regular secure video teleconferences (SVTCs) with weather experts and FEMA officials. Bush therefore knew on Wednesday, August 24, that the tropical depression had become a tropical storm as it gathered force over the Bahamas and headed for the coast. He knew by Thursday that it had hit Florida as a category 1 hurricane, compelling his brother Jeb to declare a state of emergency. He knew by Friday afternoon that Katrina had executed an ominous pivot to the northwest, veering toward the coasts of Mississippi and Louisiana with category 3 locomotion. And he knew by Saturday, August 27, that the storm had become a category 4, with a 45 percent chance of hitting New Orleans directly and producing a death toll that could make 9/11 look like a biking-induced Yard Sale.

Even here at the ranch, with lefty columnists sneering that Bush had blithely retreated into his Nowhere Land, he had much to monitor. The Israelis had recently withdrawn from Gaza, a challenge for the Palestinians to reciprocate with a commitment to peaceful self-government. In Iraq, the Sunnis were threatening to snub a proposed Iraqi constitution, compelling Bush to telephone a Shiite leader on Thursday and lobby for compromise. Of late, Bush had adopted a new paradigmatic slogan: "As Iraqis stand up, Americans will stand down." While Cindy Sheehan's Camp Casey had swelled to more than a thousand protesters and given rise to counterprotests and a full-blown media vaudeville, the White House was gearing up for a serious pushback. Bush would be giving three Iraq speeches this month—and in September, so went the plan, they would hit the airwaves with a sharp-elbowed Choice-Not-Referendum contrasting of the war president's determination versus the defeatism of the Democrats.

And so even with his mornings devoted to brush clearing and bike riding, Bush had ample substance on his plate. But the impending hurricane had become a particular concern by Sunday morning. He had already spoken by phone to FEMA's director, Mike Brown, about the prestaging of relief efforts. He had also called Louisiana Governor Kathleen Blanco to receive assurances that the voluntary evacuation of New Orleans had been reconsidered and was now mandatory. Now he decided to forgo the usual briefing by Hagin. Basically unannounced, he walked into the Crawford conference room just before noon on Sunday and sat in on a Katrina-related SVTC for the first time.

Bush sat with his reading glasses on and looked up from his map of the hurricane's expected trajectory to watch National Hurricane Center director Max Mayfield on the video screen. "I don't have any good news here at all today," Mayfield said. "This is, as everybody knows by now, a very dangerous hurricane, and the center is about two hundred twenty-five miles south-southeast of the mouth of the Mississippi River."

Bush watched as Mayfield put up slides of the hurricane, the water vapor animation, and the storm-surge forecast. The early predictions, said Mayfield, suggested that "there will be minimal flooding in the city of New Orleans itself." The NHS director followed with more slides, received questions from others hooked in to the teleconference, and then turned things over to a rainfall analyst and after that a hydrologist.

Hagin then indicated to Mike Brown that the president wanted to speak. "Yes, Mike, thank you very much," Bush said after the FEMA director had introduced him to the other conference participants. "I appreciate so very much the warnings that Max and his team have given to the good folks in Louisiana and Mississippi and Alabama. Appreciate your briefing that you gave me early this morning about what the federal government is prepared to do to help the state and local folks deal with this really serious storm.

"I do want to thank the good folks in the offices of Louisiana and Alabama and Mississippi for listening to these warnings and preparing your citizens for this, this huge storm. I want to assure the folks at the state level that we are fully prepared to not only help you during the storm, but we will move in whatever resources and assets we have at our disposal after the storm to help you deal with the loss of property. And we pray for no loss of life, of course.

"Unfortunately, we've had experience at this in recent years, and I— the FEMA folks have done great work in the past. And I'm confident, Mike, that you and your team will do all you can to help the good folks in these affected states." Then Bush thanked everyone, offered the nation's prayers, and said that "we just hope for the very best."

The video conference was far from over, but the president had said his piece. There were hard questions to ask during the noonday conference—questions that addressed the nightmare scenario of what would happen if the city's levees were breached. Were buses prestaged so that those who had no means of getting out of the city could be evacuated? Were high-level evacuation routes predetermined? Was there sufficient food and water in the meantime? Did city officials have resilient communications equipment? Was there sufficient security in the event of looting?

"No" was the answer to each. But the postdisaster questions went unasked by the president. Mellowed from his physical exertion, Bush was a silent participant for the rest of the meeting. It broke up by one in the afternoon. Bush had the rest of the day to himself.

*   *   *

Katrina made landfall the next morning. Bush talked to Mike Brown on the phone and asked him if the levees had held. Brown believed that they had. Nonetheless, 135 mph winds were hammering the city. Bush hastily convened a press conference to declare Louisiana and Mississippi disaster areas and to urge all residents of the Gulf Coast to evacuate to safer ground. It was nine thirty and Bush was already looking fatigued as he and Laura boarded Air Force One to a presidential Conversation in El Mirage, Arizona. He began his talk by acknowledging the local officials and introducing his wife. Then Bush said, "I want the folks there on the Gulf Coast to know that the federal government is prepared to help you when the storm passes. . . . When the storm passes, the federal government has got assets and resources that we'll be deploying to help you."

But he had much more to say on the subject of immigration and gas prices—two pressing domestic issues for the fall—and then even more on the progress in Iraq. After that, he turned to the Ordinary Citizens perched on their stools (two little old ladies: a nurse and a Salvation Army worker) and chatted them up on "a good deal for our seniors," his prescription drug plan. The forty-five minutes' worth of hamming it up had the effect of comfort food. His pep visibly restored, Bush headed off to now legendary Rancho Cucamonga, California, to repeat his shtick and then spend the night in San Diego.

While Bush was wowing the seniors of El Mirage, Hagin was sitting on the runway in Air Force One, participating in a SVTC with Mike Brown and Governor Blanco, among others. Hagin wanted to know if the Superdome had held up after the storm. Blanco said that it had. He also wanted to know if the levees had held. "I think we have not breached the levee," Blanco replied. "We have not breached the levee at this point in time."

In fact, Blanco was talking out of school—there had been much evidence to suggest that the 17th Street levee had been compromised—but none of her aides standing around her thought to break in and suggest that she modify her statement. Barely an hour later, the governor learned that she had been wrong. She didn't think to notify Hagin, since the images of gushing water were all over the television. And later that afternoon, a FEMA advance man named Marty Bahamonde bootlegged a helicopter, shot aerial photographs of New Orleans' multitude of underwater neighborhoods, and then placed a phone call to his boss, Mike Brown, who pledged to notify the White House right away.

And yet Bush and his staffers aboard Air Force One spent that afternoon and evening convinced that New Orleans had, as Bush would put it, "dodged a bullet." The hurricane itself had bent around the city rather than crashed through it. Hagin had heard straight from Louisiana's governor that the levees had held. Hagin also heard from Brown, who had just received Bahamonde's awful report. But Brown believed that his subordinate, though diligent, tended toward hyperbole. He did not pass on to Hagin Marty Bahamonde's grim news that the levees had been breached. The White House deputy chief of staff—Bush's de facto point man on Katrina while Andy Card was celebrating his wedding anniversary in Maine—retired for the evening without knowing that there had been a FEMA man in a helicopter seeing with his own eyes the floodwaters overtake New Orleans.

In a prior life, Hagin had been a firefighter in Ohio. His passion remained with emergency management even as he executed his care-and-feeding-of-POTUS duties. It was his experience that a fog-of-war dysclarity attended the first twenty-four hours after a disaster. Hagin's last e-mail before he went to sleep that Monday night in San Diego was from a FEMA official, who reported that the levees had held.

He let that be the last word until the fog lifted.

"I think we ought to plan on heading back," Bush told Hagin late the next morning.

They had already been through this. By seven o'clock on the morning of Tuesday, August 30, Hagin had learned that the levees had in fact not held and that 80 percent of New Orleans was under water. The president was astonished by the news. Still, it had long been Bush's pattern to shy away from tragic events. When he was governor, he had chosen not to visit the East Texas town of Jasper in the wake of three white men killing a black man and dragging him by a chain hooked to the back of their pickup truck. Jesse Jackson had been to Jasper, Gore was showing up. . . . He hated that kind of parade, found it terribly unseemly, so he called the deceased's family instead. And there had been other such incidents—wildfires, shootings at a church—from which he stood back, prompting Karen to tell him, *Sir, this is part of leadership. People expect to see their governor show up.* Which he understood, sort of—but it was not his thing, nor really a Bush family thing, to strut one's empathy in such a way.

Plus, Bush hated schedule changes.

And so when Bartlett by phone first floated to Hagin the idea of heading back to Washington after they'd learned that virtually all of New Orleans was under water, Bush did not respond affirmatively. Instead, they proceeded with the day's events. Bush motorcaded to Naval Base Coronado, where he first did an interview with Armed Forces Radio, then gave a speech commemorating the sixtieth anniversary of Japan's surrender to the Allied Forces—once again coupling that morally unambiguous war with the struggle in Iraq, assuring the troops at the base that America would "stay until the job is finished." Then on to a medical center, where he met with wounded Navy SEALS.

Even as Bush carried on with the day's entire schedule, the White House press shop was getting anxious. The news reports from New Orleans were ghastly, and the apparent disconnect between the horrors on the ground and Bush's oblivious road show was fast developing into a story of its own. There was no salvaging Bush's Iraq message—it had gone under water with New Orleans. The metastory of public perception now predominated.

Without any explanation, the advance team in charge of the press— the self-described Goatherders—rounded up the traveling pool before the designated photo op and ushered them back onto the plane. Air Force One was wheels-up an hour ahead of schedule. They were not airborne long before Bartlett did his job, making a second call from the West Wing to Air Force One and informing the president that they *really* should be getting back to Washington.

This time, Bush acquiesced. Still, there would be no rush, as had been the case when Bush zoomed back to the White House five months earlier to sign the Terri Schiavo bill. They would return to Crawford as scheduled, spend the night at the ranch, and then head out late Wednesday morning. In the interim, it fell to poor Scott McClellan to tell the pool that the sudden decision to end the president's working vacation in Crawford a few days ahead of schedule had nothing whatsoever to do with concern about public perceptions. "I don't look at it that way," Scott said. It was simply the president's "preference" now to conduct his duties in Washington rather than the Western White House.

Before taking off on Wednesday morning, August 31, the president's pilot had asked Hagin's deputy, Steve Atkiss, if he thought Bush would be interested in a slight detour from their flight pattern, so as to have an aerial view of the devastated Gulf region en route to Washington. Atkiss figured it was a no-brainer. The president couldn't very well parachute into a disaster zone on a moment's notice. The presidential apparatus was both monstrous and frail; drop it in without elaborate preparation, and it crushes everything, including itself. Better, then, to have Bush view the damage from the air than not at all. He checked with Hagin, then told the pilot, "Sure, let's do it."

But it was not as simple a proposition as Atkiss had calculated. Bartlett could imagine how the visual of Bush hovering unsullied over the wretched masses would play in the media. The flyover was the lesser of two evils—shit, what if they *didn't* make the detour? Nonetheless concerned, Bartlett called Andy Card in Maine. Card agreed: Bush would be damned either way. The chief of staff gave his "skeptical approval" to the flyover.

In an effort to narrow the distance between Bush and the tragedy below him, Goatherders took a highly unusual step. The traveling press had been irked that their photographers were increasingly getting little or no access to presidential events—that the White House instead controlled the visual message by supplying images from its staff photographers, who were, of course, paid to capture Bush in the most flattering light. On Wednesday aboard Air Force One, policy was reversed. For the first time ever during a noncampaign event, the Goatherders hastened the traveling photographers to the front of the Air Force One cabin, to capture visual evidence of Bush's concern as he viewed the damage.

The damage was unfathomable. For twenty minutes, the president passed over a wasteland. The city's highways simply gave off into the water; its rooftops seemed to float disembodied along a fetid gray river. Along the Mississippi coast, fully a half-mile inland consisted of nothing but debris—mounds of shredded wood and licorice swirls of tar. A container ship had capsized in the Gulf; its cargo of containers had rolled ashore, bowling over trees, cars, and everything else in their path. Lifelessness was the least of it. The sheer brutality of what he was observing called to Bush's mind the work of some unconscionable weapon. He simply could not contemplate this as an act of God.

McClellan went to the back of the plane, where the print media remained. The press secretary supplied a single quote from the president: "It's devastating. It's got to be doubly devastating on the ground."

It was worse than doubly devastating on the ground. In the wake of Katrina, competence had taken disaster leave. Chaos, pettiness, and ineptitude were instead ruling the day in Louisiana.

Disasters were not events to which Governor Kathleen Babineaux

Blanco was particularly suited. She was not an autocratic crisis czar in the manner of Rudy Giuliani. Blanco preferred consensus. She deliberated with her staff. No decision was concluded without the input of her husband, Raymond "Coach" Blanco. Even her closest aides could grow irritated at the watching-the-paint-dry pace of her decision making. As a physical presence, Blanco lacked the attributes of the previous Democratic governor of Louisiana, the dashing felon Edwin Edwards. She was a terrible public speaker, was wanting for pithiness, and cut a frazzled, even bereft figure for the camera—at times resembling a lonely-hearts matron who had just been fleeced by a handsome con artist. For all her attributes as an intelligent, compassionate executive, Blanco did not readily project the image of a bold and reassuring leader.

"We don't know how to deal with hurricanes in Louisiana—but we sure know how to party!" Blanco had wisecracked nervously on Sunday, August 28, during her initial meeting with FEMA director Mike Brown in Baton Rouge. Brown himself had an odd way of assuring those around him. "Now, some days you're gonna love me, and some days you're gonna hate me," he told the governor.

He added a helpful hint: "The most important thing is that you get lots of rest," he instructed Blanco. "Take power naps whenever you can." The governor's aides thought he radiated condescension.

Brown, an Oklahoma City lawyer and former commissioner of the International Arabian Horse Association, had been plucked from obscurity by his hometown pal Joe Allbaugh when the 2000 campaign's Enforcer had been marooned by Bush at FEMA. (Allbaugh's line was that Bush had passed over him for chief of staff because the men were *too* close: "Hell, it got to the point that we were finishing each other's sentences and that's not necessarily a good thing," he told reporter Chris Cooper. The dubious story circulating around FEMA—no doubt originating with Allbaugh—was that Bush had offered him any other job in the administration he wished, other than the one already promised to Andy Card . . . and that Allbaugh himself passed over the various White House and cabinet gigs in favor of the FEMA post.)

When Allbaugh stormed off in disgust after DHS incorporated FEMA in late 2002, Brown got kicked upstairs. He wasted little time mimicking his predecessor's antipathy for the new chain of command and the ceding of turf. Brown's disdain for his direct superiors, first Tom Ridge and later Mike Chertoff, was both evident and mutually felt. He haughtily dispatched his deputy, Patrick Rhode, to attend the

DHS undersecretary meetings in his stead. Still, where Allbaugh's access to his boss had gone from total to virtually zero in a span of nine years, Mike Brown was enjoying the reverse experience. By 2004, the Okie attorney suddenly found himself hovering over Florida in Marine One surveying hurricane damage with the president of the United States. He was now Bush's go-to disaster guy—direct access that came with the price of a bestowed nickname, one that he would never have answered to in the past but that, by virtue of its executive imprimatur, now stuck: Brownie.

Brownie suffered the opposite problem from that of Governor Blanco. He was glib and divaesque and camera-ready to a fault. With his well-tailored Nordstrom wardrobe and his particular brand of TV makeup—prompting one aide to refer to him as Bobby Brown, the natty R&B musician—the FEMA director arrived in Louisiana's capital in something of a tizzy. He'd been contemplating retirement—*You should've gotten out when you could!* Hagin had teased in an e-mail—and now had the makings of a category 3 or 4 hurricane to contend with. It severely displeased him that Baton Rouge's one first-class downtown hotel, the Sheraton, was fully booked (with displaced Louisianans), and that the government was instead accommodating him on the outskirts of town, in a hotel where most of the inhabitants seemed to have pets. Chertoff's people had stripped Brown of his devoted PR aide, Sharon Worthy, and saddled him with a DHS public affairs specialist, Nicol Andrews, who for all Brownie knew was a spy for Chertoff. For this last mission, he decided to rejigger the command structure. Brownie would report to the president—or really Hagin, though he often told others he'd just spoken with the president, same difference—and leave Chertoff completely out of the loop.

As Tuesday dawned with the sickening realization that the floodwaters had engulfed the Crescent City, it became clear that the Superdome had to be evacuated. Brownie did not seem particularly worried. "Help yourselves, guys," he said to the half-dozen Transportation Department officials who showed up in the FEMA director's satellite truck and were surprised to find him sitting there alone, gazing placidly at a bank of television screens. When he wasn't watching TV that morning, he was being interviewed for TV. His words were uniformly soothing, on camera and off—as when he assured Blanco that FEMA had buses on their way. He promised her this more than once throughout the day—just as FEMA logistics specialists were in turn insisting that the buses were right on schedule.

But FEMA logistics did things by the book, and that book was not written for disasters of Katrina's magnitude. The buses had not arrived by Tuesday night, nor by Wednesday morning. The first FEMA order for 450 buses did not reach Norm Mineta's Department of Transportation until later that day; another 650 buses were ordered on Thursday. Evacuees in the Superdome who had been assured that their ordeal would last a maximum of three days now saw their fourth, then fifth day consigned to a gulag of human waste. It was not until Wednesday that state troopers and FEMA coordinators gathered to map out structurally viable routes for mass passage into and out of New Orleans. Such routes were by Tuesday plainly visible to the locals. But because the city's police force had, like the Iraqi army, simply melted away, the state troopers in Baton Rouge had no one to call to determine whether such routes were safe.

For lawlessness had broken out all over the city. Looting was abundant and went thoroughly unchecked. Blanco's National Guard troops did not arrive in force until Thursday morning. Meanwhile, food delivered by the Department of Agriculture sat untouched in warehouses. A crisis was evolving in the downtown convention center, where tens of thousands had gathered of their own accord—and where there was no food or water to be had. With this gathering pandemonium, and with the evacuation buses still nowhere near New Orleans, Mike Chertoff went on the air Wednesday afternoon and spoke as if from a parallel universe, saying, "We are extremely pleased with the response that every element of the federal government, all of our federal partners, have made to this terrible tragedy."

Of course, Chertoff wasn't getting information from Brownie—not that this would have been altogether helpful, considering that the FEMA director confessed to CNN's Paula Zahn Thursday evening, "Paula, the federal government did not even know about the convention center people until today." Later that night, Mike Brown tried to convince Ted Koppel that FEMA was feeding the people stranded at the convention center. Koppel called him on the inaccuracy. The FEMA director confessed that he was in error.

Just after the interview with Koppel, Brownie broke down in tears.

As midnight approached on Thursday, the city's emergency preparedness director, retired Marine Colonel Terry Ebbert, stood outside the Superdome in pitch blackness, waiting for the puny trickle of FEMA buses to grow into a caravan. He had not slept since Sunday. Just a few minutes earlier, he had received a call from a state trooper who had seen hordes of empty buses parked near the La Place exit on Interstate 10. Apparently FEMA inspectors had pulled the buses over and were now checking the depth of the treads on the bus tires to make sure that they met safety requirements.

Thinking of this, Ebbert pulled out his BlackBerry and e-mailed a friend: *I've spent my whole life serving this country and I know human despair because I caused a lot of it but I never thought I would see it with our people in a city within the USA and if anybody in any leadership position had to stand where I'm standing now and seeing this despair and human suffering they would feel like me, I'm ashamed of being an American.*

From the moment he touched down in Washington on Wednesday afternoon, Bush's every public utterance seemed to be that of a man beset by misinformation or outright denial.

After disembarking from Marine One, he stood in the Rose Garden, flanked by Rumsfeld and a few other cabinet secretaries, and discussed what he had just seen on his flyover—which, of course, was the macrocosmic view of what TV viewers had been watching in horrific granularity for two days now, while the president was flying around the West selling hand-picked audiences on the progress in Iraq. Bush seemed unaware of just how late to the game he had come. He proceeded to rattle off the multitude of things that the federal government had done or was about to do for the city of New Orleans. That monumental failures had already occurred, resulting in massive human suffering, did not receive the president's acknowledgment.

The following morning, he told Diane Sawyer on ABC's *Good Morning America*, "I don't think anybody anticipated the breach of the levees. They did anticipate a serious storm. But these levees got breached. And as a result, much of New Orleans is flooded. And now we are having to deal with it and will." That summation was not only flip but untrue: Hagin had known to ask repeatedly about the condition of the levees, and so, by extension, had Bush.

Early that afternoon, Bush held a press conference to announce that the men standing on either side of him, his father and Bill Clinton, would lead a hurricane relief effort. As with his Rose Garden speech, the president emphasized his engagement with the New Orleans problem: "I'm in close contact with Secretary Chertoff. . . . I want to make sure I fully understand the relief efforts and the extent of the relief efforts and the progress of the relief efforts. . . . We're working hard to repair the breaches in the levees. . . . As we speak, people are moving into the New Orleans area to maintain law and order. . . ." He also said, "Bus caravans are shuttling back and forth between Houston and New Orleans to get those folks to Houston"—apparently believing that this was so, but it was not.

Bush had to get on the ground. They'd known this since Tuesday. For the first time since 9/11, Hagin figured he had better preadvance the trip himself. By the time of his arrival in New Orleans on Wednesday morning, Hagin was aware of the public relations fallout. At the same time, the last thing they needed to do was disrupt the relief effort with the bloated presidential apparatus. Hagin called his old friend Governor Haley Barbour of Mississippi, who requested that the president forestall his visit until the following Monday. Governor Bob Riley of Alabama also urged Bush to come later rather than sooner. Perhaps by oversight, Governor Blanco's opinion was not solicited.

Hagin fanned his advance men out over the Gulf. The goal, as in all disaster situations, was to place the president in a tableau of manageable suffering and allow him to connect, empathize, project hope. A site was readily located in Biloxi: a low-income neighborhood just a three-mile drive from the landing zone, hard hit but not thoroughly flattened—a "hope story," in other words.

Louisiana was another matter. Hagin's guy on the ground, Jason Recher, was first instructed to find a good visual story in Baton Rouge. Recher checked out the Emergency Operations Center, where most state officials were encamped. But it was a chaotic spectacle of haggard, deeply dispirited emergency workers. At ten o'clock on Wednesday night, Hagin called Recher and told him that the president had weighed in. "Put off Baton Rouge—he wants to go to New Orleans," Hagin said.

Taking Bush to the Superdome had been a live option until Thursday morning, when Recher flew over it in a helicopter and was overwhelmed by the stench and the near-riotous conditions below. The helicopter wheeled toward Lakeview, the city's regional airport. It was an island, with hundreds of stranded workers groping about and begging for help. Also not a "hope story."

Later Thursday afternoon, Recher discovered that the 17th Street levee was accessible by land. He thought of Bush standing at Ground Zero on September 14, 2001: *This is where Americans want to see him. Not at some emergency office or an airport. They want to see him right where it all happened.*

While weaving the logistics together, Recher tried several times to contact Mayor Nagin. At 4:45 AM Friday, the advance man was sleeping in a van when he heard his phone buzzing. It was one of Nagin's communications persons. "Where are you guys?" Recher asked.

It took some prodding before she responded, "We're hiding on the twenty-seventh floor of the Hyatt."

"Hiding?"

"Yeah. They found out he was here."

Recher decided to quit trying to make sense of this. The president was coming to New Orleans tomorrow and would like to see the mayor, he informed her. "Is there anything we can do for him in the meantime?"

"The mayor hasn't had a shower in five days," she said.

Jason Recher said that they could make arrangements to get him cleaned up.

Before lifting off Friday morning, Bush received a briefing about the convention center. It began to dawn on him that somebody had been feeding him a lot of crap about the stellar relief efforts in New Orleans. What galled him was this: The media had managed to get there; why hadn't the federal government? He marched out to the South Lawn where the press awaited him. Bartlett could see how pissed the boss was. *Not necessarily a bad thing*, he thought.

"Tell 'em," he prodded Bush.

And so, amid the happy talk of diligent efforts, Bush said it for the first time: "The results are not acceptable."

Bartlett thought that this was a big step.

But it was followed by a huge step backward at Bush's first stop in Mobile, Alabama. While walking from Air Force One to the Coast Guard hangar where Bush would say a few words, Governors Barbour and Riley spoke with gratitude about the herculean federal efforts. Both men singled out one individual for lavish praise: Michael Brown. Riley was explicit: "Whenever I've needed anything here in Alabama, all I've needed to do is call Mike Brown," he said. "Mr. President, he's doing a heck of a job."

Those words were evidently ringing in Bush's ears as he concluded his emotional talk of loss and hope by saying, "Again, I want to thank you all for—and, Brownie," he said, wheeling toward the soft-skinned man in the starched shirt, "you're doing a heck of a job. The FEMA director is working twenty-four—they're working twenty-four hours a day," he concluded as those around him warmly applauded Brownie, who was mere hours away from becoming toast.

The next port of call was the "hope story" neighborhood in Biloxi. Bush hugged a number of residents and declared that "the people have got to understand that out of this rubble is going to come a new Biloxi, Mississippi." Still brimming with determined optimism, he seemed taken aback when Associated Press reporter Jennifer Loven launched a poignant question: "Sir, you talk about fixing what's wrong and you talk about the results not being acceptable. But there are a lot of people wondering why you weren't fixing the problems yesterday or the day before, and why the richest country on earth can't get food and water to those people that need it."

"The levees broke on Tuesday in New Orleans," he began unsteadily and incorrectly. "On Wednesday, we—and Thursday we started evacuating people. A lot of people have left that city. A lot of people have been pulled out on buses. It's—"

And without warning, he descended into a tortured formulation at odds with the plainspoken utterances on which he prided himself:

"I'm satisfied with the response. I'm not satisfied with all the results."

Mayor Nagin was showering on Air Force One when Bush choppered down to Louis Armstrong International Airport. None of the other elected officials who would convene on the plane that afternoon— Bush, Blanco, Senators Landrieu and Vitter, Congressmen Jindal and Jefferson—had weathered Katrina from its epicenter as Nagin had. He had refused to vacate the city for Baton Rouge, as some had recommended. None of his communications equipment was functioning, and he had not eaten a hot meal since landfall on Monday. His own home had been destroyed. His family had relocated to Dallas. This was his first term as a public servant. The public he served was now more desperate than any American populace in recent memory. He had commiserated with them at the Superdome, had driven the ungoverned streets and choppered over the sunken neighborhoods.

Still, even by New Orleans standards, Nagin's behavior that week had been erratic. He had abdicated the command center on City Hall's seventh floor; he showed no interest in utilizing the high-tech facilities on the USS *Bataan* when it pulled in to port on Wednesday. Instead, he held camp on the twenty-seventh floor of the Hyatt, from which he could view the expanse of the awfulness like a king surveying the slaughter of his army from the perch of his castle keep . . . and which one could access only by ascending twenty-seven flights in a darkened stairwell. Despite his occasional visits to the ground level, Nagin seemed unaware of basic facts—that both the 17th Street levee and the Superdome were reachable by land, for instance. His early assessments of the damage—"We know there is a significant number of dead bodies in the water. Minimum, hundreds. Most likely, thousands."—were way off base and served only to augment the hysteria. Nagin's detachment from reality was apparent to Brownie when they met on Tuesday. Brownie later told an aide, "That man's on Valium."

But there was nothing sedate about his rant on WWL-AM 870 the day before Bush's arrival. "I've talked directly to the president," he hollered at host Garland Robinette. "I've talked to the head of Homeland Security. . . . I've talked to everybody under the sun. I've been out there. I've flown these helicopters. Been in the crowds. Talking to people. Crying. Don't know where their relatives are. I've done it all, man! And I'll tell you, man: I'll keep hearing that it is coming. This is coming. That is coming. And my answer to that today is: BS! Where is the beef? There is no beef in this city. There is no beef anywhere in southeast Louisiana and these goddamned ships which are coming— *I don't see them!* . . . I basically told [Bush] that we had an incredible crisis here and that him flying over it on Air Force One does not do it justice and that I have been all around this city and I am very frustrated because we are not able to master resources and we are outmanned in about every respect. . . . Excuse my French, everybody in America, but I am *pissed.*"

It was a cathartic howl that obscured an uncomfortable truth—that Ray Nagin had lost any semblance of control over his city. By the time he had finished eating and showering on Air Force One, the mayor was no longer "pissed" at the president. He was grateful, a bit humbled, and very much in need of a political lifeline.

Bush needed the same thing. The night before, Bartlett's press shop had put together a DVD of news footage so that the president could at last see what Americans had been witnessing on TV for days now. The epic failure to deliver aid and comfort was now seared into him. How could this have happened? Even as Bush and his aides insisted that the White House was focused on solutions, Brownie had been feeding Hagin and Card an appealing narrative for days now: Unlike Mississippi, there was no "unified command structure" in Louisiana. The fault, in other words, lay not with Brownie and

FEMA, nor with Bush or Nagin. It lay instead with Governor Blanco. As long as control rested with her, the failures would continue. Brownie, Hagin, Card, and soon Nagin were in concurrence: Bush needed to push Blanco out of the way and federalize.

Blanco played right into this storyline. "We need everything you've got," she had pleaded to the president on Monday morning, just after landfall—an abject and ultimately meaningless request, except insofar as it revealed the governor's failure to grasp the precise necessities. Two mornings later, it dawned on Blanco. "I wish I'd called for troops," she told an aide, before picking up a phone and attempting to reach Bush, then Andy Card. Picking a number out of the air, she asked for forty thousand troops to help with search and rescue. But after a briefing with her counsel, Blanco clarified herself: Her request should not be taken to mean that she wished to lose authority over the National Guard. Federalization of the Guard would cause them to relinquish their law enforcement capability under the terms of the Posse Comitatus Act. With looting rampant, disarming the Guard was the last thing New Orleans needed.

New Orleans needed more, not less. But because Blanco did not agree to federalize, her request for forty thousand troops was not approved on Wednesday—or, when she reiterated it, on Thursday. Unknown to her, back in Washington, Rumsfeld was expressing great reluctance to deploy his military to a civilian zone—and in his trademark passive-aggressive way "throwing up every obstacle you could throw up," as one senior staffer would later recall.

The governor and the president had gotten along well in the past. They first met at the Union Bethel Church faith-based event on January 15, 2004, when the newly inaugurated state executive rode with Bush to the church, handing him along the way a wish list of things Louisiana needed. "She's not a shrinking violet when it comes to describing what she would like to see in terms of responsiveness," Bush told Union Bethel's congregation that day. "I appreciate that."

But by the time of Bush's arrival at the New Orleans airport on Friday, September 2, he was convinced that Blanco *had* been, in the wake of Katrina, a "shrinking violet," and now needed to step aside so that the feds could take over. Bush wasn't readily buying the media's scapegoating of FEMA. After all, he'd just heard from the other two governors affected by the hurricane. In *their* states, Brownie had done a heck of a job. Alabama, of course, had suffered comparatively little damage. Mississippi had been walloped, but Barbour, a former White

House staffer and longtime Beltway operative, knew whom to call and which buttons to push to get the goods delivered. Those very same services were available to Blanco. And though she was the lone Democrat of the three governors, she had spoken repeatedly to Bush, Hagin, and Card throughout the week. The problem wasn't access. It was that Blanco and her team lacked the ability to exploit FEMA's resources and the wherewithal to improvise in a time of crisis.

There was some truth to this theory—and truth as well to the belief that one could not compare Biloxi to a city under water with tens of thousands of its inhabitants stranded and starving. Regardless, by the time Bush touched down, things had begun to improve in New Orleans. The buses had arrived; evacuations to Houston's Astrodome were proceeding smoothly. Joint Task Force Katrina Commander Lt. General Russ Honore had arrived in the city and was lending assistance to the ongoing search-and-rescue efforts. Three thousand Guard troops from other states had poured in; order in the streets was being restored. And to assist in coordinating relief efforts, Blanco had hired Clinton's former FEMA director James Lee Witt—though only after the first applicant for the job, Joe Allbaugh, said that he had other commitments for at least another week.

It was a full house on Air Force One. In addition to Bush and Hagin, Rove had made the trip from Washington, a sure sign that the political dimension was being attended to (though he had been side-lined with kidney stones when the levees broke on Monday). Republican Senator David Vitter, whose contempt for Blanco was undisguised, huddled with Rove. Two days earlier, Vitter had called one of Blanco's aides, saying that Rove had asked Vitter to prod her about federalizing. In the meantime, Rove was working the other side: He was arguing fiercely with Rumsfeld, who was reluctant to place the American military in a domestic disaster zone.

Brownie was on board—as was, to his chagrin, Mike Chertoff. That Bush's national security adviser, Steve Hadley, was also present was a tip-off that the issue of federalization would be on the table. The freshly scrubbed Nagin and Democratic Congressman William Jefferson seemed in awe of the plane's trappings. Senator Mary Landrieu appeared completely unstable: On the tarmac she had thrown her arms around Jason Recher, crying, "Oh, it hurts, hold me!" though they had never met before, and on the plane she repeatedly wailed, "Mr. President, this is a *disaster*! I'm telling you, this is a *catastrophe*!"

Blanco brought Bush a letter stating in writing her previous request for forty thousand troops. Bush put it to the side. "The issue is, who's responsible for securing the city of New Orleans?" he wanted to know.

Blanco indicated that it was the city's responsibility. Nagin replied that it was Blanco's.

Bush brought Nagin into his office for a private chat. Would the mayor support federalization? Nagin enthusiastically said that he would.

Bush then sent out Nagin and brought in Blanco. The compulsively deliberative governor was at a disadvantage here. Her staff had not been permitted on board. "I'd like you to think through asking us to take over until the immediate situation is stabilized," Bush began.

She spoke slowly, choosing her words with painstaking care. "None of us is standing on protocol," she acknowledged. Referring to the letter she had brought with her, Blanco added, "I'm asking for forty thousand troops, and I'm not specifying where they come from."

"Well, do you want to federalize?" Bush pressed.

The governor backpedaled. "Well, we're meeting tonight to consider the best course of action for the long term," she said.

It wasn't what Bush wanted to hear.

Marine One ferried Bush, Blanco, and Nagin over to the Coast Guard station beside the 17th Street levee. The president's feet were now officially on the ground, in the city. It reeked of debris and rot. Bush strolled around New Orleans' version of Ground Zero, patting workers on the back, saying, "It's going to get better. We're going to rebuild this place."

Nagin did the same, albeit in his own ditzy style: "Y'all come back during Mardi Gras and I'll buy you a beer."

Rove noticed that Brownie had receded into the background, looking more than a little disconsolate. "Get up there next to the president," he encouraged the FEMA director. "This is *your* deal. You need to be there if he's got questions."

Brownie edged only a little closer. Chertoff was now standing next to Bush, whose face mirrored both fatigue and deep dissatisfaction.

As they climbed back into their helicopters, Mary Landrieu lunged back toward the Coast Guard station. A small dog was wandering in circles with its tongue hanging out. "It needs water!" the senator cried out.

Rove handed her his water bottle. Landrieu hugged the dog and wept as it drank.

After Air Force One took off for Washington, Brown asked the FEMA spokesperson Nicol Andrews, "Do you think the president has lost confidence in me?"

"I don't know him as well as you do," Andrews replied. "You were with him all day? Do *you* think so?"

Brownie frowned. "Yeah," he said. "I do."

That evening, a group at the White House including Card, Hadley, and general counsel Harriet Miers worked up a reorganization plan that would put Blanco's National Guard troops under General Honoré's authority. Bush went to bed that night utterly confident that he would be standing in the Rose Garden the next morning, announcing in his Saturday radio address that he had assumed control over the military response to Katrina in Louisiana. At 11:20 PM, Card faxed the new scheme over to Blanco, requesting her signature.

He did not get it. "I want the troops," Blanco said late that evening. But she saw little that would be gained by removing her Guard commander and inserting Honoré. The debate continued all night. Card was scrambling between his office and Miers', wrestling with an emerging question: Should the president simply *usurp* the governor's authority under the Insurrection Act? The temptation was great to do so—except for the trifling matter that New Orleans was *not*, by any reasonable interpretation, in a "state of insurrection . . ." and to claim otherwise, and risk having a federal judgment slapped on the White House, would add a whole new layer of woe to Bush's Katrina tribulations.

Blanco called Card's bluff and stuck to her guns. The chief of staff finally got home by six in the morning. Shortly after Bush woke up, the two men spoke. The boss was not happy—not happy at all. He demanded to know what had gone wrong.

Card returned to the White House with Bush's angry words still reverberating in his skull. He faxed another Memorandum of Agreement to Blanco. "Governor, this is nonnegotiable," he informed her coldly.

Blanco read the document. Bush was deploying another seven thousand federal troops under Honoré's command. Nothing was mentioned about the command structure of the National Guard. The governor agreed: There was nothing to negotiate. She had won.

But seventy-two precious hours had been wasted in this seemingly pointless debate. The biggest loser therefore was not Bush. It was the people in New Orleans who died waiting for the government to stop bickering and start rescuing.

"Y'all need to cut this shit out," growled Bush to Blanco's chief of staff Andy Kopplin the following Monday.

The two stood toe-to-toe in Louisiana's Emergency Operations Center in Baton Rouge. "Listen, we didn't start this," Kopplin retorted.

The "blame game," as Bush and others in the White House were calling it, was in full swing. There was plenty of it to go around, and no level of government was spared. But the national media had no appetite for the carcasses of Ray Nagin and Kathleen Blanco. A palpable outrage at the Bush administration coursed through their coverage of Katrina's aftermath. For six years they had withstood Message Discipline, factory-packaged presidential events, and their own gullibility in the months after 9/11 . . . all the while abiding the scornfulness of their subject, a president who boasted that he did not read what they wrote and who shunned their inquiries like a man who saw no purpose to their labor. . . .

These indignities amassed against the media's pretense of restraint. Katrina sundered those levees as well. Arriving at the scene several steps ahead of the federal government, the press showed little mercy. And if their battering rams helped take down the levees of civic endurance for the Bush administration, in truth little assistance was required. Disunity, ever-rising gas prices, and a war of obscure purpose with no end in sight had long taxed the public's patience. With the tragically bungled response to Katrina, their patience had run out.

To shore up the levees and stop the bleeding, the White House pulled out all the stops. Bush showed up to the Gulf eight times in the succeeding seven weeks. He convened roundtables, hugged, drove nails into wood, wrote recovery checks like a drunken sailor. Laura made appearances of her own. After being discovered on a shoe-shopping spree and whacking tennis balls with Monica Seles in Manhattan during the height of New Orleans' misery, Condi Rice got back on message and announced a trip to her native Alabama to oversee the recovery efforts there. The VP dropped in on Gulfport, Mississippi, where a young man followed him and twice hollered out, "Go fuck yourself, Mr. Cheney!" And Bush's parents spent a day comforting evacuees in the Astrodome—a gesture somewhat undercut when Bar said during a TV interview, "What I'm hearing, which is sort of scary, is that they all want to stay in Texas. Everyone is so overwhelmed by the hospitality. And so many of the people in the arena here, you know, were underprivileged anyway, so this is working very well for them."

To the surprise of no one, including himself, Brownie was thrown overboard. Taking baby steps toward a full-throated mea culpa, Bush went from repeating, "That is unacceptable," to a more personalized yet still dodgy, "Katrina exposed serious problems in our response capability at all levels of government, and to the extent that the federal government didn't fully do its job right, I take responsibility."

Coaxing much more out of Bush was not easy. Card, Hagin, and Rove were loath to tell the president that the disaster was in any way man-made. The notion that Bush himself should have done more irritated him in a literal sort of way. "Getting water to someone—people don't think I'm in charge of *that*, do they?" he snapped.

Bush was offended by the charge that he lacked compassion, in particular for blacks. Look what he'd done in the president's Emergency Plan for AIDS Relief two years ago. Pledged $15 *billion* in worldwide aid, dwarfing the Clinton administration's commitment to the same issue. And for zero political gain. He'd consulted only his conscience—or rather, Mike Gerson had: "We're the richest country in history, and history's going to judge us harshly if we don't do this," the speechwriter had warned. And so Bush didn't wait for other countries to fill the coffers before the U.S. would match them. "It must be because I'm a Texan," he would later say. "I see a problem, I say let's solve it . . . I said, 'People are dying, let's lead.' " His PEPFAR initiative had saved the lives of thousands of blacks throughout the world. Still, Katrina was a tragedy in the homeland. As a show of leadership, far more than a donation was required of him.

Still at a remove from the heart of the tragedy, having not once visited the neighborhoods where so many had lost so much, the president was having trouble summoning empathy. He could see their pain but not feel it.

And that did not cut it. *Heck of a job* did not cut it.

Hagin's advance guy Jason Recher found Ray Nagin still ensconced in the Hyatt, though now on the fifth floor. "The president's coming to give a speech the day after tomorrow," he informed the mayor.

Now fully two weeks after landfall, Nagin had his mojo back. "Great! About time! Let's hear what the man has to say."

"We want to do it in Jackson Square," said Recher.

"Perfect location! Not destroyed, shows the life of the city . . ."

"The gates to the square are locked," Recher said.

Nagin seemed not to understand.

Jackson Square was city property, Recher reminded him. "Do you know where the keys are?"

After presiding over flood, anarchy, and mass deprivation, the mayor of New Orleans was now being confronted with a problem that he could actually solve. "Just pop the locks—cut the damn things off!" he said, laughing.

Recher thanked him and went off to fetch up some bolt cutters.

After which Scott Sforza rolled in the warm tungsten lights, so that the St. Louis Cathedral was cast in a ghostly blue—and in front of it, the president's podium set up on the grass, centered with the statue of Andrew Jackson astride his battle horse. The president approached in his motorcade from unlit streets, with members of the 82nd Airborne standing at attention and saluting in their red berets. Though this was a prime-time address, Bush wore no jacket. He took his place behind the podium, his back to the Cathedral. Standing under the dark of night on this theatrical but unpopulated stage, he seemed strangely forlorn, like a motivational speaker regaling an audience of three.

"Good evening," he began. "I'm speaking to you from the city of New Orleans—nearly empty, still partly under water, and waiting for life and hope to return. . . ."

It was not all happy talk this time. He spoke of the suffering, the sudden relocations, and the deep-rooted poverty that the hurricane had unveiled. But Bush seemed determined to punch it up with optimism. There was a forced lilt to his voice, with every sentence screwing its way up to a high note. Given the eerie setting, the effect was that of a man whistling past a graveyard.

Still, he said what he had to say. "It was not a normal hurricane—and the normal disaster relief system was not equal to it," Bush acknowledged, using a sentiment that his speechwriters had pilfered from JFK's Bay of Pigs speech. Later he added, "When the federal government fails to meet such an obligation, I as president am responsible for the problem, and for the solution." Blinking, one might have missed it—but there it was, the president owning up to his share of the blame.

The bleeding had stopped. But the patient would never be quite the same.

18

"THIS IS NOT
YOUR DAUGHTER!"

As if on cue, in rode Karen Hughes to massage the message . . . except that her port of call was not the Gulf Coast, but rather the Persian Gulf, where she'd never been before.

She had been largely out of the loop since the spring of 2002, when Karen decided that being the most powerful woman in America was not worth it if the other two men in her life (her husband, Jerry, and her son Robert) were miserable in Washington. Only a few months before her departure, she had counseled another Texan who had no truck for the Beltway: "Look, none of us likes it here. We'd all rather be back in Austin. *I've* wanted to leave. But we can't—the president needs us."

A "family-friendly decision," she had termed her resignation. It was also an income-friendly decision: Viking paid her a sweet $750,000 for her memoirs, and over the next three years Karen racked up hundreds of thousands in speaking fees even as the RNC paid for her advice to the tune of $15,000 a month. Rove tended to comment aloud on such matters. He, Bartlett, and others missed Texas and had dependents just as she had. None of them was getting rich working seventy hours a week in the West Wing. Karen's habit had long been to weigh in at the last minute, with overwhelming force, upending well-laid plans. When she did it now, afloat on an air mattress in her back-yard swimming pool in West Austin, the untanned, underpaid toilers found themselves thinking unkind thoughts about Karen Hughes.

They reminded themselves about her cornball prose—*Hug your children; We see a little more gray in the mirror*—and her superficial approach to policy. They snickered about her lobbying to make 9/11 a national holiday. And they were fond of observing that her chief contributions to the 2004 campaign—the twins' convention speech and the slogan "We've turned the corner and we can't turn back"—were losers.

There were some who said these things. But there were at least as many who would murmur among themselves, *God, I wish Karen were still here.* Unlike Rove, she had no agenda other than the president's. Unlike Card and Bartlett, she did not hesitate before walking into the valley of the shadow of death. Karen was no less guilty of doting on Bush and guffawing loudly at his jokes. But she had a moderating effect on Bush—playing soccer-mom counterweight to Rove's angry white man, which meant more than ideology: she kept Bush humble. With Karen in his ear, Bush had been bipartisan, putting his compassionate foot forward. Without her, his obstinate streak grew.

Had Karen stuck it out in Washington, would the president have zipped across the country to sign a bill keeping Terri Schiavo alive? Would he have been indifferent to Cindy Sheehan's presence in Crawford? Would he have waited until two days after the levees broke to discontinue his vacation and conduct a flyover en route to the White House? No one could say. But the very asking of these questions—and they were asked inside the administration—was proof that Karen Hughes was missed.

She missed the action, too. Soccer moms had now been identified by Dowd and Mehlman as "security moms"; the nation's safety had become a Karen Hughes issue. When Bush, while making his are-you-an-eight-year-man rounds, asked Karen in December 2004 if she would be willing to come back in some capacity, she began to talk to Condi Rice about a role in shaping America's image overseas. Such a post actually existed: Under Secretary of State for Public Diplomacy and Public Affairs. The first holder of the office, from the Clinton era, was Evelyn Lieberman, who, as a Hillary loyalist, achieved distinction by banning Monica Lewinsky from the White House. Under Bush, the office had been something of a redheaded stepchild, underfunded and given little attention by Colin Powell.

Installing Karen Hughes changed everything about the office, so it seemed at the time. Karen had the president's ear, after all. Sending her abroad with ambassadorial rank sent a signal that Bush did in fact care about the Muslim world's low opinion of America.

It was not, however, a signal that Bush himself sent. Improving America's image, like engagement with the UN, did not suffice as an end unto itself. Bush's goal was democratization, the Freedom Agenda trumpeted in his inaugural address and in virtually every foreign-policy speech thereafter. "Together," said Bush at her swearing-in ceremony on September 9, "we're going to help millions achieve the nonnegotiable demands of human dignity so they can build a better life for their children." Karen then specified these demands. They included "the rule of law, limits on the power of the state, respect for women, private property, free speech, equal justice and religious tolerance."

In other words, what Karen Hughes was billing as a "listening tour" to the Middle East would also be a nonnegotiable demanding tour.

She touched down in Cairo on September 25, 2005, and waded into a day of typical unrest. Israeli troops were storming the West Bank and arresting two hundred Palestinians. Iran's foreign minister announced that it would not "give up its right to nuclear technology." Meanwhile, in Iraq more than two dozen would be slain in suicide bomb attacks and gunfire, compelling Tony Blair to admit that he hadn't expected the "ferocity" of the Iraqi insurgency. Rove's Strategic Initiatives scribe Pete Wehner had memo'd in May that "The effects of the liberation of Iraq and the January 30th election are radiating throughout the region." By the time of Karen's arrival, "the Arab Spring" evoked by Wehner had withered on the vine.

"Thank you for that warm welcome!" she boomed as she strode down a red carpet in her smart gray suit en route to her first meeting, with an Egyptian sheikh whom Karen had characterized as "moderate" and thus "courageous" because he dared to condemn terrorism . . . though he did support nuclear development in the Arab world and, in some cases, suicide bombings. After she emerged from what she described as a "wonderful meeting with His Eminence," one of the two dozen members of the Western press who had accompanied her on the trip asked her what she had learned from the encounter.

"Well," Karen began, "I think I was able to have a wonderful meeting with His Eminence to talk with him about the common language of the heart. . . ."

There was, in fact, serious diplomacy to be conducted in Egypt. Earlier in the month, President Hosni Mubarak had received 88 percent of the vote in a sham election. His opponent had been jailed, and the leading opposition movement, the Muslim Brotherhood, had been outlawed. Though the Bush administration bestowed $2 billion in foreign aid on Egypt, America's approval rating in that country stood at a dismal 23 percent.

But Karen didn't meet with anyone from the Muslim Brotherhood. ("We are respectful of Egypt's laws," she explained carefully after consulting with an aide.) Nor did she receive an audience with Mubarak—though his prime minister assured her that the strongman was committed to transparent elections: "The door is open!" Instead, she hosted a succession of tame meet-and-greets with foreign exchange students, whom she charmed with her "four E's of diplomacy: Engagement, Exchange, Education, and Empowerment."

"This is my first visit to Saudi Arabia and I'm so excited to be here—my very first time!" she sang out upon arriving in Jeddah the following afternoon. Karen spent the evening at a *majilis*, a diverse gathering of Saudis at a private home. There, her "listening tour" began in earnest as the under secretary got an earful of vitriol: *What do you Americans REALLY want out of Iraq? Why have you permitted Israel to slaughter innocent Palestinians? Do not impose your will on the people of Saudi Arabia!*

Karen assured her hosts that America would not do such a thing. But the very next day, on the way to a speech at a women's university in Jeddah, she scribbled on a piece of paper: *Women should be full and equal participants in society. . . . My ability to drive is an important part of my freedom.* That women in Saudi Arabia should be permitted to drive was, to Karen's direct boss, Condi Rice, "just a line that I have not wanted to cross."

But Karen did. To the all-woman audience that morning, she said, "I believe that women should be full and equal participants in society. And I feel as an American woman that my ability to drive is an important part of my freedom. It has allowed me to work during my career, it has allowed me to go to the grocery store and shop for my family. It allows me to go to the doctor and it gives me a measure, an important measure, of independence. Now I understand that your culture and traditions here in Saudi Arabia are very different. And so I don't think that we should try to impose from the outside an outcome for you all. What I do think we can do is try to encourage greater participation, encourage opportunities like this for women in Saudi Arabia to speak up and speak your mind."

The audience was not upset so much as baffled. Heeding Karen's urging to "speak up and speak your mind," they vented to the traveling press: "We have *more* than equal rights!" "I don't mind if someone else does the driving!" "She didn't say enough about why she came here. . . . To me, it's like plastic surgery."

Flying to Ankara, Turkey, that afternoon, Karen defended her promulgating to reporters. "Driving is a symbol," she said. "We can't imagine not being able to drive ourselves to work, or drive to wherever. I assume every woman on this plane—we drive ourselves places."

A reporter on the plane asked Karen if anyone on her "listening tour" had yet said a negative thing about Bush, whose popularity in the Middle East roughly coincided with that of Osama bin Laden in America. Tilting her head slightly, she replied, "I haven't really heard a lot of that. I had one person at lunch raise the issue of the president mentioning God in his speeches. And I asked whether he was aware that the previous American president also cited God, and that our Constitution cites 'one nation, under God.' He said, 'Well, never mind,' and went on to something else."

Reporters checked with one another afterward. Had the Under Secretary of State for Public Diplomacy and Public Affairs really confused the Constitution with the Pledge of Allegiance?

By the last leg of the journey, it was becoming clear that a sort of metadiplomacy was under way: This was about *being seen* listening. Karen was there to *appear* conciliatory—but, just as much, to defend, and even to prod. She was not there to give ground. An exasperated reporter finally asked her, "So what are you telling them if you are not changing anything? Your word is just propaganda then. It's nothing. It's nothing else, if there is no change."

At that, Karen Hughes let out an incredulous laugh. "That's an interesting thought! Should I just throw up my hands and say, 'I give up'?"

The Message Disciplinarian did not bring the press with her on an overseas trip again after that.

During the trip, a friendly reporter told Karen that he had learned who Bush's new Supreme Court nominee was likely to be.

"Oh, that's wonderful!" Karen exclaimed when she heard the name. "Harriet would be a wonderful Supreme Court justice!"

Harriet Miers didn't want the job. She didn't want to be in Washington at all. For those who did not know her, the limits of Miers' ambitions might have been hard to gauge. For George W. Bush had made her a player in spite of herself. At the request of Bush's Dallas guru, Jim Francis, she had become the legal counsel to his gubernatorial campaign in 1993. She later served as the governor's outside counsel and accepted the unpaid position of Texas lottery commissioner. When Bush began to flirt with the presidency, Miers did whatever was asked of her. She monitored the bright lines between his '98 reelect and his national fund-raising activities. She oversaw the in-house opposition-research team. She chaired Lawyers for Bush. She spearheaded the legal efforts to establish the Wyoming residency of Dick Cheney, who had lived in Dallas for several years when Bush selected him to be his VP nominee. She moved up to Washington to help vet appointees to the Department of Justice.

But unlike most of the Bush Texans who thrilled at the chance to follow the boss to the White House, Harriet Miers was certain of her niche in life. She was a Dallas corporate lawyer. When Andy Card approached her in the transition office after *Bush v. Gore* and asked her to be Bush's staff secretary, she had no idea what the position entailed. Her reluctance was unmistakable. Card pushed back. "Go home," he told her in his avuncular but unyielding New Englander's manner, "and find a way to say 'yes.' "

She was a woman with a law firm, with relatives in Texas—but also with no husband or children, and no particularly good reason to say no to the president of the United States. She returned to Dallas and began divesting herself of her practice, while a friend of hers scouted down an apartment for her in Washington, which she moved into sight unseen. Miers' arrival went unremarked, and for years she went about her work in a state of near-perfect anonymity.

As staff secretary, her job was to review every document before it fell into the president's hands. She had interviewed previous occupants of the job and had even taken the unusual step of hiring assistants from Clinton's staff secretary. But Bush had his own requirements. He did not like mistakes and he did not like tardiness. A document had to be, as those in the White House put it, "ready for prime time." Miers interpreted this broadly. She wanted to make sure that everyone who needed to weigh in on the document had in fact been consulted. She wanted to ascertain whether anything in the document conflicted with administration policy—or (and this was far more frequent) imprudently *made* policy. She wanted to think like her boss, who had this disheartening knack for finding flaws that had escaped even her lawyer's eagle eye. Miers would play this furious game with herself: *What can he possibly ask me about this. . . .* She almost always sent a document back for correction or someone else's perusal. Bush still managed to find some repetition or flawed logic that she hadn't caught. And so she sought to do better, work harder.

But she could not be late. No one could be late. When the president expected something, *it had to be there*. Which meant late hours. Insane hours. Harriet Miers was always in by six in the morning. Always still there at eight in the evening. Usually much later. And weekends—those, too. She'd go to church on Sunday, then over to the White House. After all, she reasoned, things were happening in the world twenty-four hours a day. Always events that generated documents, which the president needed to see the following morning. When a nagging issue arose, she generally avoided calling staffers at home at night, interrupting their family lives. She would endeavor to do the research herself. This approach, she told herself, was the more efficient method.

There were others in the White House who kept inhuman hours: Card, Bartlett, Rove, Bolten. But no one could remember walking into the West Wing at any hour and not seeing Harriet Miers's light on.

She scrupulously avoided injecting her own opinions into the documents she edited. People needed to have faith in her as an honest broker. But she did in fact have an interest in policy; she was not just a pencil-pusher. She was happy to replace deputy chief Josh Bolten when he moved over to OMB in July 2003: The work was more stimulating, the hours somewhat less brutal. After the reelect, Al Gonzales took Ashcroft's job as AG, and Miers took over as White House general counsel. Full circle: Harriet Miers was once again Bush's lawyer, and content to be there, seeking nothing more exalted.

Nor had Bush sought to elevate her. Laura had joined those in the message camp lobbying for him to pick a woman to replace the suddenly deceased Chief Justice William Rehnquist. (Seldom did the first lady venture into White House policymaking. One of her few pet legislative projects was the reauthorization of the AmeriCorps national service bill. "It's very important to Laura," then-House majority leader Dick Armey was told by Office of Legislative Affairs director David Hobbs in 2002. Armey didn't care. He thought that the federally funded volunteer program was a joke and refused to voice support for it on the House floor.) Bush had already picked John Roberts to replace Sandra Day O'Connor, then slid him over to the chief justice's seat. The women's slot figured to be easy at first. The White House kept an "Evergreen" list of worthy Supreme Court candidates. It included federal judges Edith Jones, Edith Clement, and Janice Rogers Brown. Problems were revealed in the vetting of each of them. With Bush's post-Katrina numbers sinking, no one was eager for a confirmation battle. The search committee, which included Miers, dragged the net farther out, combing state after state for even the most obscure judicial candidates, as long as they were female.

Then Judge Roberts suggested Miers to Bush, who in turn ordered Card to conduct a quiet vetting. Her record was pristine. She was stunned by the offer. Having been approached for state and federal judgeships in the past, she had summarily issued her regrets. A lawyer is all she was. Bush and Laura disagreed. They maintained that she would make a fine Supreme Court justice.

Bush's base begged to differ.

They had been waiting for just this moment: a Republican president with two nominations to stack along with Antonin Scalia and Clarence Thomas as a rock-ribbed rightist judicial wedge. The base had its pets—jurists like Bill Luttig and Priscilla Owen—who could all but guarantee a conservative majority for the next three decades. Who was this *bureaucrat*, a woman who—*ack!*—had donated money to Al Gore in 1998 and had literally no documentation to suggest conservative credentials other than her service to George W. Bush?

Another trifle: *The woman was not a judge.* Her law degree was from *Southern Methodist University*! (Fine for Laura, but . . .) When the question of whether to take a position on abortion came before the Texas Bar Association, she had urged *a neutral stance*! Having no paper trail was virtuous only up to a point. Harriet Miers seemed never to have stood for *anything* . . . except Bush—which, by the jittery days of September 2005, was not good enough.

White House political director Sara Taylor knew the base—she *was* the base—and anticipated that they would fight Miers' confirmation. But Bush's inner circle didn't include her. Bartlett, Card, Hagin, Miers herself—these people weren't ideologically attuned to the yearnings of the base. Among those in the circle, only Rove understood. But he had problems of his own: Bush was not happy at all with the revelation that his top adviser had been discussing CIA operative Valerie Plame's identity with reporters. Rove raised his concerns about Miers in the initial phase of the selection process, was shouted down, and thereafter did not push it. When Mehlman, from the RNC, called Rove and warned him that he could see storm clouds brewing on the

Hill, Bush's deputy chief insisted, "She's done a lot of significant things in Texas. She was president of the state bar association."

Mehlman doubted that being the head of the Texas bar was going to give Miers any traction.

Rove had conference-called a group of religious conservatives on October 3, the day Bush formally announced Harriet Miers' nomination to the court. Blowing the conservative dog whistle, Rove told them that Miers had belonged to an evangelical church in Dallas. Two Texas jurists who knew her well were also on the phone. They strongly hinted that she would vote to overturn *Roe v. Wade*.

But the queasiness did not abate among social conservatives. Even after phone calls from Rove and Bush himself, Focus on the Family director Dr. James Dobson fretted, "This is one scary moment." At the same time, the neocons were in an uproar. Bill Kristol, Ann Coulter, and David Frum—the latter of whom had actually worked with Miers when he was one of Bush's speechwriters—noisily assailed her lack of gravitas. Rove hadn't anticipated the intellectuals going after Bush's pick. The more the president protested that Harriet Miers was a "pioneer" (for being the first female Texas Bar Association president), the more he asserted that she would not evolve on the bench (which, given that she had never been on the bench, was unknowable), the more those who knew her attested to her modesty and thoroughness, the more offended they became. As Coulter wrote, "Being on the Supreme Court isn't like winning a 'Best Employee of the Month' award. It's a real job."

Cheney hit the loudmouth circuit. "I'm comfortable that she has a conservative judicial philosophy that you'd be comfortable with, Rush," the VP told Rush Limbaugh and his radio listeners. Bush, he added, was "convinced that Harriet will do a great job on the court, as am I. And I think you'll find when you look back ten years from now that it will have been a great appointment."

For once, Rush wasn't going to take Cheney's assurances at face value. "But the question is, why do we need to wait ten years?" he replied. "There are people that he could have nominated that we would know about *now*."

For once, Rove had been a step behind: The social and intellectual conservatives had primed Limbaugh, Hannity, and other talk show hosts before the White House had.

Meanwhile, Democrats like Harry Reid and Chuck Schumer— friends Harriet Miers did not need—were singing her praises.

Bush was getting testy. It stupefied him that these conservative judicial-watch organizations were doubting his assurances about Miers. Had he ever let them down before with a federal court nominee? "Now, are you talking to those groups?" he snapped at Sara Taylor. "We need their support!"

Yes, Taylor said, she was talking to them. And they were talking back, loudly. "I feel like we're back to where we were in the primaries," she lamented to Bush. Bizarre as it seemed, his conservative bona fides were being questioned all over again.

For all of Miers' prowess at delivering "ready for prime time" documents to the president, she herself was unready. Bush had oversold her as someone who would deeply impress Senate Committee on the Judiciary members once they got to know her. Recently, they *had* been impressed—by John Roberts, a freakishly gifted meeter-and-greeter who discussed judicial opinions the way Bush knew batting averages. Miers was a diffident, unlearned contrast. The more time she spent on the Hill, the less enamored of her they became. Then a most un-Harriet-like development emerged: The questionnaire she had prepared for the Judiciary Committee was judged by chairman Arlen Specter to be not ready for prime time and was sent back for her to redo. It was also learned that Bush's impresario of small ball had at one time forgotten to pay her dues to the D.C. and Texas bar associations.

The gods were aligned against her nomination. Miers withdrew it in late October.

She retreated into her quiet cocoon and began vetting the next nominee, Samuel Alito. On Bush's orders, Harriet Miers also began to conduct mandatory classes for White House staffers. The subject— following the indictment of Cheney's chief of staff, Scooter Libby— was ethics.

Rove wasn't indicted by the Plamegate special prosecutor—that was autumn's only good news. Bush's approval rating had sunk to 39. For the first time in his political life, his presence was being interpreted as a hindrance to the Republican cause. When Congressman J. D. Hayworth of Arizona was asked whether he would welcome Bush's reelection help, his reply was, "In one word: no." Virginia gubernatorial candidate Jerry Kilgore, on the other hand, did accept the president's offer to campaign on his behalf. Kilgore was clobbered in November.

In December, Bush took responsibility for the struggle in Iraq. His aide had discussed the merits of doing so, and exactly how to go about doing it, over a period of several days. It was not, in other words, a reflexive thing at all, this taking of responsibility. The initial strategy had been to recapture the Iraq message. It had been seized from them by critics like Democratic Congressman Jack Murtha, a staunch supporter of the military who had recently demanded immediate withdrawal from Iraq. Rove wanted a hard pushback. Scott McClellan released a statement comparing Murtha to lefty filmmaker Michael Moore. In the meantime, the White House issued a document called the *National Strategy for Victory* as proof that America's presence in Iraq was headed toward a satisfactory outcome.

But defiance wasn't enough, Bartlett and Nicolle Devenish Wallace argued to Rove. There had to be some acknowledgment that things had not gone entirely as planned. "We're getting hammered," Bartlett pointed out. "We've got to change the press dynamic."

Bartlett had learned a useful communications lesson from Katrina: *Roll out the taking-responsibility deal slowly. You don't want the coverage of the boss's speech to be all about how he took responsibility.* But the president's speech shouldn't be anticlimactic, either. The balance was so delicate.

So Bush eased into responsibility-taking, as it were, through a series of speeches in which humility was slowly ratcheted up and triumphalism slowly ratcheted down, like a stepwise change in medication so as not to bring shock to the patient's body. In Annapolis on November 30, Bush stood before an audience of uniforms and said the word *victory* over and over, to rousing applause. A week later, he gave a similar speech, but to an entirely different crowd—the tweedy Council of Foreign Relations—and then a few days later he delivered an address in Philadelphia, in which he actually took questions from the audience.

Then, on December 14, at the Woodrow Wilson Center in D.C., Bush came out with it. After conceding that the Coalition had failed to find weapons of mass destruction, he continued: "As president, I'm responsible for the decision to go into Iraq—and I'm also responsible for fixing what went wrong by reforming our intelligence capabilities."

Having planted the seed of responsibility-taking, the president brought it to fruition four days later, on December 18, during his prime time address from the Oval Office. Bush's momentum had been undermined by his least favorite newpaper, the *Times*, which two days earlier had revealed the existence of a secret program authorizing the National Security Agency to eavesdrop on American residents with suspected links to Al Qaeda. The paper had held off on publishing the story for a year when Bush persuaded the *Times'* editor, Bill Keller, that the story would threaten national security. A few days prior to the story's publication, Keller had notified the White House that they intended to run with the story and were confident that Bush's concerns wouldn't be violated. Card and Hadley continued to negotiate with the editor, who promised them that they would receive a heads-up before the story ran.

At 6:50 PM on Friday, August 16, Keller called Hadley to say that they were going with the domestic-spying story. Bartlett checked the *Times'* website. The story had been up on the Web for twenty minutes before Keller's call. Bartlett was incensed. This was a classic Sunday story, not a Friday story. No other publication was chasing it. He was convinced that the *Times* had published the piece that day to influence the debate on the Hill about whether to reauthorize the Patriot Act. (And indeed, the piece did make its mark, if only temporarily: Several senators who had read the *Times'* bombshell cited it as they joined a filibuster to block renewal of the Patriot Act that evening.)

Bush was furious. Encouraged by Cheney—to whom it usually fell to wield the brass knuckles, but who said this time, "I think the president ought to give the speech"—he took the unusual step of making news in his radio address the following morning. After scolding the filibuster of the Patriot Act—"That decision is irresponsible, and it endangers the lives of our citizens"—Bush defiantly confirmed that he had authorized the NSA domestic-spying plan. "This is a highly classified program that is crucial to our national security," he said. As a result of the *Times'* disclosure, he added edgily, "our enemies have learned information they should not have, and the unauthorized disclosure of this effort damages our national security and puts our citizens at risk."

Bush made no apologies for the secret program. "It is critical to saving American lives," he said. "The American people expect me to do everything in my power under our laws and Constitution to protect them and their civil liberties. And that is exactly what I will continue to do, so long as I'm president of the United States. Thank you."

He stormed away from the press pool without further word. Then he motorcaded to the Secret Service Academy in Beltsville and went for a bike ride.

Bush made no mention of the *Times* story the next evening in his address to the nation. The game plan had been responsibility-taking, and he stuck to it. After acknowledging that the prewar intelligence had made a false case for WMDs, Bush said, "As your president, I am responsible for the decision to go into Iraq. Yet it was right to remove Saddam Hussein from power."

Though he continued to assert the war's justness, there was a hint of pain in his voice as he remarked on a mission that had "brought danger and suffering and loss. This loss has caused sorrow for our whole nation—and it has led some to ask if we are creating more problems than we're solving. . . . The work in Iraq has been especially difficult—more difficult than we expected. Reconstruction efforts and the training of Iraqi security forces started more slowly than we hoped. . . . And you will continue to see the grim results on the evening news. This proves that the war is difficult—it does not mean that we are losing. My fellow citizens: Not only can we win the war in Iraq; we *are* winning the war in Iraq."

But after that slight burst of bellicosity, Bush adopted an almost plaintive tone as he addressed "those who did not support my decision to send troops into Iraq. I have heard your disagreement, and I know how deeply it is felt. . . . I don't expect you to support everything I do, but tonight I have a request: Do not give in to despair, and do not give up on this fight for freedom."

Three days later, on December 21, at the National Naval Medical Center in Bethesda, Bush visited several wounded soldiers. One of them, a young man from Trinidad who was not an American citizen, lay in critical condition and would not live to see Christmas. Bush held the hand of the soldier's mother as she sobbed.

Through her tears, she did not see opportunity. "How could you do this!" she cried to her son's commander in chief. And then, thinking of Bush's two children, who would never face combat: *"THIS IS NOT YOUR DAUGHTER!"*

On the helicopter ride back to the White House, Bush murmured to an aide, "That big black woman was really angry at me."

He thought for a moment before adding, "I don't blame her." He turned to the window of Marine One and said nothing else.

On December 15, 2005, in the middle of the responsibility-taking, Iraqis went to the polls to elect a new government. Four U.S. senators were there to bear witness to the historic event. They choppered from Baghdad over to the town of Al Hillah, walked into a peaceful polling station, got their thumbs dipped in purple ink, and stepped outside to an awaiting press, where one of the senators, Saxby Chambliss, declared, "Today's a great day to be an Iraqi."

The following day, two of the four senators, Joe Biden and Lindsey Graham, visited the White House to brief the president on their trip. The mood in the Treaty Room was openly celebratory. "We're on the road to victory here," Bush said to the gathering, which also included Rice, Cheney, Hadley, Rumsfeld, Card, and several moderate Democratic and Republican senators: McCain, Clinton, Lieberman, Pete Domenici, Ron Wyden, and Thomas Carper. "Let me tell you what victory is. First, we'll have a new ally in the war against terror. Second, we will have an Iraqi military capable of defending Iraq's territory. And three, there will be a security force strong enough to be prevent safe haven for terrorists."

As part of "what victory is," Bush did not include democratizaton of the Middle East.

Ambassador to Iraq Zalmay Khalilzad was on the video screen with General James Casey. "Right now," said Khalilzad, "the question is, will the Sunnis give up violence for the ballot—for participating. Right now they're engaging in violence *and* participating."

General Casey reported that the training of the Iraqi army was proceeding apace. But, he conceded, they were a year behind schedule when it came to standing up a legitimate Iraqi police force. They should think of 2006, Casey said, as "the year of the police."

"I've got real concerns about the police," said Rumsfeld, shaking his head. "Real concerns." To a few in the room, a question was begged: *Would Rummy be saying this if Iraq were still the Pentagon's problem rather than the State Department's?*

After a few upbeat comments by Cheney, Rice, McCain, and Lieberman, Graham spoke up. "Well, Mr. President, we all know the parts that went well," he said. "Here are the parts that bother me." The South Carolina senator talked about Sunni prisoner abuse by Shiite jailers and the need for a nonsectarian minister of the interior—since the present one, he said, "is being controlled by some of the most extreme religious figures in the country."

What especially worried Graham, though, were the militias. "They're stronger in their region than the national army," he told Bush. "You can't have a Republican army and a Democratic army," he said, "and call it a democracy."

Bush then called on Biden. "Mr. President," said the ranking

Democrat on the Foreign Relations Committee, "we have six months that'll tell the story. Two gigantic deals have to be done *beyond* rebuilding: What kind of government are they going to have, and what kind of constitution will they end up with? I know you don't like foreign-policy-sounding things, so I won't use 'contact group.' But there's gotta be cumulative pressure from the international community on their surrogates. Iran—it isn't in their interest to have a civil war. We ought to be able to work something out with them. Even if they're bad guys."

"Condi, tell the senator what we're doing," said Bush.

Rice mentioned that she had spoken with the Germans and the French about exerting pressure on Iran. "Mr. President, you've got a shot with the Germans now," Biden replied. Referring to newly elected Angela Merkel, he said, "You've got a conservative chancellor now."

Bush agreed. "And by the way," the president said, "I did call the Emirates and the Saudis."

"It probably had some effect on Sunni participation," Biden said approvingly.

Bush asked no questions during the meeting. Nor did the secretary of state—though, as people stood, she thanked Lindsey Graham for his input and assured him that they were already on top of his concerns, which Graham found difficult to believe.

Bush intercepted Biden on his way out the door. "We've gotta do this more often," the president said.

Biden agreed, though with a caveat. "I really think you've gotta bring people down who think we should get out now," he said. "Guys like Jack Murtha who think it's the bottom of the ninth and we can't win this. You know, when Clinton bombed Kosovo and everyone was saying it was a failure, once a week he'd bring his harshest Republican critics into the Yellow Room. And they'd sit by the fireplace and he'd ask, 'What do you think?' And for an hour and a half they'd let him have it."

Biden saw a skeptical gleam in Bush's eyes. "I know you don't like hearing from those kinds of guys," the senator conceded.

Bush grabbed his arm. "I'm a tough guy," he said. "I can take it."

Nonetheless, he didn't invite Murtha or any other war critics to the White House.

On Christmas day, nine days after Biden and the other senators visited the city to laud Iraq's peaceful political participation, Al Hillah was bombarded round-the-clock with mortar shells. Four transmission towers were taken down, and two American soldiers lost their lives.

At the White House Christmas party, Bush found himself shaking hands with an African American man whose face was vaguely familiar.

"Reverend Brown," the president called out. "How's your church?"

Bush hadn't heard. The Reverend had made repeated calls to the Office of Faith Based and Community Initiatives. He tried to convey to them: *This is an OPPORTUNITY. Make our church a PARTICIPANT in, a SYMBOL of, the recovery.* Because Reverend Brown *knew* how important Union Bethel was to the president . . . But the White House hadn't delivered. FEMA hadn't delivered. The church was still in shambles. And someone, the Reverend believed, had dropped the ball. *Help bring back our church, which is so important to our community—that sends a signal. . . . Leave us hanging, after you came and got nice news coverage during a reelection year—that sends a different signal.*

Reverend Brown didn't get into all that while standing in the receiving line. He didn't mention that the congregation that had been so welcoming to Bush on January 15, 2004, had lost everything they owned and were now scattered across America. He just told the president that Union Bethel had been wrecked by the hurricane.

"I want to see it come back," Bush replied. "Because I want to come back."

I want to see it come back was not quite the same as *I want to help.* Reverend Brown thanked the president, who was already shaking hands with another guest. The Reverend gazed around him. It was a lovely party. There was nothing like this going on in Union Bethel's neighborhood.

"Look!" he said, nudging his wife. "There's Karl Rove!"

PART SIX

THE THUMPIN'

19

THE BOLTEN BOUNCE

Optimism was basic to Bush. Disgruntlements did not fester; failure was not a thing to fear. Bush could push through crises—alcohol abuse, defeat in New Hampshire, thousands killed in the homeland on his watch—with little in the way of self-doubt or residual gloom. Bush liked to say that the unconditional love of his parents and religious faith were his props. The more cynical assessment was that the privileged son of George Herbert Walker Bush could afford to roll the dice. Whatever—buoyancy was his most persistent trait. And it came naturally to him, for as long as he could remember.

As commander in chief of an increasingly unpopular war, however, Bush's optimism grew less reflexive and more self-consciously determined. Aides heard it from him, time and again: "It takes an optimistic person to lead." "Who's going to follow a leader who says, 'Follow me, things are going to get worse'?" "I'm the calcium in the backbone."

As optimism became harder to come by, the more it was required of him. Rare was the occasion when Bush lifted the veil. During an interview with NBC's Matt Lauer on the campaign trail in 2004, the president was asked if the War on Terror was winnable. The answer Bush gave was intellectually honest: "I don't think you can win it. But I think you can create conditions so that those who use terror as a tool are less acceptable in parts of the world, let's put it that way."

He kicked himself later over that one. *How can I expect the troops to fight if I don't project confidence in the mission?* That was where the rubber met the road—with those risking their lives in Iraq, and with those who had already fallen on behalf of the mission, leaving behind griev-

ing parents and spouses who jabbed their fingers in the president's
chest and said to him, no less hauntingly for its predictability, *Don't let
my son die in vain. Finish the mission.*

Bush told aides that he fed off of the loved ones' resolve. He said
that he drew strength from the soldiers who assured him that it was a
honor to serve in Iraq—and who also added, *We're doing great things
over there, we're making progress, the media doesn't get it.* . . .

The commanders and the troops never told him what was going
wrong. Just as—and Dick Cheney, Jerry Bremer, Andy Card, Joe
Hagin, Condi Rice, and Steve Hadley all observed this—the generals
on the ground never once told the president during their regular
video conferences, *Sir, we need more troops.* Not once.

All of which suggested that things were Okay.

Things were not Okay.

But it was not a good thing to say that things were not Okay.

Though it was also not a good thing to say that things *were* Okay
when they were not.

He began New Year's Day 2006 early, with a long helicopter ride from
Waco to San Antonio, arriving at the Brooke Army Medical Center at
8:40 AM. The soldiers he visited were in many cases burned beyond
recognition. As Bush exited one ward and walked down the hall
toward another, a woman intercepted him in the doorway.

"My son's in this room," she told him. "He's a huge fan of yours—
there's nothing he'd love more than to see you. But he doesn't want
you to come inside, because he's not able to salute you."

Bush began to tear up. "I don't care about that," he said. "I'd just
like to pat him on the head, or whatever. . . ."

The mother retreated into the room for a moment. Then she
returned to the president.

"He doesn't want you to see him like this," she said, apologetically
but emphatically.

Bush said that he understood.

More than three hours later, he said goodbye to the last of two
dozen or so soldiers and their families. "That was tough," he said quietly to his deputy press secretary, Trent Duffy.

Between the hospital and the limo that would ferry Bush back to
the landing zone, there remained an additional task, one that Duffy
knew the president would find particularly onorous in light of what he
had just witnessed. Screwing up his courage, Duffy strode into the val-

ley of the shadow of death: *Mr. President, we're going to do a brief press availability. . . . They're going to ask you about the NSA program. Today the* Times *reported that General Ashcroft's deputy, James Comey, had refused to certify the program while Ashcroft was in the hospital. . . . What's really important is your body language. . . .*

Bush's displeasure was unambiguous. Duffy wanted to crawl into a hole.

But then the president stepped out into the lobby and said to the waiting media, "Happy New Year to you all. Thanks, I can't think of a better way to start 2006 than here at this fantastic hospital. . . ."

As Duffy had predicted, the first question was about whether Bush was "aware of any resistance to the launching of the NSA program at high levels of your administration. . . ." Bush showed no hint of his earlier irritation. While sidestepping the question, he defended the domestic surveillance activity as a "vital, necessary program" and assured the press gaggle that it would continue.

The last questioner wanted to know what it was like for Bush to confront the sadness of critically wounded soldiers there at Brooke Army Medical Center. "There's horrible consequences to war—that's what you see in this building," he acknowledged.

But then came that determined pivot toward hope and righteousness: "On the other hand, we also see people who say, 'I'd like to go back in, Mr. President, what we're doing is the right thing.' Because many of these troops understand that by defeating the enemy there, we don't have to face them here. And they understand that by helping the country and the Middle East become a democracy, we are, in fact, laying the foundation for future peace. And I, as the commander in chief, I am resolved to make sure that those who have died in combat's sacrifice are not in vain. And I am resolved to make sure that these kids who are recovering here, that have suffered terrible injury, that their injuries are not in vain by completing the mission and laying that foundation for peace for generations to come.

"And I'm optimistic we'll achieve that objective," he concluded.

Walking out of the medical center, Bush said to his press aide, "How was that, Duffy?"

Trent Duffy—who knew that this was the boss's way of saying, *You did your job*—remarked that Bush had nailed it.

Others in the Bush administration were showing less of a talent for this enforced sunniness. In January 2006, an unprecedented stream of outsiders—conservative intellectuals, top-level aides in previous administrations—were brought into the White House for sessions with Bush, Rove, or other subordinates. During one gathering of economists, a White House aide observed, "You know, the economy's performing extremely well, things are getting better in Iraq. . . . Do you think the polls are just wrong?"

One of the visiting economists, Martin Anderson, was aghast. "No," he shot back. "I think *you're* wrong."

At another meeting, hosted by Harriet Miers and Keith Hennessey, political scientist David Brady pronounced himself impatient with all the rosiness. "As a conservative, what am I supposed to be happy about?" he demanded. "I've got no Social Security reform, a high debt, no permanent tax cuts, not a single veto. . . ."

Brady glared at Miers and Hennessey, who in turn stared at the conference table, saying nothing.

Bartlett, Rove, and Card knew by heart the modifiers that dogged the Bush White House: *disengaged; incurious; stubborn; in denial.* It was important to show otherwise, to spread the carefully calibrated twin messages of optimism and concern. The "I am responsible" offensive of December 2005 had hoisted Bush's numbers up out of the thirties. But the public—soon, once again, to be the voting public—still agitated for signs of change, if not of outright progress. Bartlett's message team had a term for the prescription. They had to "scratch that itch."

On the fifth morning of January, thirteen secretaries of state and defense from administrations past were paraded into the Roosevelt Room for a one-hour advisory session with Bush. Photographers were ushered in to capture the image of Bush in consultation with the graybeards. Then Bush introduced the ambassador to Iraq, Zal Khalilzad, who spoke by video from Baghdad. After Khalilzad's briefing came a monologue by General Casey. Then presentations by Rumsfeld and Rice. By the time they were finished, a grand total of fifteen minutes was left for discussion.

After flattering comments by Melvin Laird, Robert McNamara, and George P. Shultz, former Clinton Secretary of State Madeleine Albright could no longer contain her annoyance at the happy talk. The war in Iraq, she said, was consuming too much of the administration's energy, to the detriment of relations with China and Latin America. America was losing its friends—and, Albright added, losing focus on the nuclear ambitions of Iran and China.

Aides in the room listened with palpable discomfort. The prospect of Albright's spouting off had led some of them to argue against inviting former Democratic cabinet members. "I can't let this comment stand," Bush snapped. His administration could walk and chew gum at the same time, he said. And their alliances had never been better.

A couple of minutes later, Bush adjourned the meeting by saying that it was time for their photo op in the Oval Office. "We ought to do this quarterly!" Rove sang out as the national-security sages were shepherded into the Oval—from which, after a couple of snapshots, the president exited, leaving a number of participants to marvel at the encounter's thorough lack of substance.

But it wasn't about substance. It was about scratching that itch.

And it seemed, for a blessed moment, that the Democrats would do the scratching for them.

After the botched Harriet Miers Supreme Court nomination, the White House abandoned any further yearning for a female jurist to replace Sandra Day O'Connor. They went instead for the sure thing: Samuel Alito, a federal appellate judge of unassailable if workmanlike credentials. Determined to paint Alito as a Frankenstein's monster of the right, Democrats on the Judiciary Committee of the Senate badly overstepped. The insinuation that the soft-faced Alito was a racist caused his wife to bolt weeping from the proceedings. Alito's confirmation was thereafter assured, and it was a Choice, Not Referendum world once again.

In an instant, the Dubai Ports World deal snatched it all away.

On February 10, 2006, the government-run entity of the United Arab Emirates joined the two dozen or so foreign businesses that had been contracted to assume management over various major American port terminals. From a policy standpoint, it seemed a no-lose proposition. Foreign contracts helped fund the Bush administration's ballooning deficit. DP World would manage port operations but have no oversight of the security work of the New York, Philadelphia, Baltimore, Newark, New Orleans, and Miami ports. And the UAE's unambiguous cooperation in the War on Terror deserved to be rewarded.

That was the optimistic, and politically indifferent, view of Dubai Ports. A darker and more cynical vantage point held that two of the nineteen 9/11 hijackers had resided in the UAE, and that the terrorist plot had been bankrolled in part through Emirates' financial institutions. To suggest that this wealthy Arab country did not have

September 11's blood on its hands was naïve. When in doubt, the Bush White House erred on the side of America's security interests. The Patriot Act, the NSA domestic surveillance program, the designation of Guantánamo Bay detainees as enemy combatants, the use of waterboarding to force confessions from terrorists, the quiet post-9/11 rejiggering of racial-profiling guidelines—at no turn could anyone accuse Bush of putting America's safety second . . . until now.

And yet the Treasury Department, in keeping with its policy of insulating foreign investment from the vagaries of politics, had not notified the president that the Emirates would now be managing six American ports. He learned about it the way his Legislative Affairs director, Candi Wolff, did: through the media buzz on February 16 that Democrats—led by Senators Hillary Clinton and Chuck Schumer—were mounting a challenge to the ports deal. Wolff, who knew the pulse of the Hill, immediately smelled trouble. Bush did not. It was the weekend before Presidents' Day, and while Wolff was on the ski slopes of Utah hoping that the White House would get the matter under control, the rest of the West Wingers were dispersing for the long weekend as well. So were 534 congressmen. And what they would hear back home, from constituents agitated by the talk-radio airwaves, was: *WE ARE TURNING OUR PORTS OVER TO . . . ARABS!*

The morning after Presidents' Day, Senate majority leader Bill Frist's staff contacted the White House's Office of Legislative Affairs to say that Frist—having fielded hysterical calls from Republican members throughout the past seventy-two hours—intended to announce that he opposed the ports deal. Barely five minutes later, Frist's press release shimmied through fax machines all across the District. Then House Speaker Dennis Hastert called Candi Wolff. Hastert said that he would have to voice his opposition as well. Now seriously behind the eight ball, Wolff and others in the West Wing scrambled to find some wiggle room, a means of pacifying the natives before a minor Treasury Department agreement became a major GOP food fight.

But Bush was on a different page. He was just returning from a speech in Colorado—test-driving a new initiative to curb America's "addiction to oil"—when, as he would remember it, "Bartlett walks in and says, 'We got a problem.'" The arguments against the deal struck him as beyond the pale. Did Frist and Hastert really think Bush would compromise American security? Bush told Bartlett to bring the press pool back to his cabin on Air Force One. He did not mince words about the Republican leadership: "They ought to listen to what I have to say about this. They ought to look at the facts, and understand the consequences of what they're going to do. But if they pass a law, I'll deal with it, with a veto."

Never before had Bush exercised his veto power. Rove did not like the implications of the president doing so on an issue as easily demagogued as this one. When Ken Mehlman, at the RNC, called Rove that afternoon, wondering what the hell was going on, Rove protested, "I was trying to get him not to."

Mehlman and Candi Wolff both knew what Bush did not: that talk radio was frothing on the ports deal, and that in a midterm year, Republicans on the Hill could not afford to turn a deaf ear. But Bush refused to back down. An hour after his earlier statement, Bush disembarked from Marine One on the South Lawn and reiterated his support for the Dubai agreement. The UAE company, he said, "has played by the rules," and not awarding them the contract would "send a terrible signal to friends and allies."

Republicans were aghast at Bush's intransigence. They begged Rove, *You can't let Hillary and Schumer get to the right of us! Please, make this issue go AWAY!* On February 28, GOP senators huddled to discuss the matter. To their surprise, Cheney showed up to the meeting. (The VP had been keeping a low profile since his own unfortunate newsmaking event seventeen days prior. On February 11, Cheney had accidentally shot a friend during a quail hunt on a South Texas ranch. He had brought no communications staff with him on the trip—a terrible oversight, the White House press shop later concluded—and his slowness in notifying Bush and the national media about the mishap had been front-page news for days . . . until the Dubai deal had knocked it off.)

The older senators—John Warner of Virginia, Ted Stevens of Alaska—begged the caucus to stand behind Bush. "He's at forty in the polls," John McCain reminded the others. "He needs our help."

Then New Mexico's Pete Domenici took the floor to make his pitch for solidarity. "We're like a covey of quail!" he bellowed. "Any one of us flies off—we'll get *shot!*"

In the horrified silence that followed, Cheney the errant quail hunter quietly got up and left the room.

The Dubai Ports World agreement was scotched two weeks later— much too late to avoid significant embarrassment. The affair revealed not only the White House's tin ear but its growing dysfunctionality. How could Candi Wolff—the staffer tasked with asking for votes on the Hill—not be alerted to the president's intention to veto a controversial legislative initiative? And how, following the Harriet Miers debacle, could the White House permit yet another public spat between Bush and his own party to dominate the news for fully a month?

There was no easy answer—except that it, like the Miers bungle and the Katrina fallout, had taken place on Andy Card's watch.

Extended stay in the West Wing could exact a toll on its inhabitants similar to that incurred by a prison sentence. The brutal hours and incessant stresses turned hairs gray, stamped dark rings and an oatmealish pallor into otherwise youthful faces. Ever lurked the danger that a West Wing senior staffer—both physically and psychologically sequestered in the White House's gilded bubble—would succumb to an inmate's stunted perspective, forgetting how things played out in the world beyond 1600 Pennsylvania Avenue.

Bush, an eight-year man by choice, required comfort and routine. The notion that change was not only good but essential—that oncevital personnel would outlive their usefulness and require culling—ran counter to his impulses. Nonetheless, it was a Darwinian reality: Staffers moved on, and sometimes without waiting to be moved. Mike Gerson, having already provided the architecture for the Bush presidency's moral and intellectual framework, awakened one day in 2006 to the realization that there was no more heavy lifting for him to do. After decades serving on Capitol Hill and in the Clinton and Bush administrations, Norm Mineta received a juicy private-sector offer that he could not turn down, not even when Bush asked him to hold off until after the midterm elections in November. Nicolle Wallace's husband had moved to New York to work for the UN, providing her with a handy exit strategy from the triage of Message ER. And the president's bodyman, Blake Gottesman, followed the inclinations of his predecessor, Logan Walters, by leaving the White House to get his MBA. (Gottesman had accumulated only a year's worth of undergraduate credits before dropping out to join the Bush administration. The Harvard School of Business—where, of course, Gottesman's boss had earned his MBA—was somehow persuaded to overlook that shortcoming.) Though Bush's personal aide slipped out quietly on his last day to avoid a tearfest, he left behind a wry memento. Senior staffers noticed the next day that the porcelain bust of Churchill in the Roosevelt

Room looked . . . well . . . different. Because it *was* different. A white bust of Blake Gottesman now sat there in its place.

Nothing about Andy Card's affable servility implied megalomania. If anything, he seemed egalitarian to a fault: maintaining savage hours (second only to Harriet Miers among West Wing workaholics), stapling his own documents, devoting literally days to hand signing some eight thousand Christmas cards. He took the time to accost junior staffers in the hallways and ask them about their ailing relatives. Every so often, he went down to the Office of Records Management and asked to lunch a lifelong bureaucrat who had never before met the chief of staff, in this or any previous administration.

Having served Reagan and Bush 41, Card suffered no illusions as to a White House staffer's indispensability. But he took pride in his durability. Chiefs of staff seldom lasted more than three or four years. Here he was, going on his sixth. Reminding co-workers that he had once worked the late shift at McDonald's while attending college and supporting a wife and children, he dismissed suggestions of burnout with a chortling, "I've *always* looked this tired!"

He had offered his resignation to the president shortly after the reelect, and then again in December 2005. But Card knew that it took a hard push to get Bush to cut an eight-year man adrift, and he didn't push. Besides, the usual jackals were increasingly calling for Card's head. There was no way Bush was going to appear acquiescent to the editorial board of the *New York Times.*

The ports fiasco renewed the catcalls, and in early March, Card brought up the matter again with Bush. The chattering classes were clamoring for changes, said the chief to his boss, and "change has to be personified. We all know who they are: Donald Rumsfeld, Karl Rove, Dick Cheney, and Condi Rice." Card knew Bush wasn't going to discard Cheney or throw Rumsfeld—the personification, in Bush's mind, of the White House's "strategy for victory" in Iraq—to the jackals.

"Rove, you can't touch him till the trial's over," he continued, referring to the ongoing Valerie Plame leak investigation. "It's either gonna rain or it's gonna be sunny. And Rice is a superstar. You'd be nuts to get rid of her."

Then he proffered himself. "You can change me and there's no Senate hearing," he reminded Bush. "You don't need anyone's permission, don't need to sign a piece of paper and send it to the Hill."

What Andy Card was selling was change for change's sake—not the kind of commodity George W. Bush tended to buy. Card was proposing his resignation as a solution. He had not argued that he, Andy Card, was in fact a problem. He had not made this point because he himself did not believe it.

But others close to the president did. They observed how Card's gatekeeping had, in the wake of 9/11, become far more Sununu-like than Bush had previously envisioned, even as the chief hoarded his own access to the president. They noticed that Card could be heedless to the needs of Republicans on the Hill while overly sensitive to how a particular decision might impact this or that West Wing staffer. And they saw what outsiders could not—namely, that under Andy Card, the White House management structure had effectively collapsed. Bartlett and Rove were constantly at war. Legislative Affairs was out of the loop. While running interference for the White House on Sam Alito's Supreme Court nomination, Ed Gillespie told a fellow Republican, "I'm going crazy over here. I feel like a shuttle diplomat, going from office to office. No one will talk to each other."

Most of all, they noticed that Andy Card had lost his edge and was giving the president bad advice. For all his contacts and experience on the Hill, he failed to forecast the fate of Social Security reform. It was Card who had given the go-ahead for Bush's New Orleans flyover, which would join "Mission Accomplished" as one of the most resounding photo-op backfires of Bush's presidency. Card had begun the push for federalization of the Katrina disaster too late, and then too stridently, and lost the battle to Governor Blanco anyway. He joined the small group cheerleading Harriet Miers' doomed nomination. It was the chief of staff's business to head trouble off at the pass. But Card did not know about the Dubai Ports World agreement before it was too late. Nor had he been aware that one of his top subordinates, domestic-policy adviser Claude Allen, had resigned his position five weeks after being detained at a Gaithersburg, Maryland, Target on January 2 for shoplifting. Allen was then arrested on a similar offense on March 9. Bush learned of the matter only the following evening, through the media. He called his chief of staff that night to chew him out.

But he did not accept Card's offer to resign that night of January 10. The next day, Card repeated the offer. On Monday, the 13th, he offered again. When he brought up the matter yet again on the 15th, he found Bush somewhat more receptive but not yet committed.

Card joined Bush at Camp David that weekend. The two men rode bikes together. The chief of staff went Yard Sale on the trails, breaking his elbow in the process.

Bush hadn't told him that he had already found Andy Card's replacement.

In the Bush White House, Joshua Bolten qualified as an eccentric. He was Jewish, rode a Harley to work, kept late hours, and at one time had dated the actress Bo Derek. Bolten did not give off a sycophantic reek. His life before entering Bushworld was full enough: son of a CIA agent, graduate of Princeton and then Stanford Law, an international trade lawyer and deputy director of the Office of Legislative Affairs during the first Bush administration, and finally, a London-based executive at Goldman Sachs, when mutual friends approached him about meeting with Bush at the Governor's Mansion one evening in January 1999.

The Texas governor wore cowboy boots and splayed his legs and inhaled his hot dog in seconds flat. He seemed impressed when Bolten didn't bullshit him and instead confessed not to know much about several policy initiatives. Thereupon Bush hired him to be the campaign's policy director, and in late February 1999 Josh Bolten was installed in Karl Rove's political consulting office, in a windowless storage room with Bartlett and an assistant, and two phones for the three of them to share.

By springtime, Bolten had moved into the campaign's new headquarters at 301 Congress and proceeded to fill its cubicles with propeller-heads. These included the opposition researchers Tim Morrison and Bill Clark, who were faithful practitioners of the Atkins Diet and subsisted almost entirely on large quantities of barbecued meat. It also included one of Bob Blackwill's Harvard students, Joel Shin, a foreign-policy geek of seemingly bionic voraciousness who literally lived and slept in his cubicle until Joe Allbaugh one day ordered him to find an apartment. (Like Rice, Shin was from Birmingham, and one day he returned from his birthplace with several miniature reproductions of that city's Vulcan statue. From this the Bush foreign-policy team derived its name, the Vulcans.)

Bolten was among the firmly entrenched members of the inner circle. He worked, as Gerson would marvel, "with tremendous influence, without fingerprints." It seemed not to impress Bolten, however. Unlike Rove, who relished face time with the boss, the new deputy chief of staff was more interested in orderly policy formulation than in high-level meetings and frequently sent subordinates to them in his stead. Unlike Rove, Bolten almost never dispensed information to the press—though he was friendly with reporters, which, coupled with his vague air of mystery, caused various female journalists to develop unrequited crushes on him.

In 2003, he replaced the combative Office of Management and Budget director Mitch Daniels, who had shared Bush's scornful view of legislators. ("Don't just stand there—SPEND something!" was Daniels's oft-repeated summation of the Hill mentality.) One of Bolten's first acts was to go fishing with Alaska Senator Ted Stevens to assess White House relations with its party leaders. But the new OMB director was neither a kiss-ass nor a pushover. He did not suffer fools, and he wasted little energy charming associates or worrying about whose feelings he might hurt. Among the many things Bolten found virtuous about the president, the latter's tendency to cry—"I do tears," as Bush put it—was not one of them.

"Congratulations—that's terrific," Andy Card told Bolten after being informed of Bush's decision. "It's best for the president." Bolten could tell that Card was somewhat surprised and hurt that Bush had moved so swiftly to select a replacement. Card kept his anguish to himself, however. The evening before the announcement was to be made, the chief of staff gave a Lincoln Day dinner speech in Cincinnati on behalf of House whip John Boehner. He chose to focus on Bush's glory day of September 14, 2001—when, as Card liked to tell people, the president fulfilled all his executive duties: addressing the nation, commiserating with the suffering, and convening his war cabinet. He thought he gave one hell of a speech.

Early the next morning, March 28, he called several congressional leaders and informed them of what would be announced an hour later. Then Andy Card removed the cast from his broken arm and stepped out to face the press one last time before retiring after five and one-half years as the president's right-hand man . . . during which he had achieved much, failed here and there, but, he would later note proudly, never submitted a billable hour to an attorney.

The so-called Bolten Bounce—a sudden and noticeable spike in Bush's approval ratings—began three weeks later, when the new chief fired Scott McClellan and stripped Karl Rove of his policy portfolio.

Confidence was not exactly the word that Scott McClellan brought to mind during his two years as Bush's mouthpiece. Well liked and capable behind the scenes, he was badly out of his depth when poised against the White House press corps—looking like nothing so much as a terrified if well-fed koala bear as he peered out from behind the press room podium and recited his message lines as if at gunpoint: "As I said, the president has a bold agenda on behalf of all Americans. . . ."

Bolten quietly approached his good friend Torie Clarke, who had been Rumsfeld's press secretary before leaving for the private sector in 2003. Would she be willing to take Scott's job? Clarke informed Bolten that she would rather commit suicide. His second choice, Fox News anchor Tony Snow, did not exactly lunge at the offer, having recently recovered from cancer treatment. His insistence that he be included in key Oval Office meetings failed to endear him to his new colleagues. And when Snow botched his three run-throughs—failing even to recite the White House's Iraq talking points, which most members of the press corps now muttered in their sleep—one senior staffer predicted darkly that the new press secretary wouldn't last through the end of the year. Then Tony Snow held his first press conference, a performance so dazzling that his ruefully admiring co-workers were left to wonder why this move hadn't been made months earlier.

The decision to bust down Karl Rove was more complicated. It had been Card's idea in 2004 to "depoliticize" Rove by awarding him the post of deputy chief for policy, once held by Josh Bolten. That put Rove in charge of the White House's various policy councils—yet another responsibility for Bush's senior adviser, who, by the summer of 2005, would take on the additional burden of becoming a key figure in the ongoing Plamegate investigation. Management, both of time and of people, had never been Rove's strong suit anyway. Bolten noticed that other staffers were intimidated by Rove: They tended not to speak up at meetings he chaired, and far from encouraging others, he relished being the smartest guy in the room. Above all, Rove was doing too much—freelancing, insinuating himself into the message world (where so much of the action was), parachuting into Capitol Hill whenever it suited him, demoralizing his colleagues, and in general making a mockery of this self-styled post-Clinton "MBA presidency." Card had effectively conceded to journalist Ron Suskind in 2002 that he had little control over Rove—that the chief could only stand "in the middle of the seesaw, with Karen Hughes on one side, Rove on the other, trying to keep it in balance." (Though Suskind's two stories in *Esquire* about Hughes and Rove were reviled in the White House as hyperbolic beyond any credibility, Card never repudiated his quotes. Rove believed them, in any case, and indicated his hurt feelings to others.)

Rove did not take the news of his demotion (though no one wanted to call it that) well. He would be giving up his posh office suite on the West Wing's first floor to the new deputy chief, Joel Kaplan. Rove testily informed Mike Gerson that he would like the chief speech-writer's office suite, please. Gerson, soon to be leaving anyway, obliged him. But the new suite was windowless and drab. At seven in the morning on April 19, the day that McClellan's dismissal and Rove's reassignment were to be announced, he gathered his subordinates and explained to them that they would be moving down the hall.

His senior assistant, Susan Ralston, could see how despondent her boss was. She began to clap her hands. "It'll be great!" Ralston insisted to the startled expressions around her. "We can all sit together!"

But Rove remained cranky for weeks. His constituency was the Republican establishment—and, though he would never admit it, the media elite as well. But after the initial lampooning passed, the Beltway's dispensed wisdom was that this was less a demotion than a needed correction. This was 2006, after all. A crucial midterm year. Forget the policy councils—Rove's considerable genius was best devoted to maintaining the Republican majority. Bush's "architect" needed to be *re*politicized.

This pleased Rove. He stopped yelling at his subordinates, began giving speeches to conservative audiences and feeding off-the-record musings to reporters again.

Bolten's machinations weren't limited to personnel shuffling. He called dozens of Republican congressmen who had been feeling ne-glected by Andy Card. He worked with Joel Kaplan to reestablish order in the policy-making apparatus. And unlike Card, Bolten knew how to manage *up*: He made it his business to make sure that Bush got the news he needed to hear, not simply the news he wished to hear. He did this by forcing Bush's inner circle, especially Rove and Bartlett, to communicate with each other, and to face unpleasant truths that would then be communicated to the president. Bolten's colleagues respected him—and, because he cared only about results, frankly feared him a little . . . and that was not such a bad thing.

In a month's time, it had become Josh Bolten's West Wing. But it was still George W. Bush's White House. His pungency predomi-nated, for good or for ill. Two of Bolten's other hires were replace-ments for Treasury Secretary John Snow, who had long been deemed ineffectual, and communications director Nicolle Wallace. Bolten aggressively lobbied Goldman Sachs CEO Henry Paulson for the

Treasury slot. Paulson said no repeatedly; Bolten would not take it for an answer. The chief of staff asked Bush to turn on the charm. Bush did so, but with some reluctance. It was an honor to be working for the president, he snapped: *"He* should be begging *me!"*

Bolten settled on Education Secretary Margaret Spellings's press aide, Kevin Sullivan, to fill in for Wallace. Sullivan had been the Dallas Mavericks' media guy while Bush was running the Texas Rangers, and in his job interview, he laid it on thick with the jock stuff. "If this was a test, you passed it," Bush proclaimed at the end of their session.

Sullivan had heard all the Incurious George distillations of his new boss. In one of his first meetings with Bush, the president unspooled a discourse on Muslim extremism that astounded the new communications director with its clarity and breadth of knowledge. He told Bartlett later, "That was amazing!"

"Yeah," the counselor said ruefully. "That's the side of him that they don't see on TV."

Thinking of the side they *did* see, Kevin Sullivan inquired gently, "Is there a way to . . . you know . . . *discourage* the president from taking jabs at the media?"

"No," said Dan Bartlett. "There's really not."

20

The Phantom Fence

On April 25, Bush sat between two senators in the Cabinet Room as they yelled at each other about an issue that somehow had become theirs rather than his.

The topic was immigration-reform legislation, though it had quickly deteriorated to arcane procedural swordsmanship. Senate minority leader Harry Reid sat to Bush's left, demanding that majority leader Bill Frist cede control of the conference committee to Reid. Frist hollered back that Reid was stonewalling Republican-sponsored amendments that would clean up the bill. For several minutes the two men went at it, while Bush and ten other senators listened to the partisan bickering overtake one of the president's most enduring passions.

"This is worse than I thought," mumbled Bush to nobody in particular—somewhat bemused at first, but then progressively annoyed, and then even more so when John McCain finally interjected with a tsk-tsk: "Mr. President, I'm embarrassed that you have to see this shameful display of partisanship. This is a waste of your time."

Arlen Specter of Pennsylvania tried to return the discussion to the Hagel-Martinez bill currently stalled in the Senate immigration subcommittee. Bush's favorable comments on the legislation—which provided a two-tier pathway to citizenship for illegal workers, depending on how long they had been in the United States—led Specter to suggest that the president participate more openly in its passage. Bush knew the House leadership would rebel if he did. "Don't you go out there and say I'm supporting the bill, Arlen," he warned.

Then the pesky Republican Lindsey Graham spoke up. "Mr. President, some say that anything short of shipping every illegal alien and their family back to Mexico is amnesty," Graham drawled. "And others say that amnesty is when you're rewarded for illegal behavior by being permitted to cut in line for citizenship. Which is *your* definition?"

Bush bristled. He had stated time and again that he opposed amnesty and didn't feel that he should have to go on record once more. "You're playing prosecutor," he told the former trial lawyer. "Don't put me on the witness stand, Lindsey. You don't want me to answer that question, anyway. I don't think it's in your interest or my interest to endorse Hagel-Martinez in its entirety."

The meeting ended on a productive note, with Bush and the twelve senators agreeing on the principles outlined in the Hagel-Martinez bill. All the same, this was not as Bush had envisioned it. On the subject of immigration, he had become, at best, a backstage referee rather than an overt champion of comprehensive reform.

Bush had not expected to spend his presidency at war or responding to natural disasters. He had assumed that his preoccupations would be education, tax cuts, Social Security, perhaps missile defense—and certainly immigration. The subject hit home in rather obvious ways. Though few Mexicans worked in the oil patch during Bush's era, the culture of his home state was suffused with Hispanic influences. He grew up hearing of the agricultural Bracero Program originating during World War II and would come away with the impression that "it was a pretty compatible arrangement." (He would not recall that Texas employers were frequently cited for exploiting Mexican workers or that the state cracked down on illegal aliens with Operation Wetback in 1954.) His brother Jeb's wife, Colomba, was Mexican. He regularly jabbered in high-school-level Spanish with ballplayers in Arlington, and later with constituents as the governor of an immense border state.

The politics of the issue fascinated Bush. In 1997, then-Governor Bush expressed his disapproval of UT Law School Professor Lino Graglia, who was noisily inveighing against affirmative action. It wasn't so much that he thought Graglia was wrong, he confided to others; Bush himself was against quotas. It was that such stridency had infuriated the Hispanic Caucus and in turn put the Republican Party in a hard place. For Bush and Rove, the demographic trends told the story: The future of Texas, and indeed most of America, was not a tale of red or blue, black or white. It was about brown. The country's population was surging with Latinos, and conservatives ignored this at their peril.

"Let's just take the Hispanic issue," he told a Texas reporter in 1998 as the two sat in the governor's office and discussed Bush's desire to put a new face on conservatism. "I've found that much of the language was very divisive and was driving potential Hispanic voters away from the conservative moment, and/or the conservative leadership was driving them to the point where they didn't really feel like they had any hope for the future. The language of 'English only' is a language that basically says, 'Me, Not You . . . ' It basically sends the signal that says, 'You don't care about me.' "

Bush cared. He freely unleashed his passion on the subject during the 2000 campaign. "Family values don't stop at the Rio Grande," Bush liked to say, adding that he not only didn't blame undocumented workers from crossing over to improve their livelihoods, he welcomed it: "I think the hardworking Hispanics have enriched my state." Even as he flung red meat to the base during the South Carolina primary, he never rose to the bait when town hall questioners invited him to criticize illegal aliens. On immigration and education, Bush steadfastly bucked the Republican party line. Nor, though, could he move the line.

Throughout 2001, the subject of amnesty for illegal aliens popped up frequently in White House meetings. Gerson openly rhapsodized about such a policy. His deputy speechwriter, John McConnell, believed that such a declaration by Bush would be grand and historic—one of a litany that schoolchildren would one day recite: the Louisiana Purchase, the Emancipation Proclamation, Bush's amnesty plan. . . . The White House working group chaired by Margaret Spellings that year actively contemplated a scheme that would distinguish between citizenship and legal status. The matter of clamping down at the border received almost no attention during these meetings. Instead: Why not put eleven million undocumented people in status—*overnight*? Why not let the market drive the policy? That sentiment, if not amnesty outright, was shared by Spellings, Karen Hughes, Condi Rice, and White House counsel Al Gonzales—and by Bush, who, on July 10, 2001, stood on Ellis Island and declared, "Immigration is not a problem to be solved. It is a sign of a confident and successful nation."

Then came 9/11, and calls for greater border security drove all liberalized approaches to immigration into the bunker. But as the reelection campaign dawned, Bush and Rove had demographic trends on their minds once more. Just as they had hoped to improve on Bush's dismal showing among black voters ("Ol' Nine Percent Bush," he sometimes called himself) by sending him to Union Bethel Church in January 2004, it was decided that Bush would propose a "temporary-worker program" that same month. Even if the measure faltered on the Hill, Rove figured, the pro-immigration groups would respond to the gesture by exercising restraint against Republicans that November.

The policy sought to thread the needle. Undocumented workers would not be granted citizenship under the new proposal. But by paying a onetime fee, they would not be prosecuted for their illegal entry into the United States. Whether this amounted to amnesty depended on one's point of view. During Strategery meetings in the Old Executive Office Building, Legislative Affairs director David Hobbs warned the other senior staffers that the speech was a mistake. "Democrats are going to hate it because it's not amnesty," he predicted, "and Republicans are going to hate it because it *is* amnesty."

Hobbs was from Houston and could see that the White House bias was palpably Texas-centric. Bush, Spellings, Hughes, and Gonzales came from a vast state that readily absorbed illegal aliens. Farther north of the border, a different experience was occurring, but the White House team was largely unaware of it.

Bush delivered his temporary-worker speech in the East Room on January 7, 2004. The audience was full of enthusiastic Hispanics, a stacked deck. Outside the East Room, David Hobbs was right: Both sides found something to dislike about the speech. Afterward, Bush called his Legislative Affairs director into the Oval Office. The president was angry. He thrust into Hobbs's hands a newspaper article quoting a Republican member who said that he loved the president but hated his amnesty proposal.

"Hobbsy," he demanded, "you go up there and you tell them I'm not for amnesty!"

For the second time in his administration, Bush was forced to table his immigration initiative. "They didn't want to take it on," he remembered. "They wanted to do border security only. So okay, let us prove that we can enforce the border." Over the next few years, Bush would triple the Border Patrol's budget, a show of commitment that would lead to a policy rollout in the fall of 2005. But Bush's Katrina problems sucked all the oxygen out of his agenda for the remainder of that tortuous year. It might not have mattered anyway. Earlier in

2005, when Republican congressmen returned home to conduct town hall meetings on Social Security, their constituents had plenty to say, but not on personal accounts. The subject on their minds was the unchecked wave of illegal aliens besieging America's economy, its schools, and its culture.

A sobering irony had reared itself: The conservative base that had flourished under Bush was now turning against him. And while Bush could effortlessly roll the base during the halcyon days of 2002 through 2004, by 2006 his clout was badly diminished. Indeed, now it was Congress whose needs mattered most. Push them too far to the center, and the base would not turn out for the Republican incumbents in November. If the GOP forfeited its majority rule on the Hill—an absolutely unthinkable scenario a year beforehand—then Bush could kiss the rest of his agenda goodbye.

Nonetheless, several members made it clear to the White House: *We'll work with you on this. But you've gotta give us cloud cover.* And so the president adapted. Even as he plaintively urged Americans to consider the issue "in a way that doesn't pit one group of people against another," Bush now emphasized the need for border security. After Rove's deputy Barry Jackson emerged from two weeks of meetings with conservative think tanks with the word *assimilation* clanging in his ears, Bush suddenly began asserting publicly, for the first time ever in his presidency, that immigrants "have a responsibility to understand what America is about and have a responsibility to learn the English language." Instead of celebrating the immigrant tradition on Ellis Island, he now appeared at border states for photo ops in which he stood under the hot sun in shirtsleeves, grimacing at the porous borders.

Nearly three weeks after he met with Frist, Reid, and the other senators in the Cabinet Room, Bush gave additional cloud cover. On May 15, he addressed the nation from the Oval Office to "make it clear where I stand, and where I want to lead our country on this vital issue." The new Bush, the weakened midterm Bush, led with his paean to the base: "First, the United States must secure its borders." Bush said that he would dispatch six thousand National Guard troops to America's southern border and build more prison beds.

Virtually half of his speech had passed before the president got around to proposing a temporary worker program. And even so, Bush framed the proposal not as morally virtuous but as something needed "to secure the border effectively." For the length of time that it took to explain such a program, Bush devoted equal time to explaining why "What I've just described is not amnesty." Only at the end of the speech did he permit himself to speak from the heart about "the great American tradition of the melting pot . . . We honor the heritage of all who come here, no matter where they come from, because we trust in our country's genius for making us all Americans—one nation under God."

Five months after Bush's speech, Congress at last passed immigration legislation. The legacy they awarded George W. Bush for his five-year effort to bring Hispanics into the Republican fold was entitled the Secure Fence Act and said nothing about a temporary worker program. Instead, it authorized seven hundred miles of fencing along the southwestern border . . . though only for the sake of stilling passions before the midterms. In reality, Republican House leaders had quietly underfunded the initiative. As one of Bush's senior aides would later snicker, "The dirty little secret is: There's no fence."

Still: Under Bush's watch, a bill had been passed authorizing the walling off of Mexico. And the unlikely coalition that had been gathering weekly in the OEOB—the National Immigration Forum, La Raza, immigration lawyers, Hispanic church groups, and other individuals who had never before sided with Bush but believed in his sincere passion on the issue—would not be able to convey to *their* base that this was only dummy legislation. And so a radical backfire would ensue. The Republicans, having lost the Hispanic vote in 2004 by a mere 9 percentage points, would lose it in 2006 by 40.

Back in 1998, Governor Bush had told a Texas reporter that the same forces who were demonizing undocumented laborers were also seeking to turn homosexuality into a wedge issue. "I understand their concern about gay marriages or special rights," he said that summer day. "But I don't agree with the idea of pitting one group against another. That's exactly what's happened during the Hispanic debate, it seems like. And it may not have been the intention, but it became Us versus Them. It's impossible to lead the nation or state towards a better tomorrow by dividing into camps."

The two subjects weren't quite the same, Bush acknowledged back then, when he was still governor. To him, at least, the difference lay in his own comfort level. He could talk about the great immigrant tradition and the American dream until his voice went hoarse. As for sexual orientation, well . . ."Let me tell you my view when I was asked about gays in my staff," then-Governor Bush continued. "I said,

'How do you know?' Let me tell you my view about sex. It's private. It's not my business. *I don't want to know*. I don't want to know about your sex life, and I'm not really interested in you knowing mine. It's a private matter. It disturbs the average American—and I view myself as an average American, when someone's private life becomes part of the public discourse. People making a case for special rights based on their orientation—*I don't want to know*. I don't know if I've got a gay person on my staff, nor do I care. . . . If I were commander in chief of America, I'd say, 'Generals, what does it take to win a war? What is necessary in morale for it to be a fighting force? You all determine it and take politics out.' If the generals are comfortable with Don't Ask Don't Tell, I can live with it. . . . I wouldn't [appoint someone] based on their gaydom. Or gayhood. But I don't know. It's none of my business. I get nervous when it becomes an agenda. I'm troubled by a world in which people's sexuality is no longer a private matter. It *should* be a private matter."

That was Bush unvarnished: old-fashioned, socially libertarian, determined not to let divisiveness carry the day. He said little more than that on the campaign trail and through the early years of his presidency. But when conservative groups reacted with dismay to the Supreme Court's decision to strike down the Texas sodomy statute in the summer of 2003, Bush felt compelled to speak out in favor of the "sanctity of marriage." At the same time, he expressed reluctance toward a federally imposed ban on gay marriages . . . until December, the eve of the election season, when he told ABC's Diane Sawyer, "If necessary, I will support a constitutional amendment which would honor marriage between a man and a woman—codify that."

By February 2004, after Massachusetts and San Francisco officials began to issue marriage licenses to gays, Bush threw out the "if necessary" and unambiguously declared the need for a constitutional amendment defining marriage as that between a man and a woman. After the election was won, the freshly mandated president fell silent on the subject once again. Throughout 2005, Bush spent not so much as a dime of his political capital defending the sanctity of marriage. He seemed content to let the matter die.

But Bush's contentedness was not priority one in 2006. Holding the majority was. Seeking a campaign wedge issue, Republican House members had settled on flogging a constitutional "Marriage Protection Amendment." The president had to take a position on the subject. There was no question as to what that position would be. Left open to debate was how out front Bush would be on the matter. Bartlett and Rove scheduled a speech in the Rose Garden in which Bush would announce his support of the constitutional amendment on June 5.

At the last minute, they decided to go low-profile and hold the speech next door in the OEOB. Bush gave his endorsement before a crowd filled with religious conservatives. He spoke for ten minutes, then left without exchanging words with the press.

Tony Snow did. He told reporters that day that Bush's endorsement was made "more in sorrow than anything else, that this may in fact require a constitutional amendment."

After which Bush, having gone on the record, once again resumed his silence on the "private matter."

Katrina had blown through his presidency. But the aftershocks lingered.

After a two-month absence from the Gulf region, Bush returned to New Orleans on January 12. The advance staff had been pressing for the president to visit the city's still-ravaged neighborhoods, which he had yet to do. The message shop pushed back: *There's been enough death and destruction. We need to talk about turning the corner.*

So Bush visited a convention center in the lower Garden District, a sumptuous neighborhood largely unscathed by the hurricane. "It may be hard for you to see," he told the community leaders at that roundtable event, "but from when I first came here to today, New Orleans is reminding me of the city I used to come to visit. It's a heck of a place to bring your family. It's a great place to find some of the greatest food in the world and some wonderful fun. And I'm glad you got your infrastructure back on its feet. I know you're beginning to welcome citizens from all around the country here to New Orleans. And for folks around the country who are looking for a great place to have a convention or a great place to visit, I'd suggest coming here to the great New Orleans."

The motorcade then passed by the untrammeled rows of nineteenth-century architecture—avoiding the blight, circumnavigating as well the protesters at Jackson Square—and delivered the president to Air Force One, which took him to a recovery event in Mississippi, and after that, a GOP midterm fund-raiser in Palm Beach.

"I'm a woman who has nothing to lose," Governor Kathleen Blanco had told Andy Card during his final weeks as chief of staff. Livid over the administration's rejection of a New Orleans recovery plan hatched by Republican Congressman Richard Baker of Baton Rouge, she told Card, "If I have to, I'll declare war on this president. This is a *man-made* disaster."

Assuaging Blanco was Don Powell, Bush's hand-picked recovery czar. "Let's get to the numbers," he gently urged during that meeting in the White House. After much haggling, a sum of $4.2 billion was agreed upon for housing recovery in Louisiana.

Bush was getting it from all sides. Conservatives accused him of drafting hurricane relief checks like a Massachusetts Democrat. Liberals bashed him for insensitivity. When Sara Taylor's Office of Political Affairs looked at the numbers, the most corrosive perception was that the once-efficient executive apparatus was now widely viewed as "incompetent." The ongoing woes in Iraq fed this sentiment, but the more graspable evidence was Katrina related. The ghost of Brownie lingered: Tens of thousands of unused FEMA trailers sat in fields outside Lumberton, Mississippi, and Clinton's old hometown, Hope, Arksansas. Brown testified elaborately on Capitol Hill as to his prescience on the failures of DHS. Meanwhile, the president—while declaring, with unintended irony, New Orleans to be a "heck of a place"—had yet to set foot in the city's devastated Lower Ninth Ward.

Bartlett knew that this could not continue. On March 5, while traveling with Bush on Air Force One from Pakistan, he decided to tear up the schedule for the trip the president would take to New Orleans three days later. It was preordained that Bush would visit the Industrial Canal levee. To get there, the presidential entourage could take reality avoidance to an extreme and arrive by boat . . . or it could arrive at the levee by motorcade, passing through the Lower Ninth, where there would surely be protesters. And to drive *through* New Orleans' most damaged neighborhood without stopping would echo the August 31 flyover.

They really had no choice in the matter. Bush was going to the Lower Ninth.

The expected protesters lined the streets that Wednesday morning. But they were incidental to the searing image as the motorcade passed through block after block of boarded-up shells that once served as homes for people who once upon a time had lived here. Bush wore a frown, and his blue shirtsleeves were rolled up as he stood in the middle of a rubble-strewn street and absentmindedly jabbed at a stick that jutted out of a pile of household debris. He followed Mayor Ray Nagin into an abandoned house. The walls were bearded with black mold. Up close and in panorama, the visual was unsparing. Bush mustered a few positive sentiments about debris removal—that after this necessary step, the rebuilding could at last begin. Then he went to the Industrial Canal levee, where he announced that the $4.2 billion recently earmarked by House Appropriations Committee leaders for all the hurricane-ravaged states should instead be funneled to Louisiana in its entirety.

Advance man Jason Recher had discovered a sweet coda to this otherwise somber trip. Not far from the levee stood a mom-and-pop restaurant owned by African Americans that had been flooded up to the counter. Just that week, Stewart's Diner had reopened for business. It was stretching the schedule, Recher knew. But Bush was hungry anyway. He put in an order for red beans and rice.

Bush and the first lady sat on bar stools at the freshly repainted counter while they waited for their order. The president mentioned to the proprietress how encouraging it was to see that the Stewarts were back in business.

"It's all construction workers," Kim Stewart told him. "As soon as they finish with their work, they'll be gone. It's the locals whose business we need. And until they get their homes rebuilt, they're not coming back."

Bush said that he got it.

"If I were still an entrepreneur, I'd go to the Gulf and start a business," Bush often said to his aides. The Texan had an affinity for plucky if laid-back southern folks like the Stewarts—and they, it seemed, for him. He now made a point of visiting the Lower Ninth Ward on every trip to New Orleans. They seemed to appreciate his presence, his hugs and assurances that the city would come back. And no one got in his face and blamed him for the whole mess.

He returned for the anniversary of Katrina on the eve of August 29. Recovery, not recrimination, was the message of the trip. And so he gave an address at Easton High School, which until three weeks before the president's visit did not have electricity and was filled with moldy books and rotting furniture. (The Secret Service descended to lend an assist with debris removal.) He broke bread at the Lower Ninth Ward's Musicians' Village, where there had been no running water until it magically came on just a few days before Bush's arrival. All across the Lower Ninth, wrecked houses that had lain fallow for a year suddenly hummed with the sounds of saws and power drills.

Bush sat that morning with Laura in the pews of St. Louis Cathedral in Jackson Square. The building hadn't been hit by the hurricane, so it didn't have quite the story to it that the advance team had been seeking. Still, it was the most photogenic New Orleans church not still in disrepair. The advance boys tweaked the atmospherics by filling the grand sanctuary with suitably ordinary folks who had never attended a service at St. Louis before. The Stewarts were there—and as were all the other African American residents who worked at the diner, along with several members of their families. A Cajun fellow named Rockey Vacarella, who had driven from Louisiana to Washington in a FEMA trailer (though it turned out to be a replica of a FEMA trailer) to thank the president for his support, had also shown up. And seated to Bush's left were Ethel Williams and her daughter Wanda, residents of the Lower Ninth whose hurricane-damaged house had been awaiting recovery assistance, along with tens of thousands of other residents. But the Williamses had gotten lucky: Bush had met them during a previous visit and had enjoyed his banter with them. Now they sat in the front pew.

"I hear your roof's coming up this week," Bush confided to Ethel.

The woman hadn't known that her house was suddenly, after all this time, slotted for rehabilitation. Such a coincidence! And it amazed her that the president of the United States took the time to know such things.

After the sermon and the singing and the laying on of hands, a gigantic black man who had lost most of his vision was led up to Bush's pew. The two men embraced. "God bless you, Ernie," the president said to Ernie Ladd, the former Houston Oiler defensive end for whom Bush had worked at Project PULL in the early 1970s. He knew that Ladd had cancer and added, "God's going to watch over you."

It was an uplifting service, and the only thing missing from it were Reverend Thomas Brown and the other congregants of Union Bethel African Methodist Episcopal Church. Many of them now lived in a FEMA trailer park outside Baton Rouge—though the vast majority of that erstwhile church family remained scattered across the country, with nothing remaining from their former life to draw them back to New Orleans. The Office of Faith-Based and Community Initiatives had the Reverend's number, just as USA Freedom Corps had Tenisha Stevens's contact information. But neither of them received an invitation to the service.

God would watch over them, too, of course. But not the White House. The story was now recovery. Union Bethel, alas, did not fit the narrative.

Optimism, turning the corner, recovery—this was the upbeat election-year message, and at times the facts seemed thoroughly cooperative. The economy was just as an incumbent party would wish it to be: high job creation, low inflation, a soaring Dow Jones. On June 7, the American military scored a major victory when Al Qaeda's brutal leader in Iraq, the Jordanian Abu Musab Al-Zarqawi, was killed by two five-hundred-pound bombs.

Later that month, one of Bush's favorite foreign counterparts, Japanese Prime Minister Junichiro Koizumi, dropped into Washington for a visit. Hadley and Hagin approached Bush with a novel, feel-good spin to the trip. Koizumi was an Elvis Presley fanatic. Why not surprise him with a trip to Graceland?

"Are y'all serious?" Bush laughed. As it developed, the logistics required tipping off Koizumi in advance. Nonetheless, on June 30, Air Force One served the Elvis staple banana-and-peanut-butter sandwiches and piped in the King's music as POTUS and the PM flew to Memphis. At Graceland, Koizumi seized a microphone and proceeded to croon a few bars while Bush stood back and winced and a Memphis businessman whispered into Joe Hagin's ear, "Y'all have an unusual existence."

Three weeks later, Bush gave an address to the NAACP. He had been at war with the African American organization since the 2000 campaign, when the NAACP ran anti-Bush ads using footage of James Byrd, the East Texas black man who had been dragged to death by white supremacists. Offended by what he termed "name-calling" on the part of its leadership, Bush refused invitations to speak at the NAACP conventions each year beginning with 2001. Though no good could come from snubbing the NAACP a few months before the midterm elections, Bush adamantly refused to swallow his pride and reward with his presence an organization that had insulted him.

But the NAACP's new president, Bruce Gordon, took it upon himself to open a dialogue with Bush. Out of respect for Gordon—and not wishing to become the first president since Hoover never to speak before the NAACP—he made the one-mile trip to the Washington Convention Center on July 20. The reception for him was respectful, for the most part. But as Bush would reflect later, "It's very interesting when I proposed ideas that basically liberate people, such as that if you're trapped in a failed school you ought to go somewhere else, or a personal retirement account so that you can have your own assets—it's like, total silence."

The day before his speech, Bush also avoided becoming the first president in modern times not to exercise his veto power. The bill he chose to veto pushed the envelope on embryonic stem-cell research. The public largely favored such research. But Bush had come up with his formulation in the summer of 2001—research on existing stem lines only—and was sticking to it . . . and, in so doing, he avoided another revolt from the base.

All this was good news, politically speaking. And to promote it, Bush was now out there with uncustomary frequency. Josh Bolten made it a point to put press conferences on the schedule wherever possible. "You're good at this stuff," he would remind the president— who, Bolten believed, had spent his first term convinced that the White House press corps was trying to prod him into making a mis- statement. *It's in our body language—we LOOK like we're hunkering down, trying to get by with the minimum*, Bolten told Bush and Bartlett. The more press conferences they did, the new chief believed, the more conversational and less "gotcha" they became. The viewing public still wasn't seeing the George W. Bush who effortlessly charmed the firefighters and businessmen and killed-in-action fami- lies he met in intimate, unscripted moments.

But, Bolten thought, the gap was closing. And that was cause for optimism.

Still, the world outside America veered off message.

In January, the Palestinian voters had their say—and overwhelm- ingly elected to Parliament the Hamas party, which the Bush admin- istration had repeatedly condemned as a terrorist organization. The precarious balance in that region collapsed in June, when Hamas militants captured an Israeli soldier, prompting the latter govern- ment to launch retaliatory airstrikes. When Hezbollah to the north provoked the Israelis with airstrikes of its own, the Israeli army invaded Lebanon—a violation of the UN charter that exacerbated hostilities throughout the Arab world.

Bush was certain that these were proxy conflicts waged by Syria and Iran on Israel. But he enjoyed no leverage over either country—par- ticularly Iran, whose president, Mahmoud Ahmadinejad, had declared in April, "I am officially announcing that Iran joined the group of those countries which has nuclear technology." Eleven months prior, in the early flush of Bush's Freedom Agenda, Pete Wehner had distributed a gleeful memo that read, in part, "I suspect that by the end of the President's second term, the region will look vastly different than it did at the beginning of his first term." That prediction was threatening to come true.

In March, Bush made a surprise visit to Afghanistan, the crown jewel in the Freedom Agenda. "We're impressed by the progress that your country is making, Mr. President," Bush said to Hamid Karzai during his five-hour stay behind the walls of the presidential palace. Even as he did so, the director of the Defense Intelligence Agency was testifying to the Senate Armed Services Committee that Afghanistan was being rocked by insurgents to a degree not seen since the U.S. invasion in 2001. The Taliban was regrouping, and the nation's future was increasingly uncertain.

These events, along with North Korea's test-firing of six missiles that summer, did not make for an optimistic G-8 summit in July. Bush remained Bush, however, steadfastly pushing his Freedom Agenda while describing his meeting with the summit's host, Vladimir Putin, in a press conference. "I talked about my desire to promote institutional change in parts of the world, like Iraq, where there's a free press and free religion," Bush said pointedly to reporters. "And I told him that a lot of people in our country would hope that Russia would do the same."

The droll Russian leader saw the softball coming, and he whacked it out of the park. "We certainly would not want to have the same kind of democracy that they have in Iraq, quite honestly," Putin deadpanned.

21

"I Owe You a Strategy That'll Work"

"It's kind of sad. She's being used."

Bush made the comment while staring out a window of the residence at Cindy Sheehan, who was staging yet another protest beyond the White House gates. No Baby Boomer, including Bush, could escape the tableau's haunting familiarity. But one did not speak of it in the West Wing. One did not mention Johnson, or Nixon. One took pains never to utter the dreaded V-word. One took pains to shout it down—to invoke, if historical comparison was required, World War II.

Yet that was the Greatest Generation's war, not Bush's. For better or for worse, his life experience was informed by a messier conflict. At Yale, he once observed that era's Cindy Sheehans with wry bemusement: "I used to always wonder about people who always worried about nuclear war, trying to imagine what it would be like to walk around thinking, 'A bomb's gonna hit.' I always try to enjoy myself. I never try to be so heavy that I can't see the bright side. I'm an optimist. . . . Only later, the more I heard about how the Vietnam War was conducted, the more disillusioned I got. It was more of the fact that the soldiers weren't allowed to fight. We put people in harm's way, and it was a political war."

He was determined that the battle of Iraq not be waged politically—and, without mentioning either LBJ or Vietnam, Bush repeatedly told aides, "I'm not gonna pull out a map and look at targets." He left that to his generals. At times, during his hundreds of hours' worth of video conferences with commanders on the ground in Iraq, Bush would be probing: *Is the strategy working? What are your military counterparts doing? Do you have enough troops?* At other times, those who attended the conferences with Bush found the commander in chief overly deferential, and not terribly attuned to the specifics—nothing at all like the hyperkinetic president who steered domestic-policy meetings. *Do we need to win? Can we win? Are we winning?* Sometimes, Bush's interrogation of his generals extended no further.

His aides also observed a level of communication that seemed less than forthright. Listening to the generals drone on—*Mr. President, let me just say that the men and women of your armed forces have the greatest confidence in this mission*—Bob Blackwill and Condi Rice used to exchange disheartened glances, after which Blackwill would mutter to her, "Same briefing—it's like *Groundhog Day.*" That was in 2004. But by 2006, Josh Bolten would be thinking more or less the same thing—wondering, as he heard the generals' bravado, whether there was something in military culture that discouraged the delivery of bad news.

In fact, to the degree that such a resistance existed, at least some high-ranking officers understood its consequences. General Hugh Shelton, former chairman of the Joint Chiefs of Staff, once handed out copies of H. R. McMaster's *Dereliction of Duty* to his fellow Joint Chiefs and other Pentagon officials. McMaster's account of the military's costly refusal to admit mistakes, which Bush himself had read, was something Shelton did not wish to see repeated.

Then again, Shelton and his Joint Chiefs were, as Rumsfeld would say, "Clinton's generals."

Ironically, Dick Cheney had been secretary of defense during the first Gulf War and had been among the civilians who showed no hesitation in revising the military's tactics, often to successful effect. By 2006, the Office of the Vice President was showing far less interest in postwar Iraq than it had in building the case for war. Even as he publicly touted the administration's accomplishments in Iraq with his usual unflappable self-certainty, Dick Cheney found himself ruminating over mistakes made. Chief among them, he thought, was the decision to bring in Jerry Bremer and the Coalition Provisional Authority. Had the White House set up a provisional government before the invasion, the transfer of power would surely have been executed with greater dispatch. This was, of course, what Doug Feith and Ahmed Chalabi's Iraqi National Congress had recommended all along. Cheney regretted that the opinion jointly held by the State

Department and the NSC—namely, that Iraqi exiles would have no legitimacy in the eyes of the Iraqi public—had carried the day.

Cheney was forgetting who had been immovable in the belief that Iraqis should choose their own leader. It wasn't Colin Powell or Condi Rice. It was George W. Bush.

Bush, for his part, was not disposed to second-guessing. Throughout 2006, he read historical texts relating to Lincoln, Churchill, and Truman—three wartime leaders, the latter two of whom left office to something less than public acclaim. History would acquit him, too. Bush was confident of that, and of something else as well. Though it was not the sort of thing one could say publicly anymore, the president still believed that Saddam had possessed weapons of mass destruction. He repeated this conviction to Andy Card all the way up until Card's departure in April 2006, almost exactly three years after the Coalition had begun its fruitless search for WMDs.

Returning to a favorite trick play, Bush flew in utmost secrecy to Baghdad to meet Iraq's new leader.

As always, the clandestine trip was an operational masterpiece—even after the intended visitation date, Memorial Day weekend, fell through when Iraq's new government failed to gel. Tony Blair's recent visit to Baghdad had leaked out moments after Iraqi officials were informed. Hagin learned from the UK's mistake. The new prime minister, Nouri al-Maliki, was not informed that the president was coming until a few minutes before they shook hands on June 13, 2006.

For several months, the Bush administration had been focused on standing up a unified Iraqi government, with the hope that stability would follow. That strategy had been imperiled by the rise of sectarian militias—Sunni and Shiite confederations attacking each other and, at times, Coalition troops. The bombing of the Shia mosque in Samarra on February 22 was immediately followed by a week-long spasm of Shia-led retaliatory violence that left hundreds dead. Then things grew quiet; as Hadley had put it, Iraq "looked into the abyss and stepped back." Not far enough, however: The cycle of violence was intensifying by late May, and Hadley's deputy in charge of Iraq, Meghan O'Sullivan, wondered aloud if the Iraqi government to which the White House had devoted so much energy had ceased to be of any consequence.

So concerned were Bush's national security principals that they suggested a summit at Camp David in early June to rethink their entire Iraq strategy. But when Maliki at last selected his cabinet, that plan was scrapped. "My thinking was that the country has finally got a government under a new constitution that took about thee months to do this and finally got it together, and my job is to inspire and encourage the new government," Bush would say. And so the Camp David summit became the ruse employed to head-fake the press while Bush quietly made his way to Baghdad.

Maliki "said all the right things," Bush would remember. He didn't grill the new prime minister, though Maliki's close affiliation with clerical strongman Moktada al-Sadr was well known. And he chose to see the best in the new cabinet members, despite their inexperience. "Many were articulate, smart, capable—although I think the Sadr people weren't there," Bush recalled.

In front of the media that morning, Bush said to his Iraqi counterpart, "I'm impressed by the strength of your character and your desire to succeed. And I'm impressed by your strategy."

"What I didn't realize at the time," Bush would later say, "was how hard it was to go from words to action."

After Bush met with Maliki and his cabinet, Bush delivered an address to a gathering of troops behind the walls of the Green Zone. His language was confident if subtly tapered. Without irony, he referred to "the mission that you're now accomplishing"; with notable somberness, he acknowledged that "long deployments are tough— they're tough on you and they're tough on your families." And when he worked the rope line after the speech, he heard poignant exhortations from the soldiers that no one would have thought to utter during his last visit less than three years ago.

Hang in there, they told Bush. *You're doing the right thing. It's getting better. . . .*

Even when the optimism was drowned out by the clamor of militia death squads throughout the summer of 2006, the thinking of the Bush White House was: *It's a new government. Look how WE were in early 2001, even with institutions and expertise in place.* And in any event, Bush thought it important to resist the damning nomenclature of "civil war." The words made a difference, he told his new chief of staff Bolten. *The American people signed up for liberating the people of Iraq, getting rid of a tyrant with weapons of mass destruction—not getting caught up in a civil war. As soon as it gets labeled that way, public support's going to erode.*

"I'm concerned," Bush said one August day in the Roosevelt Room to a gathering that included Hadley, Bolten, Cheney, Rumsfeld, and Generals Abizaid and Casey along with Zal Khalilzad by secure video teleconference. "I've got to make a better case to the American people about the mistakes we've made and about how we're going to turn this around."

He was concerned about the message, but also the realities. "Do we have enough forces to deal with both the sectarian militias and Al Qaeda?" Bush wanted to know.

Abizaid and Casey were emphatic: *Yes, sir. We do.*

Bush kept pressing. "What is the average Iraqi's life like?" he said.

Khalilzad piped up: *Six million Iraqis now have cell phones, most neighborhoods have electrical power now . . .*

Bush returned to the generals, pelting them with questions about Maliki and the militias. Cheney felt compelled to offer the mollifying words—*We stand behind you 100 percent*—but Bush firmly cut in: "You understand why we have to ask these tough questions. Because I've got to be confident in the strategy, and I can't be confident unless I ask."

Still, thought Philip Zelikow, Condi Rice's State Department counsel who was attending in her stead, the meeting had a frustratingly discursive quality. Zelikow was not surprised when nothing came of it.

Meanwhile, Baghdad burned.

Maliki's security strategy that Bush had applauded in June was pronounced a failure by late July. Two of Iraq's security brigades had failed to show up. On August 1, the Coalition announced a second security plan, Operation Together Forward II. That, too, would fail, as a result of Iraqi forces refusing to crack down on al-Sadr's Mahdi militia and preventing Coalition forces from arresting key Shia death-squad leaders.

But the American public would not hear about plans gone awry. Coinciding with the five-year anniversary of 9/11, the White House rolled out a grim new election-year message: the Nature of the Enemy. On September 5 at the Capital Hilton, Bush did something he ordinarily resisted, quoting lavishly from leaders other than himself—in this case, bin Laden, al-Zawahiri, and al-Zarqawi—to underscore that they, and therefore their sworn enemy, should take seriously the stakes in Iraq. "This third world war is raging in [Iraq]," was among the bin Laden support material Bush cited. Two days later, at a speech in Atlanta, he repeated the bin Laden line. And on the evening of September 11, 2006—following two days of wearing black, commiserating with first responders, and laying wreaths at the three crash sites of the hijacked airplanes—Bush used that awful anniversary not to talk about hope, as he had done two weeks earlier in New Orleans to commemorate the Katrina anniversary . . . but instead to issue a dire warning, during a prime-time Oval Office address: "Whatever mistakes have been made in Iraq, the worst mistake would be to think that if we pulled out, the terrorists would leave us alone. They will not leave us alone. They will follow us. The safety of America depends on the outcome of the battle in the streets of Baghdad."

The Democrats were adamant to make November 2006 a referendum on Bush and Iraq. Bush intended to give them what they wanted. "Let's punch back," he had said when his aides discussed with him how to handle the October release of Bob Woodward's third Bush-related book, *State of Denial*. Woodward's first of the three, the 9/11-related *Bush at War*, had been endorsed so enthusiastically by the White House that Karen Hughes instructed Rumsfeld to sit for interviews with the *Washington Post* reporter after the SecDef indicated his preference not to do so. Woodward's second release, *Plan of Attack*, was slightly less flattering, but still relied so heavily on the vantage points of Bush and other key officials that the White House saw no choice but to embrace it, even going so far as to recommend it to readers on the Bush campaign's website.

For *State of Denial*, the White House punched back, as ordered. Bartlett took the first swings on Sunday, October 1, when he appeared on Bob Schieffer's and George Stephanopoulos's shows to rebut some of the book's passages—asserting on the latter program that Woodward "had already formulated some conclusions even before the interviewing began." Then Tony Snow's press shop proceeded to grind out lengthy memos with headings like "Setting the Record Straight: Bob Woodward." When Woodward then went on Tim Russert's show to defend his book from the White House's rebuttals, the White House press office followed with another point-by-point counterattack: "Setting the Record Straight: Bob Woodward on *Meet the Press*."

Josh Bolten hadn't read Woodward's book, but he was personally offended by its title and by what he regarded as factual inaccuracies he'd seen in the published excerpts. He was glad to see the president out there. But the sale wasn't being made, Bolten believed. They had become wedded to the belief that a show of doubt undercut Bush's ability to lead. That approach had to be modified, Josh Bolten believed. And in early October, the chief of staff began telling that to Rove and Bartlett: *We need him to make the case—but also to acknowledge our OWN internal disappointment.* In other words: demonstrate the absence of a state of denial.

Bartlett took it from there. He got Bush to agree to a press conference—never an easy feat. Then the counselor wrote a draft statement fulfilling Bolten's pitch for "acknowledgment" of the poor showing in Iraq. The president read it two nights before the October 11 press conference as he flew home from a fund-raiser aboard Air Force One. After reading it aloud to some of the staffers on the plane, Bush proceeded to mock its sentiment: *Oh woe is us, the hand-wringers have come out, the pro-defeat team is here, might as well just pack up and leave.* . . . Hagin and others joined in with the taunts. No one challenged the president's visceral distaste for Bartlett's proposed statement.

Still, Bush slept on the matter. The next morning, Bolten showed up in the Oval Office with a marked-up version of Bartlett's statement. He told the president that he thought Bartlett had the right idea. Bush agreed to look at Bolten's edits. Then Bush got out his own pen.

On the day of the press conference, Bush greeted the gaggle with an observation that the federal budget deficit had been halved. He reiterated his determination that North Korea's nuclear program be confronted through diplomatic channels. Then he turned to Iraq. "The situation is difficult in Iraq, no question about it," Bush said. Despite the violence there, Bush took pains to point out that "important political developments are also taking place" and rattled off several gambits initiated by the Maliki administration. "I fully understand the American people are seeing unspeakable violence on their TV screens," he continued. "These are tough times in Iraq. The enemy is doing everything within its power to destroy the government and to drive us out of the Middle East, starting with driving us out of Iraq before the mission is done. The stakes are high. As a matter of fact, they couldn't be higher. If we were to abandon that country before the Iraqis can defend their young democracy, the terrorists would take control of Iraq and establish a new safe haven from which to launch new attacks on America. How do I know that would happen? Because that's what the enemy has told us would happen. That's what they have said. . . ."

In the blink of an eye, Bush had gone from Acknowledgment to Nature of the Enemy. As a result, the tonal shift itself went largely unacknowledged.

*   *   *

But something else was acknowledged that month.

"I owe you a strategy that'll work," General John Abizaid said to Bush around the time of his October 11 press conference.

The president would not let on publicly that his CENTCOM commander was now conceding that the Coalition was pursuing a losing strategy in Iraq. "At this point in time in a campaign, like in mid-October," Bush would say, "you don't want to be making decisions that appear to be political. I was very conscious about any personnel and/or strategy decisions made while I was campaigning. I want our military to know that any decision I made would be a thoughtful decision, not a political one, based upon succeeding.

"I'm driven a lot by—in my mind exists many of the conversations I've had with families. It's replayed quite often. About making sure that their child is not, their memory is not—that the sacrifice is *worth* something, that it's *worth* something going in, that it's *worth* it to promote democracy, that it's *worth* it to see it through. And I feel the same way.

"I often hear those voices. I really do."

22

A Fine Line Between
Realism and Pessimism

"We're gonna hold 'em," the president said of the House and the Senate. It was not so much a prediction as a conviction. By force of his willful optimism, democracy would prevail in Iraq, and Republicans would prevail in November. He did not express doubt once—not in public, not in the Oval Office—because in fact he harbored no doubt. Rove was similarly optimistic. Every day, Rove would trot in the overnights—where the money was being moved, where the polls were trending—and Bush would study them as he would a baseball box score. "I thought we were gonna lose quite a few seats," he would later say. "But I thought we'd be able to hold on, barely."

His hunch fell short even of pseudoscientific. When Pennsylvania Senator Rick Santorum was down by 18 percentage points in the spring, Bush waved off the margin and said, "He's gonna win." He said the same thing in the summer—believing that Santorum, a strong Bush ally, would win in part because Bush announced that he would do all it took to help Santorum . . . which, as turned out, would be limited to raising money and sending Laura to Pennsylvania, since Bush's numbers were worse than even Santorum's in that state.

Bush was less certain about those Republicans who were backpedaling on Iraq. He understood the war's grind on the national psyche. But no one could make him believe that Americans were content to see defeat there. He was going to talk about Iraq, about the Nature of the Enemy, and about the Cut-and-Run Democrats, all the way until November 7.

There were many Republican incumbents—whole regions of them, particularly the Northeast—who wanted no part of Bush and his tough war talk in this dicey election cycle. Being avoided rather than embraced by others of his party was a phenomenon Bush had never encountered before. Still, all of them were happy to receive his fundraising help, and Bush provided $193 million worth of it. And when Ken Mehlman and Sara Taylor did request his presence at rallies, Bush happily obliged.

During the last five weeks of the campaign, he traveled to eighteen states. The language Bush employed was far more direct than his sly verbiage in 2002. Voters, he was now saying, "have got a stark choice." The president had honed the morass of issues down to two: terror and taxes. As to the first: "The stakes are high. The Democrats are the party of cut and run." And then the second issue: "There's no doubt in my mind that if the national Democrats had control of the House or the Senate, they'd raise your taxes."

Meanwhile, Rove, Mehlman, and Taylor were dragging out all the reliable artillery. They assisted incumbents in the Choice, Not Referendum effort to "localize" their races with negative ads about their opponents' political, professional, or personal foibles. They brought in Laura to sprinkle the sugar, Cheney to heave the meat. Most of all, they rallied the GOP's vaunted grassroots apparatus—which, after the last three elections, had attained mythic status, such that Mehlman began to worry that some of his candidates were depending unduly on the sorcery his vaunted 72-Hour Strategy (so named for the eleventh-hour intensity of its get-out-the-vote efforts) to drag them across the finish lines.

Scandals had effectively taken three sure Republican congressional districts—one in Texas, another in Florida, the third in Pennsylvania—off the boards. And yet Bush still brandished his optimism. He campaigned in Pennsylvania for the beleaguered Don Sherwood—"a good guy," he later reflected, "but he got caught up with his mistress." He trusted Jeb's assurances that they would hold the Florida seat recently vacated by Mark Foley, who admitted to inappropriate flirtations with congressional pages. And Bush flew down to Sugarland, Texas, to the district once represented by recently indicted Tom DeLay, and personally instructed the voting public to write in the name of DeLay's replacement candidate, Shelley Sekula-Gibbs, on the ballot. ("I was secretary of state, for a moment.") The Saturday before the election, he asked Mehlman for his prediction. The RNC chair figured that the GOP would lose sixteen seats, one more than was needed to lose control of the House. Bush made an argument for fourteen. Rove meticulously explained to Bolten and others how the boss's gut instinct was borne out by the data. No one in the White House seemed to believe either man.

"Aw, y'all are pessimists," he told Sara Taylor when the political director also forecast that the Democrats would retake the House.

"I'm a realist," she suggested.

Bush pondered that for a moment. "Realist—I like that," he decided. But, he added, "There's a fine line between realism and pessimism."

The line between realism and optimism turned out to be a great deal wider.

After a final mad push—fifteen cities in the last eleven days, the cornball asides about Laura and commonsense non-Washington values blending with the stark choice and the high stakes, until in an instant it was all behind him and his own ballot was duly recorded at the Crawford, Texas, firehouse—George W. Bush flew back to Washington and considered what he had experienced. The crowds, as always, had been huge. And affectionate. Things *seemed* fine. He went upstairs to the residence that afternoon and took a nap.

He woke up with, unaccountably, a bad feeling. "It's not gonna be a good night," he told Laura.

Bush spent it with familiar Election Night faces: Laura, Karl and Darby Rove, Bartlett, Don Evans, Brad Freeman, and Josh Bolten and his girlfriend Dede McClure. Rove was darting in and out, thumbs stabbing at his BlackBerry. He was looking at two early states, Indiana and Kentucky. But the final overall tracking polls weren't encouraging. The early dinner was quiet, bordering on funereal. Shortly before eight, word came in from the bellwether Third Congressional District of Kentucky—represented by five-term veteran Anne Northrup, a staunch Bush supporter for whom the president had campaigned, and whose opponent had tarred her with Bush and Iraq. Northrup was going to lose.

The men retired to Bush's office in the residence and smoked cigars (except for Rove, who was preoccupied with the returns, and Bolten, who couldn't stand cigars). Bush talked with the others about the Republican losers he would miss, and about others who deserved what they were getting.

He was back in bed by eleven.

Though Rove would later administer lipstick to the pig—*We came within 70,000 votes of keeping the House, 2,500 of hanging on to the Senate*—the defensiveness ill suited an administration that had come to power as a result of a 538-vote margin. Yes, it could have been worse, but it was bad enough: The electoral tsunami had hit his presidency. That night the Republicans lost the House by what would turn out to be a margin of 31. By the end of the next day, it would become clear that the Senate had fallen to the Democrats as well. Of the twenty-six GOP candidates who had chosen to stand by Bush's side as he campaigned for them in October and November, more than half of them had lost.

It was Iraq, it was scandal, it was fatigue—Bush thought it was a lot of things. But it was decisive. Matthew Dowd's extinct swing voters had resurrected and swung the other way. The Choice had become a Referendum.

Bush now belonged to the minority.

As the first senior staffer the president saw each morning, Josh Bolten had made it a habit to greet Bush with a formal show of gratitude: "Thank you for the privilege of serving today." Bush usually grunted something halfhearted in reply.

On the morning after the election, Bolten upped the ante. "Thank you for the privilege of serving," he said. *"Even* today."

Bush, the compulsive optimist, replied, *"Especially* today."

The routing of the GOP was not an unexpected development at the White House. Weeks before the election, Bartlett, Rove, Bolten, Hagin, and Joel Kaplan had convened to prepare for the worst. Bolten, as always, pushed for the president to hold a press conference, as a public show of sportsmanship. What few others knew at the time was that Bush would show what a sport he was in rather dramatic fashion.

He would hand Democrats the head of Donald Rumsfeld.

The defense secretary's unpopularity inside Bushworld was almost as fervent as it was outside of it. His cavalier quips (referring to the insurgents as "a few dead-enders," for example) had infuriated the communications shop. Though he had regularly dined with CIA director George Tenet, Rumsfeld openly disapproved of the agency's human intelligence capability—to the point of studying the National Security Act of 1947 to see if he could justify seizing control of the CIA during wartime. Rumsfeld waged bureaucratic war on so many fronts that NSC and State Department staffers could not hope to compete against him. No detail was too petty for Rummy, who daily issued dozens of memos he called "snowflakes" (for their blizzard-like volume) to his frazzled subordinates. At the same time, by 2005 the legendary micromanager had grown noticeably detached from Iraq policymaking, even as he refused to yield an iota of sovereignty.

One evening in April 2006, Bush invited several confidants—Dan Bartlett, Karl Rove, Josh Bolten, Andy Card, Condi Rice, Steve Hadley, Ken Mehlman, Karen Hughes, Margaret Spellings, and Ed Gillespie—to have dinner at the residence. Bush wanted their thoughts on how to buoy the sagging presidency.

Mehlman advised Bush to fire Rumsfeld. The president asked for a show of hands on the matter. Keeping Rumsfeld onboard: The president raised his hand. So did the ever-cautious Hadley. So did Rove, who thought it was a mistake to invite a confirmation hearing for a new defense secretary amid the midterm campaign. So did Bartlett, who shared with Bush the concern that dumping Rumsfeld now would make it appear that the administration was acquiescing to the Rummy-must-go sentiments expressed on April 12 by retired Major General John Batiste and on the following day by retired Major General Charles Swannack. ("My reaction," Bush would recall of the so-called Generals' Revolt, "was, 'No military guy is gonna tell a civilian how to react.'" White House aides who had hoped to see Rumsfeld fired had predicted glumly that the retired generals' remarks would prompt exactly that response from the boss. As one of them would lament, "The moment someone would say 'Fire Donald Rumsfeld,' Donald Rumsfeld would get a new lease on life.") Mehlman, Card, Bolten, Karen, Gillespie, Rice, and Spellings voted the other way. That made it 7–4 for dismissing Donald Rumsfeld.

But Bush's vote was the only one that counted. Rumsfeld stayed on throughout the 2006 campaign season, a potent symbol of intransigence for the Democrats that was sure to cost the GOP in November. Even though Bush understood this and was himself privately acknowledging Rumsfeld's liabilities to his closest aides, he'd made up his mind: no dismissals during the election cycle. To fire Rumsfeld would be to publicly repudiate a strategy that was still playing itself out on the streets of Baghdad.

Even Rumsfeld had come to believe that the strategy wasn't working. He told Bush that progress in Iraq was not going "well enough or fast enough"—a subtle encapsulation that Josh Bolten wrote down and encouraged the president to use on the campaign trail, that he might otherwise appear out of touch with what the public was seeing on its TV screens. (Months later, Rumsfeld would commit that phrase to print in a November 6 classified memo that was eventually leaked to the *New York Times*.) He began to send signals that a shift in strategy might understandably warrant a change in personnel.

The wily Rumsfeld read the writing on the wall. His doctrine of a smaller, stealthier military had been an appealing concept to Bush. But its application to Iraq had helped give rise to the current mess. Administration aides like Rice's counsel Philip Zelikow and Hadley's Iraq expert Meghan O'Sullivan had seen this coming. The deficiencies in the Coalition's fleet, they'd both concluded, had made it possible for the militias to amass power.

When asked if Bush felt in any way ill served by Rumsfeld, or if he believed that Rumsfeld had made crucial mistakes, the president responded both times, "No." He added, "See, every decision's mine." Bush took umbrage at the assertion that he had been deferential to Rumsfeld on the details, saying, "Look, I know what questions to ask. I'm in the sixth year of my presidency. We've already been through one war together." But Bolten, for one, had come to believe that Bush's interactions with the Pentagon in general and Rumsfeld in particular fell short of hands-on and needed to be changed. The chief of staff wondered if Casey and Abizaid's reluctance to ask for more troops from the president bespoke a hesitancy to challenge their superior's doctrine. Challenging Don Rumsfeld's wisdom or sovereignty—not a smart move.

By October 2006, Bush had begun to give ground. Still, he told his advisers, "I'm not making a change unless I'm comfortable with who's replacing him."

The net was not cast far. Robert Gates, Poppy Bush's former CIA director and currently the president of Texas A&M, was the only serious contender—and if he had refused the offer, there was no plan B. A close friend of Bush's from Yale had sat on a board with Gates and was the first to suggest him. When Bush mentioned this to Hadley, who had worked with Gates during 41's administration, the national security adviser responded glowingly. On the morning of Sunday, November 5, Gates—punchy from the previous night's football game against Oklahoma—met Hagin and Bolten in the parking lot of a McGregor, Texas, supermarket, a few miles outside Crawford. Bush spent two hours with him at the ranch. Then the president boarded Air Force One, bound for a campaign event in Nebraska.

Two days later, he stood in the East Room and told the White House press corps that "after a series of thoughtful conversations, Secretary Rumsfeld and I agreed that the timing is right for new leadership at the Pentagon."

On December 15, 2006, his last day as secretary of defense, Donald Rumsfeld sent out a final memo. It read:

"This is my final snowflake—as Secretary of Defense.

"Over the past six years, thousands of these memos have fallen—sometimes in blizzards and flurries and sometimes in cold and lonely isolation.

"Yet—surprising as this may seem to those who may have been buried in the deluge—there are many people in the Department who have never received a snowflake. A few souls have even requested one.

"This snowflake is especially for them.

"Its message is, perhaps typically, to the point: Thank you!

". . . Oh, and one final note. Somewhere there may be a few folks who hoped to run out the clock on their outstanding snowflakes. Well, I want you to know—You have not been forgotten!

"Nonetheless, in the spirit of the season, as my last official act as Secretary of Defense, I hereby grant a general amnesty for any outstanding snowflakes.

"The blizzard is over! Thank you all for all you do for our wonderful country. Well done!"

During the postelection press conference, Bush was generous in his appraisal of the opposition's leadership. "They ran a disciplined campaign," he said. "Their candidates were well organized and did a superb job of turning out their votes."

On the spot, he decided to show a little Acknowledgment. "Look, this was a close election," he told the reporters. "If you look at race by race, it was close. The cumulative effect, however, was not too close. It was a thumpin'."

Over and over, Bush pledged to work with the leaders of the new majority, Harry Reid and Nancy Pelosi. CBS's veteran reporter Ann Compton called him on it. "Americans have heard it before," she pointed out. "There's going to be cooperation, we're going to get along. What can you do to show Americans that there—that you'll stop and avoid any gridlock?"

"Well," Bush replied, "we had some pretty good successes early on in this administration. We got the No Child Left Behind Act passed, which was an important part of bipartisan legislation. We got some tax cuts passed with Democrat votes."

But Bush could not think of any example to cite from the years 2002 through 2006.

One of Bush's favorite reporters from Austin, Cox Newspapers' Ken Herman, asked him if "after six years in the Oval Office, you're out of touch with America for something like this kind of wave to come and you not expect it? And on a somewhat related note, does Nancy Pelosi look much like Bob Bullock to you?"

Bush laughed appreciatively. "That's an inside joke, I'm not commenting on it," he said. As for being out of touch, the president demurred in characteristic fashion.

"I'm an optimistic person, is what I am."

Clinton had spoken to him several times after the election. The predecessor reminded Bush that *his* most productive years had come at the end of his presidency.

And he had dined with the new House Speaker, Nancy Pelosi, along with majority leader Steny Hoyer, two days after the Thumpin'. Both had been very gracious and noncombative, seemingly eager to work with Bush on the nation's business. Reauthorization of No Child Left Behind, increasing the minimum wage, a comprehensive immigration package, entitlement reform—he could see a chance for a constructive relationship . . . assuming, of course, that Pelosi and Harry Reid intended to show America that Democrats knew how to lead, instead of just obstructing, in which case Bush would spend his last two years in office hammering the obstructionists on the campaign trail instead of getting work done.

In candid moments, Bush would concede that being a Uniter was one of those "process" things—a nice aspiration, maybe even the right thing to do . . . but not the end game. Perhaps, Bush said, he could do a better job of reaching out to Democrats. *But*. "The way I look at it, we got a whole lot done," he would say. "A *whole* lot done. The legislative success here has been fantastic! Should we have tried to do a 380-to-whatever victory as opposed to a 2-vote victory? I don't know. All I can tell you is: Medicare reform, trade, taxes, No Child Left Behind. I mean, we got a *lot* done! So what matters is the results, rather than whether or not everybody's feeling good about each other. I'm a results guy."

Democrats, of course, had come to discover this about him. "I had a [Democratic] member actually tell me, 'I'm not going to help you on entitlement reforms, because you'll use it to defeat our candidates.' And we'd defeated their candidates in the past, in 2002. Guy had a pretty good point."

Bush knew that it wasn't 2001 anymore. Still, he suggested, "Hopefully they'll see that we've got a position of responsibility, and why don't we show the American people we can work with the president and get things done."

That was the bright side. It was not so hard to see, really—unless one was looking at Iraq.

In early December, the Iraq Study Group delivered its report. The bipartisan panel led by Jim Baker and Lee Hamilton had spent the year receiving alarming reports from the CIA and other information sources that contrasted sharply with the administration's public rhetoric. "A lot of us kept looking at each other wondering if the situation might collapse before we had a chance to make any recommendations," one of the members, former Clinton chief of staff Leon Panetta, would say.

Throughout its investigation in 2006, the group met with Bush on several occasions. They found him engaged but far more upbeat than the realities in Iraq seemed to warrant. The strategy was working, Bush informed them in June, just after returning from his secret trip to Baghdad. On several occasions, he predicted to them that Iraq would be judged by history to be a success. Just as repeatedly, Bush invoked Truman's rehabilitation by historians. It occurred to one member of the group that the president did not so much want to hear their views as "convince us that we should be writing a report that would reflect *his* views."

At the end of August 2006, the Iraq Study Group flew to Baghdad. By then, the second Baghdad security plan was floundering. The members met with Prime Minister Maliki who, in cochairman Hamilton's belief, "didn't give the appearance of being a confident, decisive leader." They also met with the cabinet and found them both ill-equipped to do their jobs and profoundly divided along sectarian lines—not at all the "unity government" that the White House had been publicly extolling.

The group interviewed Generals Casey and Chiarelli and asked whether additional troops in Baghdad were required. Casey was categorical: "We don't need it," he said. Elaborated Chiarelli, "You're not going to win this war at the point of a bayonet. You'll only win it when you meet the Iraqi people's basic needs—water, electricity, food, sanitation, jobs." One group member, former Clinton defense secretary Bill Perry, was so surprised by the generals' unwavering posture that he interviewed them privately. The commanders on the ground repeated the sentiment: A surge of Coalition troops to Baghdad was not the ultimate solution to the sectarian bloodshed in Iraq.

The Iraq Study Group's report did not mince words. "The situation in Iraq is grave and deteriorating," were its opening words. The group's three primary recommendations to the president were that focus be shifted to training, that aid to Iraq be withheld when it failed to meet timetables, and that the Bush administration engage in diplomacy with Syria and Iran.

Bush, Rice, and Hadley had already signaled to the group that they were disinclined to negotiate with Syria and Iran. (Though the member who drafted that portion of the recommendations was Bush family friend Jim Baker.) On the morning of December 6, the president formally received the report from the members. Leon Panetta said to him, "No president can conduct a war with a divided nation and a divided Congress. Whatever you decide to do, it's got to bring the country together."

Bush nodded to Panetta but said nothing.

That same day, he had lunch with Jim Baker. "I'm thinking about these options," he told the group's cochairman. "My question, Jimmy, is: Can we get to where you want us to be without doing something in the meantime?"

Bush was referring to the possibility of a troop increase. And though that had not been among the groups's seventy-nine recommendations—indeed, it had explicitly been rejected—a compromise line in the text had been inserted: "We could, however, support a short-term redeployment or surge of American combat forces to stabilize Baghdad, or to speed up the training and equipping mission, if the U.S. commander in Iraq determines that such steps would be effective." Baker helpfully referred the president to that line on page 73.

"He's the guy who reminded me of whatever page it was," Bush would say.

A few days later, Bush went into the Tank.

The small, secure conference room inside the E-Ring, on the side of the Pentagon that faces the Potomac River, was where the Joint Chiefs of Staff conducted its briefings and was therefore unfamiliar to

Bush. Bush hosted his combatant commanders annually in the Cabinet Room, but never to discuss specific strategy. He had farmed that dialogue out to Rumsfeld, who in turn all but shut out the JCS from war policy.

Now things were changing. Rumsfeld was at the meeting—but so was his successor, Robert Gates. They sat on either side of Bush, facing the chiefs. For the next ninety minutes, the president did something he had never done before: He grilled the military commanders. "Look, I want to win," he told them. "If we have a chance to win this, I want to win. I don't want to minimize our humiliation or our losses. Because I think it's just too important. And I need to know from you how to do it."

The chiefs argued that the war could not be won militarily. Sensitive to the suggestion that the current quagmire bespoke a diplomatic failure, Condi Rice retorted, "But we can't win this thing *without* military assistance."

"We need more forces in the Army overall," said its chief, General Peter Schoomaker. Marine chief General James Conway added that the Marines had the same problem. In saying this, both men were flatly denouncing the Rumsfeld theology.

"I'll consider it," said Bush.

There was a lot to consider, he added. But, Bush informed them, "This review is going to be *my* review. I'm gonna drive it."

Steve Hadley was heartened by what he saw that day in the Tank. He believed that Bush's legacy was inextricably tied to Iraq's outcome. The one regret Bush's national security adviser didn't want the boss to have was that he had ceded control of his own legacy. He had said as much to Bush recently: *Mr. President, you've got to run it.*

A step ahead of him, Bush had replied, "I *am* running it!"

And his first decision, in running the review of Iraq, was to do something that absolutely went against his grain, but that Josh Bolten and others had persuaded him was the right thing to do: Bush would postpone his address to the nation on the war in Iraq until after the holidays. The Iraq Study Group had said it, and against the grain of his optimism, he could no longer deny it: "The situation in Iraq is grave and deteriorating."

He had a lot of listening and thinking to do.

By now, Bartlett was an old hand at such matters. Knowing that at Bush's end-of-the-year press conference the president would be hammered with questions about whether we were winning the war in

Iraq, the counselor decided to let the air out of the matter. He contacted the *Washington Post* and offered up a half-hour exclusive interview with the president for December 19, the day before the press conference.

In the Oval Office, the *Post* reporters obligingly asked the question. Bush had his reply, an echo of the recent congressional testimony of General Peter Pace: "We're not winning. We're not losing."

And so the year ended as the preceding year had, with Acknowledgment.

It was one of those things a person knew not to ask Bush: *What will you do when you retire?* Like what he thought of polls, or if he harbored regrets, or if he could do something over again, or how he believed history would regard his presidency. He just did not dwell in those nebulous strata. He focused on the here and now, stuck to Big Ideas and small comforts, rode his bike and slept well.

Plus, he wasn't done yet. "I don't think you're ever a lame duck as president," he would say . . . somewhat in defiance of the facts that he had lost control over his own base, his party was in a state of serious reassessment, the Democrats had no intention of making things easy on him, and the war he had chosen to wage was spinning badly out of control—sucking the oxygen out of his presidency, as Colin Powell had warned. If ever a scenario existed for lame-duckhood, it was now.

But then there was that bright side, the inextinguishable verity that George W. Bush had made a handy career out of being "misunderestimated." And anyway: Here he was on a December morning, feeling pretty lousy from a flu—he'd been puking all day yesterday, which was the day of his press conference—and looking frankly like a man who had spent the night before on a park bench . . . but Christmas at Camp David was only four days away, and he had all those stupid-ass holiday gatherings at the White House behind him (no wonder he was sick), and plenty of time to reflect on how to reverse the bloody tide in Iraq while getting in some excellent single-track bike rides. Today was a very light day, almost pre-9/11 in its breeziness: no public events at all, just a dental appointment and a few briefings. He sat in the Oval Office that morning, with "my man Barney" waddling in and out, congested and puffy-eyed, but hey, things could always be worse. . . . And sure, yeah, why not engage in that devil's craft of the hypothetical, imagining himself retired. To tell the truth, no one had ever asked him about it before.

"I'm gonna build a fantastic Freedom Institute," he said as he sat cross-legged in a chair. "And today the news got out that we're negotiating with SMU. I would like to build a Hoover Institute, but with a different feel to it. I want a place where young leaders—you know, the former prime minister of Mongolia, it'd be cool to pay him a stipend, have him come live in Dallas and write and lecture."

Bush admitted that he would like to make some money—"replenish the ol' coffers," as he put it. He could make "ridiculous" money on the lecture circuit. "I don't know what my dad gets. But it's more than fifty, seventy-five. . . . Clinton's making a lot of money."

He would continue reading books, of course. Never watched TV—other than football, and baseball set to low volume while he read—and had no plans to start. Bush often invited historians to the White House to talk about "history, all kinds of stuff. And they bring me their books, and if I get fascinated by them as individuals, then I want to read what their book's about. . . . Laura used to say to the girls, 'When you read, your mind can wander. You can go to distant places. Magically leave.' And you know, I'm beginning to say, 'Yeah, she's right.' "

He could see shuttling between Dallas and Crawford. "Laura's gonna want to spend a lot of time in Dallas," he said. "It's a two-hour drive. I can just envision getting in the car, getting bored, going down to the ranch."

He would be a mere sixty-two and, God willing, still in great shape, still able to sustain a heart rate of 140 during ninety minutes of biking—and hopefully, as he heard someone say once, still on track to "die young as late as possible." How the days would hold his interest after the unceasing adrenaline rush of the world's most powerful office . . . hard to imagine. Very hard and perhaps better not to dwell on. For yes, his Freedom Institute would keep him in the game—he saw it vaguely as "an institute that really, you know, just kind of imparts knowledge and deals with big issues"—but there was really only one game, with one desk, as he knew better than anyone except four other living men. And how an adrenaline-and-Big-Ideas junkie like George W. Bush would deal with the sudden, everlasting loss of that role was unknowable. Backpedal twenty years: He was a father and he was sober and otherwise had nothing whatsoever to show for himself. If they'd taken a poll of his prospects *then*?

For a man so reliant on predictability, he was the best available proof that the unknowable was really all you could rely upon.

Though here was something:

On September 19, 2006, Bush flew to New York to give his annual address to the UN. Bill Clinton happened to be in the building as well. And, as the White House advance team noticed, the former president seemed to be lingering in the corridors, aimlessly chatting with whomever, as if waiting . . . waiting . . .

Waiting for Bush, who motorcaded up to the UN building with the usual press entourage. And there inside the doorway, 43 ran into 42, and the two fell into pleasant conversation in full view of the TV cameras. All of which made the evening news, leading some White House aides to speculate uncharitably that this was another case of Clinton craving just one more tanning session in the executive limelight. One of them shared this belief later with Bush, who chose not to take a swipe at a brother in his elite and lonely fraternity.

But he did say, accompanied by the world's most famous semismirk, "Six years from now, you're not gonna see *me* hanging out in the lobby of the UN."

EPILOGUE

On January 16, 2007—six days after speaking to the nation about his new strategy for Iraq and seven days before delivering his State of the Union address—George W. Bush found time to meet with the World Series champion St. Louis Cardinals.

Receiving winning sports teams at the White House has long been a presidential ritual—a camera-ready opportunity to bask in reflected glory, and to gas on about teamwork and perseverance and other such virtues. Bush had given many such testimonials. But the day's tribute to the Cardinals was atypical in its poignancy.

He stood in the East Room of the residence, with a backdrop of muscular young men in coats and ties, and after a few icebreaking yuk-yuks he began to talk about the many losing streaks the Cardinals had endured throughout 2006. "When you're on one of those losing streaks," Bush said as he turned away from his notes and addressed the players, "it's easy to get down and to forget the goal. So, like, I'm sure the sports pages were a little rough on you for a while there, you know? Well, you endure it, as the result of character and leadership."

Bush then said that he had met with the team's manager, Tony LaRussa, in August—a month that the Cardinals began with an eight-game losing streak and the Bush administration began with its second failed Baghdad security plan. After chatting with LaRussa that day at the White House, Bush now said, "I was convinced the Cardinals were going to go all the way. You know why? Because *he* was. Because *he believed it*. And I appreciate good leadership."

Tony LaRussa had been dead certain of victory. And it had paid off.

Bush had elected to confront the violence in Baghdad with a surge of 21,500 troops—or, as he would say later, "We call it 'the reinforcement,' because words take on meaning." So does setting, and Bush's aides were quite fretful over the visuals for the January 10 prime-time address. Should he stand or sit? The Oval Office or the Map Room? Walking past the latter locale, Laura Bush observed the starkness of the rear wall. "That's not a good picture," she said, and pointed to the grandfather clock—which would either be ticking while Bush spoke or not be ticking, and neither of these scenarios was an attractive metaphor. Laura then suggested the Library, which ultimately was where Bush delivered his speech that evening—standing up, blinking at the teleprompter, and speaking in the self-consciously formal manner he tended to employ whenever there was no live audience with which he could interact.

The speech was more explicit on Acknowledgment ("The situation in Iraq is unacceptable to the American people—and it is unacceptable to me") and Responsibility ("Where mistakes have been made, the responsibility rests with me") than any of his previous addresses. Gone were the lofty allusions to the Freedom Agenda. Instead, Bush characterized Iraq as a "young democracy that is fighting for its life," and which, even in victory, "will not be perfect. But it will be a country that fights terrorists instead of harboring them."

In opting for the Surge/Reinforcement, Bush was ignoring the advice of the bipartisan Iraq Study Group. Hours before the speech, Steve Hadley briefed the group on its contents and told them, "We've actually adopted the thrust of the recommendations."

"Wait a minute," said Leon Panetta. "There are three main recommendations," and he then listed them: transitioning from a combat to a support role; making economic aid conditional to the Iraqi government's keeping its promises; and broadening diplomatic efforts to include Iran and Syria. From Hadley's briefing, it was clear to Panetta and others in the group that Bush had rejected all of these—and instead was embarking on a principally military solution, which they had explicitly warned against.

Well, except—and Hadley and others in the White House would come to know the citation by heart—*If you look at page 73 in the report, "We could, however, support a short-term redeployment or surge. . . ."*

But the Iraq Study Group wasn't Bush's problem. A Gallup poll taken after his speech indicated that only 38 percent of the American public approved of his new strategy. And for the first time in Gallup's surveying of the matter, a plurality of Americans, 47–49 percent, believed that the United States was likely to lose the war. Bush had failed to rally the public—and in turn, the new Democratic majority vowed to curtail the president's Iraq initiative, even to the point of revoking the 2002 use-of-force authorization.

The Democratic leadership had received him graciously for his January 23, 2007, State of the Union address—a relief to Bush, who had braced himself for a chillier environment. (In an early draft of the speech, Bartlett had inserted the line, *Tonight I ask for your attention rather than your applause*—anticipating, of course, that there would be none of the latter anyway.) "I wasn't sure, going in, about what the reaction would be," he said later. "After it was over, I think I congratulated the Speaker: 'Thank you, Nancy, for you and your membership treating me so cordially'—I said that when I turned around. Spent more time getting out of the hall than any of the other addresses. Signed a lot of autographs. After it was over, there were a lot of compliments for the speech—probably more than any since September 21," referring to the post-9/11 address to the Joint Session of Congress that had redefined George W. Bush, until the fallout from Iraq had redefined him once more.

The clock could not be turned back to the 2001 era of good feelings. Bush was now, and would likely remain until the end of his tenure, a highly unpopular and divisive president, and the show of civility on Capitol Hill was only that. (As an indicator that the cordial atmosphere had been choreographed, the Democratic members faithfully stood and applauded whenever Speaker Pelosi did.) Similar courtesies were extended when Bush showed up at the Democratic caucus's retreat in Williamsburg, Virginia, on February 3. The president sounded all the right notes about "the big things I'd like to see us try to accomplish." Still, the Democratic leadership had designated certain members to ask Bush less than genial questions at the end of his speech, once the reporters were ushered out of the hall.

Congressman Bennie Thompson of Mississippi expressed his chagrin over Bush's neglecting to mention the Hurricane Katrina victims in his State of the Union address. *It gave the appearance that your administration doesn't care about Louisiana and Mississippi anymore*, Thompson charged.

"Wait a minute, Bennie," Bush retorted. Since when was $110 billion in federal assistance *not caring*? The problem with the recovery, he added, lay with the state and local governments. (What Bush didn't say was that no mention of the Katrina recovery effort had appeared in *any* of the speech drafts. Everyone—Bush, the speechwriters,

Bartlett—had seen no particular need to reiterate the president's pledge sixteen months prior: *We will do what it takes, we will stay as long as it takes. . . .*)

Minnesota Congressman Tim Walz lit into Bush over his seeming indifference to veterans' issues: *Why is it, Mr. President, that you haven't mentioned veterans in your last four State of the Union addresses?* Bush managed to maintain his cool. No one could tell him that he didn't care about veterans, the president informed the freshman (who, to Rove, sounded like he was still in campaigning mode). Bush had increased funding for veterans' benefits. He'd comforted families of the fallen.

Susan Davis, whose constituents in California included a large military population, asserted that the troops were fighting a war that the rest of America had no emotional investment in. (Bush responded that if anything, the opposite was true: The war was "sapping our souls.") Jay Inslee of Washington challenged Bush to place a cap on carbon dioxide emissions. (Bush refused and defended his environmental record.) The most agreeable query came from Illinois Congressman Luis Gutierrez, a defender of Bush's immigration reform package. Gutierrez wanted to know how Bush intended to get GOP House members on board for immigration legislation—especially considering that "members of my party were brutally attacked [by Republicans] in the last election on this issue."

"*Gracias,* Luis," Bush replied with a grin. He expressed his determination to get such a measure on the House floor this year, before the presidential campaign could "overtake the debate." That sounded encouraging to Gutierrez—though the eight-term congressman found himself wondering later: *I've always expressed positive things about the president's immigration stance in the past. A lot of Democrats have. So why didn't he just reach out more? "Hi, Luis, how do we work this out"—or was it I who was supposed to call HIM?*

Twenty years before he gave these three speeches, George W. Bush was forty years old and only just then becoming a man. He had recently given up alcohol and committed his heart to Jesus Christ. These were not small things by any means. Yet there was nothing whatsoever about him that foreshadowed global significance. He was a marginally successful businessman who would spend that year and the next in the service of his father, the aspiring president. He espoused no ambition for himself, much less for the world at large. Even being a famous man's eldest son, George W. Bush was easily overlooked and seemed destined to stay that way.

Now it was 2007, and Bush was mentoring the head of the world's most frail democracy on how to lead a nation.

It was something Bush talked about every week during his SVTCs with Tony Blair: *These guys Maliki and Abbas* [the president of the Palestinian National Authority], *we've gotta nurture them. . . .* He had tried with Allawi and Ja'fari, the two previous prime ministers. But the former had little interest in policy, while the latter—definitely not Bush's kind of guy—was more inclined to recite poetry than build a democracy. By the time he first laid eyes on Maliki in Baghdad on June 13, 2006, Bush could not afford to be choosy. Iraq was out of control, here was its new leader . . . and through his willful optimism, Bush would see to it that theirs was a match made in heaven.

"I'm convinced you will succeed," he told Maliki that day. Shortly afterward, Bush acknowledged to the Iraq Study Group that "my job is to give confidence to the Maliki government." Though some in the group evinced less enthusiasm for the new prime minister, Bush had a different outlook. Maliki, he said, was "a lot better than what we've had." And in any event, the president's job was to "inspire" the novice politician.

In the months that followed, the prime minister's Shiite patron, al-Sadr, ran roughshod over Baghdad while the government arrested only al-Sadr's Sunni foes. Bush didn't lecture or threaten Maliki. When Hadley's memo criticizing Maliki was leaked to the *Times* in late November, Bush immediately contradicted it, saying that Maliki was "the right guy for the job"—and then dispatched Hadley to the Sunday talk shows, where the latter assured viewers that Maliki "has the will and desire to take responsibility."

Bush and Hadley happened to be on their way to Amman, Jordan, to meet with Maliki when the *Times* published its story about the memo. The president thought to defuse the matter right away. Pulling Hadley toward him, Bush grinned at Maliki and said, "Do you know our national security adviser, Steve Hadley?" When Maliki smiled and hugged Hadley, Bush thought, *This speaks well of the guy.*

The prime minister had been hearing rumors of a coup against him and feared that Bush and Ambassador Khalilzad supported it. Maliki therefore came armed with a security plan of his own. Though it struck Bush as ambitious in the extreme, he was delighted by Maliki's assertiveness and returned from the Middle East just as upbeat as he had been six months earlier.

Five weeks later, Bush was conducting an SVTC to brief Iraqi officials on his upcoming address to the nation on the new Iraq strategy when he suddenly said, "Let's clear the room." Maliki's aides departed, as did Bush's. Now it was just the two leaders.

"You know," Bush told his counterpart with a fatalistic laugh, "we're hanging out here together. A lot of people here don't think we can succeed. I do."

Then, challenging Maliki, the president said, "It's looking like al-Sadr's gonna run your country."

Maliki grew solemn. "I swear to *God*," he vowed, "al-Sadr will not run this country."

Bush took that in. "Well," he said, "I'll put my neck out if you put your neck out."

Bush's decision to appoint General Petraeus as the new commander in Iraq didn't please some in Maliki's government who remembered Petraeus's empowerment of former Baathists in Mosul. "I know you have concerns about this," Bush said. "But let me just tell you, leader to leader: I have a lot of respect for this man. Trust me on this."

A week later, Maliki appointed First General Aboud Jenber to be his new Baghdad security commander. General Casey contacted Bush to register his concern. Jenber, he said, was an unknown quantity. Bush got Maliki on the phone.

Maliki said to Bush, *I have a lot of respect for this man. Trust me on this.* Turning the tables on him—Bush loved it!

"He's learning to be a leader," Bush said a few weeks later. "And one of my jobs as the president and his ally is to help him be that leader without being patronizing. At some point in time, if I come to the conclusion that he can't be the leader—he's unwilling to lead or he's deceptive—then we'll change course. But I haven't come to that conclusion. As a matter of fact, his recent actions have inspired *me.*"

So far, Maliki's armed forces had begun to enforce laws across sectarian lines. His government had passed a $41 billion budget. The prime minister had yet to fulfill all his promises—most prominently, ratifying an oil-revenue-sharing deal that would grant the Sunnis a stake in the Iraqi economy. But Bush would cut Maliki some slack. "Everybody tells him the same thing—you better get moving, or else," Bush would say. "That's what I told [Senate Armed Services Committee chairman] Carl Levin. I said, 'You went to Iraq and you told him point blank, You better get moving.' I said, 'Thank you for doing that.'

"He said, 'Why don't you do the same thing?' I said, 'I've got other audiences. My message isn't just to the Iraqi government. It's to U.S. troops, the enemy, the Iraqi people. And therefore I've got to be careful about how I deliver the message. I want to be viewed more as a mentor than a scolder."

Maliki was learning leadership on the fly—and getting into a groove, Bush believed, where the more hard decisions the Iraqi made, the stronger he became. It was Bush's theory of political capital transplanted to Baghdad: The more of it you spent, the more you accrued.

"I do believe, however," said Bush in February, "that he knows he's running against the clock."

Of course, the clock ticked against them both.

As a leader, Bush himself remained a curious case—though not among his subordinates, who, with near-unanimity, revered the man down to his gristle. They were conscious, of course, that not everyone shared their admiration, and it pained many of them that their boss's finest qualities went somehow unbeheld.

And all those qualities were, in fact, there to be seen. Yet they could also be viewed somewhat less glowingly: the quickness as brusque impatience, the plain speech as intellectual laziness, the strategic vision as disrespect for the process, the boldness as recklessness, the strength as unreflective self-certainty. Neither vantage point was entirely wrong or entirely right. As was the case with Clinton, Bush 41, Reagan, Carter, and perhaps all other presidents, Bush's virtues and his vices were one and the same.

And he was not quite so simple, despite his professed contentedness to be regarded as such. Over time, some of Bush's detractors would see this for themselves, in some close setting that made it impossible for them to dispute. And so okay, he wasn't at all dumb—was clearly in charge, clearly up on things, didn't defer to Cheney or Rove, had a way of getting at the heart of the matter. . . . While over the same time frame, a very few of his otherwise admiring lieutenants would quietly descend into reassessment. Wondering: Was a man *really* all that secure with himself if he felt compelled to assert, over and over, that he never wavered, never lost a wink of sleep, and harbored no regrets? What bespoke his compulsive optimism—and was it, in the end, worth the sacrifice of credibility?

In time, a Bush observer would be rewarded with the revelation that the man defied all his stereotypes. The president relished Texas machismo. He also cried without shame. He enjoyed a reputation for shooting from the gut. Yet when the moment called for it, Bush could be quite deliberative . . . though the decisions he came to—limiting funding for stem cell research, invading Iraq, surging troops—tended to be unsurprising, thoroughly consistent with his conservative predilections. Most of all, Bush evinced an almost petulant heedlessness to the outside world. Yet he listened very much to the men and women whose loved ones he had sent off to die in Afghanistan and Iraq—was alternately "healed" and "driven" by their voices. . . . And he listened, with growing interest, to the voices of the past conjured up in history books. Not just the glorious testaments to Truman and Churchill, but the voices of women and children slaughtered in the aftermath of the Algerian revolution, or the innocents massacred on the killing fields of Cambodia. He was gambling with lives. Millions and millions of Iraqi lives. Publicly, Bush gave his critics every reason to believe that his conscience was unburdened. It was not to be believed.

Bush was an idealist, a promulgator of grand, risky visions. If risk taking was a personal need, so were the desires for routine that invariably collided with it. Even as Bush roiled America with the Freedom Agenda and the Opportunity Society, he himself required comfort—a predictable schedule, familiar food, inviolable exercise time, frequent respites at his Crawford ranch . . . and reliable aides whose fidelity he valued, in several cases, far more than expertise or sound judgment. His Harvard MBA notwithstanding, Bush could not manage with dispassion. Instead of acquiring fresh horses at the end of his first term, Bush cajoled his frazzled aides: *Are you an eight-year man?* And instead of replacing those in his administration who had become a clear liability, Bush consulted his own loyalty—and his stubbornness: like a pundit or a retired general was going to tell him how to run the White House!—and kept the loyalists on board.

He could rattle a whole room with his restlessness. Bush would lope through his schedule, early for everything, finished and off on his bike, staffers in the sway of his blitheness . . . until something would go wrong, necessitating deliberation, followed by an adrenaline-crazed galloping catch-up. New Hampshire to 9/11 to Iraq to Katrina—

this was the way it was in Bushworld. In his personal life, Laura could be counted on to, as he put it, "keep the brakes on." But his wife stayed out of governance. And though Bush could in fact be challenged with bad news or a differing point of view, and acquiesce, and even ultimately reward the bold dissenter . . . it was very hard, to stick one's arm into the fiercely whirring gears of Team Bush's institutionalized optimism and say, *Let's . . . slow . . . down. And rethink this.*

Of course, now Iraq had jammed the gears of his presidency.

But the Decider had decided: There would be a surge, or reinforcement, or whatever, and once again it was a time for hope. And Bush *was* hopeful, seemingly more than ever, to the surprise of many. "I have people walk up to me all the time," Bush said one morning in early February 2007 as he sat with his boots sprawled across his desktop in the Oval Office. Snickering, he added, "They look at you like, 'Wow.' Like they expect to see something different."

And three months later, on May 8, 2007, with every reason in the world to be wearing a Nixonian pallor—spotty progress at best in Iraq, an approval rating of 28, his press secretary Tony Snow diagnosed with a recurrence of cancer, Paul Wolfowitz forced out of office at the World Bank for showing professional favoritism to his girlfriend, former campaign strategist Matthew Dowd publicly airing his disillusionment with Bush to the *Times,* and attorney general Al Gonzales embroiled in a growing scandal over the highly suspicious dismissal of nine federal prosecutors—Bush seemed, somehow, even *more* serene. He was consuming history books with the same voraciousness with which he had pounded back the hot dog during lunch the previous December. Kissinger had recommended a book on the Algerian revolution; Rove, a copy of Lynne Olson's *Troublesome Young Men,* about the rise of Churchill. His presidency now all but consigned to history, Bush was immersed in the past, and gleaning from its portents what the future would say about America's forty-third president.

And feeling eerily ducky about it all. Would Congress somehow recultivate an appetite for a continued military presence in the Middle East? "My bet is that when all is said and done, they will," Bush said that afternoon. "The job of the president is to think over the horizon. I find that there are more and more people in Congress who are also thinking over the horizon . . . Now we've got a presence in the region—but Iraq creates a different kind of opportunity for a presence."

He imagined aloud that the surge would stabilize Iraq, which would hopefully encourage Bush's successor "to stay longer at the request of the Iraqi government. Which would have the following effect. One, it would serve as a reminder to the region that we're a force of stability. Two, it would remind certain actors that the United States is something to be reckoned with—Iran, for example, if they continue on the course they're doing . . . That's where my head is at."

But who else's head was there, contemplating dead-certain success in Iraq, instead of the very real possibility of failure?

"The danger is that the United States won't stay engaged," Bush acknowledged. "The danger is, people come to office and say, 'Let us promote *stability*—that's more important.' The problem is that in an ideological war, stability isn't the answer to the root cause of why people kill and terrorize."

Studying the past, thinking over the horizon, contemplating a hopeful future—these now brought Bush comfort. He had to lean on something. Had to keep things "relatively lighthearted" around the White House: "I can't let my worries—I try not to wear my worries on my sleeve. I don't want to burden them with that." His parents and his siblings would call Bush, expressing worry for him. He assured them, too, that he was doing just great. Sleeping well. Showing them nothing in the way of fretfulness.

The burden was there, all the same. "I think he carries a lot of it around, for sure," Laura Bush would say. "There's no doubt about it."

But to display it would be more than unseemly. "Self-pity is the worst thing that can happen to a presidency," Bush said—adding, "This is a job where you can have a lot of self-pity."

Though not on the subject of Iraq, Laura would remind him. " 'Well,' she says, '*you* chose to do this.' " Bush went on. "She reminds me that I decided to do this. Nobody decided it but me . . . I've got God's shoulder to cry on. And I cry a lot. I do a lot of crying in this job. I'll bet I've shed more tears than you can count, as president. I'll shed some tomorrow."

Catching himself, Bush let his boots fall from his desktop, leaned forward and said, "But I don't view this as a burden, being the president. I view it as a great opportunity. I truly believe we're in the process of shaping history for the good. I know, I firmly believe, that decisions I have made were necessary to secure the country. Things could've been done differently—I'm confident of that. That's what military historians do—they'll review this, diplomatic historians will review that, political historians . . .

"I made the decision to lead. And therefore there'll be times when you make those decisions—one, it makes you unpopular; two, it makes people accuse you of unilateral arrogance. And that may be true. But the fundamental question is: Is the world better off as a result of your leadership?"

That was, inarguably, the fundamental question. At the moment, Congress and the public were unambiguous on the subject: Bush's way was the wrong way. His power was waning. By the end of the year, his relevance would all but cease. And meanwhile, Iraq was a ticking time bomb.

Bush had his own calculations. In September, General Petraeus would testify before Congress about Baghdad's progress. Bush had to hope that the additional troops would quell the violence. Had to speak with utter confidence that his hopes would be realized.

"So now I'm an October–November man," Bush had said that February, a picture of rustic calm as his boots rested atop the fine historic desk. "I'm playing for October–November."

And until then? He would travel overseas, take another crack at immigration and energy legislation, study his daily Terrorist Threat Matrix, hug war widows. But the present tense was, in a sense, no longer his domain—not with the public and the legislative branch so beyond the reach of his persuasions. Americans had soured on the president and his war. The First Optimist had made pessimists out of them.

His playing field was now the future. That, of course, assumed that October–November would at last bring stability to Iraq and thereby surge his depleted mandate. Bush did in fact operate with that belief—always. New Hampshire could not change that in him. The midterms could not change that in him. What had to be believed, he believed.

"I'm not afraid to make decisions," Bush said. "Matter of fact, I *like* this aspect of the presidency."

He yearned to make more decisions. And he just knew it: After October–November, the strategy would work, Bush would be proven right, and that big ball would be back in his hands again, and he would heave it long.

Source Notes

Most of the information for this book (particularly from Part II onward) was obtained through interviews with current and former Bush administration officials. Candidly discussing often sensitive topics that were occurring more or less in real time, and for a book that would be published while the Bush administration was still in power, necessitated conducting most of these interviews "on background." Therefore, unless otherwise specified, readers should assume that the source of a particular fact was one or more current or former administration officials who divulged the information with the understanding that their identity would not be cited.

For this book, the author conducted six interviews (each roughly an hour in length) with President Bush between December 12, 2006, and May 8, 2007, as well as two interviews with Laura Bush in April and May of 2007. Additionally, the author interviewed then-Governor Bush several times—along with his wife and parents—for a lengthy profile that *GQ* Magazine published in October 1998. The Bushes talked with refreshing unguardedness back then, as did Karl Rove, who spoke expansively with the author in 1999 for a separate *GQ* profile. Only small portions of those transcripts made their way into magazine print, in part because interest in the musings of Bush and Rove was not then what it is now. With only a couple of exceptions, the quotes cited from the transcripts are published here for the first time.

Prologue

Virtually all of the material for this section came from an interview conducted with President George W. Bush on December 12, 2006. The exception is the passage that begins with, *It had become Bush's habit to take out his pen. . . .* The source for this was a senior White House official.

PART ONE. BAPTISM
1. New Hampshire

3 *Not counting state police escorts:* From scheduling records of Bush's New Hampshire campaign staff.

4 *The oceanside town awaiting the motorcade:* Details of the New Castle event were gathered from interviews with Bush campaign officials and from the following articles: "For New Castle, The Bush Campaign Kickoff Was Impressive," *New Hampshire Union-Leader,* June 15, 1999; "Bush Makes Grand Entrance," *Portsmouth Herald,* June 15, 1999; "Bush Stands Up To Questioners In N.H.," *Boston Globe,* June 15, 1999; "On The Road With George W. Bush," Salon, June 16, 1999.

5 *That week, a New Hampshire poll:* "Boston Herald Poll Also Shows Bush With Lead," Associated Press, June 15, 1999.

6 *But among the aspirants:* Details of the July 4 and July 31, 1999, events were drawn from interviews with a Bush New Hampshire campaign official and from campaign scheduling records.

6 *He loved to smoke a jogging mate:* Interview with Dr. Charles M. Younger, 1998.

6 *He sulked:* Interview with member of Bush's gubernatorial senior staff.

6–7 *"It's mean," "doer" etc.:* interview with Bush, 1998.

7 *"Cryer,"* interview with Bush, December 2006.

7 *After the triumphant swing:* Details of the North Conway event were drawn from interviews with a Bush New Hampshire campaign official.

8 *"Make it look presidential"* . . . *tell the damn Ranger security force:* Interview with senior Bush campaign official.

8 Like a hockey season: Interview with senior Bush campaign official.

8 *"We're the candidate of reasonable, cautious, prudent reform":* Interview with Karl Rove, 1999.

8 *"Things have never been better":* The Big Enchilada, Stuart Stevens, Free Press, 2001.

9 *"I understand you know box scores"* and *He dispensed nicknames:* Interviews with Bush New Hampshire campaign officials.

9 *Kasich wondered where the hell:* Interview with Bush campaign adviser.

10 *reading his Bible over breakfast:* Interview with Logan Walters.

10 *that feather pillow:* This infamous disclosure was first reported by the *New York Times* writer Frank Bruni on January 26, 2000.

10 *Judd Gregg's pale-eyed chief of staff:* Interviews with Bush New Hampshire campaign officials.

10 *"I don't know much":* Interview with senior Bush campaign official.

10 *the local gurus blamed Karen:* Interviews with Bush New Hampshire campaign officials and a senior Bush campaign official. Andy Hiller interview: Does George W. Bush Know What It Takes To Be President?, air date November 1, 1999.

11 *As soon as Hiller was done: Ten Minutes From Normal,* Karen Hughes, Penguin Group, 2004.

11 *Breathlessly, Karen phoned Josh Bolten:* Inteview with senior Bush campaign official.

11 *"Okay, you guys are supposed to be so smart":* Interview with Bush campaign aide.

12 *She wasn't like Gore's Chris Lehane:* Interview with Karen Hughes, 2005.

13 *One evening in Bedford:* Interviews with two Bush New Hampshire campaign officials.

14 *During one call-in program:* Interview with Bush New Hampshire campaign official.

14 *"Rarely is the queston asked":* from a campaign event in Florence, South Carolina, January 11, 2000, published in *The Complete Bushisms,* Jacob Weisberg, Slate.

14 *"Is he going to stand there":* Interview with three Bush New Hampshire campaign officials.

15 *"What's this, 'if I'm elected'?":* Interview with Bush campaign aide.

15 *"Boys," said the senator:* All details pertaining to McCain activities in New Hampshire are drawn from interviews with senior McCain campaign officials.

17 *At the 1992 Republican National Convention:* Interview with Mark Salter (who was present for the Bush-McCain encounter).

19 *The temptation was to blame it all:* Nearly eight years after the fact, New Hampshire-based Bush loyalists maintain, with passion and specificity, that his primary campaign was fatally misconfigured and underresourced. (Three different New Hampshire senior staffers cited Joe Allbaugh's refusal to allocate money for toilet paper in the Concord office, for example.) Just as vehemently, the Texas-based campaign staffers insist that this was not so. "They got everything they freaking wanted—*everything they wanted,*" one of the top lieutenants asserted, adding that while he was not familiar with the toilet paper anecdote, it was "probably bullshit." Difficult to dismiss, in any event, is the larger point—that the campaign, like its candidate, lacked zeal and urgency. It's now widely held in Bushworld (including by the President) that the blowout in New Hampshire was, as one key subordinate would say, "the most important thing that ever happened to the campaign." Of course, none of them felt particularly grateful at the time. But as will be evident throughout this narrative, the cycle of hubristic complacency and adrenaline-crazed recompense is a seemingly inescapable dynamic in the Bush presidency, basic as it is to the man himself.

20 *"Everything I have to say to you":* Interview with Bush campaign aide.

21 *On the icy roads:* Interview with Bush New Hampshire campaign official.

21 *"Bush is a nice guy":* Union-Leader, December 3, 1999.

22 *Sununu's former deputy:* In an interview with the author, Andy Card offered a lengthy explanation of how George W. Bush had apparently attempted to fire Sununu first—but "it didn't take," thus requiring that then-deputy chief of staff Card complete the task.

22 *"How's he doing?":* Interviews with two Bush New Hampshire campaign officials.

23 *"We're turning around":* Interview with senior Bush campaign official.

23 *"Why don't we go sledding":* Interviews with two Bush New Hampshire campaign officials.

24 *"You ready to win tonight?":* Interview with Bush New Hampshire campaign official.

24 *The first exit polls came in:* Interviews with senior Bush and McCain campaign officials.

25 *there sat the First Lady of Texas:* Interview with senior Bush campaign official.

25 *"You got defined":* Interview with Bush, December 2006.

26 *"We're going to lose today":* Interviews with senior Bush campaign officials.

26 *"Draft a statement":* Interview with Bush, December 2006.

26 *"This has . . . implications:"* Interview with Mark Salter.

26 *"Rove's on the phone":* Interviews with two senior McCain campaign officials.

27 *Doing what he did best:* Interviews with Bush New Hampshire and senior campaign officials.

2. Texas

28 *"I learned from my mother":* Interview with Bush, December 2006.

29 *It was never a boy's idea:* Details of Bush's youth and young adulthood are drawn from interviews with a number of his former classmates and Texas friends unless otherwise noted.

30 *The posturings of history professor Staughton Lynd:* Interview with Bush, 1998.

31 *And, famously, he enlisted in the National Guard:* All information is drawn from Bush's military files. National Guard: "Lt. Bush is a dynamic outstanding young officer:" memo from Lt. Colonel Jerry B. Killian to 147th Fighter Group, November 3, 1970. "I have applied:" Statement of Intent, May 27, 1968. May physical: Killian memo to Bush, May 4, 1972. Calling five days after the deadline, "wants to transfer:" Killian memo to file, May 19, 1972. Suspended: Killian memo, August 1, 1972. Requested an early discharge: application for discharge, September 18, 1973.

31 *carry the candidate's pillow:* Interview with White House official.

32 *"You wanna go mano a mano right here?":* As far as I can tell, the earliest citation of this anecdote Skip Hollandsworth's profile of Bush, "Born To Run," *Texas Monthly,* May 1994.

32 *"Georgie would've never won that fight":* Interview with Bush family friend.

32 *Instead, he let the old man hook him up:* Interviews with former Projecct PULL supervisors Ernie Ladd, Muriel Henderson and Edgar Arnold, 1998.

33 *There was a cute little kid named Jimmy Dean:* 2000 Republican National Convention Bush campaign video; *God and George W. Bush: A Spiritual Life,* Paul Kengor, HarperCollins, 2004.

33 *once bringing in a friend:* Interview with Bush friend Sam Greeley.

34 *The men who took him in:* Interviews with Ralph Way, Buzz Mills, and Delmon Hodges.

34 *"I've been talking to Dad":* Interview with Delmon Hodges.

34 *"Do you make any money?":* Interview with Clay Johnson.

35 *"That's how I've come to feel about the Yale experience:"* Bush commencement speech at Yale, May 21, 2001.

35 *"You guys from Midland:"* Interview with Joe O'Neill.

35 *"Do you know who you just arrested?":* "President Bush Once Thanked Maine Officer," *Boston Globe,* November 4, 2000.

35 *"Well, they got George last night on a DUI:"* Interview with Delmon Hodges.

35 *That meant a $150 fine:* Maine Bureau of Motor Vehicles record.

36 *"the best thing that could have happened:"* *Boston Globe,* November 4, 2000.

36 *"You can't win against Kent Hance,":* Interview with Bush, 1998.

36 *"You can't learn lessons by reading:"* interview with Bush, 1998.

36 *"go-to girl for dime bags":* *The Family: The Real Story of the Bush Dynasty,* Kitty Kelley, Random House, 2004.

36 *"What's a dime bag?":* Interview with White House official.

36 *He stayed up past midnight:* Interview with Joe O'Neill.

36 *"A man would answer:"* interview with Barbara Bush, 1998.

37 *"wasn't given a Chinaman's chance:"* *Midland Record-Telegram*, May 18, 1978.

37 *"red as a coffee can:"* Interview with Ralph Way.

37 *"You don't ever get over losing:"* Interview with Jim Bradshaw.

38 *he assured his bookkeeper:* Interview with Kim Dyches.

38 *"floundering":* Interview with Texas writer.

38 *"How do we know we can trust you":* *A Charge To Keep: My Journey to the White House*, George W. Bush, HarperCollins, 1999.

38 *who knew from past campaigns:* Interview with Sally Atwater.

38 *"we just stayed up all night and drank:"* Interview with Bush, 1998.

39 *had "been telling him for a few years":* Interview with Laura Bush, 1998.

39 *"obviously I was searching:"* Interview with Bush, 1998.

39 *and in fact George W. Bush was never able to recall:* Interview with Bush family friend.

39 *"Let her gut it out:"* Interview with Mary Matalin, 1998.

39 *an apoplectic George W. tried in vain:* Interview with a senior Bush campaign official.

39 *"people had to move on:"* Interview with Barbara Bush, 1998.

39 *Laura would later tell a Texas reporter:* Interview with Paul Burka.

40 GEORGE BUSH JR.: Interview with Wally Wilkerson.

40 *"George, you've got no base here":* Interview with Jim Francis.

40 *Beginning with that first season in 1989:* Information pertaining to Bush's ownership of the Texas Rangers is drawn from interviews with current and former Rangers officials, unless otherwise noted.

42 *"Well, I guess you don't like it":* Interview with Randy Galloway.

42 *"I'll never forget:"* Interview with Bush, December 2006.

43 *This did not escape the attention:* Interviews with Jim Francis and Shari Waldie.

43 *"The great irony is":* Interview with a senior Bush campaign official.

44 *"A show horse, not a workhorse":* Interview with former Bullock senior aide.

44 *"I can't* believe *a governor would say":* Interview with a Bush campaign aide.

44 *"I didn't ask you here to back me":* Interview with Sandy Kress.

44 *"Teach me about juvenile law":* Interview with Judge Hal Gaither.

44 *And he showed up at Karl Rove's shabby Austin office:* Interview with Marvin Olasky.

44 *Rove suggested a fourth*: Interview with Karl Rove, 1999.

45 "I am a capitalist!": Interview with Karen Hughes.

46 *at an event for Republican governors:* Interview with a senior White House official.

46 *"Blacks didn't come out for me":* Interview with a Texas reporter.

47 *"I know you don't like clothes":* Interview with Barry Smith.

48 *"You're not even from Texas":* Interview with former Bullock chief of staff Bruce Gibson.

49 *And on George W.'s fiftieth birthday:* Interviews with Joe O'Neill and Don Evans.

49 *Bush imposed on the governor's office:* Information pertaining to Bush's style of management is drawn from interviews with his former personal aide Logan Walters and other gubernatorial staff members.

50 *Early on the afternoon of February 18, 1998:* Information relating to Bush's 1998

visit to the Marlin juvenile facility is drawn from the author's article, "The Child Bush Left Behind," *GQ*, May 2004, from then-Governor Bush's scheduling records and from a subsequent March 2006 interview with the former juvenile in question, Johnny Baulkmon.

53 *The swing through California:* Information pertaining to Bush's April 1998 visit to the home of George P. Shultz is drawn from interviews with Shultz, John Cogan, Michael Boskin, and other participants, as well as from scheduling records.

54 *"I'm doing everything in my power":* Interview with a senior Bush campaign official.

55 *"He's definitely gonna run":* Interview with a Bush campaign adviser.

55 *"I'm just not gonna do this":* Interview with Karen Hughes.

55 *sweating completely through his clothes:* Interview with Logan Walters.

55 *a Dallas attorney named Harriet Miers:* Interview with a senior Bush campaign official. Miers, in an interview with the author, at first denied that she had performed such a task for the campaign, then said, "I don't know, exactly. I'd have to go back and see. I had different kinds of responsibilities."

55 *What do you think we should do about this?":* Interview with a senior Bush campaign official.

55 *"I'd made a conscious decision":* Interview with Bush, December 2006.

56 *"You're ruining our lives!":* Interview with Laura Bush, April 2007.

56 *She and Barbara had seen:* Interview with Bush, December 2006. In an interview with the author, Laura Bush recalled her husband having told Jenna, "Your mother and I are living our lives. And that's what we raised you and Barbara to do, to live your lives."

56 *Bush upstairs having a yelling match:* Interview with a Bush campaign adviser.

57 *"He was talking to you!":* Interview with Karen Hughes. Bush later acknowledged to media adviser Mark McKinnon that Pastor Craig's sermon (a copy of which unfortunately does not exist, according to Hughes) was "what did it," i.e., convinced him to run for the presidency.

57 *"That's three times the amount":* Interview with a Bush family friend.

57 *"useful impatience":* Interview with Marvin Olasky.

58 *"What do we have an army for, anyway?":* Interview with a senior Bush campaign official.

58 *"If the American people wanted an economist for president":* Interview with a Bush campaign aide.

3. South Carolina

59 *"Logan?":* Interview with Logan Walters.

59 *"How bad's it gonna get?":* Interview with a Bush South Carolina campaign official.

61 *"Look, you're the reformer":* Interview with a Bush campaign aide. In an interview with the author, Quayle confirmed this dialogue. For her part, Karen Hughes maintains that it was she who first told Bush that he, not McCain, was the true reformer. The campaign aide privy to the Quayle-Bush conversation recalls Hughes being in the room and taking notes.

61 the base: "The Republican Insurgent: McCain and Bush Revving Up Their Campaigns," *New York Times*, February 3, 2000.

61 *And one of the opposition's South Carolina advisers:* Interview with a McCain South Carolina campaign adviser.

61 *The latter didn't sit well:* Interview with a senior Bush campaign official.

62 *That was all Karen Hughes had cared about:* Interview with Karen Hughes.

62 *All the heavies were present:* Information pertaining to the Hyatt meeting of Bush operatives was produced from interviews with eight of the participants.

64 *"If we don't win this, it's over":* Interview with a senior Bush campaign official.

64 *It fell to Karen:* Interview with Karen Hughes.

64 *His chief of staff, Mark Salter:* Interviews with Mark Salter and Ted Sampley.

66 *She phoned 301 Congress:* Details pertaining to the Austin meeting of Bush operatives were gleaned from interviews with five of the participants.

67 *"That's not right":* Interview with a senior McCain campaign official.

68 *"For the very reason y'll are sitting cheering it":* Interviews with two McCain South Carolina campaign advisers.

69 *The morning after the "Desperate" spot aired:* The Big Enchilada, Stuart Stevens.

69 *On Thursday, the day of the shoot:* Details from the shooting of the "Integrity" ad were furnished from interviews with three of the participants

70 *He was feeling juiced:* Interview with a Bush South Carolina campaign adviser.

71 *"I want the negative stuff off":* Interviews with three senior McCain campaign officials.

73 *"a calculating and conniving politician":* Bob Jones, "Explaining McCain," *World Magazine*, February 19, 2000.

73 *"feel free to copy and/or send it to others":* The quotation is from a CNN transcript, February 14, 2000. When contacted by the author, the professor at Bob Jones University who had written the e-mail acknowledged that he had "misconstrued the public data" about McCain's children but insisted that he had not intended for his e-mail to be disseminated beyond his circle of friends. The professor refused to show the full four-page e-mail to the author.

74 *His aides quietly discussed busting:* Interview with a McCain South Carolina campaign adviser.

74 *chief of staff Mark Salter had chased a man:* Interviews with Mark Salter and a McCain South Carolina campaign adviser.

74 *"didn't just steal a page":* Interview with a McCain South Carolina campaign adviser.

75 *McCain was greeted by five hundred:* Interview with a Bush South Carolina campaign adviser.

77 *The Bush people had never bought this story:* Interviews with two Bush South Carolina campaign advisers.

77 *A part-time auto mechanic:* Interviews with a Bush South Carolina campaign adviser and a senior Bush campaign official.

78 *"Buddy":* Interviews with two senior McCain campaign officials and with McCain. That McCain had responded to Bush's overture with profanity has been widely reported, though likely without firsthand confirmation.

78 *a "victory party":* Interview with a Bush South Carolina campaign adviser.

78 *Meanwhile, Bush's people had located:* Interview with a senior Bush campaign official.

79 *That night was Karen Hughes's worst:* Interview with Karen Hughes.

79 *Rove was pale:* Interview with a Bush campaign adviser.

80 *Henry McMaster confided to McCain:* Interview with McCain.

81 *"What's he gonna say":* Interview with McCain.

PART TWO. "THROUGH OUR TEARS"
4. The Building of Bushworld

87 *On this particular evening:* Interview with the reporter to whom Bush told this story. Bush himself did not recall this anecdote but also said, "I'm sure the guy's not making it up."

88 *He had a six-toed cat named Ernie:* When the Bushes moved to the White House, Ernie's propensity for clawing furniture compelled them to bequeath the cat to Bush's longtime friend Brad Freeman in Los Angeles.

88 *he befriended a ponytailed El Paso biker:* Interview with Adair Margo.

88 *he demanded a fruit salad every day: Produce News,* January 19, 2001.

88 *"Let's see what ol' Henry's up to":* Interview with a reporter who fished with Bush.

89 *"I don't know what's going to come on my desk":* Interview with Bush, December 2006.

90 *Dick Cheney's first run was to Capitol Hill:* Interview with a participant at the meeting; also, see "After the Republican Fall," Lincoln Chafee, *New York Times,* November 12, 2006.

91 *"Nice tie":* Interview with Logan Walters.

92 *his mother-in-law:* Interview with Laura Crawford, who sat with Jenna Welch as the mattresses were being replaced.

92 *retrofitting the White House gym:* Interviews with Laura Bush, Logan Walters, and a senior administration official.

92 *Bush had assigned:* Interview with Clay Johnson.

95 *He'd met George W. Bush back in 1979:* Interview with Andy Card.

97 *"And when did you begin to think seriously":* transcript of a December 11, 2001, AEI-sponsored discussion between Rove, Norm Ornstein, and Tom Mann of the Brookings Institution.

97 *In 1960, nine-year old Karl Christian Rove:* Interview with Rove, 1999.

97 *"Imagine being the college chairman during that time":* Interview with Rove, 1999.

97 *"Your great reward is I'll win":* Interview with Rove, 1999.

97 *His fourth-floor office:* Interview with a former Rove associate.

101 *"The danger for me":* Interview with Rove, 1999.

101 *"Dudeness!":* The author was the recipient of this salutation by Rove.

103 *At his insistence, a memo was generated:* More than once during the author's interviews with Bush, the president made a point of emphasizing his accessibility to his staff. His father's "walk-in access" list, Bush said, consisted of one name: "John Sununu."

107 *On the morning of January 31, 2001:* Interview with one of the senators who participated in the event.

107 *Not long after that:* Interview with one of the Cabinet members who participated in the meeting. Colin Powell denies that Bush locked him out; the other Cabinet member is certain that he was.

107 *Bush held a grand total of one state dinner:* In an interview with the author, Laura Bush offered one explanation for her husband's reluctance to throw state dinners, at least after September 11, 2001: "George hosted, I think literally, a hundred and twenty heads of state, more than ever before, for working lunches or working dinners. Everyone from around the world came to meet with the President after September 11th . . . And it was not a time that you had parties. You didn't—it wasn't like we thought, well, we can't have parties. It was like it never even occurred to us. It just wasn't that sort of mood at the White House. You just didn't have celebrations. I mean, it was jut not the way it would be, although we did see all these heads of state, a million of them."

108 *"Sorry, Margaret, you're cut out":* When asked by the author if he had ever felt double-crossed by a reporter, Bush immediately responded with Warner's name.

108 *"I don't spend a lot of time":* Transcript of an October 1, 2002, on-background interview with Bush by three reporters.

5. Doing A Few Things Right

109 *"I know there's a lot of talk":* The encounter with Tom Daschle is memorialized by Daschle in his book *Like No Other Time,* Crown Publishers, 2003. Daschle vividly recalled the scene during an interview with the author, and in a separate interview, a key former aide remembered Daschle emerging from the meeting and saying with puzzlement, "He told me he didn't want me to ever lie to him." Bush evinced skepticism to the author that he would ever have said such a thing. He repeatedly brought up the matter in later interviews—though even more frequently, the president acknowledged that his memory of past details was not good.

109 *"really not a bad guy":* Interview with a Daschle senior staffer.

110 *"No, Dick":* Interview with Dick Armey.

110 *"My dad's Vision Thing":* Interview with a Republican senator.

111 *"In my administration":* Details from Bush's January 22, 2001, meeting with Democratic elders were provided by participants Jody Powell and Bill Gray III, as well as by an adviser to the late Paul Simon.

112 *"Africa?":* Details from Bush's January 31, 2001, meeting with the Congressional Black Caucus came from interviews with two of the participants.

113 *"That guy's the exact opposite of me":* Interview with a senior Bush adviser.

114 *"voice-interactive virtual reality stations":* Interview with Bush, 1998.

114 *"I am an activist":* Interview with Bush, 1998.

114 *"I know how you've been calling for disaggregation":* Interview with Sandy Kress.

115 *"Your brother used this desk":* Interview with Sandy Kress.

115 *the desk had been built in 1880:* As the White House website indicates, the desk was built in 1880 from the timber of the H.M.S. *Resolute,* an abandoned British warship, and since that time has been used by every American president except Johnson, Nixon, and Ford. It became iconic in the photograph of John F. Kennedy Jr. sitting underneath the desk.

117 *Like other moderates:* Jeffords declined to be interviewed for this book, but his

own book, *My Declaration of Independence* (Simon & Schuster, 2001), recounts his point of view on the matters of Bush's tax cuts, Jeffords' dedication to the issue of special education and ultimately his split from the Republican party.

117 *Karen Hughes anxiously phoned:* Karen Hughes, *Ten Minutes From Normal*, 2004.

118 *At one point, the two men sat in the green room:* Interview with Andy Card.

118 *"I want to be helpful":* Interview with a Baucus senior staffer.

120 *Administration aides had turned the other way:* Interview with a Baucus senior staffer.

121 *While in Trieste:* Whitman declined to be interviewed for this book, instead (through a spokesperson) directing the author to her own book, *It's My Party Too* (The Penguin Press, 2005), as the repository of her point of view. That book, in addition to interviews with several senior administration officials, comprise the source material for the CO2 episode.

122 *"lima green bean":* "Back in the Spotlight," *Time* magazine, March 28, 2004.

123 *It did surprise her:* Interview with Karen Hughes.

125 *"I must confess I am wrestling with a difficult decision":* Though Kass himself declined to be interviewed by the author ("I belong to that apparently vanishing race that does not discuss private conversations with outsiders, not even well-meaning and thoughtful ones," he wrote in an e-mail), Karen Hughes took extensive notes of his conversation with Bush and read them to reporters during her August 10, 2001, press availability.

125 *"I think it's really important":* Interview with Dr. LeRoy Walters.

6. Then . . .

128 *"It's like the pig and the chicken":* Interview with Bush, 1998.

130 *Just after the gaffe:* Interview with Joe Biden.

131 *The fact that Bush's dad:* Transcript of an on-background interview with Condi Rice and a reporter, May 17, 2002.

132 *"Your human capital":* Transcript of an on-background interview with Condi Rice and a reporter, May 15, 2002.

132 *"You know, I found that story very interesting":* Transcript of a June 2001 interview with Bush by *Wall Street Journal* columnist Peggy Noonan.

132 *Outside the door:* Interview with Logan Walters.

132 *"Let's not get stuck in history":* Karen Hughes, *Ten Minutes From Normal*, 2004.

132 *"Let's not be Brezhnev and Nixon":* Transcript of an on-background interview with Condi Rice and a reporter, May 17, 2002.

133 *On Sunday morning:* Interview with a Bush family friend.

134 *Bush stayed that evening:* "The Day Before Everything Changed, Bush Touched Locals' Lives," *Sarasota Herald-Tribune*, September 10, 2002.

134 *Accompanying him on the predawn run:* Interview with Dick Keil.

134 *But Bush was feeling uncharacteristically languid:* Interview with Sandy Kress.

141 *In truth, Bush was pissed off:* Ari Fleischer, *Taking Heat*, HarperCollins, 2005.

142 *"The foreman lives there":* Interview with Logan Walters.

144 *"I'm the kind of guy":* Transcript of an October 1, 2002, interview with Bush by a reporter.

144 *"I'm not staying in there"*: Interview with Bush, December 2006.

145 *He couldn't sleep:* Interviews with Bush, December 2006, and with Laura Bush.

154 Release all foreign nationals: Bob Woodward, *Bush At War,* Simon & Schuster, 2002.

155 *"We've got a crisis"*: Interview with Robert McCleskey.

158 *The vest was what worried him:* Details of Bush's experiences throwing out the first pitch at Miller Park and Yankee Stadium were furnished by Bush and two senior administration officials.

158 *"I'll bet you ten thousand dollars"*: Interview with Robert McCleskey.

PART THREE. DARK CITY ON A HILL
7. Nightmare Scenario

164 The bazaar's open: Interview with Andy Card.

166 *"My God"*: Transcript of a January 28, 2003, on-background interview with Bush conducted by three reporters.

166 *"this is a time when the U.S. has unparalleled power"*: Transcript of an August 19, 2002, on-background interview with Rice by a reporter.

166 *"dragging it across the finish line"*: Transcript of a December 11, 2002, on-background interview with Rice by a reporter.

166 *he would receive a formal Terrorist Threat Matrix:* Interview with Philip Zelikow.

167 *Something was weighing on Bush:* Interview with Ari Fleischer.

169 *"No backing off"*: Interview with Ari Fleischer.

169 *On the Truman Balcony:* Interview with Dick Armey.

169 *The weekly White House breakfasts:* Interview with a participant.

173 *"We better talk through that now, not later"*: Transcript of a September 25, 2002, on-background interview with Rice by a reporter.

173 *"You cannot lead a divided state"*: Interview with Bush, 1998.

173 *"Dad made a mistake"*: Interview with a Bush family friend.

8. Drumbeats

175 *"perhaps within a year"*: Cheney speech to the VFW, August 26, 2002.

175 *"less than a year away"*: Cheney interview by Don Imus, MSNBC, January 20, 2005.

175 *"I've been in this business a long time"*: Rice transcript, September 25, 2002.

177 *"I really appreciate your holding these hearings"*: Interview with Joe Biden.

178 *"I don't believe that America will justifiably make"*: Interview with Dick Armey.

179 *Thinking to himself:* Interview with Andy Card.

180 *"The American people gotta know"*: Interview with Bush, December 2006.

181 *"You don't have to tell me about Iraq"*: Rice transcript, September 25, 2002.

182 *"For a guy who's used to clapping and cheering"*: Interview with Bush, December 2006.

182 *"I did the UN a favor"*: Transcript of a January 28, 2003, on-background interview with Bush conducted by four reporters.

183　*"When the president of the United States walks in":* Interview with Bush, December 2006.

185　*"the speech that nobody listened to":* Transcript with Bush and four reporters, January 28, 2003.

186　*Steve Hadley, indicated to a colleague discomfort:* Interview with Philip Zelikow.

186　*"the confirmation":* Interview with Andy Card.

187　*Saddam's heart "is of stone":* Details of the January 10, 2003, meeting between Bush and the Iraqi exiles were gleaned from interviews with Kanan Makiya, Andy Card, Ari Fleischer, and one other participant. Two written sources—Fleischer's book *Taking Heat,* and a translated extract from a January 24–30, 2003, article in *al-Mutamar,* the weekly newspaper of the Iraqi National Congress—provided additional details.

189　*"It's important for the world to see":* Transcript with Bush and four reporters, January 28, 2003.

189　*"It's going to be hard":* Interview with Andy Card.

190　*"I usually don't address churches":* Text of a November 3, 1996, speech given by Bush at Westlake Hills Presbyterian Church.

190　*"I would never justify my faith":* Transcript with Bush and four reporters, January 28, 2003.

190　*During the past several weeks:* Interview with Laura Bush, April 2007.

190　*This time, he prayed as he walked:* Bob Woodward, *Plan of Attack,* Simon & Schuster, 2004.

9. The Grid

191　*"We spent hours":* Interview with Bush, February 2007.

193　*"an implication of finality":* Interview with Donald Rumsfeld.

196　*"was properly calibrated":* Interview with Donald Rumsfeld.

197　*It was a disaster:* Interviews with Randall Richardson, Robyn McGuckin, Stephen Browning, and Nick Horn.

198　*"exquisite understanding":* Interview with a DIA analyst. Rumsfeld also confirmed to the author that the DIA had produced highly revealing data on the electrical grid for the purposes of targeted bombing.

198　*Its numbers were way off:* As one top State Department official admitted in an interview with the author, the Project's report "wasn't a plan." Its estimate of prewar generating capacity as 9,600MW was wildly off the mark, and it chose to make a case study of Kurdistan—no doubt because intelligence was lacking elsewhere, but that region's power supply was far greener than elsewhere in the country.

199　*"We are not supposed to engage":* Interview with Stephen Browning.

199　*Frantically, they began to pull:* Interviews with Stephen Browning and Nick Horn.

199　*Rumsfeld would insist to reporter Bob Woodward:* Bob Woodward, *State of Denial,* Simon & Schuster, 2006.

199　*"This is a huge mistake":* Interview with Stephen Browning.

200　*"What's the strategy?":* Interview with Nick Horne.

200 *"I don't understand this, Pete":* Interview with Stephen Browning.

201 *"blue sky" exercise:* Interview with Robyn McGuckin.

201 *Every plant manager:* Details of this conference came from interviews with Stephen Browning, Nick Horne, Randall Richardson, and Robyn McGuckin.

201 *"We need to put a goal out there and execute it":* Interview with Stephen Browning.

202 *The electricity team couldn't believe:* Details of the 4400 Project came from interviews with Browning, Horne, Richardson, and McGuckin; from papers produced by Home for the UN; from the paper, "Iraqi Power Sector: CPA's Legacy and Lessons," by McGuckin and Tom Wheelock; and from two senior administration officials.

207 *"We're not still doing business":* Interview with Randall Richardson.

207 *With Iran:* Interviews with Randall Richardson and Tommy Crangle.

207 *several Syrian officials:* Interviews with Randall Richardson and Nick Horne.

209 *"The idea":* Interview with Bush, February 2007.

209 *"Absolutely":* Interview with Bush, December 2006.

209 *"You end up with 25–28 million":* Interview with Donald Rumsfeld.

209 *"Mr. President":* Interview with Ari Fleischer.

211 *"We simply don't have enough troops":* Interview with Stephen Browning.

211 *"Well, the policy":* Interview with Bush, December 2006.

212 *"This isn't open for discussion":* Interview with Stephen Browning.

10. Thanksgiving

225 *his black pug, Buddyroo:* Interview with Dick Keil.

217 *"Welcome to Free Iraq, Mr. President":* L. Paul Bremer III, *My Year In Iraq*, Simon & Schuster, 2005.

PART FOUR. A CHOICE, NOT A REFERENDUM
11. The One-Legged Runner

221 *"I did not come here to negotiate":* Interviews with two participating senators.

223 *he received a call:* Interview with Clark Kent Ervin. Christopher Hitchens could not recall the incident but speculated, in an email exchange, "Probably one of our team was hoping to introduce him to someone at Foggy Bottom, to even things up a bit." With respect to his friend Chalabi, Hitchens added, "You are not wrong to say that Ahmad had a good deal of influence in DC at the time, but his position was partly the outcome of, and partly a cause of, the ongoing fratricide between departments."

226 *"You killed my son":* Interview with Andy Card.

227 Don't let my son die in vain: The frequency of this admonition to the president has been verified in interviews with Bush, Andy Card, Joe Hagin, and Josh Bolten.

227 *Bush visited the wounded:* Details of the president's interactions with Staff Sergeant Michael McNaughton are drawn from interviews with McNaughton and Sgt. Dave Silva.

12. "You Know Where I Stand"

236 *The admaker walked into the Yellow Room:* Interview with Mark McKinnon.

237 *sitting in a chair:* Interview with Karen Hughes.

237 *When* GQ *magazine reporter Michael Hainey:* "A Beer With John Kerry," *GQ,* September 2004.

239 *"How can you throw away":* Interview with Karen Hughes.

239 *While playing up Kerry's exploits:* "Kerry To File Complaint Tying Bush To Attack Ads," *Los Angeles Times,* August 21, 2004.

239 *The Bush campaign had been notified:* The author was shown a preview of the first Swift Boat ad by a member of the Bush campaign, who told the author that Karl Rove had informed him that the TV spot would be running in selected cities the following day.

240 *and so, oddly, did Kerry:* Interview with a senior adviser to the Kerry campaign.

242 *Depending on which staff:* The author interviewed senior aides in both the Daschle and McCain camps and received thoroughly contradictory accounts as to the seriousness with which McCain took Daschle's overture to him about switching parties.

244 *"Barbara and Jenna decided":* Interview with Bush, December 2006. In a separate interview, Laura Bush recalled to the author that "Jenna called and told me she dreamed her daddy had lost and she hadn't campaigned for him, and she felt this huge guilt and sense of loss."

245 *They expressed their displeasure:* Interview with a Bush family friend.

245 *"Should I be nervous":* Interview with a Bush campaign adviser.

245 *"The energy":* Interview with Bush, December 2006.

13. Ask President Bush

247 *"We've got to remind people":* Interview with Karen Hughes.

251 *he melted down:* Details of the 2000 Crawford debate prep session were furnished through interviews with Karen Hughes, Senator Judd Gregg, a senior campaign adviser, and two administration officials.

254 *"He's not gonna attack":* Interview with Karen Hughes.

256 *"I think we've got a problem":* Interview with Karen Hughes.

256 *"They're going to report":* Interview with Karen Hughes.

258 *as John Edwards had in the summer of 2002:* On the Senate floor that summer, Edwards said of Saddam Hussein, "We know that he is doing everything he can to build nuclear weapons, and we know that each day he gets closer to achieving that goal." Later that year, Edwards told the author, in the presence of a senior aide, that he believed his focusing on Saddam's pursuit of nuclear weapons, rather than on weapons of mass destruction, would prove to be the most compelling argument for going into Iraq among the likely Democratic contenders. Well before these remarks, however, Edwards was behaving hawkishly on the subject of Iraq. For example, on February 24, 2002, the senator appeared on CNN's "Late Edition" and said, "I think Iraq is the most serious and imminent threat to our country."

258 *He knew almost nothing:* Interview with a senior Bush campaign official.

260 *Mehlman's ground team in Florida:* Interviews with a Bush campaign aide in Florida and with a senior Bush campaign official.

261 *"Why are you saying":* Interview with senior Bush campaign official.

14. "Stand with Me"

269 *"Karl says there's some problems with these numbers":* Interview with Karen Hughes.

270 *"Fuck, these exit polls are so screwed up":* The author was present at the pub in question and witnessed Dowd's remarks to campaign staffers.

PART FIVE. COMEUPPANCE
15. Eight-Year Men

277 *One cold Saturday:* Interview with one of the participants in the bicycle ride.

278 *"Eight years is a* hell *of a long time":* Interview with Adair Margo.

282 *He took a pass:* Asked about this, Rumsfeld told the author, "I can't recall the meeting. I can tell you that my view was we absolutely *had* to do something about Afghanistan. I have *no* recollection about discussing Iraq or even having it discussed at that meeting."

283 *"I've known President Bush":* Transcript of an on-background briefing with a reporter, July 8, 2002.

283 *"my relationship with the president":* Transcript of an on-background briefing with a reporter, June 20, 2002.

284 *"my husband":* Rice's slip of the tongue was first reported by Deborah Schoeneman in *New York* magazine, April 26, 2004.

284 *the African American women who convened:* Told to the author by one of the participants; confirmed by a former top aide to Rice.

284 *never fiction:* Transcript of an on-background briefing with a reporter, August 29, 2002.

284 *"Children and I are not the happiest combination":* Transcript of an on-background briefing with a reporter, December 4, 2002.

284 *there were few African American males:* Interview with a Rice friend.

284 *As an oil entrepreneur in Midland:* Interview with Kim Dyches.

285 *a recently divorced Mexican American woman:* Interview with Cecilia Levine.

285 *"How come you don't have kids":* Interviews with two female reporters.

285 *"You never cede control":* December 4, 2002, transcript.

285 *there was a presence to him:* Interview with a Rice friend.

286 Austin Powers *cracked her up:* Interview with a Rice friend.

286 *"People don't understand":* Interview with a Rice friend.

286 *"I suppose there are people":* Transcript of an on-background briefing with a reporter, February 14, 2002.

287 *"Fighting fire with fire":* Interview with Karen Hughes.

16. Big Ball, Long Bomb

292 *"the mantle of the presidency"*: Interview with Karen Hughes.
292 *"much higher comfort level"*: Interview with Joe O'Neill.
292 *"Cheney spoke 5 percent of the time"*: Interview with Philip Zelikow.
293 *A month after his reelection:* Details from the December 2004 meeting between Bush and the four congressmen were gleaned from interviews with two senior aides of the participants, and from an interview with Andy Card.
295 *In early January:* Interview with an attendee of the meeting.
296 *A few weeks later:* Interviews with two senior aides of Democratic attendees.
298 *"I can't get you one Democratic vote"*: Interview with a Baucus aide.
300 *Baucus was in a lethal stew:* Interview with a Baucus aide.
302 *"This has to happen"*: Interview with a Baucus aide.
302 "This has to happen": Interview with a senior Democratic official.

17. Heck Of A Job

305 *One sweltering summer day:* Details of Bush's August 2005 bike rides came from interviews with two individuals who rode with Bush.
306 *"Find me a ranch"*: Interview with Byron Cook.
307 *he would gather the dishes:* Interviews with Laura Bush and a friend.
307 *The twins had celebrated:* Interviews with a Bush family friend and with Laura Bush.
311 *"you all are nice and intelligent people"*: One of the administration officials participating in this encounter remembers Sheehan saying this; the other conveyed to the author that "that's not what she said, but she was courteous and respectful."
311 *That afternoon at the Broken Spoke Ranch:* "Bush Passes War Protesters En Route To Fundraiser," *USA Today,* August 12, 2005.
312 *Towey called the church's pastor:* Details of Bush's trip to Union Bethel, and of the church's Katrina-related travails, were drawn from interviews with the Reverend Thomas Brown Jr., Tenisha Stevens, three other church members and two administration officials.
316 *As always, he rode hard:* Interview with one of the participants in the bicycle ride.
319 *"I think we have not breached the levee"*: "The Day Storm Hit, Bush Was Worried About Levees," *New Orleans Times-Picayune,* March 1, 2006.
319 *Barely an hour later:* Interviews with two Blanco advisers.
320 Sir, this is part of leadership: Interview with Karen Hughes.
322 *The traveling press had been irked:* Disgruntlement over the administration's determination to control the visual message had been festering well before 2005. See, for example, "Glimpses Of A Leader, Through Chosen Eyes Only," *New York Times,* July 13, 2003. In a letter to Dan Bartlett on July 30, 2005, Susan Walsh, president of the White House News Photographers Association, protested that "Limiting our access to these events [involving the president] is a disservice to the public here in Washington and around the world." Later in the year, *U.S. News & World Report* made the decision to discontinue sending one of its photographers along with the traveling pool, on the grounds that "We really don't get much access from this White House," according to its director

of photography. "U.S. News Quits White House Photo Pool," *Photo District News*, December 1, 2005.

323 *She was not an autocratic crisis czar:* Interviews with two Blanco advisers.

323 *"We don't know how to deal with hurricanes":* Interview with a federal government official who was present for this conversation.

323 *"Take power naps":* Interviews with two Blanco advisers.

323 *"Hell, it got to the point":* Christopher Cooper and Robert Block, *Disaster: Hurricane Katrina and the Failure of Homeland Security*, Times Books, 2006.

326 I've spent my whole life: Interview with Terry Ebbert.

328 *"Whenever I've needed anything here in Alabama":* Interview with a senior aide to Governor Bob Riley.

330 *Despite his occasional visits to the ground level:* In an interview with the author, a senior aide to Nagin maintained that the mayor had conducted daily flyovers of the city. If this is true, Nagin did not make his tours known to local officials, the press, or the Bush administration—and in any event, White House officials found him to be far less knowledgeable about the condition of his city than, for example, Governor Blanco and Senator Landrieu.

331 *"I wish I'd called for troops":* Interview with a Blanco adviser.

331 *"throwing up every obstacle":* Rumsfeld denied to the author that he had played an obstructionist role in the matter: "Our position was this was a matter handled in the White House by Andy Card and the president, and the DHS had the principal responsibility, and we were simply available and waiting." He did, though, indicate his disapproval of Blanco's stipulation that she have control over federal troops. "I had a minimum of high regard for that," he told the author. "It just isn't the way a chain of command ought to work."

332 *though only after the first applicant for the job:* Interviews with three Blanco advisers. One of them recalled that Allbaugh had professional commitments for at least two more weeks; another had been led to believe that Allbaugh's wife was ill. Allbaugh himself would not respond to repeated requests for an interview.

333 *"The issue is":* Quoted passages here are drawn from notes taken by a participant in the meeting.

334 *"I want the troops":* Interview with a Blanco adviser.

334 *Card was scrambling:* Interview with Andy Card.

335 *"Y'all need to cut this shit out":* Interview with a Blanco adviser who witnessed the encounter.

336 *"It mst be because I'm a Texan":* Interview with Bush 2007.

18. "This Is Not Your Daughter!"

338 *As if on cue:* Except where otherwise noted, the material describing Hughes and her trip to the Middle East is drawn from interviews the author conducted with Hughes and others while accompanying her on the trip for a *GQ* article.

344 *Laura had joined those in the message camp:* In an interview with the author, Laura Bush averred somewhat, saying, "Well, I didn't get into the thing of telling George who to nominate, but I love Harriet and I know she would have been great. . . . Of course, I would like for it to be a woman. I mean, why not?"

345 *Problems were revealed in the vetting:* Interview with Andy Card and other senior administration officials.

346 *"This is one scary moment":* From a transcript of the October 6, 2005, RNC/White House conference call.

346 *"Being on the Supreme Court":* "This Is What Advice And Consent Means," AnneCoulter.com, October 5, 2005.

350 *Four U.S. senators:* The author accompanied the senators on the trip to Iraq.

351 *The following day, two of the four senators:* Interviews with Lindsey Graham and Joe Biden, the latter of whom took notes of the briefing

353 *Al Hillah was bombarded around the clock:* Interview with an American soldier who was stationed in Al Hillah during the bombing.

353 *Bush found himself shaking hands:* Interview with Rev. Thomas Brown Jr.

PART SIX. THE THUMPIN'
19. The Bolten Bounce

360 *One of the visiting economists:* Interview with Martin Anderson.

360 *At another meeting:* Interview with David Brady.

360 *On the fifth morning of January:* Details from the meeting with past secretaries of Defense and State were drawn from interviews with two of the former secretaries, with two administration officials, and from David E. Sanger's "Visited by a Host of Administrations Past, Bush Hears Some Chastening Words," *New York Times,* January 6, 2006.

362 *"Bartlett walks in":* Interview with Bush, December 2006.

363 *On February 28:* Details of the GOP Senate caucus meeting were taken from an interview with one of the senators present.

365 *in early March, Card brought up the matter:* Interview with Andy Card.

368 *"I do tears":* Interview with Bush, December 2006.

368 *never submitted a billable hour:* Interview with Andy Card.

369 *"in the middle of the seesaw":* Ron Suskind, "Mrs. Hughes Takes Her Leave," *Esquire,* July 2002.

20. The Phantom Fence

372 *On April 25:* Details of Bush's meeting with the senators were taken from interviews with two of the participating senators and from three senior administration officials.

373 *"it was a pretty compatible arrangement":* Interview with Bush, December 2005.

373 *In 1997, then-Governor Bush expressed:* Interview with a former senior adviser to Gov. Bush.

374 *"Let's just take the Hispanic issue":* Interview with Bush, 1998.

374 *"I think the hardworking Hispanics":* "Bush Blasts Anti-Immigrant Forces," *Cedar Rapids Gazette,* January 6, 2000.

375 *"Ol' nine per cent Bush":* Interview with Bush, December 2006.

375 *"They didn't want to take it on":* Interview with Bush, December 2006.

377 *"I understand their concern":* Interview with Bush, 1998.

379 *"I'm a woman who has nothing to lose":* Interview with a Blanco senior adviser who was present during the conversation.

381 *"It's all construction workers":* Interview with Kim Stewart.

382 *"I hear your roof's coming up this week":* Interview with Ethel and Wanda Williams.

382 *"God bless you, Ernie":* Interview with Ernie Ladd.

384 *"It's very interesting":* Interview with Bush, December 2006.

21. "I Owe You A Strategy That'll Work"

386 *"It's kind of sad":* Interview with Adair Margo, who was present and staying in the White House residence when Bush uttered this remark.

386 *"I used to always wonder":* Interview with Bush, 1998.

387 Once handed out copies: Interview with a former Pentagon official.

388 *He repeated this conviction to Andy Card:* Interview with Andy Card.

389 *"My thinking was that the country":* Interview with Bush, February 2007.

389 *"said all the right things":* Interview with Bush, February 2007.

390 *"I'm concerned":* Interview with Philip Zelikow.

393 *"I owe you a strategy that'll work":* Interview with Bush, February 2007.

393 *"At this point in time in a campaign":* Interview with Bush, February 2007

22. A Fine Line Between Realism And Pessimism

394 *"I thought we were gonna lose quite a few seats":* Interview with Bush, December 2006.

395 *"a good guy":* Interview with Bush, December 2006.

395 *"I was secretary of state":* Interview with Bush, December 2006.

396 *"It's not gonna be a good night":* Interview with Bush, December 2006.

396 *Bush spent it:* Details of Election Night at the residence were drawn from interviews with five of those who were present, including Bush and Laura Bush.

397 *studying the National Security Act of 1947:* Interview with a senior Pentagon official.

398 *"My reaction":* Interview with Bush, February 2007.

399 *Months later, Rumsfeld would commit:* "Rumsfeld Memo On Iraq Proposed 'Major' Change," *New York Times,* December 3, 2006.

399 *"No":* Interview with Bush, February 2007.

401 *Clinton had spoken to him:* Interview with Bush, December 2006.

401 *"The way I look at it":* Interview with Bush, December 2006.

402 *"A lot of us kept looking at each other":* Interview with Leon Panetta.

402 *The strategy was working:* Interviews with two Iraq Study Group members.

402 *"convince us that we should be writing":* Interview with an Iraq Study Group member.

402 *"didn't give the appearance":* Interview with Lee Hamilton.

402 *"We don't need it":* Interviews with two Iraq Study Group members.

403 *"No president can conduct a war":* Interview with Leon Panetta.

403 *"I'm thinking about these options"*: Interview with Bush, February 2007.

403 *"He's the guy who reminded me"*: Interview with Bush, February 2007.

405 *"I don't think you're ever a lame duck as president"*: Interview with Bush, December 2006.

406 *"I'm gonna build a fantastic Freedom Institute"*: Interview with Bush, December 2006.

Epilogue

409 *"We call it 'the reinforcement' "*: Interview with Bush, February 2007.

410 *"Wait a minute"*: Interview with Leon Panetta.

411 *"I wasn't sure"*: Interview with Bush, February 2007.

412 *"members of my party"*: Interview with Luis Gutierrez.

413 *When Hadley's memo:* "Bush Adviser's Memo Cites Doubts About Iraqi Leader," *New York Times*, November 29, 2006.

413 *"Do you know our national security adviser"*: Interview with Bush, February 2007.

414 *"Let's clear the room"*: Interview with Bush, February 2007.

414 *"He's learning to be a leader"*: Interview with Bush, February 2007.

414 *"Everybody tells him the same thing"*: Interview with Bush, May 2007.

417 *"I have people walk up to me"*: Interview with Bush, February 2007.

417 *Kissinger had recommended:* Interview with Bush, May 2007.

417 *"My bet is"*: Interview with Bush, May 2007.

418 *"I think he carries a lot of it around"*: Interview with Laura Bush.

418 *"Self-pity is the worst thing"*: Interview with Bush, May 2007.

419 *"So now I'm an October–November man"*: Interview with Bush, February 2007.

419 *"I'm not afraid"*: Interview with Bush, February 2007.

??? *"David Petraeus is gonna have to be the person"*: Interview with Bush, May 2007.

Author's Note
and Acknowledgments

What I have undertaken here is a literary narrative of a sitting president. My energies were especially directed toward exploring the character of Bush and his subordinates through first-hand interviews. This is the value I have attempted to bring to the ongoing study of our forty-third chief executive. This book does not pretend to compete with the fine existing works on the particular subjects of the Florida recount, the Iraq war, 9/11, and Hurricane Katrina. For that matter, the document-intensive search for the truth relating to the various Bush-era scandals (Plamegate, Jack Abramoff, the nine dismissed federal prosecutors, etc.) is its own separate enterprise.

The source material for this book consists primarily of interviews with current and former Bush administration officials, including the president himself. Such access to the Bush White House is unique, and gaining it was not an overnight proposition.

Throughout the 1990s, I was a close observer of then-Governor George W. Bush—first as a staff writer for *Texas Monthly*, and later as an Austin-based correspondent for *GQ*. For the latter publication, I wrote a lengthy profile of Bush in the summer of 1998 and spent a great deal of time with him, his family, and his close associates. The governor thought the piece was fair, and that was nice, and that was that, or so I figured at the time.

The notion of penning a straightforward literary narrative of a sitting president—particularly one as consequential as Bush—did not strike me as an especially novel idea. And yet by the summer of 2004, no such book of America's forty-third president had either been published or was in the works. My decision to change this was met in

Bushworld with approval of a highly guarded nature. I benefited greatly from the endorsement given by my old friend, the president's media adviser Mark McKinnon. Bush's former counselor, Karen Hughes, also gave early and much-appreciated encouragement.

His counselor until July 2007, Dan Bartlett, served as wary gate-keeper. We first met in his West Wing office in January 2005, a couple of days after the president's second inaugural address. Bartlett offered no assurances about access to the president, instead suggesting speechwriter Mike Gerson and Office of Strategic Initiatives director Pete Wehner as interviewees. In the ensuing months, I took what was given, pressed where I could. Bartlett, in the meantime, was doing his job, which included keeping watch over my machinations. By the summer of 2006, he judged that it might not be a bad idea for me to visit with the president in the Oval Office. I'm deeply grateful to Bartlett for this leap of faith—made without any promises on my part or stipulations on his. Viewed through the twenty-four-hour news cycle, there was nothing my book had to offer the Bush White House. I was aiming for a larger, more lasting portrait. Dan Bartlett saw the value of that, and he has my lasting gratitude for it.

That said, it was George W. Bush's decision alone to spend time with me. Belying the gut-instinct stereotype he himself promulgates, Bush spent several months mulling this over. He consulted Bartlett, Karl Rove, his wife Laura, and others. Some advised him to cooperate, others not. My first interview with him—offered with no promises of a follow-up—was on December 12, 2006, the day the president reluctantly decided to postpone his address to the nation on a new strategy for Iraq. He was not in the most accommodating of moods that day. Nonetheless, at the conclusion of our talk, Bush stood and said, "Okay, we'll do another."

We did six in all—averaging about an hour each—from that day through May 8, 2007. From the outset, the president was expansive and informal. Session by session, he became even more so. Though he was helpful in filling in and clarifying details, I found Bush to be at his best when allowed to meander, offering himself up impressionistically. His contribution to this book, obvious in places though it may be, cannot therefore be quantified by quotes. At the time of this writing, George W. Bush is not a terribly popular character. But he remains a surprising one. In the span of a few minutes' worth of discourse, he would swerve from reflective to edgy to amused, and yet somehow retain a cohesive, authentic persona. With or without his cooperation, my principal aim in this text was to render Bush as a many-shaded literary character. Whether or not he agrees with my depiction of him here, I hope he'll concur that my book is the better for his assistance. I'm thankful for the privilege of spending this time with him.

Some two hundred other individuals agreed to be interviewed for this book. Several of these—Laura Bush, Vice President Dick Cheney, Secretary of State Condoleezza Rice, former Secretary of Defense Donald Rumsfeld, and senior adviser Karl Rove—are household names. Others, while somewhat less celebrated, were at least as valuable in sharing information. [These include, but are by no means limited to: White House chiefs of staff Andy Card and Josh Bolten; deputy chief of staff for operations Joe Hagin; communications directors Nicolle Wallace, Kevin Sullivan, and the aforementioned Dan Bartlett; political affairs directors Ken Mehlman, Matt Schlapp, and Sara Taylor; legislative affairs directors Nicholas Calio, David Hobbs, and Candida Wolff; advance directors Brian Montgomery, Steve Atkiss, and Jason Recher; speechwriters John McConnell, Matthew Scully, William McGurn, and the aforementioned Michael J. Gerson; counsel Harriet Miers; personal aides Israel Hernandez and Logan Walters; national security adviser Steve Hadley; Coalition Provisional Authority administrator Paul Bremer; campaign strategists Matthew Dowd, Ed Gillespie, Jim Francis, Stuart Stevens, Russ Schriefer, and the aforementioned Mark McKinnon; and director of scheduling Brad Blakeman. I spoke as well with dozens of other current and former White House officials; with over half a dozen Cabinet secretaries; with numerous NSC, Pentagon, and State Department officials; with several members of the Iraq Study Group (including its two chairmen, James A. Baker III and Lee Hamilton); with a multitude of Bush family friends; and with the senior advisers to both the Bush and McCain primary campaigns in New Hampshire and South Carolina. Additionally, scores of sources on Capitol Hill from both sides of the aisle (among them Senators John McCain, Judd Gregg, Lindsey Graham, Joe Biden, Mary Landrieu, and Chuck Hagel) were helpful with their insights and recollections. Most of my sources were interviewed more than once, sometimes as many as a dozen times. It goes without saying that my book owes a great debt to their generosity.

My 1998 *GQ* story on Bush was edited by that magazine's longtime managing editor, my friend Marty Beiser. He had just settled in to his new job as an editor at Free Press when I came upon the idea to write this book. I'm fortunate beyond words that Marty and Free Press's editor in chief, Dominick Anfuso, immediately grasped the value of my project and determined to make it theirs. The encouragement and wisdom offered up by Marty, and by my agent, the immortal Sloan Harris, were floating objects to hang on to when the riptides threatened to pull me under. I'm also grateful to Free Press's highly attentive copyediting supervisor Carol de Onís for her skill and patience. Indeed, I'm humbled by Free Press's across-the-board commitment to this project and in particular would like to thank president Martha Levin, director of marketing Carisa Hays, publicist Nicole Kalian, and Marty Beiser's assistant, Kirsa Rein.

Jim Nelson, Andy Ward, and Mark Kirby of *GQ* magazine, where I've worked for the past decade, helped sustain this project—first by permitting me to write stories that kept me in the Bush wheelhouse, and later by granting me time off so that I could plunge into the manuscript. My most productive writing hours were spent at Stanford University's Hoover Institution and the Virginia Center for the Creative Arts, each of which awarded me fellowships in 2006. And though no one but me is to blame for the research represented herein, Sarah Schmidt provided invaluable assistance in gathering newspaper clippings and transcribing hoards of interview tapes.

I began this book with a crucial handful of Washington friends and made many others along the way: Undying thanks to Jim and Jessica Shahin, Ann Hornaday, Jim and Susan Duffy, Daniella Landau, Peter Bergen, Brad Garrett, Elisa Poteat, Norm Kurz, John Anderson, Robert Traynham, and Lara Andre for their companionship and encouragement. In addition, Anne Kornblut's early and unwavering belief in this project is something I'll always appreciate.

I have been blessed with a multitude of advocates in my life. First among these are my family: my parents and my brother John (to whom I've dedicated this book), and my cousin Joe Jaworski. But I must also cite my wonderful friends Michael MacCambridge, Lisa DePaulo, Skip Hollandsworth, Mimi Swartz, Evan Smith, Lee Smith, Hal Crowther, and the aforementioned Mark McKinnon as those who, through gestures great and small, helped sustain me throughout this episodic slog. Hardly least: For a very long time, the lovely and talented Meg Littleton has shown me great support and tolerance in my monomaniacal literary pursuits. She will forever have my gratitude.

INDEX

ABOUT THE AUTHOR

Robert Draper has been a national correspondent for *GQ* magazine for the past decade, and previous to that was senior editor at *Texas Monthly*. He lives in Washington, D.C. He is the author of a novel, *Hadrian's Walls* (Knopf), and of *Rolling Stone Magazine: The Uncensored History* (Doubleday).